# The Spy and the Traitor

# The Spy and the Traitor

*The Greatest Espionage Story of the Cold War*

## BEN MACINTYRE

VIKING
*an imprint of*
PENGUIN BOOKS

VIKING

UK | USA | Canada | Ireland | Australia
India | New Zealand | South Africa

Viking is part of the Penguin Random House group of companies
whose addresses can be found at global.penguinrandomhouse.com.

First published 2018

005

Copyright © Ben Macintyre, 2018

The moral right of the author has been asserted

Lyrics from 'Brothers in Arms' copyright © Mark Knopfler and Crockford Management.
Reproduced by permission

Set in 12/14.75 pt Bembo Book MT Std
Typeset by Jouve (UK), Milton Keynes
Printed and bound in Great Britain by Clays Ltd, Elcograf S.p.A.

A CIP catalogue record for this book is available from the British Library

HARDBACK ISBN: 978–0–241–18665–7
TRADE PAPERBACK ISBN: 978–0–241–18666–4

In memory of Joanna Macintyre (1934–2015)

'He had two lives: one open, seen and known by all who cared to know . . . and the other running its course in secret.'

Anton Chekhov, 'The Lady with the Dog'

# Contents

# List of Illustrations

## Illustration Acknowledgements

**Section 1:** p. 1 *top, bottom* private collection; p. 2 *top, bottom* private collection; p. 3 private collection; p. 4 *top left, top right* private collection; p. 4 *bottom* Avalon; p. 5 private collection; p. 6 *top* World History Archive/Alamy Stock Photo; p. 6 *bottom* akg-images/Ladislav Bielik; p. 7 *top, bottom* private collection; p. 8 *top, bottom* private collection; p. 9 private collection; p. 10 *top* Ritzau Scanpix/TopFoto; p. 10 *bottom left* Bettmann Archive/Getty Images; p. 10 *bottom right* Ritzau Scanpix/TopFoto; p. 11 *top left* Time Life Pictures/FBI/The LIFE Picture Collection/Getty Images; p. 11 *top right* Jeffrey Markowitz/Sygma/

# Introduction
## 18 May 1985

For the KGB's counter-intelligence section, Directorate K, this was a routine bugging job.

It took less than a minute to spring the locks on the front door of the flat on the eighth floor of 103 Leninsky Prospekt, a Moscow tower block occupied by KGB officers and their families. While two men in gloves and overalls set about methodically searching the apartment, two technicians wired the place, swiftly and invisibly, implanting eavesdropping devices behind the wallpaper and skirting boards, inserting a live microphone into the telephone mouthpiece, and video cameras in the light fittings in the sitting room, bedroom and kitchen. By the time they had finished, an hour later, there was barely a corner in the flat where the KGB did not have eyes and ears. Finally, they put on face masks and sprinkled radioactive dust on the clothes and shoes in the closet, sufficiently low in concentration to avoid poisoning, but enough to enable the KGB's Geiger counters to track the wearer's movements. Then they left, and carefully locked the front door behind them.

A few hours later, a senior Russian intelligence officer landed at Moscow airport on the Aeroflot flight from London.

Colonel Oleg Antonyevich Gordievsky of the KGB was at the pinnacle of his career. A prodigy of the Soviet intelligence service, he had diligently risen through the ranks, serving in Scandinavia, Moscow and Britain with hardly a blemish on his record. And now, at the age of forty-six, he had been promoted to chief of the KGB station in London, a plum posting, and invited to return to Moscow to be formally anointed by the head of the KGB. A career spy, Gordievsky was tipped to ascend to the uppermost ranks of that vast and ruthless security and intelligence network that controlled the Soviet Union.

A stocky, athletic figure, Gordievsky strode confidently through the airport crowds. Inside him, though, a low terror bubbled. For Oleg Gordievsky, KGB veteran, faithful secret servant of the Soviet Union, was a British spy.

Recruited a dozen years earlier by MI6, Britain's foreign-intelligence service, the agent codenamed NOCTON had proven to be one of the most valuable spies in history. The immense amount of information he fed back to his British handlers had changed the course of the Cold War, cracking open Soviet spy networks, helping to avert nuclear war and furnishing the West with a unique insight into the Kremlin's thinking during a critically dangerous period in world affairs. Both Ronald Reagan and Margaret Thatcher had been briefed on the extraordinary trove of secrets provided by the Russian spy, though neither the American President nor the British Prime Minister knew his real identity. Even Gordievsky's young wife was entirely unaware of his double life.

Gordievsky's appointment as KGB *rezident* (the Russian term for a KGB head of station, known as a *rezidentura*) had prompted rejoicing among the tiny circle of MI6 officers privy to the case. As the most senior Soviet intelligence operative in Britain, Gordievsky would henceforth have access to the innermost secrets of Russian espionage: he would be able to inform the West what the KGB was planning to do, before it did it; the KGB in Britain would be neutered. And yet the abrupt summons back to Moscow had unsettled the NOCTON team. Some sensed a trap. At a hastily convened meeting in a London safe house with his MI6 handlers, Gordievsky had been offered the option to defect and remain in Britain with his family. Everyone at the meeting understood the stakes: if he returned as official KGB *rezident* then MI6, the CIA and their Western allies would hit the intelligence jackpot, but if Gordievsky was walking into a trap he would lose everything, including his life. He had thought long and hard before making up his mind: 'I will go back.'

Once again, the MI6 officers went over Gordievsky's emergency escape plan, codenamed PIMLICO, and drawn up seven years earlier in the hope that it would never have to be activated. MI6 had never exfiltrated anyone from the USSR before, let alone a KGB officer. Elaborate and hazardous, the escape plan could be triggered only as a last resort.

Gordievsky had been trained to spot danger. As he walked through Moscow airport, his nerves ragged with internal stress, he saw signs of peril everywhere. The passport officer seemed to study his papers for an inordinate length of time, before waving him through. Where was the official who was supposed to be meeting him, a minimal courtesy for a KGB colonel arriving back from overseas? The airport was always stiff with surveillance, but today the nondescript men and women apparently standing around idly seemed even more numerous than normal. Gordievsky climbed into a taxi, telling himself that if the KGB knew the truth, he would have been arrested the moment he set foot on Russian soil, and already on his way to the KGB cells, to face interrogation and torture, followed by execution.

As far as he could tell, no one followed him as he entered the familiar apartment block on Leninsky Prospekt, and took the lift to the eighth floor. He had not been inside the family flat since January.

The first lock on the front door opened easily, and then the second. But the door would not budge. The third lock on the door, an old-fashioned deadbolt dating back to the building of the apartment block, had been locked.

But Gordievsky never used the third lock. Indeed, he had never had the key. That must mean that someone with a skeleton key had been inside, and on leaving had mistakenly triple-locked the door. That someone must be the KGB.

The fears of the previous week crystallized in a freezing rush, with the chilling, paralysing recognition that his apartment had been entered, searched and probably bugged. He was under suspicion. Someone had betrayed him. The KGB was watching him. The spy was being spied upon by his fellow spies.

PART ONE

# 1.   The KGB

Oleg Gordievsky was born into the KGB; shaped by it, loved by it, twisted, damaged and very nearly destroyed by it. The Soviet spy service was in his heart and in his blood. His father worked for the intelligence service all his life, and wore his KGB uniform every day, including weekends. The Gordievskys lived amid the spy fraternity in a designated apartment block, ate special food reserved for officers, and spent their free time socializing with other spy-families. Gordievsky was a child of the KGB.

The KGB, the *Komitet Gosudarstvennoy Bezopasnosti* or committee of state security, was the most complex and far-reaching intelligence agency ever created. The direct successor of Stalin's spy network, it combined the roles of foreign- and domestic-intelligence gathering, internal-security enforcement and state police. Oppressive, mysterious and ubiquitous, the KGB penetrated and controlled every aspect of Soviet life. It rooted out internal dissent, guarded the communist leadership, mounted espionage and counter-intelligence operations against enemy powers, and cowed the peoples of the USSR into abject obedience. It recruited agents and planted spies worldwide, gathering, buying and stealing military, political and scientific secrets from anywhere and everywhere. At the height of its power, with more than one million officers, agents and informants, the KGB shaped Soviet society more profoundly than any other institution.

To the West, the initials were a byword for internal terror and external aggression and subversion, shorthand for all the cruelty of a totalitarian regime run by a faceless official mafia. But the KGB was not regarded that way by those who lived under its stern rule. Certainly it inspired fear and obedience, but the KGB was also admired as a Praetorian Guard, a bulwark against Western imperialist and capitalist aggression, and the guardian of communism. Membership of this elite and privileged force was a source of admiration and pride.

Those who joined the service did so for life. 'There is no such thing as a former KGB man,' the former KGB officer Vladimir Putin once said. This was an exclusive club to join; and an impossible one to leave. Entering the ranks of the KGB was an honour and a duty to those with sufficient talent and ambition to do so.

Oleg Gordievsky never seriously contemplated doing anything else.

His father, Anton Lavrentyevich Gordievsky, the son of a railway worker, had been a teacher before the Revolution of 1917 transformed him into a dedicated, unquestioning communist, a rigid enforcer of ideological orthodoxy. 'The Party was God,' his son later wrote, and the older Gordievsky never wavered in his devotion, even when his faith demanded that he take part in unspeakable crimes. In 1932, he helped enforce the 'Sovietization' of Kazakhstan, organizing the expropriation of food from peasants to feed the Soviet armies and cities. Around 1.5 million people perished in the resulting famine. Anton saw state-induced starvation at close quarters. That year, he joined the office of state security, and then the NKVD, the Peoples' Commissariat for Internal Affairs, Stalin's secret police and the precursor of the KGB. An officer in the political directorate, he was responsible for political discipline and indoctrination. Anton married Olga Nikolayevna Gornova, a 24-year-old statistician, and the couple moved into a Moscow apartment block reserved for the intelligence elite. A first child, Vasili, was born in 1932. The Gordievskys thrived under Stalin.

When Comrade Stalin announced that the Revolution was facing a lethal threat from within, Anton Gordievsky stood ready to help remove the traitors. The Great Purge of 1936–8 saw the wholesale liquidation of 'enemies of the state': suspected fifth columnists and hidden Trotskyists, terrorists and saboteurs, counter-revolutionary spies, Party and government officials, peasants, Jews, teachers, generals, members of the intelligentsia, Poles, Red Army soldiers and many more. Most were entirely innocent. In Stalin's paranoid police state, the safest way to ensure survival was to denounce someone else. 'Better that ten innocent people should suffer than one spy get away,' said Nikolai Yezhov, chief of the NKVD. 'When you chop wood, chips fly.' The informers whispered, the torturers and executioners set to work, and the Siberian gulags swelled to bursting. But as in every revolution, the enforcers themselves inevitably became suspect. The NKVD began to investigate and purge itself. At the height of the bloodletting, the Gordievskys' apartment block was raided more than a dozen times in a six-month period. The arrests came at night: the man of the family was led away first, and then the rest.

It seems probable that some of these enemies of the state were identified by Anton Gordievsky. 'The NKVD is always right,' he said: a conclusion both wholly sensible, and entirely wrong.

A second son, Oleg Antonyevich Gordievsky, was born on 10 October 1938, just as the Great Terror was winding down, and war was looming. To friends and neighbours, the Gordievskys appeared to be ideal Soviet citizens, ideologically pure, loyal to Party and state, and now the parents to two strapping boys. A daughter, Marina, was born seven years after Oleg. The Gordievskys were well fed, privileged and secure.

But on closer examination there were fissures in the family façade, and layers of deception beneath the surface. Anton Gordievsky never spoke about what he had done during the famines, the purges and the terror. The older Gordievsky was a prime example of the species *Homo Sovieticus*, an obedient state servant forged by communist repression. But underneath he was fearful, horrified and perhaps gnawed by guilt. Oleg later came to see his father as 'a frightened man'.

Olga Gordievsky, Oleg's mother, was made of less tractable material. She never joined the Party, and she did not believe that the NKVD was infallible. Her father had been dispossessed of his watermill by the communists; her brother sent to the Eastern Siberian Gulag for criticizing collective agriculture; she had seen many friends dragged from their homes and marched away in the night. With a peasant's ingrained common sense, she understood the caprice and vindictiveness of state terror, but kept her mouth shut.

Oleg and Vasili, separated in age by six years, grew up in wartime. One of Gordievsky's earliest memories was of watching lines of bedraggled German prisoners being paraded through the streets of Moscow, 'trapped, guarded and led like animals'. Anton was frequently absent for long periods, lecturing the troops on Party ideology.

Oleg Gordievsky dutifully learned the tenets of communist orthodoxy: he attended School 130, where he showed an early aptitude for history and languages; he learned about the heroes of communism, at home and abroad. Despite the thick veil of disinformation surrounding the West, foreign countries fascinated him. At the age of six, he began reading *British Ally*, a propaganda sheet put out in Russian by the British embassy to encourage Anglo-Russian understanding. He studied German. As expected of all teenagers, he joined the Komsomol, the Communist Youth League.

His father brought home three official newspapers and spouted the communist propaganda they contained. The NKVD morphed into the KGB, and Anton Gordievsky obediently followed. Oleg's mother exuded a quiet resistance that only occasionally revealed itself in waspish, half-whispered asides. Religious worship was illegal under communism, and the boys were raised as atheists, but their maternal grandmother had Vasili secretly baptized into the Russian Orthodox Church, and would have christened Oleg too had their horrified father not found out, and intervened.

Oleg Gordievsky grew up in a tight-knit, loving family suffused with duplicity. Anton Gordievsky venerated the Party and proclaimed himself a fearless upholder of communism, but inside was a small and terrified man who had witnessed terrible events. Olga Gordievsky, the ideal KGB wife, nursed a secret disdain for the system. Oleg's grandmother secretly worshipped an illegal, outlawed God. None of the adults in the family revealed what they really felt – to each other, or anyone else. Amid the stifling conformity of Stalin's Russia, it was possible to believe differently in secret but far too dangerous for honesty, even to members of your own family. From boyhood, Oleg saw that it was possible to live a double life, to love those around you while concealing your true inner self, to appear to be one person to the external world and quite another inside.

Oleg Gordievsky emerged from school with a silver medal, head of the Komsomol, a competent, intelligent, athletic, unquestioning and unremarkable product of the Soviet system. But he had also learned to compartmentalize. In different ways, his father, mother and grandmother were all people in disguise. The young Gordievsky grew up around secrets.

Stalin died in 1953. Three years later he was denounced, at the 20th

Party Congress, by his successor, Nikita Khrushchev. Anton Gordievsky was staggered. The official condemnation of Stalin, his son believed, 'went a long way towards destroying the ideological and philosophical foundations of his life'. He did not like the way Russia was changing. But his son did.

The 'Khrushchev Thaw' was brief and restricted, but a period of genuine liberalization that saw the relaxation of censorship and the release of thousands of political prisoners. These were heady times to be young, Russian and hopeful.

At the age of seventeen, Oleg enrolled at the prestigious Moscow State Institute of International Relations. There, exhilarated by the new atmosphere, he engaged in earnest discussions with his peers about how to bring about 'socialism with a human face'. He went too far. Some of his mother's nonconformity had seeped into him. One day, he wrote a speech, naïve in its defence of freedom and democracy, concepts he barely understood. He recorded it in the language laboratory, and played it to some fellow students. They were appalled. 'You must destroy this at once, Oleg, and never mention these things again.' Suddenly fearful, he wondered if one of his classmates had informed the authorities of his 'radical' opinions. The KGB had spies inside the Institute.

The limits of Khrushchev's reformism were brutally demonstrated in 1956 when the Soviet tanks rolled into Hungary to put down a nationwide uprising against Soviet rule. Despite the all-embracing Soviet censorship and propaganda, news of the crushed rebellion filtered back to Russia. 'All warmth disappeared,' Oleg recalled of the ensuing clampdown. 'An icy wind set in.'

The Institute of International Relations was the Soviet Union's most elite university, described by Henry Kissinger as 'the Russian Harvard'. Run by the Ministry of Foreign Affairs, it was the premier training ground for diplomats, scientists, economists, politicians – and spies. Gordievsky studied history, geography, economics and international relations, all through the warping prism of communist ideology. The Institute provided instruction in fifty-six languages, more than any other university in the world. Language skills offered one clear pathway into the KGB and the foreign travel that he craved. Already fluent in German, he applied to study English, but the courses were oversub-scribed. 'Learn Swedish,' suggested his older brother, who had already joined the KGB. 'It is the doorway to the rest of Scandinavia.' Gordi-evsky took his advice.

The Institute library stocked some foreign newspapers and period-icals which, though heavily redacted, offered a glimpse of the wider world. These he began to read, discreetly, for showing overt interest in the West was itself grounds for suspicion. Sometimes at night he would secretly listen to the BBC World Service or Voice of America, despite the radio-jamming system imposed by Soviet censors, and picked up 'the first faint scent of truth'.

Like all human beings, in later life Gordievsky tended to see his past through the lens of experience, to imagine that he had always secretly harboured the seeds of insubordination, to believe his fate was somehow hardwired into his character. It was not. As a student, he was a keen communist, anxious to serve the Soviet state in the KGB, like his father and brother. The Hungarian Uprising had caught his youthful imagination, but he was no revolutionary. 'I was still within the system but my feelings of disillusionment were growing.' In this he was no different from many of his student contemporaries.

At the age of nineteen, Gordievsky took up cross-country running. Something about the solitary nature of the sport appealed to him, the rhythm of intense exertion over a long period, in private competition with himself, testing his own limits. Oleg could be gregarious, attract-ive to women and flirtatious. His looks were bluntly handsome, with hair swept back from his forehead and open, rather soft features. In repose, his expression seemed stern, but when his eyes flashed with dark humour, his face lit up. In company he was often convivial and comradely, but there was something hard and hidden inside. He was not lonely, or a loner, but he was comfortable in his own company. He seldom revealed his feelings. Typically hungry for self-improvement, Oleg believed that cross-country running was 'character building'. For hours he would run, through Moscow's streets and parks, alone with his thoughts.

One of the few students he grew close to was Stanislaw Kaplan, a fellow runner on the university track team. 'Standa' Kaplan was

Czechoslovakian, and had already obtained a degree from Charles University in Prague by the time he arrived at the Institute as one of several hundred gifted students from the Soviet bloc. Like others from countries only recently subjugated to communism, Kaplan's 'individuality had not been stifled', Gordievsky wrote, years later. A year older, he was studying to be a military translator. The two young men found they shared compatible ambitions and similar ideas. 'He was liberal-minded and held strongly sceptical views about communism,' wrote Gordievsky, who found Kaplan's forthright opinions exciting, and slightly alarming. With his dark good looks, Standa was a magnet to women. The two students became firm friends, running together, chasing girls and eating in a Czech restaurant off Gorky Park.

An equally important influence was his idolized older brother, Vasili, who was now training to become an 'illegal', one of the Soviet Union's vast global army of deep undercover agents.

The KGB ran two distinct species of spy in foreign countries. The first worked under formal cover, as a member of the Soviet diplomatic or consular staff, a cultural or military attaché, accredited journalist or trade representative. Diplomatic protection meant that these 'legal' spies could not be prosecuted for espionage if their activities were uncovered, but only declared *persona non grata*, and expelled from the country. By contrast, an 'illegal' spy (*nelegal*, in Russian) had no official status, usually travelled under a false name with fake papers, and simply blended invisibly into whatever country he or she was posted to. (In the West such spies are known as NOCs, standing for Non-Official Cover.) The KGB planted illegals all over the world, posing as ordinary citizens, submerged and subversive. Like legal spies, they gathered information, recruited agents and conducted various forms of espionage. Sometimes, as 'sleepers', they might remain hidden for long periods before being activated. These were also potential fifth columnists, poised to go into battle should war erupt between East and West. Illegals operated beneath the official radar and therefore could not be financed in ways that might be traced, nor communicate through secure diplomatic channels. But unlike spies accredited to an embassy, they left few traces for counter-intelligence investigators to follow. Every Soviet embassy contained a permanent KGB station, or *rezidentura*, with a number of KGB officers in various official guises, all under the command of a *rezident* (head of station in MI6 parlance, or station chief to the CIA). One task facing Western counter-intelligence was working out which Soviet officials were genuine diplomats, and which were really spies. Tracking down the illegals was far harder.

The First Chief Directorate (FCD) was the KGB department responsible for foreign intelligence. Within this, Directorate S (standing for 'special') trained, deployed and managed the illegals. Vasili Gordievsky was formally recruited into Directorate S in 1960.

The KGB maintained an office inside the Institute of International Relations, staffed by two officers on the lookout for potential recruits. Vasili mentioned to his bosses in Directorate S that his younger brother, proficient in languages, might be interested in the same line of work.

Early in 1961, Oleg Gordievsky was invited in for a chat, and then told to go to a building near the KGB headquarters in Dzerzhinsky Square, where he was politely interviewed, in German, by a middle-aged woman, who complimented him on his grasp of the language. From that instant, he was part of the system. Gordievsky did not seek to join the KGB; this was not a club you applied to. It chose you.

Gordievsky's time at university was nearing an end when he was sent to East Berlin for a six-month work-experience posting, as a translator in the Russian embassy. Thrilled at the prospect of his first trip abroad, Gordievsky's excitement spiked when he was called into Directorate S for a briefing on East Germany. The communist-ruled German Democratic Republic was a Soviet satellite, but that did not make it immune from the attentions of the KGB. Vasili was already living there as an illegal. Oleg readily agreed to make contact with his brother and carry out a few 'small tasks' for his new, unofficial employer. Gordievsky arrived in East Berlin on 12 August 1961, and travelled to a student hostel inside the KGB enclave in the suburb of Karlshorst.

Over the previous months, the stream of East Germans fleeing to the West through West Berlin had reached a torrent. By 1961, some

3.5 million East Germans, roughly 20 per cent of the entire population, had joined the mass exodus from communist rule.

Gordievsky awoke the next morning to find that East Berlin had been invaded by bulldozers. The East German government, prompted by Moscow, was taking radical steps to staunch the flow: the construction of the Berlin Wall was under way, a physical barrier to cut off West from East Berlin and the rest of East Germany. The 'Anti-Fascist Protection Wall' was, in reality, a prison perimeter, erected by East Germany to keep its own citizens penned in. More than 150 miles of concrete and wire, with bunkers, anti-vehicle trenches and chain fencing, the Berlin Wall was the physical manifestation of the Iron Curtain, and one of the nastiest structures man has ever built.

Gordievsky watched in horrified awe as East German workers tore up the streets alongside the border to make them impassable to vehicles, and troops unrolled miles of barbed wire. Some East Germans, realizing that their escape route was closing fast, made desperate bids for freedom by clambering over the barricades or attempting to swim the canals that formed part of the border. Guards lined up along the frontier with orders to shoot anyone attempting to cross from East to West. The new wall made a powerful impression on the 22-year-old Gordievsky: 'Only a physical barrier, reinforced by armed guards in their watchtowers, could keep the East Germans in their socialist paradise and stop them fleeing to the West.'

But Gordievsky's shock at the overnight construction of the Berlin Wall did not prevent him faithfully carrying out the orders of the KGB. Fear of authority was instinctive, the habit of obedience ingrained. Directorate S had provided the name of a German woman, a former KGB informant; Gordievsky's instructions were to sound her out and establish if she was prepared to continue providing information. He found her address through a local police station. The middle-aged woman who answered the door seemed unfazed by the sudden arrival of a young man holding a bunch of flowers. Over a cup of tea, she made it clear she was prepared to continue cooperating with the KGB. Gordievsky eagerly wrote up his first KGB report. Only months later did he realize what had really happened: 'It was I, rather than she, who was being tested.'

That Christmas he linked up with Vasili, who was living under a false identity in Leipzig. Oleg did not reveal to Vasili his horror at the construction of the Berlin Wall. His older brother was already a professional KGB officer, who would not have approved of such ideological wavering. Just as their mother had concealed her true feelings from her husband, so the brothers kept their secrets from one another: Oleg had no idea what Vasili was really doing in East Germany, and Vasili had no clue what Oleg was really feeling. The brothers attended a performance of the *Christmas Oratorio*, which left Oleg 'intensely moved'. Russia seemed 'a spiritual desert' by comparison, where only approved composers could be heard, and 'class hostile' church music, such as Bach's, was deemed decadent and bourgeois, and banned.

Gordievsky was profoundly affected by the few months he spent in East Germany: he had witnessed the great physical and symbolic division of Europe into rival ideologies; he had tasted cultural fruits denied to him in Moscow; and he had started spying. 'It was exciting to have an early taste of what I might do if I joined the KGB.'

In reality, he already had.

Back in Moscow, Gordievsky was told to report for duty at the KGB on 31 July 1962. Why did he join an organization enforcing an ideology he had already started to question? KGB work was glamorous, offering the promise of foreign travel. Secrecy is seductive. He was also ambitious. The KGB might change. He might change. Russia might change. And the pay and privileges were good.

Olga Gordievsky was dismayed to learn that her younger son would be following his father and brother into the intelligence service. For once, she openly voiced her anger at the regime, and the apparatus of oppression that sustained it. Oleg pointed out that he would not be working for the internal KGB but in the foreign section, the First Chief Directorate, an elite organization staffed by intellectuals speaking foreign languages, doing sophisticated work that required skill and education. 'It's not really like the KGB,' he told her. 'It's really intelligence and diplomatic work.' Olga turned away, and left the room. Anton Gordievsky said nothing. Oleg detected no pride in his father's demeanour. Years later, when he came to understand the full scale of Stalinist repression, Gordievsky wondered whether his father, now approaching retirement, had been 'ashamed of all those crimes and atrocities committed by the KGB, and simply afraid to discuss the work of the KGB with his own son'. Or perhaps Anton Gordievsky was struggling to maintain his double life, a pillar of the KGB too terrified to warn his son against what he was getting into.

In his last summer as a civilian, Gordievsky joined Standa Kaplan at the Institute's holiday camp on the Black Sea coast. Kaplan had decided to stay on for an additional month, before returning to join the StB, Czechoslovakia's formidable intelligence service. The two friends would soon be colleagues, allies in espionage on behalf of the Soviet bloc. For a month, they camped under the pines, ran every day, swam, sunbathed, and discussed women, music and politics. Kaplan was increasingly critical of the communist system. Gordievsky was flattered to be the recipient of such dangerous confidences: 'There was an understanding between us, a trust.'

Soon after his return to Czechoslovakia, Kaplan wrote a letter to Gordievsky. In among the gossip about the girls he had met and the fine time they would have together if his friend came to visit ('We'll empty all the pubs and wine cellars in Prague'), Kaplan made a highly significant request: 'Oleg, might you have a copy of *Pravda* with Yevtushenko's poem about Stalin?' The poem in question was 'Heirs of Stalin' by Yevgeny Yevtushenko, a direct attack on Stalinism by one of Russia's most outspoken and influential poets. The poem was a demand that the Soviet government ensure that Stalin would 'never rise again' and a warning that some in the leadership still hankered for the brutal Stalinist past: 'By the past, I mean the neglect of the people's welfare, false charges, the jailing of the innocent . . . "Why care?" some say, but I can't remain inactive. / While Stalin's heirs walk this earth.' The poem had caused a sensation when it was published in the official newspaper of the Communist Party, and had also been reprinted in Czechoslovakia. 'It had a powerful effect on some of our people, with a certain tinge of discontent,' Kaplan wrote to Gordievsky. He said he wanted to compare the Czech translation to the original Russian. But in reality Kaplan was sending a coded message of complicity to his friend, an acknowledgement that they shared the sentiments expressed by Yevtushenko and, like the poet, would not remain inactive in the face of Stalin's legacy.

The KGB's 'Red Banner' elite training academy, deep in the woods fifty miles north of Moscow, was codenamed School 101, an ironic and entirely unconscious echo of George Orwell's Room 101 in *Nineteen Eighty-Four*, the basement torture chamber where the Party breaks a prisoner's resistance by subjecting him to his worst nightmare.

Here Gordievsky and 120 other trainee KGB officers would be inducted into the deepest secrets of Soviet spycraft: intelligence and counter-intelligence, recruiting and running spies, legals and illegals, agents and double agents, weapons, unarmed combat and surveillance, the arcane arts and language of this strange trade. Some of the most important instruction was in surveillance detection and evasion, known as 'dry-cleaning', or *proverka* in KGB jargon: how to spot when you were being followed, and dodge surveillance in a way that would appear accidental rather than intentional, since a target that is obviously 'surveillance aware' is likely to be a trained intelligence operative. 'The intelligence officer's behaviour shouldn't cause suspicion,' the KGB instructors declared. 'If a surveillance service notices that a foreigner is blatantly checking for a tail, it will be stimulated to work more secretly, more tenaciously, and with more ingenuity.'

Being able to make contact with an agent without being watched – or even while under surveillance – is central to every clandestine operation. In Western spy parlance, an officer or agent operating undetected is said to have gone 'black'. In test after test, the KGB students would be sent off to link up with a specific person at a precise location, drop off or pick up information, try to identify whether and how they were being followed, throw off the tail without appearing to do so, and arrive at the designated place spotlessly dry-cleaned. Surveillance was the responsibility of the KGB's Seventh Directorate. Professional watchers, highly trained in the art of tailing a suspect, would take part in the exercises, and at the end of each day the student-trainee and the surveillance team compared notes. *Proverka* was exhausting, competitive, time-consuming and nerve-shredding; Gordievsky found he was very good at it.

Oleg learned how to set up a 'signal site', a secret sign left in a public place – a chalk-mark on a lamppost for example – that meant
nothing to a casual observer but would tell a spy to meet at a certain
place and time; how to make a 'brush contact', physically passing a
message or item to another person without being spotted; how to
make a 'dead-letter drop', leaving a message or cash at a particular
spot to be picked up by another without making direct contact. He
was taught codes and ciphers, recognition signals, secret writing,
preparation of microdots, photography and disguise. There were
classes on economics and politics, as well as ideological tuition to
reinforce the young spies' commitment to Marxism–Leninism. As
one of Oleg's fellow students observed, 'these clichéd formulas and
concepts had the character of ritual incantations, something akin to
daily and hourly affirmations of loyalty'. Veteran officers, who had
already served abroad, gave lectures on Western culture and etiquette
to prepare recruits for understanding and combating bourgeois
capitalism.

Gordievsky adopted his first spy-name. Soviet and Western intelligence services used the same method for choosing a pseudonym – it
should be close to the real name, with the same initial letter, because
that way if a person addressed you by your real name, someone who
only knew you by your spy-name might well assume he or she had
misheard. Gordievsky chose the name 'Guardiyetsev'.

Like every other student, he swore eternal loyalty to the KGB: 'I
commit myself to defend my country to the last drop of blood, and
to keep state secrets.' He did this without qualms. He also joined the
Communist Party, another requirement of admission. He might have
his doubts – many did – but that did not preclude him from joining
the KGB and the Party with wholehearted commitment and sincer-
ity. And, besides, the KGB was thrilling. So, far from being an
Orwellian nightmare, the year-long training course at School 101
was the most enjoyable period of his young life, a time of excitement
and anticipation. His fellow recruits were selected for their intelligence and ideological conformity, but also for the spirit of adventure
common to all intelligence services. 'We had chosen careers in the
KGB because they held out the prospect of action.' Secrecy forges

intense bonds. Even his parents had little idea where Oleg was, or what he was doing. 'To make it into service in the FCD was the concealed and open dream of the majority of young officers of state security, but only a few were made worthy of this honor,' wrote Leonid Shebarshin, who attended School 101 at around the same time as Oleg and would end up a KGB general. 'The . . . work united intelligence officers in a unique camaraderie with its own traditions, discipline, conventions, and special professional language.' By the summer of 1963, Gordievsky had been fully adopted into the KGB brotherhood. When he swore to defend the Motherland to his last breath and his last secret, he meant it.

Vasili Gordievsky was working hard for Directorate S, the illegals section of the FCD. He had also started to drink heavily – not necessarily a drawback in a service that prized the ability to consume vast amounts of vodka after work without falling over. An illegals specialist, he moved from place to place under different aliases, servicing the undercover network, passing on messages and money to other hidden agents. Vasili never told his younger brother what he was doing, but he hinted at exotic locations, including Mozambique, Vietnam, Sweden and South Africa.

Oleg hoped to follow his brother into this exhilarating undercover world overseas. Instead, he was told to report to Directorate S in Moscow, where he would be preparing documentation for other illegals. Trying to mask his disappointment, on 20 August 1963 Gordievsky climbed into his best suit and reported for work at KGB headquarters, the complex of buildings that stands near the Kremlin, part prison, part archive, the bustling nerve-centre of Soviet intelligence. At its heart stood the sinister Lubyanka, a neo-Baroque palace originally built for the All-Russia Insurance Company, whose basement housed the KGB torture cells. Among KGB officers, the KGB control centre was known as 'The Monastery' or, more simply, 'The Centre'.

Instead of going undercover in some glamorous foreign location, Gordievsky found himself shuffling paper, 'a galley slave' filling out forms. Each illegal required a fake persona, with a convincing backstory, a new identity with complete biography and forged paperwork. Each illegal had to be sustained, instructed and financed, requiring a complex arrangement of signal sites, dead drops and brush contacts.

Britain was seen as particularly fertile ground for planting illegals, since there was no system of identity cards in the country, and no central registration bureau. West Germany, America, Australia, Canada and New Zealand were all prime targets. Placed in the German section, Oleg spent his days creating people who did not exist. For two years, he lived in a world of double lives, sending counterfeit spies into the outer world, and meeting those who had returned.

The Centre was stalked by living ghosts, heroes of Soviet espionage in their dotage. In the corridors of Directorate S, Gordievsky was introduced to Konon Trofimovich Molody, alias 'Gordon Lonsdale', one of the most successful illegals in history. In 1943, the KGB had appropriated the identity of a dead Canadian child called Gordon Arnold Lonsdale, and given it to Molody, who had been raised in North America and spoke faultless English. Molody/Lonsdale settled in London in 1954 and, posing as a jovial salesman of jukeboxes and bubblegum machines, recruited the so-called Portland Spy Ring, a network of informants gathering naval secrets. (A KGB dentist had drilled several unnecessary holes in his teeth before he left Moscow, which meant Molody could simply open his mouth and point out the KGB-made cavities to confirm his identity to other Soviet spies.) A tip-off from a CIA mole had led to Molody's arrest and conviction for espionage, although even at his trial the British court was uncertain of his real name. When Gordievsky met him, Molody had just returned to Moscow after being swapped for a British businessman arrested on spying charges in Moscow. A similarly fabled figure was Vilyam Genrikhovich Fisher, alias Rudolf Abel, the illegal whose spying in the US had earned him a thirty-year sentence before he was exchanged for the downed U2 pilot Gary Powers in 1962.

But the most famous Soviet spy in semi-retirement was British. Kim Philby had been recruited by the NKVD in 1933, rose up the ranks of MI6 while feeding vast reams of intelligence to the KGB, and finally defected to the Soviet Union in January 1963, to the deep and abiding embarrassment of the British government. He now lived in a comfortable flat in Moscow, attended by minders, 'an Englishman to his fingertips', as one KGB officer put it, reading the cricket scores in old copies of *The Times*, eating Oxford marmalade and frequently drinking himself into a stupor. Philby was revered as a legend within the KGB, and he continued to do odd jobs for Soviet intelligence, including running a training course for English-speaking officers, analysing occasional cases, and even helping to motivate the Soviet ice hockey team.

Like Molody and Fisher, Philby gave lectures to star-struck young spies. But the reality of life after KGB espionage was anything but happy. Molody took to drink and died in mysterious circumstances on a mushroom-picking expedition. Fisher became deeply disillusioned. Philby attempted to kill himself. All three would end up celebrated on Soviet postage stamps.

To anyone who cared to look closely (and few Russians did), the contrast between the myth and reality of the KGB was self-evident. The Centre was a spotlessly clean, brightly lit, amoral bureaucracy, a place at once ruthless, prissy and puritanical where international crimes were conceived with punctilious attention to detail. From its earliest days, Soviet intelligence operated without ethical restraint. In addition to collecting and analysing intelligence, the KGB organized political warfare, media manipulation, disinformation, forgery, intimidation, kidnapping and murder. The Thirteenth Department, or 'Directorate for Special Tasks', specialized in sabotage and assassination. Homosexuality was illegal in the USSR, but homosexuals were recruited to entrap gay foreigners, who could then be blackmailed. The KGB was unapologetically unprincipled. Yet it was a prudish, hypocritical and moralistic place. Officers were forbidden to drink during working hours, though many drank prodigiously at all other times. Gossip about the private lives of colleagues swirled around the KGB, as in most offices, with the difference that in the Centre scandal and tittle-tattle could destroy careers and end lives. The KGB took an intrusive interest in the domestic arrangements of its employees, for no life was private in the Soviet Union. Officers were expected to get married, have children, and stay married. There was calculation as well as control in this: a married KGB officer was considered less likely to defect while abroad, since his wife and family could be held as hostages.

Two years after joining Directorate S, Gordievsky concluded that he was not going to follow in his brother's footsteps as a deep-cover spy posted abroad. But Vasili himself may have been the main reason Oleg was rejected for illegals work: according to KGB logic, having more than one family member abroad, and particularly having two in the same country, might be an inducement to defect.

Gordievsky was bored and frustrated. A job that had seemed to promise adventure and excitement had turned out to be humdrum in the extreme. The world beyond the Iron Curtain he had read about in Western newspapers seemed tantalizingly out of reach. So he decided to get married. 'I wanted to go abroad as soon as possible and the KGB never sent unmarried men abroad. I was in a hurry to find a wife.' A woman with German-language skills would be ideal, since they might then be posted to Germany together.

Yelena Akopian was training to be a German teacher. She was twenty-one, half Armenian, intelligent, dark-eyed and sharply witty. She was a mistress of the one-line put-down, which he found attractive and alluring, for a time. They met at the home of a mutual friend. What sparked between them had less to do with passion than a shared ambition. Like Oleg, Yelena longed to travel abroad, and imagined a life far beyond the confines of the cramped flat where she lived with her parents and five siblings. Gordievsky's few previous relationships had been brief and unsatisfying. Yelena seemed to offer a glimpse of what a modern Soviet woman might be, less conventional than the female students he had met before, with an unpredictable sense of humour. She pronounced herself a feminist, although in 1960s Russia the term was strictly limited. He told himself that he loved her. They got engaged, Gordievsky later reflected, 'without much real thought or self-examination on either side', and then married, without fanfare, a few months later, for reasons that were less than romantic: she would improve his chances of promotion, and he was her passport out of Moscow. This was a KGB marriage of convenience, though neither admitted it to the other.

Late in 1965 came the break Gordievsky had been waiting for. A slot opened up for a post running illegals in Denmark. His cover job would be that of a consular official dealing with visas and inheritances; in reality, he would be working for 'Line N' (standing for *nelegalniy*, or illegals), responsible for the operational fieldwork of Directorate S.

Gordievsky was offered the job managing a network of under-cover spies in Denmark. He accepted with alacrity and delight. As Kim Philby observed after he was recruited into the KGB in 1933: 'I did not hesitate. One does not look twice at an offer of enrolment in an elite force.'

## 2.   Uncle Gormsson

Oleg and Yelena Gordievsky landed in Copenhagen on a glittering frosty day in January 1966, and entered a fairy tale.

As one MI6 officer later remarked: 'If you had to choose a city to demonstrate the advantages of Western democracy over Russian communism, you could hardly do better than Copenhagen.'

The capital of Denmark was beautiful, clean, modern, rich and, to the eyes of a couple newly emerged from the drab oppression of Soviet life, almost impossibly alluring. Here were sleek cars, shiny office buildings, smart designer furniture and smiling Nordic people with magnificent dentistry. There were teeming cafés, bright restaurants serving exotic food, shops selling a bewildering array of goods. To Gordievsky's famished eyes, the Danes seemed not just brighter and more alive, but culturally nourished. He was astounded by the range of books available in the first library he entered, but even more surprised to be allowed to borrow as many as he wanted, and keep the plastic bag he took them away in. There seemed to be very few policemen.

The Soviet embassy consisted of three stucco villas on Kristiania-gade in the northern part of the city, more like a grand gated hotel than a Soviet enclave, with immaculate sweeping gardens, a sports centre and a social club. The Gordievskys moved into a newly built apartment, with high ceilings, wooden floors and a fitted kitchen. He was allocated a Volkswagen Beetle, and a cash advance of £250 every month for entertaining contacts. Copenhagen seemed to be alive with music: Bach, Handel, Haydn, Telemann, composers he had never been allowed to hear in Soviet Russia. There was a very good reason, he reflected, why ordinary Soviet citizens were not permitted to travel abroad: who but a fully indoctrinated KGB officer would be able to taste such freedoms and resist the urge to stay?

Of the twenty officials in the Soviet embassy, just six were genuine diplomats, while the rest worked for the KGB or the GRU, Soviet military intelligence. The *rezident*, Leonid Zaitsev, a charming and conscientious officer, seemed oblivious to the fact that most of his underlings were incompetent, lazy or crooked, and usually all three. They expended far more energy on fiddling their expenses than actually spying. The broad remit of the KGB was to cultivate Danish contacts, recruit informants and target possible agents. This, Gordievsky swiftly realized, was 'an invitation to corruption', since most officers simply invented their interactions with Danes, falsified bills, made up their reports and pocketed their allowances. The Centre does not appear to have noticed the anomaly that few of its personnel in Copenhagen spoke good Danish, and some spoke none at all.

Gordievsky was determined to show that he was not like the rest. Already proficient in Swedish, he set about learning Danish. His mornings were spent processing visa applications, in obedience to his cover job in the consulate; the spying began at lunchtime.

The KGB illegals network in Scandinavia was patchy. Much of Gordievsky's work was administrative: leaving money or messages at dead drops, monitoring signal sites, and maintaining clandestine contact with the undercover spies, most of whom he never met face to face, or knew by name. If an illegal left orange peel under a specific park bench, this meant: 'I am in danger', whereas an apple core indicated: 'I am leaving the country tomorrow.' These complex arrangements sometimes descended into farce. At one signal site, Oleg left a bent nail on a windowsill in a public toilet to indicate to an illegal that he should pick up cash at a predetermined dead-drop site. The answering signal from the undercover agent, acknowledging that the message had been received, was a beer bottle cap left in the same place. On returning to the spot, Oleg found the cap from a bottle of *ginger* beer. Was ginger beer, in spy signalling, the same as ordinary beer? Or did this have another meaning? After an intense all-night discussion with colleagues back at the *rezidentura* he reached the conclusion that the spy did not see any difference between one bottle cap and another.

In Denmark, births and deaths were registered by the Protestant Church, and recorded by hand in large ledgers. With the help of a skilled forger from Moscow, any number of new identities could be fabricated from scratch by altering church records. He began cultivating clerics to gain access to the registers, and organizing burglaries at various churches. 'I was breaking new ground,' he said later. The church registers of Denmark contain a number of Danes entirely invented by Oleg Gordievsky.

In the meantime, he set about recruiting informants, agents and clandestine couriers. 'That's the main purpose of our life here,' Zaitsev told him. After months of cultivation, working under the alias 'Gornov' (his mother's maiden name), he persuaded a schoolteacher and his wife to act as a 'live letterbox', passing messages to and from illegals. He befriended a Danish policeman, but after a few meetings began to wonder whether he was recruiting the man, or the other way around.

Less than a year after his arrival in Copenhagen, Gordievsky was joined by a KGB officer of a very different stamp from the others. Mikhail Petrovich Lyubimov was a booming, cheerful, highly intelligent Ukrainian whose father had served in the Cheka, the Bolshevik secret police. Lyubimov had graduated from the Moscow State Institute of International Relations four years ahead of Gordievsky, and then wrote a thesis for the KGB entitled *English National Character and Its Use in Operational Work*. In 1957, on KGB orders, he seduced an American girl at the World Youth Festival in Moscow. Four years later, he was deployed to Britain as a Soviet press attaché, while recruiting informants within trade unions, student groups and the British establishment. He spoke English with a fruity upper-class accent, larded with old-fashioned Britishisms (What ho! Pip pip!), making him sound like a Russian Bertie Wooster. Lyubimov had developed a fascination for all things English or, more accurately, the aspects of English culture that he liked: whisky, cigars, cricket, gentlemen's clubs, tailored tweed, billiards and gossip. British intelligence nicknamed him 'Smiley Mike'. The British were the enemy, and he adored them. In 1965 he had tried and failed to recruit a British cipher clerk, and the intelligence service promptly attempted to recruit him. When he declined the offer to spy for Britain, he was declared *persona non grata* and sent back to Moscow – an experience that did nothing whatever to dent his rampant Anglophilia.

At the end of 1966, Lyubimov was posted to Copenhagen as chief of political intelligence (the 'PR Line', in KGB nomenclature).

Gordievsky took to Lyubimov immediately. 'It is not the winning that counts but playing the game,' Lyubimov boomed, as he regaled the younger man with tales of his life in Britain, recruiting spies while sipping Glenlivet in panelled clubrooms. Lyubimov adopted Gordievsky as his protégé, and said of the younger man: 'He impressed me with his splendid knowledge of history. He loved Bach and Haydn, which inspired respect, particularly compared to the rest of the Soviet colony in Denmark, who spent all their time on fishing trips, shopping, and amassing as many material possessions as they could.'

Just as Lyubimov had fallen in love with Britain, so Gordievsky found himself smitten by Denmark, its people, parks and music, and the liberty, including the sexual freedom, that its citizens took for granted. The Danes had an open attitude towards sex, progressive even by European standards. One day Oleg visited the city's red-light district, and on a whim entered a shop selling pornographic magazines, sex toys and other erotica. There he bought three homosexual porn magazines, and took them home to show Yelena. 'I was just intrigued. I had no idea what homosexuals did.' He placed the magazines on his mantelpiece, an open exhibition of a freedom unavailable in Soviet Russia.

'I blossomed as a human being,' he wrote. 'There was so much beauty, such lively music, such excellent schools, such openness and cheeriness among ordinary people, that I could only look back on the vast, sterile concentration camp of the Soviet Union as a form of hell.' He took up badminton, and found that he loved the game, particularly relishing the game's deceptive element. 'The shuttlecock, slowing down in the final few seconds of flight, gives a player a chance to use his wits and change his shot at the last moment.' The last-minute change of shot was a skill he would perfect. He attended classical-music concerts, devoured library books, and travelled to every corner of Denmark, sometimes on spy business, but mostly for the sheer pleasure of being able to do so.

For the first time in his life, Gordievsky felt that he was not being watched. Except that he was.

The Danish Security and Intelligence Service, the *Politiets Efter-retningstjeneste*, or PET, was tiny but highly effective. Its stated duty was to 'prevent, investigate and combat operations and activities that pose a threat to the preservation of Denmark as a free, democratic and safe country'. PET strongly suspected that Oleg Gordievsky posed just such a threat, and from the moment the young Russian diplomat with a taste for classical music arrived in Copenhagen, it had been keeping an eye on him.

The Danes routinely monitored Soviet embassy personnel, but lacked the resources for round-the-clock surveillance. Some of the telephones inside the embassy were bugged. KGB technicians, mean-while, had successfully penetrated the PET radio networks, and a listening post within the embassy routinely picked up messages pass-ing between the Danish surveillance teams. Yelena Gordievsky was now working for the KGB alongside her husband, listening to these messages and translating them into Russian. As a result, the KGB could often work out the positioning of PET surveillance cars, and establish when its officers were free of surveillance. Each suspected KGB officer had a codename: Gordievsky was referred to in PET radio messages as 'Uncle Gormsson', a reference to a tenth-century king of Denmark, Harald 'Bluetooth' Gormsson.

The Danish security service had little doubt that Gordievsky (alias Gornov, alias Guardiyetsev, alias Uncle Gormsson) was a KGB spy working under diplomatic cover.

One evening Oleg and Yelena were invited to dinner by their policeman friend and his wife. While they were out, PET entered their flat and planted listening devices. Gordievsky had been some-what suspicious of the invitation from the Danish couple and so, in accordance with his School 101 training, he had taken the precaution of squeezing a blob of glue between the hall door and its frame. When they returned from dinner, the invisible glue seal had been broken. From then on, Gordievsky was careful about whatever he said at home.

The mutual snooping was erratic and piecemeal, on both sides. KGB officers, trained in the art of dry-cleaning, frequently managed to slip off the Danish radar. But, just as often, Gordievsky and his colleagues believed they had successfully gone 'black' when they had not.

Either PET was monitoring Copenhagen's red-light district or the Danes were shadowing Gordievsky, when he was spotted entering the sex shop and buying homosexual porn magazines. A married Russian intelligence officer with a taste for gay porn is vulnerable, a man with secrets who might be blackmailed. The Danish security service made a careful note, and passed on this interesting nugget of information to selected allies. For the first time in Western intelligence files, a question mark appeared alongside Gordievsky's name.

Oleg Gordievsky was evolving into a most effective KGB officer. Lyubimov wrote: 'He indisputably stood out among his colleagues as a result of his excellent education, thirst for knowledge, love of reading, and, like Lenin, visits to public libraries.'

The only cloud on his horizon was his marriage, which seemed to be wilting as fast as his cultural inner life was blooming. A relationship begun with little warmth grew steadily chillier. Gordievsky wanted children; Yelena, emphatically, did not. A year into the posting, his wife revealed that before leaving Moscow she had aborted a pregnancy without consulting him. He felt deceived, and furious. A fierce bundle of energy, he found his young wife strangely passive and unresponsive to the new sights and sounds around them. He began to feel that his marriage was 'one more of convention than love' and his 'feeling of emptiness' grew steadily stronger. Gordievsky described his attitude towards women as 'respectful'. In reality, like many Soviet men, he had old-fashioned ideas about matrimony, and expected his wife to cook and clean without complaint. A skilled KGB translator, Yelena insisted there were 'better things for a woman to do than housework'. Oleg might be open to many of the new influences in Western society, but he drew the line at women's liberation; what he called Yelena's 'anti-domestic tendencies' became a source of increasing frustration. He took a cookery course, hoping to shame Yelena into doing more cooking herself; she either did not notice or did not care. Her one-line retorts, which he had once found witty, now merely irritated him. When he felt he was in the right, Gordievsky could be obdurate and inflexible. To work off his frustration, he ran every day in Copenhagen's parks, alone, for hour after hour, returning home too exhausted to quarrel.

While cracks were appearing in the marriage, seismic upheavals were taking place within the Soviet bloc.

In January 1968, Alexander Dubček, the reformist First Secretary of Czechoslovakia's Communist Party, set about liberalizing his country and loosening the Soviet yoke by relaxing controls on travel, free speech and censorship. Dubček's 'Socialism with a Human Face' promised to limit the power of the secret police, improve relations with the West, and eventually hold free elections.

Gordievsky observed these events with rising excitement. If Czechoslovakia could loosen Moscow's grip, then other Soviet satellites might follow suit. Within the Copenhagen KGB *rezidentura* opinion was sharply divided over the significance of the Czech reforms. Some argued that Moscow would intervene militarily, as it had done in Hungary in 1956. But others, including Gordievsky and Lyubimov, felt certain the Czech revolution would flourish. 'Oleg and I were sure the Soviet tanks would not go into Prague,' wrote Lyubimov. 'We bet a whole crate of Tuborg.' Even Yelena, usually so politically disengaged, seemed galvanized by what was happening. 'We saw Czechoslovakia as our one hope for a liberal future,' wrote Gordievsky. 'Not only for that country but for our country as well.'

Back at Moscow Centre, the KGB viewed the Czech experiment in reform as an existential threat to communism itself, with the potential to tip the balance of the Cold War against Moscow. Soviet troops began massing on the Czech frontier. The KGB did not wait for the Kremlin's signal and set about combating the Czech 'counter-revolution' with a small army of spies. One of these was Vasili Gordievsky.

As one brother watched with mounting enthusiasm as the Prague Spring bloomed, the other was sent to nip it in the bud.

Early in 1968, more than thirty KGB illegals slipped into Czechoslovakia, with orders from the KGB's chief, Yuri Andropov, to sabotage the Czech reform movement, infiltrate 'reactionary' intellectual circles and abduct prominent supporters of the Prague Spring. Most of these agents travelled disguised as Western tourists, since it was assumed that the Czech 'agitators' would be more likely to reveal their plans to apparently sympathetic foreigners. Among the targets were intellectuals, academics, journalists, students and writers, including Milan Kundera and Václav Havel. It was the largest intelligence operation the KGB had ever mounted against a Warsaw Pact ally.

Vasili Gordievsky travelled on a false West German passport under the name Gromov. The older Gordievsky brother had already demonstrated his mettle as a KGB kidnapper. Yevgeni Ushakov had been operating as an illegal for several years in Sweden, mapping the country and deploying a network of sub-agents in anticipation of a possible Soviet invasion. But in 1968 the Centre concluded that this spy, codenamed FAUST, had developed a persecution complex and must be removed. In April 1968, Vasili Gordievsky drugged Ushakov and then successfully exfiltrated him via Finland to Moscow, where he was placed in a psychiatric hospital, before being released and fired from the KGB. Vasili was awarded a KGB medal for 'impeccable service'.

The next month, he and a KGB colleague set out to kidnap two of the leading émigré figures in the Czech reformist movement: Václav Černý and Jan Procházka. A distinguished literary historian, Professor Černý had been sacked from Charles University by the communist regime for speaking out in defence of academic freedom. Procházka, a writer and film producer, had publicly denounced official censorship and demanded 'freedom of expression'. Both were living in West Germany. The KGB was convinced (wrongly) that the pair headed an 'illegal anti-state' group dedicated to 'subverting the foundations of socialism in Czechoslovakia', and must therefore be eliminated. The plan was simple: Vasili Gordievsky would befriend Černý and Procházka, convince them that they were in imminent danger of assassination by Soviet hitmen, and offer a 'temporary hiding place'. If they refused to come voluntarily, they would be subdued using 'special substances', then handed over to operatives from the Special Actions department of the KGB and driven across the border into East Germany in the boot of a car with diplomatic number plates – by diplomatic convention, such vehicles were usually not subject to search. The plan did not work. Despite Gordievsky's urgings, Černý refused to believe 'that he was in any greater danger than usual'; Procházka was accompanied by a bodyguard, and spoke only Czech, which Gordievsky did not understand. After two weeks of trying, and failing, to persuade the Czech dissidents to come with him, Gordievsky aborted the kidnapping.

Vasili Gordievsky, alias Gromov, then crossed the border into Czechoslovakia, and joined the small, highly trained gang of Soviet illegals and saboteurs posing as tourists. Their task was to mount a series of 'provocation operations', intended to give the false impression that Czechoslovakia was about to erupt in violent counter-revolution. They distributed false evidence suggesting that Czech 'rightists', backed by Western intelligence, were planning a violent coup. They fabricated inflammatory posters calling for the overthrow of communism, and planted arms caches, wrapped in packages conveniently marked 'Made in the USA', which were then 'discovered' and denounced as proof of an imminent insurrection. The Soviet authorities even claimed to have discovered a 'secret American plan' to take over the communist government and install an imperialist stooge.

The older Gordievsky brother was at the forefront of KGB efforts to defame and destroy the Prague Spring; like his father, he never questioned the rectitude of what he was doing.

Oleg had no idea his brother was in Czechoslovakia, let alone of the skulduggery he was perpetrating. The brothers never discussed the subject, then or later. Vasili guarded his secrets and Oleg, increasingly, guarded his. As spring turned to summer, and the march towards a new Czechoslovakia seemed to gather pace, Gordievsky insisted that Moscow would never intervene militarily. 'They can't invade,' he declared. 'They won't dare.'

On the night of 20 August 1968, 2,000 tanks and more than 200,000 troops, principally Soviet but with contingents from other Warsaw Pact countries, rolled across the Czechoslovakian frontiers. There was no hope of opposing the Soviet juggernaut, and Dubček called upon his people not to resist. By morning, Czechoslovakia was an occupied country. The Soviet Union had emphatically demonstrated the 'Brezhnev doctrine': any Warsaw Pact country attempting to renounce or reform orthodox communism would be brought back into the fold, by force. The Prague Spring was over, and a new Soviet winter began.

Oleg Gordievsky was appalled and disgusted. As angry Danish protestors gathered outside the Soviet embassy in Copenhagen to denounce the invasion, he felt a deep shame. Witnessing the building of the Berlin Wall had been shocking enough, but the invasion of Czechoslovakia offered even more blatant proof of the true nature of the regime he served. Alienation from the communist system turned, very swiftly, to loathing: 'This brutal attack on innocent people made me hate it with a burning, passionate hatred.'

From the telephone in the corner of the embassy lobby, Gordievsky called Yelena at home, and in a torrent of expletives damned the Soviet Union for crushing the Prague Spring. 'They've done it. It's unbelievable.' He was close to tears. 'My soul was aching,' he later recalled, but his mind was clear.

Gordievsky was sending a message. He knew that the embassy phone was bugged by the Danish security service. PET was also eavesdropping on his home telephone. Danish intelligence would surely pick up this semi-subversive conversation with his wife, and take note that 'Uncle Gormsson' was not the unquestioning cog in the KGB machine he appeared to be. The telephone call was not exactly an approach to the other side. Rather, it was a hint, an emotional brush contact, an attempt to make the Danes, and their allies in Western intelligence, aware of his feelings. It was, he later wrote, a 'first, deliberate signal to the West'.

The West missed the signal. Gordievsky reached out, and nobody noticed. In the torrent of material intercepted and processed by the Danish security service, this small but significant gesture passed undetected.

As the grim news from Czechoslovakia sunk in, Gordievsky's thoughts turned to Stanislaw Kaplan, his outspoken friend at university. What must Standa be feeling as the Soviet tanks rolled into his country?

Kaplan was outraged. After leaving Russia, he had worked at the Ministry of the Interior in Prague before joining the Czech state intelligence service, the StB. His dissident sympathies carefully concealed, Kaplan watched the events of 1968 with bleak dismay, but said nothing. The crushing of the Prague Spring prompted a wave of mass emigration, and some 300,000 people would flee Czechoslovakia in the wake of the Soviet invasion. Kaplan began collecting secrets, and prepared to join them.

Gordievsky's tour of duty in Denmark was approaching its end when a telegram arrived from Moscow: 'Cease operational activity. Stay to make analysis but no more operations.' Moscow Centre had concluded that the Danes were showing an unhealthy level of interest in Comrade Gordievsky, having probably worked out he was a KGB officer. Radio intercepts showed that, since his arrival, he had been tailed, on average, every other day, more than any other member of the Soviet embassy staff. Moscow did not want a diplomatic incident, so for his final months in Copenhagen Gordievsky was put to work researching a KGB manual about Denmark.

Gordievsky's career, and conscience, was at a crossroads. His anger over events in Czechoslovakia simmered, but had yet to cohere into anything approaching a decision. Leaving the KGB was unthinkable (and probably impossible), but he wondered whether he might be able to switch from running illegals and join Lyubimov in the political-intelligence department, work which seemed more interesting, and less squalid.

Gordievsky trod water, professionally and personally: he carried out his consular duties, bickered with Yelena, nursed his secret antipathy for communism, and gorged himself on Western culture. At a party in the home of a West German diplomat, he fell into conversation with a young Danish man, who was exceptionally friendly and evidently quite drunk. The Dane seemed to know a lot about classical music. He suggested they go on to a bar. Gordievsky politely declined, explaining that he needed to get home.

The young man was an agent of the Danish intelligence service. The conversation had been the opening gambit in an attempted homosexual entrapment. Prompted by Oleg's apparent taste for gay pornography, the Danes had set a honeytrap, one of the oldest, grubbiest and most effective techniques in espionage. PET was never quite sure why it failed. Had the highly trained KGB officer spotted the attempted seduction? Or perhaps the honey in the trap was simply not to his taste. The true explanation was simpler. Gordievsky was not gay. He had not realized he was being chatted up.

Outside fiction, spying seldom goes exactly according to plan. In the wake of the Prague Spring, Gordievsky sent a veiled message to Western intelligence, which had not been spotted. The Danish intelligence service attempted to ensnare him, based on a false premise, and had missed by a mile. Each side had made an approach, and neither had connected. And now Gordievsky was going home.

The Soviet Union he returned to, in January 1970, was even more repressive, paranoid and dingy than the one he had left three years earlier. The communist orthodoxy of the Brezhnev era seemed to leech away all colour and imagination. Gordievsky was repelled by his own homeland: 'How shabby everything seemed.' The queues, the grime, the suffocating bureaucracy, fear and corruption stood in grim contrast to the bright and bountiful world he had left in Denmark. The propaganda was ubiquitous, officials alternately servile and rude, everyone spied on everyone else; the city stank of boiled cabbage and blocked drains. Nothing worked properly. Nobody smiled. The most casual contact with foreigners provoked immediate suspicion. But it was the music that gnawed at his soul, the patriotic mush blaring out of loudspeakers on every street corner, written to communist formulas, bland, booming and inescapable, the sound of Stalin. Gordievsky felt under daily assault from what he called this 'totalitarian cacophony'.

He was sent back to Directorate S, while Yelena got a job in the Twelfth Department of the KGB, the section responsible for bugging and eavesdropping on foreign diplomats. She was assigned to the unit listening in on Scandinavian embassies and diplomatic personnel, and promoted to lieutenant. The marriage was now little more than a 'working relationship', though they never spoke about their work, or discussed much of anything else in the grim flat they shared in east Moscow.

The next two years were, in Oleg's words, 'an in-between, inconsequential time'. Although he had been promoted and was better paid, his job was little different to the one he had left three years before, preparing identities for illegals. He applied to learn English, hoping this might lead to a posting in the US, Britain or one of the Common-wealth countries, but was told there was no point, since the Danes had apparently identified him as a KGB officer, and it was therefore unlikely he would be sent abroad to a Western country. Morocco was a possibility. He began learning French, with little enthusiasm. Sunk in the grey conformity of Moscow, Gordievsky suffered acute cultural withdrawal symptoms. He was restless, resentful, increasingly lonely and stuck.

In the spring of 1970, a young British intelligence officer was leafing through a 'personal file' that had recently arrived from Canada. Geoffrey Guscott was slightly built, bespectacled, multilingual, highly intelligent and dogged. More George Smiley than James Bond, he already had the look of an avuncular university tutor. But appearances could not have been more deceptive. According to one colleague, Guscott 'probably personally inflicted more damage on Soviet intelligence than anyone else in history'.

Brought up in south-east London, the son of a printer who had left school at fourteen, Guscott had a working-class background that set him apart from the majority of MI6 officers. He won a scholarship to Dulwich College, and then a place at Cambridge to read Russian and Czech. On graduation in 1961, a letter arrived from out of the blue, inviting Guscott to a meeting in London. There he met a cheery veteran of British intelligence who described his experiences as a wartime spy in Vienna and Madrid. 'I had a yen to travel, and it seemed to me exactly what I wanted to do,' recalled Guscott. At the age of twenty-four, he was enrolled in Britain's foreign-intelligence agency, known to itself as the Secret Intelligence Service, or SIS, but referred to by just about everyone else as MI6.

In 1965, Guscott was posted to Czechoslovakia, as the tide of reform was beginning to rise. For three years he ran a spy codenamed FREED, an officer in the Czech intelligence service, and by the time of the Prague Spring in 1968 he was back in London, responsible for the recruitment of Czech officials, inside and outside Czechoslovakia. The Soviet invasion sent the Czech desk into overdrive. 'We had to grab every opportunity we could.'

The file on Guscott's desk, codenamed DANICEK, concerned the recent defection of a junior officer named Stanislaw Kaplan from the Czech intelligence service.

Kaplan had taken a holiday in Bulgaria soon after the Prague Spring. There he had vanished, before reappearing in France, where he formally defected to the French intelligence service. Kaplan explained that he wished to settle in Canada. The Canadian intelligence service had a close relationship with MI6, and an officer was sent from London to debrief the defector. The Canadians undoubtedly informed the CIA of Kaplan's defection. The young Czech officer was eager to cooperate. By the time it landed on Guscott's desk, the DANICEK dossier was several inches thick.

Kaplan was described as intelligent and forthright, 'a cross-country runner who enjoyed the opposite sex'. He brought useful details about the workings of Czech intelligence, and his years as a student in Moscow. As a matter of routine, defectors were asked to identify anyone they knew of potential interest to Western intelligence. Kaplan's file contained around 100 names, mostly Czechoslovakian. But five of the 'personalities' listed by Kaplan were Russians, and one of these stood out.

Kaplan described his friendship with Oleg Gordievsky, a fellow long-distance runner destined for the KGB, who had evinced 'clear signs of political disillusionment'. During the Khrushchev Thaw, the two friends had discussed the limitations of communism: 'Oleg was a man who was not closed off, a thinking man who was aware of the horrors of the past, a person not so different from him.'

Guscott cross-referenced the name and found that an Oleg Gordievsky had been sent to Copenhagen in 1966 as a consular official. Relations between PET and MI6 were close. The Danish intelligence file on Gordievsky indicated that he was almost certainly a KGB officer, probably providing support to illegals. Nothing could be pinned on him directly, but he had evaded surveillance several times in a way that suggested professional training. He had made suspicious contact with a policeman and several priests. A bug planted in his apartment revealed that his marriage was in trouble. His visit to a sex shop and his purchase of gay pornography had prompted 'a clumsy blackmail attempt', without result. Gordievsky had returned to Moscow in January 1970, and vanished into the maw of the Centre, doing heaven knew what.

Guscott made a note in the Gordievsky file that if this able, elusive, possibly gay KGB officer who had once harboured freethinking ideas reappeared in the West, he might be worth approaching. Oleg was 'flagged' as a 'person of interest', and given the codename SUNBEAM.

In the meantime, Britain had KGB spies to deal with closer to home.

On 24 September 1971, the British government ejected 105 Soviet intelligence officers, the largest expulsion of spies in history. The mass eviction, codenamed Operation FOOT, had been brewing for some time. Like the Danes, the British closely monitored accredited Soviet diplomats, journalists and trade representatives, and had a clear idea which were authentic and which were spies. The KGB had become ever more brazen in its espionage, and MI5, the British Security Service, was itching to strike back. The trigger was the defection of Oleg Lyalin, a KGB officer posing as the representative of the Soviet knitwear industry. So far from selling communist cardigans, Lyalin was the most senior representative of the KGB's Thirteenth Department, the sabotage section responsible for drawing up contingency plans in the event of war with the West. He was given the MI5 codename GOLDFINCH, but he sang like a canary: among the secrets he revealed were plans to flood the London Underground, assassinate key figures in British public life, and land a sabotage team on the Yorkshire coast. These revelations furnished the pretext MI5 had been waiting for. Every known spy was kicked out, and one of the largest KGB stations in the world was reduced, overnight, to naught. The KGB would spend the next two decades struggling to restore the *rezidentura* to its former potency.

Operation FOOT took Moscow completely by surprise, and provoked consternation within the First Chief Directorate. With its headquarters at Yasenevo, near Moscow's outer ring road, the department responsible for foreign intelligence had undergone rapid expansion under Brezhnev, multiplying from 3,000 officers in the

1960s to more than 10,000. The mass expulsion was seen as a major debacle. The head of the section responsible for Britain and Scandinavia was sacked (the two regions were, for historical reasons, lumped together in the KGB departmental structure, along with Australia and New Zealand) and replaced by Dmitri Yakushin.

Known as the 'Grey Cardinal', Yakushin was an aristocrat by birth but a Bolshevik of conviction, a committed communist with the airs of a nobleman and a voice like a pneumatic drill. He had fought in a tank regiment during the war, specialized in pig husbandry at the Soviet Agriculture Ministry, and then transferred to the KGB, rising to become deputy head of the American department. Unlike most of the senior KGB brass he was a cultured man who collected rare books, and spoke his mind, very loudly. Gordievsky's first brush with the Grey Cardinal was extremely alarming.

One night, listening in secret to the BBC World Service, Gordievsky learned that Denmark, in a knock-on effect from Operation FOOT, had expelled three of his former colleagues, KGB officers working under diplomatic cover. The next morning he mentioned the news to a friend in the Danish section. Five minutes later, his telephone rang, and a deafening blast echoed down the line: 'Comrade Gordievsky, if you insist on spreading rumours around the KGB about alleged expulsions in Demark, you will be PUNISHED!' It was Yakushin.

Oleg feared the sack. Instead, a few days later, after the BBC report was confirmed, the Grey Cardinal summoned him to his office, and got straight to the point, at around 100 decibels. 'I need someone in Copenhagen. We have to rebuild our team there. You speak Danish . . . How would you fancy working in my department?' Gordievsky stammered that he would like nothing better. 'Leave it to me,' Yakushin bellowed.

But the head of Directorate S declined to let him go, with the pettiness typical of a boss determined to retain a member of staff just because another boss has tried to poach him.

There matters rested, frustratingly, until Vasili Gordievsky, the brother who had got him into the KGB, helped to speed Oleg's promotion by the radical expedient of dropping dead.

Vasili had been drinking heavily for years. In South-East Asia he contracted hepatitis and was advised by doctors never to touch another drop of alcohol. But he continued, and swiftly drank himself to death at the age of thirty-nine. He was given a full military funeral by the KGB. As three KGB officers fired automatic weapons in salute, and the flag-draped coffin was lowered into the floor of the Moscow crematorium, Gordievsky reflected how little he had really known about the man he called 'Vasilko'. His mother and sister, clutching each other in grief and awed by the turnout of KGB dignitaries, knew even less. Anton wore his KGB uniform and told everyone he was proud of his son's service to the Motherland.

Oleg had slightly feared his mysterious older brother. He remained entirely unaware of Vasili's illegal activities in Czechoslovakia. The brothers had seemed outwardly close, but in reality they had been separated by a wide gulf of secrecy. Vasili died a decorated KGB hero, and Oleg's stock rose accordingly, providing a small 'moral lever' in his efforts to prise himself out of Directorate S, and into Yakushin's British–Scandinavian department. 'Now that my brother had died as a result of his work for Directorate S, it would be hard for the boss to refuse my request.' With extreme reluctance, the illegals section let him go. The Soviets applied for a Danish visa, stating that Gordievsky would be returning to Copenhagen as Second Secretary at the Soviet embassy; in reality, he was now a political-intelligence officer of the KGB's First Chief Directorate – the post formerly occupied by Mikhail Lyubimov.

The Danes could have turned down the visa, since Oleg was a suspected KGB officer. Instead, they decided he should be allowed to return, and watched closely. London was informed.

The question of his sexuality was raised again. Gordievsky, it seemed, had not reported the homosexual approach made two years earlier. Had he done so, MI6 surmised, he would probably not have been sent abroad a second time because, in the distorted thinking of the KGB, any officer targeted by Western intelligence was immediately rendered suspect. MI6 assumed that Oleg had decided to conceal the attempted seduction, when he had merely failed to notice it. 'The presumption was that he had kept it to himself,' wrote one officer. If

Gordievsky was hiding a guilty secret from his bosses, and if Standa Kaplan was right about his political leanings, the Russian might be worth another approach.

MI6 and PET prepared a welcoming reception.

# 3. SUNBEAM

Richard Bromhead was Our Man in Copenhagen, and didn't much mind who knew it.

The MI6 head of station in Denmark was an old-fashioned, public-school-educated Englishman, a cheerful, back-slapping cove who referred to the people he liked as 'complete darlings' and those he did not as 'prize shits'. Bromhead was descended from poets and adventurers. The family was pedigreed and penniless. He attended Marlborough College, and then performed National Service in Germany, where he found himself in charge of 250 German prisoners in a former camp for British POWs. ('The Kommandant was an Olympic rower. Charming chap. We had a ball.') He went to Cambridge University, studied Russian, and claimed to have forgotten every word the moment he left. He was turned down by the Foreign Office, then failed to get a job in a bakery, decided to become an artist, and was living on onions in a run-down London flat and drawing pictures of the Albert Memorial when a friend suggested he apply for a job in the Colonial Office. ('They wanted me to go to Nicosia. I said: "Lovely. Where's that?"') In Cyprus, he wound up as Private Secretary to the Governor, Hugh Foot. ('It was great fun. There was an MI6 officer living in the garden, lovely chap, recruited me.') Inducted into 'The Firm', he was posted first to the UN in Geneva under deep cover, and then to Athens ('Place immediately broke out in revolution. Ha, ha.'). Finally, in 1970, at the age of forty-two, he was appointed senior MI6 officer in Copenhagen. ('I was supposed to go to Iraq. Not sure what happened.')

Tall, handsome and immaculately tailored, always ready for a joke and another drink, Bromhead swiftly became a familiar figure on the Copenhagen diplomatic-party circuit. He referred to his clandestine work as 'mucking about'.

Richard Bromhead was one of those Englishmen who put a great deal of effort into appearing to be a lot more stupid than they really are. He was a formidable intelligence officer.

From the day he arrived in Copenhagen, Bromhead set about making the lives of his Soviet adversaries a misery. In this project he joined forces with the deputy head of PET, a jocular lawyer named Jørn Bruun who 'delighted in actively harassing Bloc – and especially Russian – diplomats and other staff, in ways which cost practically nothing and were virtually undetectable'. To assist in what Bromhead called his 'teasing operations', Bruun allocated him two of his best officers, Jens Eriksen and Winter Clausen. 'Jens was small with a long fair moustache. Winter was enormous, roughly the size of a large door. I called them Asterix and Obelix. We got on frightfully well.'

One of their chosen targets was a known KGB officer named Bratsov. Whenever this man was followed into a particular Copenhagen department store, Clausen would commandeer the loudspeaker system and announce: 'Would Mr Bratsov of KGB Ltd please come to the information desk.' After the third such summons, the KGB sent Bratsov back to Moscow. Another victim was a keen young officer in the KGB station who tried to recruit a Danish MP, who promptly informed PET. 'This MP lived in a town that was two hours' drive from Copenhagen. We would get him to call up the Russian and say: "Come here immediately, I've got something frightfully important to tell you." The Russian would then drive to the home of the MP, who filled him full of vodka and fed him lots of nonsense. He would then drive back, pretty squiffy, file a long report for the KGB, and finally get to bed at six in the morning. Then the MP would call him up at nine and say: "Come here immediately, I've got something frightfully important to tell you." Eventually the Russian had a nervous breakdown and packed it in. Ha, ha. The Danes were super.'

Gordievsky's visa was approved. Bromhead was instructed by MI6 to get close to the new arrival and, when the moment seemed right, sound him out. PET would be kept informed of developments, but agreed that the case should be run in Denmark by MI6.

Oleg and Yelena Gordievsky arrived back in Copenhagen on 11 October 1972. It felt like a homecoming. The enormous Danish undercover cop nicknamed Obelix discreetly followed them out of the arrivals hall.

In his new role as a political-intelligence officer, Gordievsky would no longer be running illegals, but actively gathering secret intelligence and trying to subvert Western institutions. In practice this meant seeking out, cultivating, recruiting and then controlling spies, contacts and informants. These might be Danish government officials, elected politicians, trades unionists, diplomats, businessmen, journalists or anyone else with privileged access to information of interest to the Soviet Union. They might even, ideally, work in Danish intelligence. As in other Western countries, a few Danes were committed communists, prepared to take orders from Moscow; others might be willing to trade intelligence for money (the grease that oils the wheels of so much espionage), or susceptible to other forms of persuasion, coercion or inducement. In addition, PR Line officers were expected to undertake 'active measures' to influence public opinion, sow disinformation where necessary, cultivate opinion-formers sympathetic to Moscow and place articles in the press that painted the Soviet Union in a positive (and often false) light. The KGB had long excelled in the dark art of manufacturing 'fake news'. Under KGB taxonomy, foreign contacts were classified in order of importance: at the top was an 'agent', someone who consciously worked for the KGB, usually for ideological or financial reasons; below that was a 'confidential contact', a person sympathetic to the Soviet cause, willing to help clandestinely, but possibly unaware that the friendly man from the Soviet embassy worked for the KGB. A grade below that were numerous more open contacts, people whom Gordievsky, in his cover role as Second Secretary, would be expected to meet anyway in the course of his work. There was a wide gulf between a confidential contact, who might merely be approachable and sympathetic, and a spy prepared to betray his country. But one could evolve into the other.

Gordievsky slipped easily back into Danish life and culture. Mikhail Lyubimov had returned to Moscow to a senior role in the British–Scandinavian department, and Gordievsky stepped into his shoes. This new form of intelligence work was exciting but frustrating; Danes are almost too nice to be spies, too honest to be subversive, and too polite to say so. Every attempt to recruit a Dane bumped into an impenetrable wall of courtesy. Even the most ardent Danish communists baulked at treachery.

But there were exceptions. One was Gert Petersen, leader of Denmark's Socialist People's Party and later a Member of the European Parliament. Petersen, codenamed ZEUS and categorized as a 'confidential contact' by the KGB, passed on classified military information gleaned from Denmark's Foreign Policy Committee. He was well informed, and very thirsty. Gordievsky was startled, and rather impressed, by the quantity of beer and schnapps he was able to consume at KGB expense.

The new *rezident* in Copenhagen, Alfred Mogilevchik, appointed Gordievsky as his deputy. 'You've got the brains, the energy and the ability to deal with people,' Mogilevchik told him. 'Also, you know Denmark and speak the language. What else do I need?' Gordievsky was promoted to major.

Professionally, Gordievsky was gliding smoothly upwards through the KGB ranks; internally, he was in turmoil. Two years in Moscow had exacerbated his alienation from the communist regime, and returning to Denmark had deepened his dismay at Soviet philistinism, corruption and hypocrisy. He began to read more widely, collecting books that he would never have been permitted to own in Russia: the works of Alexander Solzhenitsyn, Vladimir Maximov and George Orwell, and Western histories that exposed the full horror of Stalinism. News filtered through of Kaplan's defection to Canada. His friend had been tried *in absentia* by a Czechoslovakian military court for revealing state secrets and sentenced to twelve years in prison. Gordievsky was shocked, but also left wondering whether the West had registered his cry of protest after the Prague Spring. If so, why was there no response? And if Western intelligence did ever try to sound him out, would he accept or reject the advance? Gordievsky later claimed that he was primed and waiting for a tap on the shoulder from the opposition, but the reality was more complicated than memory, as it almost always is.

Back on the diplomatic-party circuit, Gordievsky frequently spotted the same tall, affable Englishman.

Richard Bromhead had two photographs of Gordievsky, both supplied by the Danes, one taken covertly during his previous posting and the latest from his visa application.

'It was a stern face that I had studied, but not unpleasant. He looked hard-bitten and tough and I could not imagine how, even in the circumstances the London report had described, anyone could have thought him to be homosexual. Nor did he look like a man it would be easy for a Western intelligence officer to approach, in any sense.' In common with others of his time and class, Bromhead believed that all homosexuals behaved in certain ways that made them easy to identify.

Their first direct encounter took place in Copenhagen town hall, the red-brick edifice called the Rådhus, at the opening of an art exhibition. Bromhead knew that a Soviet delegation would attend. As a regular at the 'diplomatic lunch club', where real diplomats and spies intermingled, he had made the acquaintance of several Soviet officials. 'I was on quite good terms with a horrible little man who came from Irkutsk, poor chap.' Bromhead spotted the diminutive Irkutskian among a group of Soviet diplomats including Gordievsky, and sauntered over. 'Without seeming to put any special emphasis on it, I was able, while greeting them, to include Oleg in the general greeting. I didn't ask his name, and he didn't volunteer it.'

The two men fell into a halting conversation about art. 'When Oleg spoke, the sternness disappeared,' wrote Bromhead. 'He had a ready smile, with a genuinely humorous aspect to it, often lacking in other KGB officers. The new arrival seemed natural and genuinely amused by life. I liked him.'

Bromhead reported back to London that the target had been contacted. The main problem was communication. Bromhead had forgotten almost all his Russian, spoke only a smattering of Danish and a very little German – the language he had used to order around German POWs was not, in these circumstances, very suitable. Gordievsky spoke fluent German and Danish, but no English at all. 'We managed at a superficial level,' said Bromhead.

The Soviet, British and American embassies backed onto one another, in an odd diplomatic triangle, separated by a graveyard. Despite the frigidity of the Cold War, there was considerable social interaction between Soviet and Western diplomats, and over the following weeks Bromhead contrived to be invited to several parties attended by Gordievsky. 'We nodded to each other over the heads of fellow guests at a few diplomatic receptions.'

Recruiting a rival intelligence officer required a complicated *pas de deux*. Too obvious an approach would scare Gordievsky away, but too subtle a signal would be missed. MI6 wondered if Bromhead had the delicacy needed for this kind of dance. 'He was very gregarious, but a bit of a bull in a china shop, and well known in the Soviet embassy, where he'd been identified as MI6.' Characteristically, Bromhead simply decided to throw a party and invited Gordievsky, along with some other Soviet officials. 'PET produced a lady badminton player. The thinking was that this lady and Gordievsky would have a common interest.' Lene Køppen was a student dentist who would go on to win the world title in ladies singles badminton. She was extremely pretty, and entirely unaware she was being used as bait. The approach was 'not necessarily sexual', according to one MI6 case officer. But if Gordievsky turned out to be heterosexual, and badminton led to bed, then so much the better. It didn't. Gordievsky had two drinks, chatted briefly and inconsequentially to Køppen, and left. As Bromhead had predicted, the Russian was proving friendly but unapproachable, socially, sportingly and sexually.

Back in London, Geoffrey Guscott was now on the Soviet desk. He discussed the SUNBEAM case with Mike Stokes, a senior officer who had been the case officer to Oleg Penkovsky, the West's most successful Soviet spy to date. Penkovsky was a colonel in the GRU, the KGB's military counterpart. For two years, starting in 1960, he was run jointly by MI6 and the CIA, supplying scientific and military intelligence to his handlers in Moscow, including the placement of Soviet missiles in Cuba – information that enabled President John F. Kennedy to gain the upper hand during the Cuban Missile Crisis. In October 1962, Penkovsky was caught, arrested, interrogated by the KGB, and in May 1963 executed. Stokes was a 'huge, inspiring physical presence' who knew a great deal about recruiting and running Soviet spies. Together, Stokes and Guscott hatched an ambitious plan: a 'litmus test' of Gordievsky's sympathies.

On the evening of 2 November 1973, Oleg and Yelena had just finished dinner (a joyless, almost silent occasion) when there was a loud
knock on the door of the apartment. Gordievsky found Standa Kaplan,
his Czechoslovakian friend from university, smiling on the doorstep.

Gordievsky was stunned, and then suddenly very scared.

'*Bozhe moi!* My God. Standa! What the hell are you doing here?'

The men shook hands, and Gordievsky ushered Kaplan inside,
knowing that, in doing so, the game was changing irrevocably.
Kaplan was a defector. If one of Gordievsky's KGB neighbours saw
him enter the flat, that alone would be grounds for suspicion. Then
there was Yelena. Even if their marriage had been sound, as a loyal
KGB officer she might feel obliged to report her husband's encounter
with a known traitor.

Gordievsky poured his old friend a whisky, and introduced him to
Yelena. Kaplan explained that he was now working for a Canadian
insurance company. He had come to Copenhagen to see a Danish
girlfriend, found Oleg's name in the diplomatic list, and decided on a
whim to look him up. Kaplan seemed unchanged, the same open face
and jaunty manner. But a slight tremor in the hand on the whisky
glass betrayed him. Gordievsky knew he was lying. Kaplan had been
sent by a Western intelligence service. This was a trial, and a very
dangerous one. Was this the long-awaited response to the telephone
call placed five years earlier after the crushing of the Prague Spring?
If so, who was Kaplan working for? The CIA? MI6? PET?

The conversation was fractured and twitchy. Kaplan described
how he had defected from Czechoslovakia, reaching Canada via
France. Gordievsky mumbled something non-committal. Yelena
looked anxious. After just a few minutes, Kaplan drained his glass
and got to his feet. 'Look, I'm disturbing you. Let's meet for lunch
tomorrow and we can have a proper talk.' Kaplan suggested a small
restaurant in the city centre.

Closing the door, Gordievsky turned to Yelena and remarked how
strange it was that Kaplan should appear unannounced. She said
nothing. 'What a funny coincidence that he should turn up in Copenhagen,' he said. Her expression was unreadable, but tinged with
apprehension.

Gordievsky arrived deliberately late for lunch, having satisfied himself that he was not being followed. He had barely slept. Kaplan was waiting at a table in the window. He seemed more relaxed. They chatted about old times. Seated at a café table across the road, a well-built tourist was reading a guidebook. Mike Stokes was keeping watch.

Kaplan's visit had been minutely planned and rehearsed. 'We needed a plausible reason for Kaplan contacting him,' said Guscott. 'On the other hand, we wanted him to realize he was being tapped up.'

Kaplan's instructions were to talk about his defection, the new-found joys of living in the West and the Prague Spring. And then gauge Gordievsky's reactions.

Gordievsky knew he was being assessed. He felt his shoulders tense, as Kaplan recalled the dramatic events of 1968 in Czechoslovakia. Gordievsky merely observed that the Soviet invasion had come as a shock. 'I needed to be extremely careful. I was walking on the edge of an abyss.' When Kaplan described the details of his defection and his pleasant new life in Canada, Gordievsky nodded in a way that seemed encouraging, without being obvious. 'I thought it essential that although I should put out positive signals, I should not lose control of the situation.' He had no idea who had sent Kaplan to test him, and he was not about to ask.

In every courtship, it is important not to appear overeager. But Gordievsky's caution was more than mere flirtation technique. Though he had wondered whether Western intelligence would contact him following his outburst over events in Czechoslovakia in 1968, he was still not entirely sure he wanted to be seduced, or who was wooing him.

At the end of lunch, the two old friends shook hands, and Standa Kaplan disappeared into the crowds of shoppers. Nothing definitive had been said. No declarations or promises had been made. But an invisible line had been crossed. Gordievsky reflected: 'I knew that I had given away enough for him to put in a positive report.'

Stokes debriefed Standa Kaplan in a Copenhagen hotel room and then flew back to London to report the results to Geoffrey Guscott: Gordievsky had been surprised by Kaplan's sudden appearance, but not horrified or angry; he had seemed interested and sympathetic,

and expressed his astonishment at the Soviet invasion of Czechoslovakia. And, most importantly, Gordievsky had given no hint that he
would file a report to the KGB on his unexpected meeting with a
convicted anti-communist traitor. 'This was fascinating. This was
what we wanted to hear. Gordievsky was plainly being very cautious, but if he had not reported it, he would be taking a first, big
step. We needed to make it clear, without being too obvious, that we
were in the market. We needed to engineer a chance meeting.'

Richard Bromhead was 'absolutely bloody freezing'. It was seven in
the morning, snow had fallen overnight, and the temperature was
minus six. A steel-grey dawn was struggling up over Copenhagen.
SUNBEAM seemed most inaptly named. For three successive
mornings, at this 'ungodly hour', the MI6 man had sat in his wife's
tiny, unheated car, on a deserted, tree-lined street in the northern
suburbs, peering through the fogged windscreen at a large concrete
building, and wondering if he was getting frostbite.

Danish surveillance had established that Oleg Gordievsky played
badminton every morning with a young woman named Anna, a student member of the Danish Young Communists, at a suburban sports
club. Bromhead staked out the place, choosing to drive his wife's
inconspicuous blue Austin rather than his own Ford with diplomatic
plates. He parked in a spot with a direct line of sight to the door of
the club, but kept the engine switched off since the steam from the
exhaust might attract attention. On the first two mornings, 'Oleg
and the girl eventually appeared about 7.30, shook hands, and went to
their respective cars. She was young, with short dark hair, athletic
and slim but not particularly pretty. They didn't look as though
they were lovers, but I couldn't be sure. They might simply be prudent in public.'

On this, the third morning of sub-zero surveillance, Bromhead
decided he could stand the waiting no longer. 'My toes were completely frozen.' Judging the approximate moment when the game
should be over, he entered the club through the unlocked front door.
There was no one in reception. Oleg and his partner were almost certainly the building's only occupants. If he found them *in flagrante* on

the floor of the badminton court, Bromhead reflected, this could be tricky.

Gordievsky was between serves when the British spy came into view. He immediately recognized Bromhead. In his tweed suit and heavy overcoat he looked incongruous in the empty sports complex, and unmistakably British. Oleg raised his racquet in greeting, and then turned to finish the game.

The Russian did not seem surprised to see him. 'Perhaps he was expecting me?' thought Bromhead. 'Such an experienced and observant officer could well have noticed my car on one of the previous days. Once again, his friendly smile. Then deadly serious application to the game.'

In fact, as he played on, and Bromhead observed from a spectator's bench, Gordievsky's mind was whirling. Everything was slotting into place: Kaplan's visit, the party at Bromhead's house, and the fact that the genial British official seemed to have been at every social event he had attended in the last three months. The KGB had identified Bromhead as a probable intelligence officer, with a reputation for 'extrovert behaviour', and 'turning up at embassy parties whether he had been invited or not'. The Englishman's appearance in the deserted badminton court at this hour in the morning could mean only one thing: MI6 was trying to recruit him.

The game came to an end, Anna headed to the showers, and Gordievsky sauntered over, a towel around his neck, hand outstretched. The two intelligence officers assessed one another. 'Oleg displayed no sign of nervousness,' Bromhead wrote. Gordievsky noted that the Englishman, who usually radiated 'ebullient self-confidence', seemed for once deadly serious. They spoke a combination of Russian, German and Danish, into which Bromhead inserted some incongruous French.

'Would you be able to talk to me, tête-à-tête? I would love to have a private conversation, some place where we would not be overheard.'

'I would like that,' said Gordievsky.

'It would be very interesting for me to have that sort of conversation with a member of your service. I think you are one of the few who would speak honestly to me.'

Another line crossed: Bromhead had revealed he knew Gordi-evsky was a KGB officer.

'Could we have lunch?' Bromhead continued.

'Yes, of course.'

'It might be more difficult for you to meet up than for me, so why don't you name a restaurant that would suit you?'

Bromhead had expected Gordievsky to choose some obscure, dis-creet rendezvous spot. Instead he suggested they meet, in three days' time, at the restaurant in the Østerport Hotel, directly across the main road from the Soviet embassy.

As he drove away in his wife's battered car, Bromhead was elated, but also uneasy. Gordievsky had seemed strangely calm, apparently unperturbed by the approach. He had chosen a restaurant so near his own embassy that a hidden microphone would be able to relay their conversation to listeners across the road. They could be spotted by Soviet officials, who frequently dined at the hotel. For the first time, it struck Bromhead that he might be the target, not the initiator, of an attempted enlistment. 'Oleg's behaviour and choice of restaurant made me strongly suspect I was being played at my own game. It was all just too easy. It didn't feel right.'

Back at the embassy, Bromhead fired off a cable to MI6 headquar-ters: 'For God's sake, I think *he's* trying to recruit *me*!'

But Gordievsky was merely establishing his cover. He, too, returned to his embassy, and told the *rezident*, Mogilevchik: 'This fellow from the British embassy has invited me to lunch. What do I do? Should I accept?' The question was passed on to Moscow, and an emphatic reply immediately boomed back from Dmitri Yakushin, the Grey Cardinal: 'YES! You should be aggressive and not shy away from an intelligence officer. Why not meet him? TAKE AN OFFENSIVE POSITION! Britain is a country of high interest to us.' This was Gordievsky's insurance policy. Having obtained official permission to go ahead, he could now make 'sanctioned contact' with MI6, without the KGB suspecting his loyalty.

One of the oldest gambits in intelligence is 'the dangle', when one side appears to make a play for someone on the other, lures him into complicity and gains his trust, before exposing him.

Bromhead wondered if he was the target of a KGB dangle. If not, was Gordievsky genuinely trying to recruit him? Should he pretend to be interested, and see how far the Soviets were prepared to go? For Gordievsky, the stakes were even higher. The visit from Kaplan and Bromhead's subsequent approach might all be part of an elaborate plot, in which he revealed his hand only to be exposed. Yakushin's blessing provided some protection, but not much. If he fell victim to an MI6 dangle, his career in the KGB would be over. He would be recalled to Moscow. He would doubtless fall victim, retrospectively, to the KGB logic that anyone the other side attempted to recruit was, *prima facie*, suspect.

James Jesus Angleton, the famously paranoid post-war chief of counter-intelligence at the CIA, described the spying game as a 'wilderness of mirrors'. Already, the Gordievsky case was reflecting and refracting in strange ways. Bromhead was still pretending to arrange a casual meeting between fellow intelligence officers, albeit on different sides of the Cold War – while wondering if he was being recruited himself. Gordievsky was pretending to his KGB bosses that this was a stab in the dark by British intelligence, a chance encounter leading to lunch – while wondering if MI6 might be planning to stitch him up.

Three days later, Bromhead walked through the cemetery behind the embassies, crossed the busy Dag Hammarskjölds Allé, entered the Østerport Hotel, and took a seat in the restaurant with his back to the window, where he could 'keep a close watch on the main entrance to the dining room'. PET had been informed the lunch was taking place, but Bromhead had insisted there should be no surveillance present, in case Gordievsky spotted it and backed out.

'I carefully examined all the other people in the restaurant, to see if I could recognize any other member of the Soviet embassy staff, whose pictures were all filed in our office. Everyone seemed to be an innocent Dane, or an equally innocent tourist. I sat back, wondering if Oleg would come.'

Gordievsky entered the dining room exactly on time.

Bromhead detected 'no hint of special nervousness, though his style was intrinsically taut, poised for action. He saw me at once. *Had he already been told which table I had reserved?* I wondered, as my mind raced into conventional spy fever. Oleg smiled his usual friendly smile and walked over.'

Bromhead felt a 'friendly atmosphere from the start' as they tucked into the Østerport's excellent Scandinavian buffet. The conversation ranged across religion, philosophy and music. Oleg made a mental note that his companion had done his homework, and 'took trouble to talk about subjects of interest to me'. When Bromhead remarked how odd it was that the KGB deployed so many officers abroad, Gordievsky's response was 'non-committal'. The Russian mostly spoke Danish; Bromhead replied in a messy mixture of Danish, German and Russian, a linguistic smorgasbord that made Gordievsky laugh, though 'there didn't seem to be any malice' in his amusement. 'He seemed to be totally relaxed, and was obviously aware that we were both intelligence officers.'

When coffee and schnapps had been served, Bromhead asked the crucial question. 'Will you have to file a report about our meeting?'

The reply was revealing: 'Probably, yes, but I'll make it a very neutral one.'

Here, finally, was the hint of collusion, not a flash of leg exactly, but the glimpse of an ankle.

Even so, Bromhead left the lunch 'more puzzled than ever'. Gordievsky had hinted that he was, in part, concealing the truth from the KGB. But he was also behaving exactly like a man who believed he was the hunter, not the prey. Bromhead sent a memo to MI6 headquarters: 'I emphasized my fear that it had been much too easy, and the strong impression I had that he was being so nice to me because he wanted to recruit me.'

Gordievsky also reported back to his bosses; a long, insipid document, concluding that the meeting had 'been of interest', but framed to emphasize 'the apparent importance of my own initiative'. The Grey Cardinal was delighted.

And then something quite extraordinary happened; which was nothing at all.

The Gordievsky case went dead. For eight months there was no contact whatever. Quite why this happened remains a mystery.

In Geoffrey Guscott's words: 'Looking back, you think: "How dreadful, the case just went into the long grass for months." We were waiting for the Danes to report, waiting for Bromhead to come back. But nothing happened. Bromhead took his eye off it – he was pursuing two or three others and it was such a long shot, you think it is never going to happen.' Perhaps Bromhead's suspicions had applied the brakes harder than he intended. 'If you push too hard, too quickly, it can go wrong,' said Guscott. 'When it goes right, it is often because you don't push.' In this case, MI6 failed to push at all: 'It was a cock-up.'

But it was a cock-up which, in the long run, worked. Gordievsky was concerned when weeks passed without an effort by Bromhead to renew contact, then dismayed, then quite angry, and finally oddly reassured. The pause gave him time for reflection. If this had been a dangle, MI6 would have moved much faster. He would wait. Give the KGB time to forget the contact with Bromhead. In spying, as in love, a little distance, a little uncertainty, an apparent cooling on one side or the other, can stimulate desire. In the eight frustrating months that followed lunch at the Østerport Hotel, Gordievsky's enthusiasm grew.

On 1 October 1974, the tall Englishman reappeared at the badminton court in the dawn light, and suggested they meet again. Bromhead's reason for suddenly re-establishing contact was that he was being redeployed to Northern Ireland as an undercover officer, to conduct operations against the IRA. He would be leaving in a few months. 'There was not much time left. I had decided, therefore, to waste no more of it,' Bromhead later wrote, with a briskness that suggests he was fully aware he had been wasting time. They agreed to meet at the SAS hotel, run by Scandinavian Airlines, a brand-new building never frequented by Soviet officers.

Bromhead was waiting at a corner table in the bar area when Oleg arrived. Asterix and Obelix, the two PET agents, had arrived some time earlier, and were sitting at the opposite end of the bar, trying to look inconspicuous behind a potted palm tree.

'With his usual clockwork punctuality, Oleg walked through the door on the stroke of one o'clock. The light was dim in the corner I had chosen, and for a moment Oleg looked around. To prevent him taking too much notice of the surveillants, I rose quickly to my feet. He came straight over, with his familiar smile.'

The atmosphere was immediately different. 'I felt it was time I took the initiative,' Gordievsky later recalled. 'I was alive with anticipation. He had sensed this, and felt the same.' Bromhead moved first. MI6 had authorized him to indicate this was more than a flirtation: 'After our drinks had been brought, I went straight to the point.'

'You're KGB. We know you have worked in Line N of the First Chief Directorate, the most secret of all your departments, which is running illegals all over the world.'

Gordievsky did not hide his surprise.

'Would you be prepared to talk to us about what you know?'

Gordievsky gave no reply.

Bromhead pressed on. 'Tell me, who is the PR Line deputy in your section, the person in charge of political-intelligence gathering and agent-running?'

There was a pause, and then the Russian broke into a broad grin. 'I am.'

Now it was Bromhead's turn to be impressed.

'I had toyed with the idea of talking about world peace and so on, but my intuition about Oleg told me not to try any such blarney. But everything was still too easy. My suspicious mind was unable to accept this man at face value. My instinct was telling me that he was a remarkably nice person and I could trust him. My training and experience of KGB officers, on the other hand, was screaming caution.'

Another marker had been put down, and both knew it. 'All at once we were almost colleagues,' wrote Gordievsky. 'At last we began to speak in plain language.'

Bromhead now administered the 'acid test'.

'Would you be prepared to meet me, in private, in a safe place?'

The Russian nodded.

Then he said something that flicked an invisible light from amber to green. 'No one is aware that I am meeting you.'

After their first encounter, Oleg had informed his superiors, and written up a report. This meeting was unsanctioned. If the KGB discovered he had contacted Bromhead and kept it secret, he was doomed.

By informing MI6 that he had told no one, he was making his switch of allegiance perfectly clear, and putting his life in their hands. He had crossed over.

'This was a big step,' Guscott later recalled. 'It was the equivalent, in adultery, of saying: "My wife doesn't know I'm here."' Gordievsky felt a flood of relief, and a fluttering surge of adrenalin. They agreed to meet again, in three weeks, in a bar on the edge of the city. Gordievsky departed first. Bromhead a few minutes later. Finally, the two Danish undercover intelligence officers emerged from behind a pot plant.

The courtship was over: Major Gordievsky of the KGB was now working with MI6. SUNBEAM was up and running.

In that one cathartic moment, in the corner of a Copenhagen hotel, all the strands of a long-brewing rebellion had come together: his anger at his father's unacknowledged crimes, his absorption of his mother's quiet resistance and his grandmother's hidden religious beliefs; his detestation of the system he had grown up in and his love of the Western freedoms he had discovered; his simmering outrage over the Soviet repressions of Hungary and Czechoslovakia and the Berlin Wall; his sense of his own dramatic destiny, cultural superiority and optimistic faith in a better Russia. From now on Oleg Gordievsky would live two distinct and parallel lives, both secret, and at war with one another. And the moment of commitment came with the special force that was central to his character: an adamantine, unshakable conviction that what he was doing was unequivocally right, a whole-souled moral duty that would change his life irrevocably, a righteous betrayal.

When Bromhead's report landed in London, the senior officers of MI6 were gathered for a conference at the Service's secret training base in Fort Monckton, a Napoleonic-era fortress near Portsmouth on England's south coast. At 10 p.m., a small group gathered to consider Bromhead's report, and decide a course of action. 'The question of whether this was a provocation was raised time and again,' said Geoffrey Guscott. Would a senior KGB officer really be willing to risk his life by meeting secretly with a known MI6 operative? On the other hand, would the KGB dare to dangle one of its own officers?

After a tense debate, it was agreed to press ahead. SUNBEAM might seem too good to be true; but it was also too good to pass up.

Three weeks later, Bromhead and Gordievsky met in the dark, almost empty bar: both had carefully dry-cleaned themselves *en route*; both were 'black'. Their conversation was businesslike, but halting. The lack of a common language was a serious impediment. The English and Russian spies had established an understanding; they just couldn't fully understand what was being said. Bromhead explained that since he would soon be leaving Copenhagen, responsibility for handling future meetings would be transferred to a colleague, a senior intelligence officer who spoke fluent German and could therefore converse with Gordievsky more easily. Bromhead would select a convenient safe house in which to meet, make the introductions, and then bow out of the case.

The secretary of the Copenhagen MI6 station lived in a flat in the residential suburb of Charlottenlund. The place was easy to reach by subway, and the secretary would make herself scarce at the appropriate time. Bromhead suggested he meet Gordievsky in the doorway of a butcher's shop near the flat, at 7 p.m., in three weeks' time. 'The doorway provided a convenient shadow from the bright street lights. Also, it was difficult to post any watcher near that doorway, without their being clearly visible in the surroundings. By that time of day the place would be deserted, and all the Danes would be cosy and tucked up with their TVs.'

Gordievsky arrived at seven on the dot. Bromhead appeared moments later. After a silent grasping of hands, the Englishman said: 'Come, I'll show you the way.' The safe flat, or 'OCP' in spy jargon, standing for Operational Clandestine Premises, was barely 200 yards away, but Bromhead took a circuitous route, in case anyone was following. 'The night was cold, with drifting snowflakes.' Both men were bundled up inside overcoats. Gordievsky was silent, plunged in thought: 'I was not afraid of being kidnapped, but I knew that things were now serious: this was the real start of operations. For the first time I was entering enemy territory.'

Bromhead unlocked the door of the flat, ushered Gordievsky in, and poured them both stiff whiskies and soda.

'How long have you got?' asked Bromhead.

'About half an hour.'

'I'm quite surprised you turned up. Are you not running a grave risk seeing me like this?'

Gordievsky paused, and 'in a very measured way' replied: 'It might be dangerous, but at this moment I do not think it will prove to be so.'

Bromhead carefully explained, in his odd jumble of languages, that he would be flying back to London the next morning and then on to Belfast. But he would return in three weeks, meet Gordievsky in the butcher's doorway, bring him here to the flat, and introduce his new case officer. A small group of PET officers knew what was happening, but the case would be run exclusively by MI6. For Gordievsky's safety, Bromhead assured him, only a tiny handful of people inside British intelligence would ever know he existed, and most of these would never learn his real name. In intelligence language, someone made party to a secret operation is 'indoctrinated'; the case would involve the smallest number of indoctrinees possible, and would be run under the tightest security since there might be Soviet spies within PET or MI6, ready to report back to Moscow. Even the CIA, the intelligence service of Britain's closest ally, would be kept 'out of the loop'. 'With these factors in our favour, we could put our relationship on sound foundations, and begin serious cooperation.'

As he bid Gordievsky farewell, Bromhead reflected how little he really knew about the smiling, apparently nerveless Russian KGB officer, who seemed ready to risk his life by colluding with MI6. The question of money had never arisen. Nor had Oleg's own safety, or that of his family, or whether he wished to defect. They had talked generally about culture and music, but not about politics, ideology or life under Soviet rule. Gordievsky's motivation had not been discussed. 'I never asked him why he was doing it. There just wasn't time.'

Those questions were still niggling Bromhead when he arrived the next morning in MI6's London headquarters. The controller of the Sovbloc division was reassuring. 'He was very experienced in KGB matters and suitably cautious, but said this was a unique situation which had to be exploited to the full. It was the first time any KGB officer had responded positively to a British approach "from cold".' The Soviets were far too paranoid, he said, to dangle someone with access to real secrets. 'They had never offered up a serving KGB staff officer . . . They just didn't trust their own not to go off in a relationship with a [Western] case officer.'

The MI6 bosses were optimistic. SUNBEAM could prove to be a breakthrough case. Gordievsky seemed genuine. Bromhead was not so sure. The Russian spy had yet to produce a single shred of useful intelligence, let alone an explanation for what he was doing.

Transferring an agent from one case officer to another is a complex and sometimes fraught process, particularly when the spy is newly recruited. In January 1975, three weeks after leaving Copenhagen, Bromhead was 'infiltrated as quietly and anonymously as possible back into Denmark': he flew to Gothenburg in Sweden, where he was met by the PET officer Winter Clausen. Squeezed into the passenger seat of a Volkswagen alongside Obelix's 'vast and grinning bulk', he crossed the border into Denmark, and checked into a 'suitably impersonal and suburban' hotel in Copenhagen's Lyngby shopping centre.

Philip Hawkins, the new handler, flew in from London on a false passport. 'You will like him,' Bromhead had told Gordievsky. He was not entirely sure this was true. 'I certainly didn't like him. I thought he was a prize shit.' This was neither accurate nor fair. Hawkins was a barrister by training: severe, precise and not a bit like Bromhead.

After meeting Gordievsky at the butcher's shop, Bromhead escorted him to the safe flat, where Hawkins was waiting. Gordievsky took in his new case officer. 'He was tall and physically powerful, and I immediately felt ill at ease with him.' Hawkins spoke formal, rather stiff German, and seemed to be eyeing his new agent 'in a hostile, almost threatening manner'.

Bromhead shook hands gravely with Gordievsky, thanked him for what he was doing, and wished him good luck. As he drove away, Bromhead felt a mixture of feelings: regret, for he liked and admired the Russian spy, anxiety at the lingering possibility of a KGB plot and deep relief that, for him, the case was over.

'I was profoundly glad my role had ended,' Bromhead wrote. 'I couldn't rid myself of the thought that I might have constructed a bottomless "heffalump trap" into which my service was clearly determined to plunge headlong.'

# 4.    Green Ink and Microfilm

Why does anyone spy? Why give up the security of family, friends and a regular job, for the perilous twilight world of secrets? Why, in particular, would someone join one intelligence service, and then switch loyalty to an opposing one?

The nearest parallel to Gordievsky's secret defection from the KGB may be the case of Kim Philby, the Cambridge-educated Englishman who made the same journey but in the opposite direction, as an MI6 officer secretly working for the KGB. Like Philby, Gordievsky had undergone a profound ideological conversion, although one man was drawn to communism and the other repelled by it. But Philby's conversion occurred before he had managed to get himself recruited by MI6 in 1940 with the explicit intention of working for the KGB against the capitalist West; Gordievsky had joined the KGB as a loyal Soviet citizen, never imagining that he might one day betray it.

Spies come in many shapes. Some are motivated by ideology, politics or patriotism. A surprising number act out of avarice, for the financial rewards can be alluring. Others find themselves drawn into espionage by sex, blackmail, arrogance, revenge, disappointment, or the peculiar oneupmanship and comradeship that secrecy confers. Some are principled and brave. Some are grasping and cowardly.

Pavel Sudoplatov, one of Stalin's spymasters, had this advice for his officers seeking to recruit spies in Western countries: 'search for people who are hurt by fate or nature – the ugly, those suffering from an inferiority complex, craving power and influence but defeated by unfavourable circumstances . . . In cooperation with us, all these find a peculiar compensation. The sense of belonging to an influential and powerful organization will give them a feeling of superiority over the handsome and prosperous people around them.' For many years, the KGB used the acronym MICE to identify the four mainsprings of spying: Money, Ideology, Coercion and Ego.

But there is also romance, the opportunity to live a second, hidden life. Some spies are fantasists. Malcolm Muggeridge, former MI6 officer and journalist, wrote: 'Intelligence agents, in my experience, are even bigger liars than journalists.' Espionage attracts more than its share of the damaged, the lonely and the plain weird. But all spies crave undetected influence, that secret compensation: the ruthless exercise of private power. A degree of intellectual snobbery is common to most, the secret sense of knowing important things unknown to the person standing next to you at the bus stop. In part, spying is an act of the imagination.

The decision to spy on one's own country, in the interests of another, usually emerges from the collision of an outer world, often rationally conceived, and an inner world, of which the spy may be unaware. Philby defined himself as a pure ideological agent, a devoted secret soldier in the communist cause; what he did not admit was that he was also motivated by narcissism, inadequacy, his father's influence and a compulsion to deceive those around him. Eddie Chapman, the wartime crook and double agent known as Agent ZIGZAG, considered himself a patriotic hero (which he was), but he was also greedy, opportunistic and fickle, hence his codename. Oleg Penkovsky, the Russian spy who furnished the West with crucial intelligence during the Cuban Missile Crisis, hoped to prevent nuclear war, but he also wanted prostitutes and chocolates brought to his London hotel, and demanded to meet the Queen.

The outer world that propelled Oleg Gordievsky into the arms of MI6 was political and ideological: he had been profoundly influenced, and alienated, by the building of the Berlin Wall and the crushing of the Prague Spring; he had read enough Western literature, knew enough of his nation's real history, and seen enough of democratic freedoms to know that the socialist nirvana reflected in communist propaganda was a monstrous lie. He had been brought up in a world of unquestioning obedience to a dogma. Once he had rejected that ideology, he became committed to attacking it with all the fervour of the convert, as deeply and irreversibly opposed to communism as his father, brother and contemporaries were committed to it. A creature of the system, he understood the ruthless cruelty of the KGB at first hand. Alongside political repression lay cultural philistinism: with the passionate fury of an aficionado, he hated ersatz Soviet music and the censorship of the Western classical canon. He demanded a different, better soundtrack to his life.

But the inner world that drove Oleg is more obscure. He relished the romance and the adventure. He was undoubtedly rebelling against his father, the obedient, guilt-ridden KGB yes-man. A secretly religious grandmother, a quietly nonconformist mother, and a brother dead in the service of the KGB at the age of thirty-nine, may all have exerted a subconscious influence, driving him towards mutiny. He had little respect for most of his colleagues, KGB time-servers, ignorant, lazy and on the fiddle, who seemed to win promotion by political manoeuvring and toadying. He was cleverer than most of those around him, and knew it. Gordievsky's marriage had grown cold at that time; he found it hard to make close friends. He was looking for revenge, for fulfilment, but also for love.

All spies need to feel they are loved. One of the most powerful forces in espionage and intelligence work (and one of its central myths) is the emotional bond between spy and spymaster, agent and handler. Spies want to feel wanted, part of a secret community, rewarded, trusted and cherished. Eddie Chapman established close relationships with both his British and German handlers. Philby was recruited by Arnold Deutsch, a famously charismatic KGB talent scout, whom he described as 'a marvellous man . . . He looked at you as if nothing more important in life than you and talking to you existed at that moment.' Exploiting and manipulating that hunger for affection and affirmation is one of the most important skills of an agent-runner. There has never been a successful spy who did not feel that the connection with his handler was something more profound than a marriage of convenience, politics or profit: a true, enduring communion, amid the lies and deception.

Gordievsky sensed several emotions radiating off Philip Hawkins, his new English case officer; but love was not among them.

The eccentric and ebullient Richard Bromhead had appealed to Gordievsky by seeming 'terribly English'. He was just the sort of bravura Englishman Lyubimov had described with such enthusiasm.

Hawkins was Scottish, and colder by several degrees. Upright, clipped, as stiff and brittle as an oatcake. 'He felt it was his duty not to be smiley and nice, but to look at the case with a lawyerly eye,' said one colleague.

Hawkins had been responsible for interrogating German prisoners during the war. For several years he worked on Czech and Soviet cases, including a number of defectors. Most importantly, he had direct experience of handling a spy inside the KGB. Back in 1967, an English-woman living in Vienna contacted the British embassy to report that she had taken in an interesting new lodger, a young Russian diplomat who seemed receptive to Western ideas and quite critical of commun-ism. She was teaching him to ski. She was probably also sleeping with him. MI6 gave him the codename PENETRABLE, began to make inquiries, and discovered that the West German intelligence service, the BND, 'was also in on the chase', and had already made an approach to PENETRABLE, a KGB trainee, which had yielded a positive response. It was agreed to run PENETRABLE as a joint Anglo-West German agent. The case officer on the British side was Philip Hawkins.

'Philip knew the KGB backwards,' said one colleague. 'He was paid to be sceptical. He was the obvious person to run Gordievsky, he spoke German, and he was available.' He was also nervous, and covered his anxiety with a display of aggression. His task, as he saw it, was to find out if Oleg was lying, how much he was prepared to divulge and what he wanted in return.

Hawkins sat Gordievsky down, and launched into a courtroom-style cross-examination.

'Who is your *rezident*? How many KGB officers are there in the station?'

Gordievsky had expected to be welcomed, praised and congratu-lated on the momentous choice he was making. Instead, he was being hectored, interrogated as if he were a captive enemy rather than a cooperative new recruit.

'The inquisition continued for some time, and I did not like it.'

Through Gordievsky's mind ran the thought: 'This can't be the true spirit of the British intelligence service.'

The grilling paused for a moment. Gordievsky raised his hand,

and issued a declaration: he would work for British intelligence, but only under three conditions.

'First, I don't want to damage any of my colleagues in the KGB station. Second, I don't want to be secretly photographed or recorded. Third, no money. I want to work for the West out of ideological conviction, not for gain.'

Now it was Hawkins's turn to be affronted. Inside his mental courtroom, witnesses under cross-examination did not set rules. The second condition was moot. If MI6 decided to record him he would never know since the recording would, by definition, be secret. His pre-emptive refusal to accept financial compensation was more worrying. It is an axiom of spycraft that informants should be encouraged to accept gifts or money – although not so much that they would not want more, or would be tempted to extravagant expenditure that might attract suspicion. Cash makes a spy feel valuable, establishes the principle of payment for services rendered, and can be used, if necessary, as a lever. And why did he wish to shield his Soviet colleagues? Was he still loyal to the KGB? In reality, Gordievsky was partly protecting himself: if Denmark started ejecting KGB officers, the Centre might begin looking for an internal traitor, and eventually alight on him.

Hawkins remonstrated: 'Now we know what your position in the station is, we'll think not twice but three times before we or our allies take a decision to expel anyone.' But Gordievsky was adamant: he was not going to identify his fellow KGB officers, their agents and illegals, and they should be left alone. 'These people are not important. They are nominally agents but they are not doing any harm. I don't want them to get into trouble.'

Hawkins reluctantly agreed to relay his conditions to MI6, and laid out the *modus operandi*. He would fly to Copenhagen once a month, and stay for a long weekend during which they could meet twice, for at least two hours. The meetings would take place in another safe flat (provided by the Danes, though Gordievsky was not told this), in the northern suburb of Ballerup, a quiet area at the end of an underground line, on the other side of the city from the Soviet embassy. Gordievsky could travel by rail, or by car and park some distance away. There was little chance of being spotted there by his embassy colleagues, and if Soviet surveillance was deployed in the vicinity, he would probably know about it. Danish surveillance was more of a problem. Gordievsky was a suspected KGB officer and had been monitored by PET in the past. Loud alarm bells would ring should he be spotted going to a secret rendezvous in the suburbs. No more than half a dozen people in PET were aware that MI6 was running a Soviet agent, and only a couple of these knew his name. One of them was Jørn Bruun, the head of PET counter-intelligence and Bromhead's old ally. Bruun would ensure that his men were not tailing Gordievsky on the days he met his British handler. Finally, Hawkins handed over an emergency telephone number, secret ink and a London address to which he could send any urgent messages between meetings.

Both men left the flat feeling disgruntled. The first contact between spy and case officer had not been a happy one.

Yet in some ways the appointment of the brusque and unsmiling Hawkins turned out well. He was a professional, and so was Gordievsky. The Russian was in the hands of someone who took his job, and Gordievsky's safety, extremely seriously. To use Bromhead's favourite phrase, Hawkins was not mucking about.

So began a series of monthly meetings, in a one-bedroom flat on the third floor of a nondescript apartment block in Ballerup. The place was simply furnished with Danish furniture. The kitchen was fully equipped. The rent was paid jointly by the intelligence services of Britain and Denmark. A few days before the first meeting at the new OCP, two PET technicians disguised as electricity company workers inserted microphones in the overhead lights and electric sockets, and ran connecting wires behind the skirting boards into the bedroom where, behind a panel above the bed, they installed a tape recorder. The second of Gordievsky's conditions had been violated.

The meetings were initially tense, gradually more relaxed and in time exceptionally fruitful. What had started in an atmosphere of prickly suspicion would slowly evolve into a highly efficient relationship, based not on affection, but on grudging mutual respect. In lieu of love, Gordievsky accepted Hawkins's professional approval.

The best way to test whether someone is lying is to ask a question

to which you already know the answer. Hawkins was well versed in
the structure of the KGB. Gordievsky described, with impressive
accuracy, every directorate, department and sub-department of the
sprawling, complex bureaucracy inside Moscow Centre. Some of this
Hawkins already knew; a great deal he did not: names, functions,
techniques, training methods, even rivalries and internal disputes,
promotions and demotions. The level of detail proved that Gordievsky was straight: no 'dangle' would have dared reveal so much. He
never once asked Hawkins for information about MI6, or made any
of the moves a double agent attempting to infiltrate an enemy service
might make.

The spymasters at MI6 headquarters were soon convinced of Gordievsky's bona fides. 'SUNBEAM was the real thing,' concluded
Guscott. 'He was playing it fair and square.'

That conviction was redoubled when Gordievsky began to describe, in minute detail, the activities of Directorate S, the illegals
section where he had worked for a decade before moving to the
political wing: how Moscow planted its spies, disguised as ordinary
civilians, all over the world, including 'the immense and highly
sophisticated operation to create false identities': forging documents,
manipulating registration records, burying moles, and the complex
methodology for contacting, controlling and financing the army of
Soviet illegals.

Before every meeting, Hawkins unclipped the panel in the bedroom, inserted a fresh cassette, and switched on the tape recorder. He
took notes, but then carefully transcribed each recorded conversation,
translating from German to English. Each hour of recording took three
or four times as long to process. The resulting report was then handed
to a junior MI6 officer in the British embassy, who sent it back to London with the cassette tape in the diplomatic bag, which was immune
from search. At MI6 headquarters, the reports were eagerly awaited.
British intelligence had never run a spy so deep within the KGB. As a
trained intelligence officer, Gordievsky understood exactly what MI6
was looking for. At School 101 he had been taught techniques for memorizing large quantities of information. His powers of recall were
prodigious.

Relations between agent and case officer slowly improved. For hours they would sit, on either side of a large coffee table. Gordievsky drank strong tea, and occasionally asked for a beer. Hawkins drank nothing. There was little in the way of small talk. Gordievsky found it hard to like this uptight Scot with the air of an 'austere Presbyterian priest', but he respected him. 'He was not an easy man with whom to joke, but he was dedicated and hardworking, always making notes, preparing himself well and asking good questions.' The British case officer frequently arrived with a shopping list of questions, which the Russian would memorize and attempt to find answers for before the next meeting. One day Hawkins asked Gordievsky to look over one of his reports, a comprehensive write-up, in German, of the illegals system Oleg had described. The Russian was impressed; clearly Hawkins was a master of German shorthand, for not a single detail had been omitted. Only later did it strike him: MI6 must be bugging the apartment. Oleg decided not to make a fuss over the broken promise, reflecting that he would probably have done the same.

'I was much easier in my mind,' wrote Gordievsky. 'My new role gave a point to my existence.' That role, he believed, was nothing less than undermining the Soviet system, in a Manichean struggle between good and evil that would eventually bring democracy to Russia, and allow Russians to live freely, read what they wanted, and listen to Bach. In his day job for the KGB, he continued to make Danish contacts, draw up articles for pro-Soviet journalists and generally service the patchy intelligence-gathering system of the Copenhagen *rezidentura*. The more energetic he appeared, the greater his chances of promotion, and the better his access to important information. It was an odd situation: trying to demonstrate his proficiency to the KGB, without actually damaging Danish interests; setting up spy operations with one hand, and then unpicking them with the other, by informing Hawkins of every move; keeping his eyes and ears open for useful information and gossip, without seeming too inquisitive.

Yelena remained wholly ignorant of what her husband was up to. 'A spy has to deceive even his nearest and dearest,' Gordievsky later wrote. But Yelena was no longer either near or dear to him. Indeed, he felt sure that if she discovered the truth, as a loyal KGB officer, she would shop him. Gordievsky knew what the KGB did to traitors. Regardless of Danish or international law, he would be seized by the operatives of the Special Actions department, drugged, bundled onto a stretcher bound in bandages to conceal his identity, and flown to Moscow, where he would be interrogated, tortured and then killed. The Russian euphemism for the summary death sentence was *vyshaya mera*, 'highest measure': the traitor was taken into a room, made to kneel, and then shot in the back of the head. Sometimes the KGB was more imaginative. It was said that Penkovsky had been cremated alive and his death filmed, as a warning to potential turncoats.

Despite the pressure of a double life and the peril this entailed, Gordievsky was content, waging his solitary campaign against Soviet oppression. And then he fell in love.

Leila Aliyeva was a typist for the World Health Organization in Copenhagen. The daughter of a Russian mother and a father from Azerbaijan, she was tall and striking, with a shock of dark hair and deep brown eyes behind long eyelashes. In contrast to Yelena, she was shy and unworldly, but when she relaxed her laugh was loud and infectious. She loved to sing. Like Oleg, Leila came from KGB stock: her father, Ali, had risen to the rank of major-general in the Azeri KGB, before retiring to Moscow. Brought up a Muslim, she had had a sheltered childhood. Her few boyfriends to date had been carefully vetted by her parents. She started work as a typist in a designer firm, then worked as a journalist on the Communist Youth League newspaper and then applied, through the Ministry of Health, for a secretarial job at the World Health Organization. Like every Soviet citizen seeking to work for a foreign organization abroad, Leila was thoroughly vetted for ideo-logical dependability before being permitted to travel to Copenhagen. She was twenty-eight, eleven years younger than Oleg. Soon after her arrival in Denmark, Leila was invited to a reception given by the ambassador's wife, who asked her what she did in Moscow.

'I was a journalist,' Leila replied. 'And I would like to write some-thing about Denmark.'

'Then you must meet the press attaché at the embassy, Mr Gordievsky.'

And so Oleg Gordievsky and Leila Aliyeva began working together on an article for the Communist Youth magazine about the slum district of Copenhagen. It was never published. But very swiftly their collaboration deepened. 'She was sociable, interesting, original, witty and eager to be liked. I fell in love at first sight, [and] our love flared up quickly.' Free from her parents' controlling supervision, Leila threw herself into the affair with abandon.

'At his first appearance he seemed so grey,' Leila recalled. 'If you saw him in the street you would not notice him. But when I started to talk to him, my jaw dropped. He knew so much. He was so interesting, with this brilliant sense of humour. Slowly, slowly, I fell in love with him.'

For Gordievsky, Leila's gentle personality and simple sweetness seemed a tonic after Yelena's shrewish disdain. He had become used to calculation in his human relationships, constantly assessing his own actions and words, and those of others. Leila, by contrast, was natural, outgoing and uninhibited: Oleg felt adored, for the first time in his life. Gordievsky introduced his young lover to a new world of literature, containing ideas and realities banned in Russia. At his urging she read Solzhenitsyn's *Gulag Archipelago* and *The First Circle*, depicting the dark brutality of Stalinism. 'He gave me books from his library. I took it to my heart, this waterfall of truth. He educated me.' Leila knew from the outset, without ever being told, that Gordievsky was a KGB officer. The thought that his interest in such books might conceal a deeper dissidence never crossed her mind. In whispered trysts, they made extravagant plans. They imagined having children. The KGB frowned on adultery, and even more on divorce. 'Our meetings were very secret. Any photo that could be evidence of adultery would be used against him, and punished very severely. He would have been expelled in 24 hours.' They would have to be patient. But, then, he was used to a slow and secret courtship.

Gordievsky worked hard at both his jobs. He played a lot of badminton. Leila shared her flat with two roommates, and Yelena was often at home, so he and Leila would meet for secret assignations, covert and thrilling. But here was another layer of deception, and anxiety: he was now betraying Yelena on two levels, professional and personal. Exposure of either one could spell disaster. He covered the tracks of his double infidelity with precision and care. Every few days, he would send a disguised message to Leila, and commit adultery in a different Copenhagen hotel; every four weeks, he would make his way to an unremarkable flat in a boring Danish suburb, and commit treason. Over the course of a year, he established a system of evasion, eluding both Soviet surveillance and the suspicions of his wife. His relationships, with both Leila and MI6, were deepening. He felt safe. Which he was not.

One winter evening, a young Danish intelligence officer was heading home to Ballerup when he spotted a car with diplomatic number plates parked in a side street, far from the diplomatic enclaves. The young man was curious. He was also trained, and mustard keen. On closer inspection, he recognized the car as belonging to the Soviet embassy. What was a Soviet diplomat doing in the suburbs, at 7 p.m. on a weekend?

A dusting of snow had fallen, and fresh footprints led away from the car. The PET officer followed them for about 200 yards, to an apartment block. A Danish couple were leaving as he approached, and obligingly held the front door open for him. Wet footprints crossed the marble floor to the stairs. He followed them to the door of a flat on the second floor. From inside came the sound of low voices, speaking a foreign language. He noted down the address and number plate.

The following morning, a report landed on the desk of Jørn Bruun, the head of Danish counter-intelligence: a Soviet diplomat suspected of working for the KGB had been traced to a Ballerup flat where he was overheard speaking an unidentified language, possibly German, to a person or persons unknown: 'There is something suspicious here,' the report concluded. 'We should do something about it.'

But before the machinery of Danish surveillance could leap into motion, Jørn Bruun switched off the engine. The report was expunged from the file. The overzealous young officer was commended for his perceptiveness and then 'fobbed off' with a vague explanation as to why the lead was not worth pursuing. Not for the first time, a security service had, by its diligence, very nearly wrecked an ongoing case.

Gordievsky was shaken to learn how close he had come to being rumbled. 'The mishap gave us a shock whose after-effects lingered.' Henceforth he would travel to Ballerup by underground.

His refusal to name names waned as the months passed. Not that there were many names to name. The network of Soviet agents and informants in Denmark was, he revealed, pitifully small. There were Gert Petersen, the thirsty politician; an overweight policeman in the Danish immigration department who passed on occasional titbits; and several illegals planted around the country, waiting for the Third World War. The KGB officers in Copenhagen, Oleg explained, spent far more time inventing contacts in order to justify their expenses than actually meeting anyone. This reassuring intelligence was passed on to PET. The Danes were careful not to sweep up the few spies Gordievsky fingered, since this would immediately have pointed to an informant within the KGB. Instead, PET decided to keep tabs on the handful of Danish KGB contacts, and wait.

If the KGB had few spies worthy of the name in Denmark, the same was not true of Denmark's Scandinavian neighbours.

Gunvor Galtung Haavik was an inconspicuous employee in the Norwegian Ministry of Foreign Affairs, a former nurse who worked as a secretary and interpreter and was now nearing retirement. She was tiny, sweet-natured and rather shy. She was also a veteran, highly paid spy of thirty years' standing, who had been secretly awarded the Soviet Order of Friendship 'for strengthening international understanding' – which, in a way, she had, by handing over several thousand classified documents to the KGB.

Haavik's story was a classic tale of KGB manipulation. At the tail end of the war, with Norway still under Nazi occupation, she was working in a military hospital in Bodø when she fell in love with a Russian prisoner of war, Vladimir Kozlov. He neglected to tell her that he was already married, with a family back in Moscow. She helped him escape to Sweden. After the war, as a fluent Russian speaker, she was hired by the Norwegian Foreign Ministry and sent to Moscow as secretary to the Norwegian ambassador. There, her love affair with Kozlov was rekindled. The KGB got wind of the illicit romance, and provided an apartment where they could meet: then they threatened to expose the adulterous relationship to the Norwegians and exile Kozlov to Siberia, unless Haavik agreed to spy for them. For eight years she passed over reams of top-secret material, and continued to do so after being posted back to the Foreign

Ministry in Oslo. Norway, the northern flank of NATO, shared a 120-mile Arctic border with the USSR, and was regarded by the KGB as 'the key to the north'. Here the Cold War was fought with icy ferocity. Haavik, codenamed GRETA, met eight different KGB handlers at least 270 times. She continued to receive cash from Moscow, and messages from Kozlov (or rather the KGB pretending to be her Russian lover). A gullible, heartbroken spinster bullied into cooperating with the KGB, she was not even a communist.

Arne Treholt was as conspicuous and glamorous as Haavik was not. The son of a popular Norwegian Cabinet minister, a prominent journalist and member of Norway's powerful Labour Party, he was flamboyant, handsome and outspoken in his left-wing views. Treholt was going places, fast. He burnished his celebrity credentials by marrying a Norwegian television star, Kari Storække. The *New York Times* described him as 'one of the golden young men of public life in Norway'. Some thought he might end up as Prime Minister.

But in 1967 Treholt's trenchant opposition to the Vietnam War attracted the attention of the KGB. He was approached by Yevgeny Belyayev, an intelligence officer working undercover as a consular official in the Soviet embassy. Treholt later told police (a statement he subsequently recanted) that he had been recruited through 'sexual blackmail' after an orgy in Oslo. Belyayev encouraged Treholt to accept cash in return for information, and in 1971, at the Coq d'Or restaurant in Helsinki, he introduced him to Gennadi Fyodorovich Titov, the new KGB *rezident* in Oslo. Titov's ruthlessness had earned him the nickname 'the Crocodile', although with his large round spectacles and waddling gait he looked more like a particularly malicious owl. Titov had a 'reputation as the most accomplished flatterer in the First Chief Directorate'. Treholt liked flattery. He also liked a free lunch. Over the next decade, he and Titov dined together, at the KGB's expense, on fifty-nine occasions. 'We had glorious lunches,' Treholt recalled, many years later, 'where we discussed Norwegian and international politics.'

Norway lay outside Gordievsky's remit, but the Scandinavian countries were lumped together in KGB thinking, and each station was aware, to some extent, of the activities of the others. In 1974, a new KGB officer named Vadim Cherny was posted to Denmark from Moscow, where he had been working in the Scandinavian–British section of the FCD. Cherny was a mediocre officer, and an inveterate gossip. One day he let slip that the KGB was running a woman agent, codenamed GRETA, inside Norway's diplomatic service. A few weeks later he mentioned that the KGB had recruited another, 'even more important' agent inside the Norwegian government, 'someone with a journalistic background'.

Gordievsky passed this information on to Hawkins, who reported it back to MI6 and PET.

These two highly valuable leads were conveyed to Norwegian counter-intelligence. The source was heavily camouflaged: Norway was told the report was reliable, but not who or where it came from. 'This was not information Oleg was supposed to have in the course of his work, but stuff he had picked up – so we decided it could not be traced back directly to him.' The Norwegians were grateful, and thoroughly alarmed. Gunvor Haavik, the demure senior secretary at the Foreign Ministry, had been under suspicion for some time. Gordievsky's warning provided crucial confirmation. Fashionable young Arne Treholt had also popped up on the radar after being spotted in the company of a known KGB operative. Both would now be closely watched.

The Norwegian connection illustrated a central challenge of the Gordievsky case, and a conundrum of spying in general: how to make use of high-grade intelligence without compromising its source. An agent deep inside the enemy camp may unmask spies in your own camp. But if you arrest and neutralize them all, then you alert the other side to the spy within their own camp, and you endanger your source. How could British intelligence take advantage of what Gordievsky was revealing without burning him?

From the start, MI6 opted to play the long game. Gordievsky was still a young man. The information he supplied was excellent, and would only improve with time and promotion. Too much haste or hunger for information might scupper the case, and destroy Gordievsky. Security was paramount. The Philby disaster had taught Britain the perils of betrayal from within. The tiny group of officers in MI6 indoctrinated into the secret were told only what they needed to know. Inside PET, even fewer were aware of Gordievsky's existence.

The information he supplied was passed on sparingly to allies, some-times using intermediaries or 'cutouts', in nuggets carefully masked to appear as if they had come from elsewhere. Gordievsky was reveal-ing secrets hand over fist, but MI6 ensured his fingerprints were nowhere upon them.

The CIA was not informed about SUNBEAM. The so-called 'special relationship' was particularly warm in the intelligence sphere, yet the 'need to know' principle applied, in both directions. The CIA, it was agreed, certainly did *not* need to know that Britain had a major spy deep within the KGB.

Intelligence services do not like their officers to remain in one place indefinitely lest they become too comfortable; in the same way, agent-runners are rotated, to ensure that they do not lose objectivity or end up too heavily invested in one case or a single spy.

In accordance with this principle, the KGB *resident* in Copenhagen, Mogilevchik, was duly replaced by Gordievsky's old friend Mikhail Lyubimov, the amiable Anglophile with the taste for Scotch and tweed tailoring. The two men immediately resumed their friendship. Lyubi-mov was on his second marriage. The break-up of his first had caused a hiccup in his KGB career, but he was now in the ascendant again. Gor-dievsky admired this 'genial, relaxed fellow', with his worldly, wry take on the world. They spent long evenings together, chatting and drinking, discussing literature, art, music and espionage.

Lyubimov could see that his friend and protégé would go far. The bosses considered Gordievsky 'competent and erudite' and he was good at his job. 'Oleg behaved impeccably,' wrote Lyubimov. 'He didn't get involved in any of the infighting, was always ready to pro-vide whatever I wanted, modest like a true communist, didn't strive for promotion . . . some in the embassy staff didn't like him: "arro-gant", they called him, "too clever by half". But I didn't see these as vices. Don't most people think they are clever?' Only in retrospect did Lyubimov recall some telltale signs. Gordievsky had largely stopped going to diplomatic parties, and other than Lyubimov, he seldom socialized with other KGB officers. He buried himself in dis-sident literature. 'In his flat were books by certain authors banned in our country which I, as his senior colleague, advised him to keep out of sight.' The two couples often had dinner together, when Gordievsky would tell jokes, drink a little too heavily, and make a show of being happily married. A remark by Yelena stuck in Lyubimov's memory. 'He's not really an extrovert at all,' she said. 'Don't imagine he's being sincere with you.' Lyubimov knew the marriage was under severe strain, and paid no attention to the warning.

One evening in January 1977, Gordievsky arrived at the safe flat as usual to find Philip Hawkins waiting with a bespectacled younger man, whom he introduced as 'Nick Venables'. Hawkins explained that he would soon take up a new posting abroad, and this man was his replacement.

The new case officer was Geoffrey Guscott, the high-flyer who, seven years earlier, had read Kaplan's file and flagged up Gordievsky as a potential target. Guscott had been acting as Hawkins's desk officer and was therefore familiar with every aspect of the Gordievsky case. But he was nervous. 'I thought I knew enough to handle it, but I was still quite young. MI6 said: "You'll cope." But I wasn't so sure.'

Gordievsky and Guscott took to one another at once. The English officer spoke fluent Russian, and from the start they used the familiar form of address. Both were long-distance runners. But, more than that, in contrast to Hawkins, Guscott seemed to value Oleg as an individual, not just as a source of information. 'Inspiring in every way, always cheerful, always sincerely apologetic about any mistakes he made', Guscott was a kindred spirit who now devoted himself to the case full time, in deep secrecy. Within MI6, only his secretary and immediate superiors knew what he was doing. The SUNBEAM case moved up a gear.

MI6 offered to supply a miniature camera. With this Gordievsky could photograph documents inside the *rezidentura*, and then hand over the undeveloped film. Oleg declined. The risk of being caught was too high: 'One glimpse through a half-open door and everything would be finished.' Possession of a British-made mini-camera was about as incriminating as evidence could get. But there was another way to smuggle documents out of the KGB station.

Messages and instructions from Moscow arrived in the form of long reels of microfilm, transported via the Soviet 'diplomatic bag', an accepted part of international law used to pass information securely to and from embassies without interference from the host country. The *rezident*, or more usually the cipher clerks, then cut the film into strips and distributed these to the relevant sections or 'Lines': Illegals (N), Political (PR), Counter Intelligence (KR), Technical (X) and so on. Each length of film might include a dozen or more letters, memos or other documents. If Gordievsky could smuggle the microfilm strips out of the embassy during his lunch hour, he could transfer them to Guscott, who could copy them, and then hand them back. The entire process would take less than half an hour.

Guscott passed a request to the MI6 technical department at Hanslope Park, a country house estate in Buckinghamshire surrounded by leafy parkland and a security cordon of barbed wire and guard posts. Hanslope was (and is) one of the most secretive and heavily guarded outstations of British intelligence. During the war, the Hanslope boffins produced an astonishing array of technical gadgets for spies, including secure radios, secret ink and even garlic-flavoured chocolate – issued to spies parachuting into occupied France to ensure their breath smelled convincingly French on landing. Had Q, the technical wizard in the James Bond series, actually existed, he would have worked at Hanslope Park.

Guscott's request was at once simple and challenging: he needed a small, portable device that could copy a strip of microfilm, secretly and swiftly.

Sankt Annæ Plads is a long, tree-lined public square in the centre of Copenhagen, not far from the Royal Palace. At lunchtime, particularly in good weather, the place is thronged with people. One spring day in 1977, a well-built man in a business suit entered the telephone kiosk at the end of the park. As he was dialling, a tourist wearing a backpack stopped to ask directions, and then walked on. In that moment, Gordievsky slipped a roll of microfilm into Guscott's jacket pocket. Jørn Bruun had ensured there was no PET surveillance. A junior officer from the MI6 station loitered on a nearby bench.

Guscott rushed to a nearby PET safe house, locked himself in an upstairs bedroom, and took from his backpack a pair of silk gloves and a small flat box, six inches long by three inches wide, roughly the size of a pocket diary. He drew the curtains, turned off the light, unwound the microfilm strip, inserted one end into the little box, and pulled it through.

'It was quite a sweaty-palm procedure, fiddling in the dark. I always knew that if I couldn't do the operation in time, I would have to abort. And if I damaged the microfilm, it was a real problem.'

Exactly thirty-five minutes after the first brush contact, the two men performed another at the other end of the park, imperceptible to anyone but a highly trained surveillance officer, and the reel was back in Gordievsky's pocket.

The flow of documents out of the KGB *rezidentura* and into the hands of MI6 swelled to a torrent: initially just the PR Line instructions from Moscow Centre, of which Gordievsky was the recipient, then gradually expanding to include microfilm strips issued to other officers, which they frequently left on desks or in briefcases during the lunch hour.

The rewards were great, but so were the risks. With each transfer of stolen material, Gordievsky knew he was taking his life in his hands. Another KGB officer might return unexpectedly from lunch and find his microfilm instructions missing, or Gordievsky might be spotted filching material not intended for his eyes. If he was found to be in possession of microfilm outside the embassy, he was doomed. Each brush contact, Guscott observed with ringing understatement, was 'highly charged'.

Gordievsky was terrified, but determined. Each contact left him fizzing with the gambler's rush of a successful gambit, but wondering whether his luck could hold. Even in the coldest weather, he returned to the *rezidentura* in a muck sweat of fear and excitement, hoping his colleagues would not notice his shaking hands. The contact sites followed a deliberately irregular pattern: a park, a hospital, a hotel toilet, a station. Guscott parked a car nearby, in case the copying process had to be carried out inside the vehicle, using a lightproof fabric bag.

Despite every precaution, there was no accounting for accidents. On one occasion, Guscott arranged to make a brush contact at a railway station in the north of the city. He placed himself by a window in the station café, and drank a coffee while waiting for Gordievsky to appear and leave a roll of microfilm under a ledge in the nearby telephone kiosk. The Russian duly appeared, made the drop and walked away, but before Guscott could get to the kiosk, a man stepped into it ahead of him, and began making a telephone call. A long telephone call. The minutes slipped past, as the man obliviously chattered on, inserting one coin after another. There was only a thirty-minute window in which to pick up the film, copy it, and return it at a second contact site in another location, and it was closing fast. Guscott loitered outside the telephone box, hopping from foot to foot, exhibiting an anxiety that was not feigned. The man on the telephone ignored him. Guscott was on the point of barging in and grabbing the roll, when the man finally hung up. Guscott reached the second brush contact site with less than a minute to spare.

As Lyubimov's deputy and confidant, Gordievsky had access to many of the microfilms, and 'the volume of tape blossomed'. Scores, and eventually hundreds, of documents were extracted and copied, with details of codenames, operations, directives and even the entire 150-page confidential review compiled by the embassy, a complete picture of Soviet diplomatic strategy in Denmark. The information was carefully parcelled out back in London, disguised, and then distributed, piecemeal: to MI5, if it affected national security, and occasionally, if sufficiently important, to the Foreign Office. Of Britain's allies, only the Danes received direct intelligence from the SUNBEAM files. Some of the material – notably that relating to Soviet espionage in the Arctic – was shown to the Foreign Secretary, David Owen, and the Prime Minister, James Callaghan. No one was told where it had come from.

Guscott flew to Denmark more frequently, and stayed for longer, moving into the Ballerup flat for three days at a stretch. The two spies would carry out a microfilm exchange at lunchtime on Friday, then meet at the flat on Saturday evening and again the next morning. His romantic trysts with Leila, and his espionage assignations with Guscott, meant that Gordievsky was away from home for longer and longer periods. He told Yelena he was busy with secret KGB work that was none of her business. She may or may not have believed him.

Gordievsky's conditions for cooperation diluted, and then

evaporated. The Russian knew he was being recorded. He abandoned his own refusal to reveal names, and identified every KGB officer, every illegal and every source. Finally, he agreed to accept money. Guscott told him that, 'from time to time', sterling would be deposited for him in a London bank, as a contingency, a measure of Britain's gratitude, and an unstated acknowledgement that, eventually, he would defect to the UK. Gordievsky might never be able to spend his espionage earnings, but he valued the gesture, and accepted the cash.

Gordievsky was more valuable than money, and there was another, highly symbolic way to show it: a personal thank you letter from the chief of MI6.

Maurice Oldfield, the most senior spy in Britain, signed himself 'C', in green ink, a practice first adopted by the founder of MI6, Mansfield Cumming, who imported it from the Royal Navy, where ships' captains customarily write in green ink. The tradition has been adopted by every MI6 chief since. Guscott typed a letter of thanks and congratulations from Oldfield to Gordievsky, in English, on thick cream notepaper, which the head of the Service signed with a green flourish. Guscott translated it into Russian, and presented both the original and the translation to Gordievsky at their next meeting. Oleg's face lit up as he read the encomium. Guscott took the letter away again when they parted: a personal letter signed in green ink from Britain's spymaster-in-chief was not the sort of souvenir to keep in his possession. 'It was a way to reassure Oleg that we took him seriously and put it on a formal footing, to establish a personal connection and show Oleg he was dealing with the organization itself. That all helped to settle him down, and marked the maturity of the case.' At the next meeting, Gordievsky produced his reply to Oldfield. The correspondence between SUNBEAM and 'C' remains in the MI6 archives, proof of the personal touch on which successful spying depends.

Gordievsky's letter was his testament.

I must emphasize that my decision is not the result of irresponsibility or instability of character on my part. It has been preceded by a long spiritual struggle and by agonizing emotion, and an even deeper disappointment at developments in my own country and my own experiences have brought me to the belief that democracy, and the tolerance of humanity that follows it, represents the only road for my country, which is European in spite of everything. The present regime is the antithesis of democracy to an extent which Westerners can never fully grasp. If a man realizes this, he must show the courage of his convictions and do something himself to prevent slavery from encroaching further upon the realms of freedom.

*

Gunvor Haavik arranged to meet her KGB controller, Aleksandr Printsipalov, on the evening of 27 January 1977. The Russian was waiting when she arrived at the rendezvous, a dark side street in an Oslo suburb. So were three officers of the Norwegian security service, who pounced. After a 'violent struggle', the Soviet officer was finally subdued, and some 2,000 kroner was found in his pocket, the latest payment to GRETA. Haavik offered no resistance. Initially, she admitted only to her love affair with the Russian Kozlov, but finally she broke down: 'I shall now tell it how it is. I have been a Russian spy for nearly thirty years.' She was charged with espionage and treason. Haavik died of a sudden heart attack in prison six months later, before her case came to trial.

In the diplomatic fallout, Gennadi Titov, the KGB *rezident*, was expelled from Oslo, and news that an important agent had been arrested in Norway filtered swiftly down to the KGB station in Denmark, prompting a flurry of speculation among the officers, and, in the case of one of them, a 'cold prickle' of fear. Gordievsky assumed his tip-off had led directly to her arrest. Everyone connected to the case would now be interviewed. If the talkative Cherny remembered his idle conversation about GRETA with Gordievsky from a few months earlier, and was brave enough to report it, the KGB molehunters might start to pick up the trail. The weeks passed without a tap on his shoulder and Gordievsky slowly relaxed, but the incident was a sobering warning: if the information he passed over was acted on too obviously, it would lead to his destruction.

Yelena Gordievsky was nobody's fool. Her husband was up to

something. Increasingly, he was away overnight, and for weekends, offering only the most curt explanations for his absences. Yelena knew, without having to be told, that her husband was having an affair. She accused him, angrily; he denied it, unconvincingly. A series of 'unpleasant scenes' ensued in the flat, loud and doubtless overheard by their KGB neighbours. This was followed by a furious, wordless silence. The relationship was all but dead, but they were both trapped. Like Gordievsky, Yelena did not want her own KGB career to be damaged by scandal, and wanted to remain in Denmark. A break-up would see them both on the next plane to Moscow. They had married in obedience to KGB rules, and they must stay married, at least in name, for the same reason. But the marriage went black.

One day, Guscott asked Gordievsky if he was under any 'undue stress'. Clearly, the Danish eavesdroppers had overheard the domestic turmoil and flying crockery in his apartment, and reported back to MI6. He reassured his case officer that, although his marriage might be coming apart, he was not. But it was another reminder that he was being watched, even by those who were now his friends.

Leila was an emotional haven. Compared to the grim compromises in his crumbling marriage, the moments of intimacy with her seemed all the sweeter for being snatched and hurried, seized in one hotel room or another. 'We made plans to marry as soon as I could disentangle myself,' he wrote. Yelena was all elbows and anger, whereas willowy, dark-haired Leila was soft, kind, funny. She had been born and bred into the KGB. Her father, Ali, had been recruited in his early twenties, in his hometown of Shaki in northwest Azerbaijan. Her mother, one of seven children of a poor Moscow family, was also KGB, and had met her future husband on a training course in Moscow soon after the war. But, unlike his wife, Gordievsky never felt she was watching him, assessing him. Her very naïvety was an antidote to the complexity of his life. He loved her as he had never loved anyone before. But he was simultaneously engaged in a tumultuous secret affair with MI6. His emotional desires and his espionage stood in direct conflict. Divorce and remarriage would damage not only his KGB career, but also his prospects of obtaining more valuable intelligence for MI6. Love often begins with an outpouring of naked truth, a passionate baring of the soul. Leila was young and trusting, and she believed utterly in her handsome, considerate lover. 'I never felt I stole him from Yelena. Their marriage was finished. I idolized him. I put him on a pedestal. He was perfect.' But, unbeknown to her, he was never fully present. 'Half my existence and my thoughts had to remain secret.' He wondered if his double life would make an authentic marriage of minds impossible: 'Could I establish the close, warm relationship I longed for?'

He finally confided to Mikhail Lyubimov that he was having an affair with a young secretary at the World Health Organization, and hoped to marry her. His friend and boss was sympathetic, but realistic. From personal experience, Lyubimov knew that his protégé's prospects would suffer when the KGB puritans discovered the situation. After his own marriage failed, Lyubimov had been demoted and ignored for several years. 'A divorced Oleg was doomed to get a dull backroom job,' he wrote. The *rezident* promised to put in a good word with the bosses.

Gordievsky and Lyubimov had grown even closer. In the summer of 1977, they travelled together to the Danish coast for a weekend break. On the beach one afternoon, Lyubimov described how, as a young KGB officer in 1960s London, he had cultivated various figures on the left, including a fiery Labour MP named Michael Foot who was seen by Moscow as a potential 'agent of influence', someone who could be fed pro-Soviet ideas, and reproduce them in articles and speeches. The name meant nothing to Gordievsky.

Lyubimov might be 'a friend for life', but he was also a prime source of intelligence. Everything Gordievsky gleaned from him was passed back to MI6, including documents personally addressed to the *rezident* under his codename, KORIN. The friendship was also a betrayal. Lyubimov later reflected: 'Oleg Gordievsky was playing me like a penny whistle.'

After each meeting, Guscott reported personally to Oldfield. During one of these debriefing sessions, the case officer described how Lyubimov was being 'chatted up' by the new head of station in Copenhagen, and seemed very friendly. 'SUNBEAM will eventually leave Denmark, so we should be looking for a replacement target.

Who better than Lyubimov? He is very Anglophile, and has been tapped up once already. You would like him. He's also a raging snob, and he might respond well to an approach by someone senior.' Thus was born a radical idea. Maurice Oldfield, the chief of MI6, would fly to Copenhagen and try to recruit the KGB *rezident*, in person. The Director of Counter-Intelligence was having none of it: 'C' could not be risked on an active operation, and if it went wrong then attention would be drawn to Gordievsky. 'The plan was kyboshed, thank God,' said one intelligence officer. 'It was insane.'

Gordievsky wrote: 'I felt relief and euphoria that I was no longer a dishonest man working for a totalitarian regime.' Yet this honesty demanded emotional deception, fraud in a virtuous cause, a sacred duplicity. He was telling MI6 every secret truth he could find, while lying to his colleagues and his bosses, his family, his best friend, his estranged wife and his new lover.

## 5.   A Plastic Bag and a Mars Bar

On Westminster Bridge Road in Lambeth, not far from Waterloo Station, stood Century House, a large, ugly, twenty-two-storey office block of glass and concrete. The building was wholly unremarkable. The men and women who passed in and out looked like all the other office workers in the area. But an inquisitive observer might have noticed that the security guard in the lobby was more muscular, and a good deal more alert, than the regulation issue. He might also have wondered why so many telephone engineering vans were parked outside the office at odd times of day. He might have spotted that the workers kept irregular hours, and the chunky electric bollards guarding the underground car park. But had the inquisitive observer hung around long enough to notice these things, he would have been arrested.

Century House was the headquarters of MI6, and the most secret premises in London. Officially, it did not exist, and nor did MI6. It was a place so discreet and deliberately commonplace that new arrivals often wondered if they had mistakenly been sent to the wrong address. 'There were even those who were recruited into the Service,' wrote one former officer, 'but did not realize until after they had completed a week or two's work there.' The public remained perfectly ignorant of the real purpose of this undistinguished building, and those few officials and journalists who did know what it was for kept mum.

The Sovbloc controllerate took up the whole of the twelfth floor. In one corner stood a cluster of desks occupied by the P5 section, the team running Soviet operations and agents, and liaising with the Moscow MI6 station. Only three people in P5 knew of the Gordievsky case. One of them was Veronica Price.

Price was forty-eight in 1978, unmarried, dedicated to the Service and one of those brisk, practical, quintessentially English women who brooks no nonsense, least of all from men. The daughter of a solicitor who had been badly wounded in the First World War ('bits of shrapnel fell out of him for the rest of his life'), she grew up with a strong sense of patriotic rectitude, but also a streak of drama inherited from her mother, a former actress. 'I didn't want to be a lawyer. I wanted to travel.' Having failed to get into the Foreign Office due to inadequate shorthand, she wound up as a secretary in MI6. She served in Poland, Jordan, Iraq and Mexico, but it took MI6 nearly twenty years to realize that Veronica Price's skills went far beyond typing and filing. In 1972 she took an exam to become one of the first women officers in the British secret service. Five years later, she was appointed deputy to the head of P5. Every day, she commuted to Century House from the Home Counties, where she lived with her widowed mother, her sister Jane, several cats and a large collection of bone china. Price insisted on doing things properly. She was very sensible and, as one colleague put it, 'completely single-minded'. She liked solving problems. In the spring of 1978, Veronica Price was indoctrinated into the Gordievsky case, and so it was that she found herself grappling with a problem that had never faced MI6 before: how to smuggle a spy out of Soviet Russia.

A few weeks earlier, Gordievsky had arrived at the safe flat looking tired and preoccupied.

'Nick, I need to think about my security. For the first three years I didn't think about it, but soon I will be returning to Moscow. Can you organize an escape from the Soviet Union for me, in case I come under suspicion? If I go back, is there some way I can get out?'

Disquieting rumours had begun to circulate: Moscow Centre suspected a spy was operating within the KGB. The gossip did not suggest the leakage was coming from Denmark, or even Scandinavia, but the mere hint of an internal investigation was enough to provoke a nasty shiver of apprehension. What if MI6 had itself been penetrated? Was another Philby lurking inside British intelligence, ready to expose Gordievsky? There was no guarantee he would eventually get another foreign posting, particularly if he divorced, and he might find himself trapped in the Soviet Union for ever. Gordievsky wanted to know there was a chance he could get out if he needed to.

Spiriting the Russian spy out of Denmark would have been child's play, requiring only a call to his emergency number, a night in a safe house, a false passport and a ticket to London. But engineering an escape from Moscow, if the KGB rumbled him, was a very different prospect, and probably impossible.

Guscott's response was sobering. 'We cannot make any promises, and we cannot give a hundred per cent guarantee that you can escape.'

Gordievsky knew the probability of success was much lower than that. 'Of course,' he replied. 'That is absolutely clear. Just give me the possibility, just in case.'

The Soviet Union was in effect an enormous prison, incarcerating more than 280 million people behind heavily guarded borders, with over a million KGB officers and informants acting as their jailers. The population was under constant surveillance, and no segment of society was more closely watched than the KGB itself: the Seventh Directorate was responsible for internal surveillance, with some 1,500 men deployed in Moscow alone. Under Leonid Brezhnev's inflexible brand of communism, paranoia had increased to near Stalinist levels, creating a spy-state pitting all against all, in which phones were tapped and letters opened and everyone was encouraged to inform on everyone else, everywhere, all the time. The Soviet invasion of Afghanistan, and the resulting spike in international tension, had intensified KGB internal scrutiny. 'Fear by night, and a feverish effort by day to pretend enthusiasm for a system of lies, was the permanent condition of the Soviet citizen,' writes Robert Conquest.

Infiltrating, recruiting and maintaining contact with spies inside the Soviet Union was extremely difficult. The few agents enlisted or inserted behind the Iron Curtain tended to vanish, without warning or explanation. In a society permanently on the alert for espionage, the life expectancy of a secret agent was short. When the KGB net closed, it did so with brutal speed. But, as a serving KGB officer, it seemed possible Gordievsky might get wind of an imminent threat to his safety, giving him just enough time to attempt an emergency escape.

This was exactly the sort of challenge Veronica Price relished, and she was already something of a specialist in the art of exfiltration. In the mid-1970s, she had arranged Operation INVISIBLE, the smuggling of a husband-and-wife team of Czech scientists across the border into Austria. She had also sprung a Czech intelligence officer codenamed DISARRANGE out of Hungary. 'But the Czechs and the Hungarians didn't have the KGB,' she said. 'Russia was much, much harder', and the distance to reach safety much farther. Quite apart from losing the agent, a failed escape would hand the Russians a major propaganda weapon.

One possibility was by sea. Price began investigating whether, using forged documents, a fugitive might be able to board a commercial liner or merchant vessel sailing from one of the Russian ports. But the docks and harbours were as heavily policed as the frontiers and airports, and producing forgeries was virtually impossible since official Russian documents included watermarks, like banknotes, that could not be replicated. A motorboat might possibly ferry an escaping spy to safety across the Black Sea to Turkey, or across the Caspian to Iran, but there was a strong chance of being intercepted by Soviet patrol vessels, and sunk. The long Turkish and Iranian land borders with the USSR were hundreds of miles from Moscow and heavily defended by guards, minefields, electric fences and barbed wire.

The diplomatic bag could be used to transport sensitive items across borders, principally documents, but also drugs, weapons and, conceivably, people. Opening a parcel marked as diplomatic luggage was technically a violation of the Vienna Convention. Libyan terrorists smuggled guns into Britain this way. The Soviets themselves had attempted to expand the definition of a diplomatic bag, by claiming that a nine-tonne truck filled with crates and destined for Switzerland should be exempt from search. The Swiss refused. In 1984 a fugitive diplomat in London, the brother-in-law of the newly deposed Nigerian President, was drugged, blindfolded, put in a wooden crate labelled 'extra cargo' and addressed to the Ministry of International Affairs in Lagos. He was discovered by customs officials at Stansted airport and released. A man-sized diplomatic bag emerging from the British embassy in Moscow would not pass unnoticed.

One by one, each option was rejected as unfeasible, or insanely risky.

But there was another tradition of international diplomacy that might possibly be manipulated to Gordievsky's advantage.

According to long-standing convention, cars driven by embassy staff with diplomatic number plates are not usually subject to search when crossing international frontiers – an extension of diplomatic immunity, whereby diplomats are granted safe passage and protection from prosecution under the laws of the host country. But this was a convention, not a legal rule, and Soviet border guards felt little compunction in searching any car that aroused suspicion. Still, it was a small gap in the fortified wall surrounding Russia: a spy hidden inside a diplomatic car might conceivably slip through this chink in the Iron Curtain.

The Russian border with Finland was the nearest East–West frontier to Moscow, though still a twelve-hour drive from the Russian capital. Western diplomats regularly visited Finland for rest and recreation, shopping or medical treatment. They usually travelled by car, and the Russian border guards were used to seeing diplomatic vehicles pass through the checkpoints.

But getting an escapee into a car posed another conundrum. The British embassy, consulate and all diplomatic residences were securely guarded by KGB officers in police uniform. Any Russian attempting to enter was stopped, searched and closely interrogated. Moreover, British embassy cars were routinely tailed by KGB surveillance wherever they went, and diplomatic vehicles were serviced by KGB mechanics who, it was assumed, fitted them with hidden bugs and tracking devices.

After weeks of attacking the problem from every angle, Veronica Price framed a plan, peppered with conditionals: if Gordievsky could alert the MI6 station in Moscow that he needed to escape; if he could make his own way to a rendezvous point near the Finnish border without being followed; if a diplomatic car driven by an MI6 officer could throw off KGB surveillance for long enough to pick him up; if he could be hidden securely inside the vehicle; and if the Soviet border guards adhered to diplomatic convention and let them pass through without investigation . . . then he might escape to Finland. (Where he could still be arrested and sent back to Russia by the Finnish authorities.)

It was the longest of long shots. But it was the best shot Veronica Price could come up with. Which meant it was the best shot available.

The MI6 head of station in Moscow was instructed to find a suitable rendezvous point near the Finnish border where a fugitive might be picked up. He drove to Finland from Leningrad, as if on a shopping trip, and identified a lay-by which could serve as the pickup point, about thirty-six miles short of the border and close to the road sign marked 'Kilometre Post 836', indicating the distance from Moscow. Militia posts ten miles apart (known as GAI posts, an abbreviation for State Automobile Inspectorate) monitored the movement of all traffic, but especially foreign cars. The lay-by was almost equidistant between two of them. If the MI6 pickup car paused for a few minutes, assuming it was not being tailed by the KGB, the next militia post would probably not spot the delay. The area was heavily wooded, and a track arced off to the right in a wide D-shaped loop, shielded from the road by a line of trees, before rejoining the highway. A large rock, the size of a London terraced house, marked the entrance to the lay-by. The MI6 officer took some photographs out of the car window, and motored on south towards Moscow. Had he been spotted, the KGB would surely have wondered why a British diplomat wanted to photograph a big rock in the middle of nowhere.

Veronica Price's plan also required a 'signal site', where Gordievsky could indicate when he wanted to pass on a message, or needed to escape.

Many of the British diplomats in Moscow, including the MI6 station of two officers and a secretary, were housed in the same complex on Kutuzovsky Prospekt, known as Kutz, a wide avenue to the west of the Moscow River. On the other side of the avenue, in the shadow of the Soviet Gothic tower, the Hotel Ukraine, was a bread shop, beside a set of hoardings displaying bus timetables, concert performances and copies of *Pravda*. The place was usually thronged with people reading the newspapers, and the bread shop was much used by foreigners from the well-guarded housing complex opposite.

The plan envisaged that at 7.30 p.m. every Tuesday when Gordievsky was in Moscow, a member of the MI6 station would 'police' the signal site. The spot was actually visible from parts of the housing complex; an MI6 officer would head out with the excuse of buying bread, or time his return from work to be passing the site at exactly the right moment.

The exfiltration plan could be activated in only one way: Gordievsky must be standing by the bread shop at 7.30, holding a plastic bag from a Safeway supermarket. Safeway bags bore a large red S, an immediately recognizable logo that would stand out in the drab Moscow surroundings. Gordievsky had lived and worked in the West, and there would be nothing particularly remarkable about his holding such an object. Plastic bags were prized, especially foreign ones. As an additional recognition signal, Gordievsky should wear a grey leather cap he had recently purchased, and a pair of grey trousers. When the MI6 officer spotted Gordievsky waiting by the bread shop with the all-important Safeway bag, he or she would acknowledge the escape signal by walking past him, carrying a green bag from Harrods and eating a chocolate bar, either a KitKat or a Mars bar – 'a literally hand-to-mouth expedient', as one officer remarked. The chocolate eater would also be wearing something grey – trousers, skirt or a scarf – and would make brief eye contact but not stop walking. 'Grey was an unobtrusive colour, and therefore helpful in averting pattern accumulation by watchers. The downside being that it was all but invisible in the murk of a long Moscow winter.'

The escape signal having been flown, the second stage of the plan would swing into operation. Three days later, on the Friday afternoon, Gordievsky should catch the overnight train to Leningrad. There was no suggestion Yelena would be coming too. On arrival in Russia's second city, he would take a taxi to the Finland Station, where Lenin famously arrived to launch the Revolution in 1917, and take the first train to Zelenogorsk up the coast on the Baltic Sea. From there he would catch a bus heading for the Finnish border and get off at or near the rendezvous point, about sixteen miles south of the border town of Vyborg and twenty-six miles from the frontier itself. At the lay-by he should hide in the undergrowth, and wait.

Meanwhile two MI6 officers driving a diplomatic car would have set off from Moscow, and spent the night in Leningrad. The precise timings were dictated, and complicated, by Soviet bureaucracy: official permission to travel had to be obtained two days before departure, and special export number plates needed to be attached to the diplomatic car. The garage performing this function was only open on Wednesdays and Fridays. If Gordievsky flew the signal on Tuesday, then the car paperwork could be completed by one o'clock on Friday afternoon and the MI6 team could depart later that day so as to arrive at the rendezvous site at exactly 2.30 in the afternoon of Saturday, a gap of just four days. They would drive into the lay-by, as if intending to have a picnic. When the coast was clear, one of the officers would open the bonnet of the car: that would be Gordievsky's signal to emerge from hiding. He would immediately climb into the boot of the car, where he would be wrapped in a space blanket to deflect the infrared cameras and heat detectors believed to be deployed at Soviet borders, and given a tranquillizer pill. He would then be driven across the border into Finland.

The escape plan was codenamed PIMLICO (see map on page 273).

In MI6, as in most secret services, codenames were in theory allocated randomly from an officially approved list. Usually, they were real words, and deliberately anodyne in order to give no hint of what they referred to. But spies frequently cannot resist the temptation to choose words that resonate or offer some subtle, or less than subtle, clue to reality. The keeper of MI6's codewords was a secretary called Ursula (her real name). 'You rang Ursula and asked her for the next name on the list. But if you didn't like it you could go back and try to get her to give you a better one. Or you could get a whole set of codewords for different aspects of the case, and then choose the one you liked best.' The wartime MI5 codename for Stalin (meaning man of steel) was GLYPTIC, meaning an image carved in stone; the Germans codenamed Britain GOLFPLATZ, or golf course. Codewords could even be used as a veiled insult. There was some snorting in Century House when a CIA cable accidentally revealed that the American codename for MI6 was UPTIGHT.

PIMLICO sounded quintessentially British – and Britain was where, if it worked, Gordievsky would end up.

At their next meeting Gordievsky listened politely as Guscott outlined PIMLICO. He studied the photographs of the rendezvous spot, and attended carefully to the arrangements for the escape signal at Kutuzovsky Prospekt.

Gordievsky thought long and hard about Veronica Price's escape plan, and then pronounced it completely unworkable.

'It was a very interesting, imaginative plan for escape – but so complicated. There were so many details, unrealistic conditions for the signal site. I didn't take it seriously.' He committed the plan to memory, and inwardly prayed that he would never have to remember it. Back in Century House, sceptics said PIMLICO would never work. 'I took it very seriously,' Price later recalled. 'A lot of others didn't.'

In June 1978, Mikhail Lyubimov ushered Gordievsky into his office at the Soviet embassy in Copenhagen and told him he would soon be returning to Moscow. The end of his second, three-year posting in Denmark was no surprise, but it raised a number of issues, for his marriage, his career and his espionage.

Yelena, now fully aware of her husband's long affair with a secretary, agreed to a divorce once they were back in Moscow. Leila's job with the World Trade Organization was also coming to an end, and she would be returning to Russia as well in a few months. Gordievsky wanted to remarry as soon as possible, but he was under no illusions about the impact a divorce would have on his career. Gordievsky had risen far and fast within the KGB, and at the age of forty he was now being considered for a major promotion, to the post of deputy head of the Third Department, with responsibility for Scandinavia. But he had made rivals and enemies along the way, and the puritanical backbiters at Moscow Centre would be itching for an excuse to cut down the tall poppy. 'They'll go for you,' warned Lyubimov, speaking from personal experience. 'Not only will they condemn you for the divorce, they'll also accuse you of having had an affair *en poste*.' The *resident* sent a report to Moscow commending Gordievsky as a 'thorough, politically right-thinking officer, strong in all aspects, a good linguist, and a competent writer of reports'. Lyubimov also wrote a covering letter to the department head describing Gordievsky's marital problems and urging leniency, in the hope this might 'soften the blow'. Both men knew that, given the ferocious moralism of Moscow Centre, he was probably heading back to a long stint in the doghouse.

With his return to Moscow looming, and his professional future uncertain, Gordievsky might have taken this opportunity to end his career as a spy, and go to ground. MI6 had always made it clear that he could bale out and take sanctuary in the UK at any point. He might understandably have decided that, rather than return to the grim privations and repression of Soviet life, he would now like to defect to the West and, if possible, take his lover with him. But the possibility of defecting does not seem to have crossed his mind. He would go back to Russia, nurture in secret his newfound allegiance to Britain, gather what secrets he could, and bide his time.

'What are your ambitions for your time in Moscow?' Guscott asked him.

'I want to find out the most secret, the most important, the essential elements in the Soviet leadership,' Gordievsky replied. 'I want to find out how the system works. I will not be able to find everything, because the Central Committee keeps secrets even from the KGB. But I will find whatever I can.' Here lay the essence of Gordievsky's rebellion: to find out as much as he could about the system he loathed, the better to destroy it.

Like long-distance running, successful espionage requires patience, stamina and timing. Gordievsky's next job was likely to be in the Third Department, covering Britain and Scandinavia. He would study the KGB from within, gathering whatever information might be useful to Britain and the West. Once any fuss about his divorce and remarriage subsided, he would probably resume his upward climb through the KGB ranks, as Lyubimov had done. Perhaps in as little as three years, he might land another foreign posting. He would pace himself during the next lap. Whatever might arise in Moscow, his commitment would continue. He would stay in the race.

A spy deep within the KGB was the ultimate prize of every Western intelligence agency. But as the chief of the CIA, Richard Helms, observed, infiltrating an agent into the KGB was 'as improbable as placing resident spies on the planet Mars'. The West had 'very few Soviet agents inside the USSR worthy of the name', which meant that 'reliable intelligence of the enemy's long-range plans and intentions [was] practically non-existent'. British intelligence now had an opportunity to exploit their man inside the KGB to the full, by extracting any and every secret he came across.

Instead, MI6 decided to do the opposite.

In an act of self-discipline and self-denial almost unique in intelligence history, Gordievsky's spymasters did not encourage him to remain in contact in Moscow or try to feed back secrets. Instead, the agent-runners of Century House opted to let their spy lie fallow. Once he was back in Moscow, Gordievsky would be left entirely alone.

The reasoning was simple, and flawless: in Russia, it would be impossible to run Gordievsky as he had been handled in Denmark. There was no safe house in Moscow, no friendly local intelligence service willing to watch his back, no reliable fallback should he be rumbled. The level of surveillance was too intense, with every British diplomat – and not just suspected intelligence officers – under constant watch. The history of running agents in the Soviet Union proved that overeagerness was almost always fatal, as shown by Penkovsky's grim demise. Sooner or later (and usually sooner) the spy was uncovered by the all-seeing state, captured and liquidated.

As one MI6 officer put it: 'Oleg was too good to jeopardize. We had something so precious that we had to exercise restraint. There was enormous temptation to continue contact in the Soviet Union, but the Service lacked confidence that we would be able to do this sufficiently often and securely. There was a good chance that we would burn him up.'

Guscott informed Gordievsky that MI6 would not seek to communicate with him in Moscow. There would be no attempt to set up clandestine meetings, or harvest intelligence. But if Gordievsky needed to make contact, he could.

At 11 a.m., on the third Saturday of every month, MI6 would send an officer to loiter under the clock in Moscow's Central Market just off the Garden Ring Road, a bustling spot where a foreigner would not look out of place. Again, he or she would be carrying the Harrods bag and wearing some grey clothing. 'The purpose of this was twofold: if Oleg just wanted reassurance that we were continuously looking out for his interests, he could see us but not make himself visible. If he wanted to make a brush contact and pass on a physical message, he would make himself visible by means of the grey cap and Safeway bag.'

If he appeared with the bag and cap, then the brush contact plan went into a second phase. Three Sundays later, he should go to St Basil's Cathedral in Red Square, and ascend the spiral staircase at the rear of the building at exactly 3 p.m. Again, for ease of recognition, he should wear his grey cap and grey trousers. An MI6 officer, probably a woman wearing a grey item of clothing and holding something grey in both hands, would time her descent from the upper floor, and in the constricted space, passing abreast, he could then pass her a written message.

The brush contact should only be initiated if he uncovered information with a direct impact on British national security, such as a Soviet spy inside the UK government. MI6 had no way to respond to such a message.

If he needed to escape, he could activate the exfiltration plan by standing at the bread shop on Kutuzovsky Prospekt with his Safeway bag at 7.30 on a Tuesday evening. MI6 would monitor the site every week.

Having rehearsed the plans, Guscott handed over a hardback copy of the OUP edition of Shakespeare's sonnets. It looked like an ordinary souvenir that a Russian might take home from the West. In reality, it was an ingenious *aide-mémoire*, a gift from Veronica Price. Beneath the endpaper, the paper covering the inside of the back cover, was a small sheet of cellophane, on which Operation PIMLICO was written out, in Russian: the details of the timings, recognition clothing, escape signals, the rendezvous point after the 836 kilometre marker and the distances between key points. Gordievsky should place the book in the bookshelf of his Moscow apartment. To refresh his memory before attempting to escape, he could soak the book in water, peel back the endpaper, and extract the plastic sheet. As a further security measure, the place names were changed from Russian to French: Moscow was 'Paris'; Leningrad was 'Marseilles', and so on.

If the KGB found the 'crib' while he was still heading for the border, it would not necessarily give away the precise escape route.

Guscott finally handed over a London telephone number. If and when Gordievsky found himself outside the Soviet Union, and felt it was safe to do so, he should call the number. Someone would always answer. The Russian wrote down the number in his notebook, backwards, amid a jumble of jottings.

Some months earlier, Gordievsky had passed Guscott an important morsel of information, plucked off the Scandinavian grapevine: the KGB, or the military GRU, and possibly both, had recruited an important spy in Sweden. Details were sketchy, but the mole appeared to work for one of the Swedish intelligence agencies, civilian or military. MI6 discussed the tip-off with the Danes, and discreet inquiries were made. 'It didn't take long to nail him,' said Guscott. 'We soon had enough to identify this man with near-certainty.' Sweden was an important ally, and evidence that the Swedish intelligence community had been penetrated by the Soviets was too important not to share. Guscott now explained to Gordievsky that this information had been passed to Stockholm without revealing its origin, and would soon be acted on. He made no objection. 'By now he trusted us to protect him as the source.'

Gordievsky and Guscott shook hands. For twenty months, without detection, they had met at least once a month, exchanging hundreds of secret documents. 'This was a real friendship, a real affinity,' Guscott said, many years later. But it was a strange sort of amity, one that had grown up within strict limits. Gordievsky never knew the real name of Nick Venables. The spy and his handler had never shared a restaurant meal. 'I would like to have gone for a run with him, but we could not,' said Guscott. Their relationship had taken place entirely within the walls of a safe house, always with a tape recorder running. Like all spy relationships it was compromised and coloured by deception and manipulation: Gordievsky was undermining a political regime he reviled, and gaining the dignity he craved; Guscott was running a long-term, deep-penetration agent inside the enemy's citadel. But it also meant more than that, to both of them: theirs was an intense emotional bond forged in secrecy, danger, loyalty and betrayal.

With the copy of Shakespeare's sonnets in a Safeway bag, Gordievsky left the safe flat for the last time, and headed into the Danish night. From now on, the affair would be run at long distance. In Moscow, Gordievsky would be able to communicate with British intelligence if he wanted to, but MI6 had no means of initiating contact with him. He could try to escape if he needed to, but the British could not initiate the escape plan. He was on his own. British intelligence could only watch, and wait.

If Gordievsky was prepared to run the race without knowing when it might end, then so was MI6.

At the First Chief Directorate headquarters in Moscow Centre, Gordievsky presented himself to the head of the Third Department, explained that he was getting a divorce and planned to remarry, and watched his career shrivel up in front of him. The department chief was a short, fat Ukrainian called Viktor Grushko, cheerful, cynical and wholly obedient to the moralistic culture of the KGB. 'This changes everything,' said Grushko.

Gordievsky, the high-flyer, was brought down to earth with a thump, just as Lyubimov had predicted. Instead of becoming department deputy, he was banished to the personnel section, accompanied by a strong whiff of moral disapprobation. 'You've had an affair while on assignment,' some of his colleagues gloated. '*Very* unprofessional.' His work was as tedious as it was inconsequential. Frequently he was relegated to night duty officer. Although still a senior officer, he had 'no definite function'. Once again, he was stuck.

The divorce was concluded with unemotional Soviet dispatch. The judge addressed Yelena: 'Your husband is divorcing you because you don't want to have children, and he does. Is that right?' Yelena snapped back: 'Not at all! He fell in love with a pretty girl. Nothing else.'

By now, Yelena had been promoted to the rank of captain. She returned to her old job, eavesdropping on foreign embassies. As the injured party in the divorce her KGB career was unaffected, but she never forgave Gordievsky, and she never remarried. When the senior women officers in the KGB gathered to drink tea together, Yelena would rage about her ex-husband's disloyalty: 'He's an insincere shit, a deceiver, a man with a false front. He is capable of any sort of betrayal.' Gossip about Gordievsky's infidelity swilled around the lower reaches of the KGB. Most dismissed Yelena's remarks as the bitterness of a divorcée. 'What else do you expect from a deserted wife?' remarked a colleague in the Third Department. 'Neither I, nor anyone else, ever thought to report the matter.' But perhaps someone did.

A month after Gordievsky's return, his father died at the age of eighty-two. Only a small handful of elderly KGB officers attended the cremation. At a wake in the family flat, packed with more than thirty relatives, Gordievsky gave a speech extolling his father's work for the Communist Party and the Soviet Union – an ideology and a political system he was now actively conspiring to undermine. Years later, Gordievsky reflected that his father's death might have been a 'liberation' for his mother. In fact, the person secretly liberated by his father's demise was Gordievsky himself.

Anton Lavrentyevich never told his family what he had done as a secret policeman during the famines and purges of the 1930s. Only years after his death did Gordievsky learn that his father had been married before he met Olga, and may have had children by this earlier, hidden marriage. Oleg, in turn, never explained to his father the nature of his work for the KGB, let alone his new loyalty to the West. The old Stalinist would have been appalled, and terrified. The lies that had riddled the relationship between father and son continued to the grave. Gordievsky had secretly detested all that his father stood for, the blind obedience to a cruel ideology, the cowardice of the *Homo Sovieticus*. But he had also loved the old man, and even respected his obstinacy, a trait they shared. Between father and son, love and deception ran in tandem.

Gordievsky's remarriage was as swift and efficient as his divorce. Leila returned to Moscow in January 1979, and the wedding took place a few weeks later in a register office, followed by a family dinner at her parents' apartment. Olga was pleased to see her son so happy. She had never much cared for Yelena, regarding her daughter-in-law as a beady-eyed KGB careerist. The couple set up home in a new flat at 103 Leninsky Prospekt, on the eighth floor of an apartment block owned by a KGB cooperative. 'Our relationship was warm and close,' wrote Gordievsky. 'Everything I had always longed for.' The deception at the heart of this marriage was masked by the simple domestic pleasures of buying furniture, putting up bookshelves, and hanging the paintings brought from Denmark. Oleg missed the music and freedoms of the West. But Leila returned to the Soviet way of life without complaint or question: 'Real happiness is to queue all night, and then get what you want,' she said. Soon she was pregnant.

Gordievsky was put to work writing a history of the Third Department, a non-job that offered an insight into past Soviet espionage, but none into current operations. Only once did he glimpse a file on the desk of a colleague in the Norwegian section, with a heading that ended OLT — the first half of Treholt's name being covered up by another paper. Here was further indication that Arne Treholt was an active KGB agent. The British would be interested in this, he reflected, but not enough to run the risk of attempting to inform them.

He made no attempt to contact MI6. An exile in his own country, he nursed his secret allegiance with lonely pride. In the whole of Russia, there was probably only one man who would have understood what Gordievsky was feeling.

Kim Philby might be ageing, lonely and frequently plastered, but he was as intellectually sharp as ever. No one understood better, from long first-hand experience, the double life of the spy, how to avoid detection, and how to catch a mole. He remained a figure of legend inside the KGB. Gordievsky had brought back a Danish book about the Philby case, and asked the Englishman to sign it for him. The book came back with the inscription: 'To my good friend Oleg — Don't believe anything you see in print! Kim Philby.' They were not friends, though they had much in common. For thirty years, Philby had secretly served the KGB from inside MI6. He now lived in comfortable semi-retirement, but his expertise in treachery remained at the disposal of his Soviet masters.

Soon after Gordievsky's return, Philby received a request from the Centre, asking him to evaluate the Gunvor Haavik case and assess what had gone wrong. Why had the veteran Norwegian spy been arrested? For weeks, Philby pored over the Haavik files and then, as he had done so many times in his long career, arrived at the correct conclusion: 'The leak which betrayed the agent could only have come from inside the KGB.'

Viktor Grushko summoned senior officers to his office, including Gordievsky. 'There are signs that the KGB is leaking,' Grushko declared, before presenting Philby's meticulous conclusions in the Haavik case. 'This is particularly worrying, because the pattern of events suggests *that the traitor may be in the room at this moment*. He could be sitting here among us.'

Gordievsky felt a jolt of fear, and pinched his leg, hard, through his trouser pocket. Haavik had met more than a dozen KGB handlers during her long espionage career. Gordievsky had never been involved in running the case, and had no responsibility for Norway. Yet he was sure that his tip-off to Guscott had led directly to Haavik's arrest, and now, thanks to an elderly British spy with a nose for deception, the cloud of suspicion was wafting perilously close. He felt the nausea rise in his throat. Returning to his desk in a state of concealed shock, he wondered what else he had told MI6 that might come back to threaten him.

Stig Bergling once described the life of a secret agent as 'grey, black, white and dull with fog and brown coal smoke'. His own career as a Swedish policeman, intelligence officer and Soviet mole was luridly colourful.

Bergling had worked as a policeman before enrolling in the surveillance unit of the Swedish security service, known as SÄPO, tasked with monitoring the activities of suspected Soviet agents in Sweden. In 1971 he was appointed SÄPO liaison with the Swedish Defence Staff, with access to highly classified information, including details of all Sweden's military defence facilities. Two years later, while working as a UN observer in Lebanon, he made contact with Aleksander Nikiforov, the Soviet military attaché and GRU officer in Beirut. On 30 November 1973, he sold a first cache of documents to the Soviets for $3,500.

Bergling spied for two reasons: money, which he greatly liked, and the overbearing attitude of his superior officers, which he didn't.

Over the next four years he supplied the Soviets with 14,700 documents, revealing Sweden's defence plans, weapons systems, security codes and counter-espionage operations, and communicating with his Soviet handlers using secret ink, microdots and shortwave radio. He even signed a receipt that read: 'Money for information to the Russian intelligence service', which meant, of course, that he was now vulnerable to blackmail by the KGB. Bergling was quite stupid.

Then came Gordievsky's tip-off pointing to a Soviet agent in Swedish intelligence. The MI6 Director of Counter-Intelligence flew to Stockholm, and informed the Swedish security service that it had a spy in its midst.

By this time Bergling had become head of SÄPO's investigation office, a reservist officer in the Swedish army and, secretly, a colonel in Soviet military intelligence.

The Swedish investigators closed in. On 12 March 1979, at Sweden's behest, he was arrested at Tel Aviv airport by Shin Bet, the Israeli security service, and handed over to his former colleagues in SÄPO. Nine months later he was convicted of espionage and sentenced to life imprisonment. Bergling had earned a small fortune from his Soviet spymasters. The damage he inflicted on Sweden's national defence cost an estimated £29m to repair.

One by one, the Soviet spies fingered by Gordievsky were being picked off. As a result, the West was probably safer. But Gordievsky was not. With internal suspicion building inside the Third Department, his career in the doldrums, but now happily married and expecting his first child, Gordievsky might, once again, have chosen to make a break with the past, sever all contact with MI6, hope the KGB never discovered the truth and lie low for the rest of his life. Instead, he picked up the pace. His career needed a kick-start. He must get himself posted to the West, perhaps even to Britain itself.

He would learn to speak English.

The KGB offered a 10 per cent salary rise to officers who passed an official foreign-language course, with a maximum of two languages. Gordievsky already spoke German, Danish and Swedish. He enrolled anyway. At forty-one, he was the oldest student on the

KGB English course, which was designed to take four years; he completed it in two.

If his KGB colleagues had been paying closer attention, they might have wondered why Gordievsky was in such a hurry to learn a new language without any financial incentive, and why he was suddenly so interested in the UK.

Gordievsky bought a two-volume Russian–English dictionary and immersed himself in British culture – or as much of it as Soviet citizens were allowed to see. He read Churchill's *History of the Second World War*, Frederick Forsyth's *The Day of the Jackal* and Fielding's *Tom Jones*. Mikhail Lyubimov, who had returned from Copenhagen to take up a prestigious position as head of the First Chief Directorate think-tank, recalled how his friend 'frequently dropped in for a chat and asked for sage advice about England'. Lyubimov was delighted to oblige, happily expatiating on the joys of London clubland and Scotch whisky. 'What an irony!' Lyubimov later wrote. 'There I was giving advice on England to an English spy.' Leila also helped him with his studies, testing him at night on his English vocabulary and picking up some of the language herself. 'I was so envious of his ability. He could learn thirty words in one day. He was brilliant.'

At Lyubimov's suggestion, Gordievsky began reading the novels of Somerset Maugham. A British intelligence officer during the First World War, in his fiction Maugham brilliantly captures the moral fogginess of espionage. Gordievsky was particularly taken with the character of Ashenden, a British agent sent to Russia during the Bolshevik revolution: 'Ashenden admired goodness, but was not outraged by wickedness,' wrote Maugham. 'People sometimes thought him heartless because he was more often interested in others than attached to them.'

To further improve his English, Gordievsky helped to translate Kim Philby's reports. Like other government officials of his generation, Philby wrote and spoke a convoluted form of upper-class bureaucratic English. 'Whitehall Mandarin', a languid drawl with extended vowels, was exceptionally difficult to render in Russian, but it offered a useful primer in the arcane language of British officialdom.

The British and Scandinavian sections operated side by side within the Third Department. Gordievsky began cultivating anyone who might assist him to transfer to the British side. In April 1980, Leila gave birth to a daughter, Maria, and the proud father invited Viktor Grushko, his department head, and Lyubimov to come and celebrate with him. 'Grushko and I were invited to a dinner of Azerbaijani delicacies, prepared by his mother-in-law,' Lyubimov recalled. 'She told us about the merits of her husband, who had worked in the Cheka [the Bolshevik secret police]. Gordievsky showed off the paintings he had collected in Denmark.'

The problem with buttering up the boss is that bosses tend to move on, which can mean a lot of wasted butter.

Mikhail Lyubimov was suddenly and ignominiously fired from the KGB. Like Gordievsky, he fell foul of the Centre's moralists, but his sin was worse: with his second marriage failing, he had fallen in love with the wife of another officer, and then failed to inform the KGB before his next appointment. He was dismissed without appeal. Lyubimov had been a useful source of secrets, but also a patron, adviser, ally and close friend. The irrepressible Lyubimov declared his intention to become a novelist, the Russian Somerset Maugham.

Viktor Grushko was promoted to deputy head of the FCD, and succeeded as head of the Third Department by Gennadi Titov, 'the Crocodile', the former *rezident* in Oslo and Arne Treholt's case officer. The new head of the Scandinavian–British section was Nikolai Gribin, a glamorous figure who had served under Gordievsky in Copenhagen in 1976, but had since leapfrogged ahead of him in the KGB hierarchy. Gribin was slim, neat and handsome. His party piece was to pick up a guitar and strum mournful Russian ballads until everyone in the room was weeping. He was exceptionally ambitious, and made an art of cultivating senior officers. 'The bosses thought him a splendid fellow.' Gordievsky, by contrast, regarded Gribin as a creep, 'a typical toady and careerist'. But he needed his support. Gordievsky held his nose, and poured on the sycophancy.

In the summer of 1981, Gordievsky passed his final exam. His English was far from fluent, but he was now at least theoretically qualified for a posting to Britain. In September, a second daughter, Anna, was born. Leila was proving to be a 'first-class mother', and an attentive and dutiful wife. 'She was marvellous in the home,' Oleg reflected. Gordievsky was no longer a figure of scandal. An early sign of re-habilitation came when he was asked to write the department's annual report. He began to attend more important meetings. Even so, he was beginning to wonder if he would ever gain access to secrets import-ant enough to justify resuming contact with MI6.

Back in Century House, the SUNBEAM team was pondering exactly the same question. Three years had passed without a whisper from Gordievsky. The signal site on Kutuzovsky Prospekt was care-fully monitored, and Operation PIMLICO, the escape plan, was kept in permanent readiness. A full dress rehearsal was staged: the head of station and his wife drove to Helsinki along the exfiltration route; Guscott and Price met them on the other side of the Finnish border, and then drove all the way north to the border with Norway. In Moscow, every Tuesday evening at 7.30, whatever the weather, a member of the MI6 station or one of their wives, would monitor the pavement outside the bread shop, a Mars bar or KitKat at the ready, and watch for a man in a grey cap holding a Safeway bag. Every third Saturday in each month, an MI6 officer carrying a Harrods bag would stand near the clock in the Central Market, pretending to shop, alert for the brush contact signal. 'Her Majesty's Government still owes me £10 for one winter tomato, probably the only one in Moscow,' one officer recalled.

Gordievsky never appeared.

That year, Geoffrey Guscott was appointed MI6 head of station in Sweden – in part because if the Swedish-speaking Gordievsky was sent abroad again, there was a chance he might pop up in Stockholm. He never did. The case had gone into deep hibernation, from which it showed no signs of waking.

Then came a heartbeat, clear evidence of life, courtesy of the ever-reliable Danish intelligence service. PET was also intrigued to know what had become of the Russian spy. A Danish diplomat who regu-larly visited Moscow was asked to inquire, casually, during his next trip, about Comrade Gordievsky, the charming Russian consular official who spoke such good Danish. Sure enough, at the next recep-tion attended by the visiting Dane, there was Gordievsky, looking confident and healthy. The Danish diplomat reported back to PET that Gordievsky had remarried and was now the father of two daughters. The confirmed sighting was swiftly relayed to MI6.

The most significant element in the PET report, however, and one that sent a surge of excitement through the SUNBEAM team, was contained in a single remark dropped by Gordievsky over the cocktails and canapés.

With studied insouciance, Gordievsky had turned to the Danish diplomat and observed: 'I am now learning to speak English.'

# 6.  Agent BOOT

Gennadi Titov had a problem. The head of the Third Department of the First Chief Directorate had a vacancy for a KGB officer in the Soviet embassy in London, but nobody to fill it, at least no one who could be relied on to kowtow to Gennadi Titov – a prime qualification for the job.

The Crocodile was one of those people, familiar in every large bureaucracy, who dispenses patronage on the understanding that the recipient will thereafter be a slave. Titov was boorish, scheming, unctuous towards his superiors and sneering to his underlings. 'One of the most unpleasant and unpopular officers in the whole of the KGB' in Gordievsky's estimation, he was also one of the most powerful. Expelled from Norway after the arrest of Gunvor Haavik, he had a reputation as a crack spymaster, and continued to run Arne Treholt at long distance, meeting him regularly for enormous lunches in Vienna, Helsinki and elsewhere. On his return to Moscow in 1977, Titov had won swift promotion by playing brutal office politics, flattering his bosses and appointing his cronies to key positions. Gordievsky loathed him.

The Centre had been struggling to rebuild its London station ever since 1971, when more than 100 KGB officers were expelled in Operation FOOT. There were simply not enough able, English-speaking officers to make up the shortfall. The KGB had comprehensively penetrated the British establishment during the 1930s, inflicting enormous damage through Philby and the so-called Cambridge spy ring, but its inability to repeat this feat was a source of deep frustration. Various illegals had been infiltrated into the country, and a number of KGB officers were working as journalists or trade representatives, but there was a dearth of spies who could operate effectively under formal diplomatic cover.

In the autumn of 1981, the KGB's deputy head of the PR Line in the UK, ostensibly a counsellor at the Soviet embassy in London, returned

to Moscow. The first candidate to replace him was rejected by the Foreign Office because he was suspected by MI5, rightly, of clandestine
activities. To fill this plum posting, the KGB needed someone with
experience abroad, who spoke English, had a record as a legitimate diplomat, and would not be vetoed out of hand by the British.

Gordievsky began dropping hints that he, and only he, met the crite-
ria. Nikolai Gribin, the newly appointed head of the British–Scandinavian
section, was encouraging, but Titov wanted his own creature in London, and hitherto Gordievsky had not demonstrated the requisite degree
of subservience. A period of intense jockeying ensued, with Titov
attempting to manoeuvre his own candidate into the post, while
Gordievsky exhibited what he hoped was the right combination of
enthusiasm, obsequiousness and fake humility; he lobbied without
being obvious, quietly disparaged any rivals, and soft-soaped the Crocodile until the suds flew. Finally Titov relented, though he doubted the
British would grant a visa. 'Gordievsky's well known in the West,' he
remarked. 'They may easily reject him. But let's try anyway.'

Gordievsky was extravagant in his gratitude. Inwardly, he relished
the revenge he might soon inflict on the Crocodile. The wife of a KGB
officer on the way up, Leila was also overjoyed at the prospect of moving to Britain, in her mind a land of almost mythical fascination. The
two little girls were growing fast: Maria was a sturdy toddler, energetic
and independent, Anna was just uttering her first words in Russian.
Leila imagined herself taking her well-dressed, English-speaking
daughters to school in London, shopping for food in vast and overflow-
ing supermarkets, and exploring the ancient city. Soviet propaganda
portrayed Britain as a place of downtrodden workers and rapacious
capitalists, but her time in Denmark had already introduced Leila to the
realities of life in the West and she had briefly visited London in 1978 as
part of the Russian delegation to a World Health Organization conference. Like many couples embarking on a shared adventure, the prospect
of building a new family life in a foreign country brought them even
closer: together they excitedly imagined a place of wide streets, endless
classical-music concerts, delicious restaurants and elegant parks. They
would be able to wander the city, read whatever they wanted, and make
new British friends. Gordievsky described to Leila the Englishmen he

had met in Copenhagen: witty, sophisticated people, full of laughter and generosity. Denmark had been exciting, but they would be even happier in London, he said. When they first met, four years earlier, Gordievsky had painted a picture of how they would travel the world, a successful KGB officer with his beautiful young wife and their growing family; now he was making good on that promise, and she loved him all the more. But Gordievsky also imagined scenes he did not share with Leila. The KGB *rezidentura* in London was one of the most active in the world, and he would be handling secrets of the first importance. He would re-establish contact with MI6 as soon as it was safe to do so. He would spy for Britain, in Britain, and one day, perhaps soon, perhaps years hence, he would tell MI6 he was finished. Then he could defect, finally reveal his double life to his wife, and they would remain in Britain, for ever. This, he did not tell Leila.

For both husband and wife, the London posting was the fulfilment of a dream; but they were different dreams.

Gordievsky was issued with a new diplomatic passport. The visa application form was filled out, and sent to the British embassy in Moscow. From there, it was dispatched to London.

Two days later, James Spooner, the head of MI6's Soviet section, was sitting at his desk in Century House when a junior entered and breathlessly declared: 'I've got some big news.' She handed over a sheet of paper. 'Look at this visa application that has just come through from Moscow.' The accompanying letter stated that Comrade Oleg Antonyevich Gordievsky had been appointed counsellor at the Soviet embassy, and requested the British government to issue a diplomatic visa forthwith.

Spooner was ecstatic. But you would never have been able to tell.

The son of a doctor and Scottish senior social worker, at school Spooner had belonged to a club for 'particularly gifted boys'. He emerged from Oxford University with a first-class degree in history and a passion for medieval architecture. 'He was outstandingly clever, and exceptionally precise in his judgements, but it was hard to tell what he was really thinking,' said one contemporary. Spooner joined MI6 in 1971, another club for the particularly gifted. Some predicted he had the makings of a future chief of the Service. MI6 has a reputation for swashbuckling, for taking risks and following hunches; Spooner was the reverse. He tackled the complexities of intelligence work like an academic historian (he would later commission the first authorized history of MI6), assembling the evidence, sifting the facts, arriving at a conclusion only after consideration and reconsideration. Spooner was not a man who rushed to judgement; rather, he approached judgement very slowly, incrementally and fastidiously. In 1981 he was just thirty-two, but had already served as an MI6 officer operating under diplomatic cover in Nairobi and Moscow. He spoke good Russian, and was fascinated by Russian culture. During his time in Moscow, the KGB had attempted to involve him in a classic 'dangle', an approach by a Soviet naval officer offering to spy for Britain. As a result Spooner's posting was cut short. In early 1980, he had taken over P5, the operational team, including Veronica Price, running Soviet agents inside and outside the Soviet bloc. In many ways he was the polar opposite of Gennadi Titov, his counterpart in the KGB: allergic to office politics, immune to flattery and rigorously professional.

The SUNBEAM file was one of the first to land on his desk.

With Gordievsky in Moscow, incommunicado and professionally becalmed, the case had floated in limbo. 'It was obviously right not to make contact,' said Spooner. 'The strategic decision-making was very good. We were playing for the long term. Of course we had no idea what was going to happen. We had no reason to think he was going to get to London.'

But now Gordievsky was coming in from the cold, and after three years of inaction and suspense James Spooner, Geoffrey Guscott, Veronica Price and the SUNBEAM team swung into action. Spooner called in Price and showed her the visa application. 'I was really quite pleased,' said Price, which was her equivalent of being wildly over-excited. 'This was terrific. It was just what we had hoped for.'

'I must go away and think,' she told Spooner.

'Don't think too long,' said Spooner. 'This needs to get to "C".'

Issuing a visa for Gordievsky was not a straightforward task. On principle, any suspected KGB officer was automatically barred from entering Britain. Under normal circumstances, the Foreign Office would make a preliminary inquiry, and discover that Oleg had twice been posted to Copenhagen. A routine information request to the Danes would reveal that he was listed in their files as a suspected intelligence officer, and the visa would be summarily rejected. But these circumstances were not normal. MI6 needed Gordievsky to be admitted to Britain without delay, and with no questions asked. The immigration authorities could simply be instructed to issue the visa, but that might arouse suspicions since it would signal that there was something different about Gordievsky. The secret could not be allowed to seep outside MI6. Once alerted, PET was pleased to help. Told by MI6 that the Foreign Office would soon come asking questions, the Danes 'massaged the record', and responded that while there had been suspicions, there was no proof Gordievsky was KGB. 'We managed to leave enough doubt, so that the visa went through normally. We said: "Yes, he's been flagged by the Danes, but it's not completely certain."' As far as the Foreign Office and immigration authorities were aware, Gordievsky was just another Soviet diplomat, possibly spooky but perhaps not, and certainly not worth making a fuss about. The British passport office usually took at least a month to issue diplomatic visas; Gordievsky's permit to enter Britain as an accredited diplomat arrived in just twenty-two days.

In Moscow, that seemed suspiciously swift. 'It's very strange they granted you the visa so quickly,' an official in the Russian Foreign Ministry observed darkly when Gordievsky went to pick up his passport. 'They *must* know who you are – you've been abroad so much. When your application went in, I felt sure they'd turn it down. They've rejected so many requests lately. You can count yourself *very* fortunate.' The sharp-eyed official probably kept his suspicions to himself.

The KGB bureaucracy was much slower. Three months later, Gordievsky was still awaiting formal permission to leave the USSR. The Fifth Department of Directorate K, the KGB's internal-investigation wing, was looking into Gordievsky's background, and taking its time. He began to wonder if there was a problem. In Century House, too, anxiety levels were rising. Geoffrey Guscott, in Sweden, was told to stand ready to fly to London at a moment's notice, to receive Gordievsky on arrival. But he did not arrive. Had something gone wrong?

As the weeks of waiting stretched out, Gordievsky spent his time profitably perusing the files in KGB headquarters – one of the most secretive and impenetrable places on earth, unless you were on the inside. The internal-security system in Moscow Centre was both complex and crude. The most secret operational files were kept in a locked cabinet in the office of the department head. But the other paperwork was retained in the various section offices, and in individual safes handled by the officers overseeing different aspects of the department's work. Every evening, each officer locked his safes and filing cabinets, placed the keys in a small wooden box, and then sealed this with a lump of Plasticine into which he pressed his individual stamp – like the wax seals used on ancient documents. The duty officer then collected up the boxes, and placed them in another safe in Gennadi Titov's office. That key was again placed in a small box, and sealed in the same way with the duty officer's stamp, before being deposited in the office of the secretariat of the First Chief Directorate, which was manned around the clock. The system took up a great deal of time, and a lot of Plasticine.

Gordievsky occupied a desk in Room 635, the political section of the British department. In three large metal cupboards were files on individuals in the UK regarded by the KGB as agents, potential agents or confidential contacts. Room 635 housed only active cases. Redundant material was moved to the main archive. The files were stored in cardboard boxes, three to a shelf, each box containing two files, sealed with string and Plasticine. To unseal a file required a signature from the department head. In the British cupboard were six files on individuals classified as 'agents', and another dozen listed as 'confidential contacts'.

Gordievsky began exploring, building up a picture of the KGB's current political operations in Britain. The deputy department head, Dmitri Svetanko, teased him for swotting: 'Don't waste too much time reading, because when you get to Britain you will realize what it is like.' Gordievsky continued his research, hoping his reputation for diligence would be enough to offset any suspicions. Every day he would sign out a file, break the seal, and discover another Briton the KGB was either fishing for or had its hooks into.

These individuals were not spies, properly speaking. The PR Line primarily sought political influence and secret information; its targets were opinion-formers, politicians, journalists and others in positions of power. Some of these were considered conscious 'agents', knowingly supplying information, secret or otherwise, in a clandestine way; others were classed as 'confidential contacts', helpful informants with varying degrees of knowing complicity. Some accepted hospitality, holidays or money. Others, merely sympathizers to the Soviet cause, were not even aware the KGB was cultivating them. Most would have been astonished to know that they merited a codename and a file in a locked steel cupboard inside KGB headquarters. Nonetheless, these were people of a different calibre to the nobodies the KGB station had pursued in Denmark. Britain was a major target. Some of the cases stretched back decades. And some of the names were shocking.

Jack Jones was one of the most respected figures in the trade union movement, a crusading socialist once described by the British Prime Minister Gordon Brown as 'one of the world's greatest trade union leaders'. He was also a KGB agent.

A former Liverpool dock worker, Jones had fought for the Republicans in the International Brigades during the Spanish Civil War, and by 1969 he had risen to become General Secretary of the Transport and General Workers' Union (TGWU), once the largest union in the Western world with more than two million members, a position he held for almost a decade. An opinion poll in 1977 found that 54 per cent of voters considered Jones to be the most powerful person in Britain, with greater influence than the Prime Minister. Genial, outspoken and intransigent, Jack Jones was the public face of the unions. His private world was more dubious.

Jones had joined the Communist Party in 1932, and remained a member until at least 1949. He was first approached by Soviet intelligence while recuperating from wounds sustained during the Spanish Civil War. A bugging operation at Communist Party headquarters in London revealed that Jones, according to one MI5 report, was 'prepared to pass to the Party Government and other information which has been passed to him confidentially in his trade union capacity'. The KGB formally listed him as an agent, codenamed DRIM (the Russian transliteration of 'Dream'), between 1964 and 1968, when he handed over 'confidential Labour Party documents which he obtained as a member of the NEC [National Executive Committee] and the Party's international committee as well as information on his colleagues and contacts'. He accepted contributions towards his 'holiday expenses', and was 'regarded by the KGB as a "very disciplined, useful agent"', passing on 'intelligence about what was happening in No. 10 Downing Street, about the leadership of the Labour Party, and about the trades union movement'. The Prague Spring in 1968 led Jones to break off his relationship with the KGB, but the files indicated that there had been sporadic contact in the years since. He had retired from the TGWU in 1978, pointedly turning down a peerage, but he remained a forceful figure on the left. Gordievsky noted 'clear indications in the file that the KGB wished to revive its association with him'.

A second dossier was devoted to Bob Edwards, the left-wing Labour MP, another former dock worker, Spanish Civil War veteran, trade union leader and long-term KGB agent. In 1926, Edwards had led a youth delegation to the USSR, and met both Stalin and Trotsky. Over a long political career, Edwards had proved a willing informant, with access to high-grade secrets. 'There is no doubt,' MI5 later concluded, that the MP 'would have passed on all he could get hold of' to the KGB. He was secretly awarded the Order of the People's Friendship, the third-highest Soviet decoration, in recognition of his undercover work. His case officer at that time, Leonid Zaitsev (Gordievsky's former boss in Copenhagen), met Edwards in Brussels to show him the medal in person, before taking it back to Moscow for safekeeping.

In addition to the big fish, the files contained a number of smaller fry, such as Lord Fenner Brockway, the veteran peace activist, former MP and General Secretary of the Labour Party. Over many years of dealings with the KGB, this 'confidential contact' had accepted a great deal of hospitality from Soviet intelligence without ever, it seemed, producing anything of much value in return. By 1982 he was ninety-four years old. Another file related to a journalist on the *Guardian* newspaper, Richard Gott. Back in 1964, while working for the Royal Institute of International Affairs, Gott had been approached by a Soviet embassy official in London, the first of several contacts with the KGB. He relished his brush with the spy world. 'I rather enjoyed the cloak-and-dagger atmosphere which will be familiar to anyone who has read the spy stories of the Cold War,' he later said.

1 (top) A KGB family: Anton and Olga Gordievsky, with their two younger children, Marina and Oleg (aged about ten).

2 (bottom) The Gordievsky siblings: Vasili, Marina and Oleg, in about 1955.

3 (top) **Moscow Institute of International Affairs track team: Gordievsky, far left; Stanislaw 'Standa' Kaplan, second right. Kaplan, a future Czechoslovakian intelligence officer, would defect to the West and play a key role in the recruitment of his old university friend.**

4 (bottom) **The long-distance runner training on the shores of the Black Sea.**

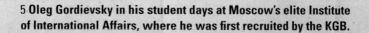

5 Oleg Gordievsky in his student days at Moscow's elite Institute of International Affairs, where he was first recruited by the KGB.

6 (top left) Anton Gordievsky in the KGB uniform he habitually
wore. 'The Party is always right,' he insisted.

7 (top right) Vasili Gordievsky, a highly successful KGB 'illegal', who operated undercover
in Europe and Africa, and drank himself to death at the age of thirty-nine.

8 (bottom) The Lubyanka: the KGB headquarters known as 'The Centre', part
prison, part archive, and the nerve-centre of Soviet intelligence.

9 **Oleg Gordievsky in KGB uniform: an ambitious, loyal and highly trained officer.**

10 (top) The construction of the Berlin Wall, August 1961. The spectacle of the physical barrier being erected between East and West made a profound impression on the 22-year-old Gordievsky.

11 (bottom) The Prague Spring, 1968. A lone protestor defies a Soviet tank. Gordievsky was appalled when 200,000 Soviet troops invaded Czechoslovakia to crush the reform movement.

12 **Covert surveillance photographs of Gordievsky taken by the Danish intelligence service (PET) during his postings to Copenhagen. For years, these were the only images available to MI6 of the Russian intelligence officer codenamed SUNBEAM.**

13 (top) Playing badminton doubles with an unidentified partner in Copenhagen. The KGB officer was first directly approached by MI6 while on the badminton court.

14 (bottom) On the Baltic coast with Mikhail Lyubimov, the KGB *rezident* in Copenhagen and Gordievsky's close friend and patron.

15 **Travelling in Denmark with Lyubimov (standing), his wife, Tamara (left), and Gordievsky's first wife, Yelena.**

Scandinavian spies.

16 (top) Arne Treholt (left), rising star of the Norwegian Labour Party, with his KGB handler Gennadi 'The Crocodile' Titov (centre), on the way to one of their fifty-nine lunches.

17 (bottom left) Stig Bergling, the Swedish policeman and security service officer who became a Soviet spy in 1973.

18 (bottom right) Gunvor Galtung Haavik, the inconspicuous secretary at the Norwegian Ministry of Foreign Affairs who spied for the KGB for more than thirty years under the codename GRETA. Seen here immediately after her arrest in 1977.

19 (top right) Aldrich Ames at around the time he joined the CIA. He would eventually betray the entire CIA spy network inside the Soviet Union, sending many agents to their deaths.

20 (top left) A handwritten message from Ames to his KGB handlers, arranging a 'dead drop' of intelligence information.

21 (bottom) Ames with his second wife, Maria de Rosario Casas Dupuy. 'She was a breath of fresh air,' said Ames. She was also demanding, extravagant and extremely expensive.

22 (top) Sergey Chuvakhin, the Russian arms control specialist selected by Ames as his first point of contact in the Soviet embassy in Washington DC. 'I did it for the money,' he later said.

23 (bottom) Colonel Viktor Cherkashin, chief of counter-intelligence at the Soviet embassy and Ames's first KGB spymaster.

24 (top) Vladimir Kryuchkov, head of the First Chief Directorate and later head of the KGB.

25 (bottom) Yuri Andropov, the KGB chairman whose extreme paranoia prompted Operation RYAN, a demand for evidence of a Western 'first strike' that brought the world close to nuclear war. In 1982 he succeeded Leonid Brezhnev as Soviet leader.

26 (top right) Colonel Viktor
Budanov of K Directorate, the
counter-intelligence branch.
The 'most dangerous man in
the KGB', he personally
interrogated Gordievsky
in May 1985.

27 (left) Nikolai Gribin, the
charismatic, guitar-playing
head of the KGB's British-
Scandinavian section and
Gordievsky's immediate boss.

28 (bottom right) Viktor Grushko, the
Ukrainian deputy head of the First
Chief Directorate, and Gordievsky's
mostsenior inquisitor.

**KUTUZOVSKY PROSPEKT SIGNAL SITE**

1. Ukraine Hotel
2. 7/2 Kutuzovsky Prospekt (known to diplomats as 'Kutz') the diplomatic block
3. Militia Post-KGB guard
4. Bread shop
5. Newspaper hoardings = signal site
6. 'Raz' point (where it was permitted to do a U-turn)
7. Trees
8. 'Beriozka' - hard currency shop

MOSCOW RIVER

RSFR COUNCIL OF MINISTERS (The White House)

To Kremlin and Embassy

KUTUZOVSKY PROSPEKT

Flats

Kutz car park

Kutz

N

7/2 Kutuzovsky Prospekt ('Kutz') compound for foreign residents

Ukraine Hotel

MI6 flat

SIGNAL SITE

BREAD SHOP

**29 (top) The signal site.**

30 Leila Aliyeva, Gordievsky's second wife, pictured at around the time they first met in Copenhagen. She was twenty-eight, the daughter of KGB officers, working as a typist for the World Health Organization. They married in Moscow in 1979.

The contacts resumed in the 1970s. The KGB gave him the codename RON. He accepted Soviet-paid trips to Vienna, Nicosia and Athens. Gott later wrote: 'Like many other journalists, diplomats and politicians, I lunched with Russians during the Cold War . . . I took red gold, even if it was only in the form of expenses for myself and my partner. That, in the circumstances, was culpable stupidity, though at the time it seemed more like an enjoyable joke.'

Like all spy agencies, the KGB was prone to wishful thinking and invention when reality got in the way. Several of those identified in the files were simply left-wingers, perceived as potentially pro-Soviet. The Campaign for Nuclear Disarmament was regarded as a particularly fertile recruiting ground. 'Many were idealists,' Gordievsky noted, 'and most "gave" their "help" unwittingly.' Every target was given a codename. But that did not make them spies. As is often the case in intelligence work, the political files contained a great deal of material that was simply culled from newspapers and journals, and then dressed up by the KGB in London to appear secret, and therefore important.

But there was one dossier that stood out from all the others. The cardboard box contained two folders, one 300 pages thick, the other perhaps half that size, bound with old string and sealed with Plasticine. The file was labelled BOOT. On the cover the word 'agent' had been crossed out, and 'confidential contact' inserted. In December 1981, Gordievsky broke the seal and opened the file for the first time. On the first page appeared a formal introductory note: 'I, senior operational officer Major Petrov, Ivan Alexeyevich, herewith open a file on the agent Michael Foot, citizen of the UK, giving him the pseudonym Boot.'

Agent BOOT was the Right Honourable Michael Foot, distinguished writer and orator, veteran left-wing MP, leader of the Labour Party and the politician who, if Labour won the next election, would become Prime Minister of Britain. The Leader of Her Majesty's Loyal Opposition had been a paid KGB agent.

Gordievsky recalled how, back in Denmark, Mikhail Lyubimov had described his efforts to woo an up-and-coming Labour MP in the 1960s. In his memoirs, with a heavy-elbowed nudge to anyone in the know, Lyubimov referred to the London pub where he did his recruiting as 'The Lyubimov and Boot'. Gordievsky knew that

Michael Foot had risen to become one of the most prominent politicians in Britain. For the next fifteen minutes he flipped through the file, his pulse rising.

Michael Foot occupies a peculiar position in political history. In later years, he became a figure of ridicule, mocked as 'Worzel Gummidge' for his dishevelled appearance, donkey jacket, thick spectacles and knobby walking stick. But for two decades he was a towering figure on the left of the Labour Party, a highly cultured writer, an eloquent public speaker and a politician of vigorous conviction. He became that most peculiar of British animals, a National Treasure. Born in 1913, he began his career as a journalist, edited the socialist newspaper *Tribune*, and was elected to Parliament in 1945. His first Cabinet appointment came in 1974, as Secretary of State for Employment under Harold Wilson. The Labour leader James Callaghan was defeated by Margaret Thatcher in 1979 and resigned eighteen months later. Foot was elected leader of the Labour Party on 10 November 1980. 'I am as strong in my socialist convictions as I have ever been,' he said. Britain was deep in recession. Thatcher was unpopular. Opinion polls put Labour more than ten percentage points ahead of the Conservatives. The next general election was due in May 1984, and there seemed a good chance that Michael Foot could win it, and become Prime Minister.

The BOOT file, if it became public, would put paid to that in an instant.

Major Petrov clearly had a sense of humour, and had been unable to resist the pun on Foot/Boot when choosing a codename. But the rest of the dossier was deadly serious. It described, step by step, how a twenty-year relationship with Foot had evolved since the late 1940s, when the KGB decided that he was 'progressive'. At their first meeting with Foot, in the offices of *Tribune*, KGB officers posing as diplomats slipped £10 into his pocket (worth roughly £250 today). He did not object.

One sheet in the file listed the payments made to Foot over the years. This was a standard form, with the date, amount and name of the paying officer. Gordievsky scanned the figures and estimated there had been between ten and fourteen payments during the 1960s, of between £100 and £150 each, so roughly £1,500 in total, worth more than £37,000 today. What happened to the money is unclear. Lyubimov later told Gordievsky that he suspected Foot might have 'kept some for himself', but the Labour MP was not a mercenary man, and it seems more likely the cash was used to prop up *Tribune*, which was perennially broke.

Another page listed the case officers who had run Agent BOOT out of the London *rezidentura*, by both real name and codename: Gordievsky immediately noted Lyubimov, codenamed KORIN. 'I quickly looked through the list. One of my objectives was to see if there was somebody else I knew, and find out who were the officers able to manipulate such a man.' There was also an index, five pages long, an inventory of every person mentioned by Foot in conversation with the KGB.

The meetings took place roughly once a month, frequently over lunch at the Gay Hussar restaurant in Soho. Every rendezvous was carefully planned. Three days beforehand, Moscow sent an outline of what should be discussed. The resulting report was read by the PR Line chief in London, then the *rezident*, before being sent on to Moscow Centre. At each stage, there was an evaluation of the developing case.

Gordievsky read a couple of reports in detail, and skim-read another half a dozen. 'I was interested in the language and style of those reports and what they reflected of the relationship – they were better than I expected. The reports were not very imaginative, but they were intelligent, well written. This was a very developed relationship, sympathetic on both sides, with confidentiality on both sides, they spoke with cordiality, and lots of specifics, saturated with real information.' Lyubimov had been particularly skilled at running Foot, and paying him. 'Mikhail Petrovich would put money in an envelope and put it in his pocket – he had such elegant manners that he could do it in a convincing way.'

What did the KGB get in return? Gordievsky recalled: 'Foot freely disclosed information about the Labour movement to them. He told them which politicians and trade union leaders were pro-Soviet, even suggesting which union bosses should be given the present of Soviet-funded holidays on the Black Sea. A leading supporter of the Campaign for Nuclear Disarmament, Foot also passed on what he knew about debates over nuclear weapons. In return, the KGB gave him drafts of articles encouraging British disarmament which he could then edit and publish, unattributed to their real source, in *Tribune*. There was no protest by Foot to the KGB over the Soviet invasion of Hungary in 1956, and he quite often visited the Soviet Union to a top-level welcome.'

Foot was exceptionally well informed. He provided details on internal machinations within Labour, as well as the Party's attitude towards other hot topics: the Vietnam War, the military and political consequences of Kennedy's assassination, the development of Diego Garcia as a US base, and the Geneva Conference of 1954 to settle outstanding issues from the Korean War. Foot was in a unique position to provide the Soviets with political insight, and receptive to the Soviet line. The manipulation was subtle. 'Michael Foot would be told: "Mr Foot, our analytical people came to the conclusion it would be useful if the public knew such and such." Then the officer would say: "I have prepared some material . . . take it and use it, if you like it." They discussed what would be nice to publish in the future, in his own paper and others.' Never was it acknowledged that Foot was being served raw Soviet propaganda.

BOOT was a peculiar sort of agent, who did not exactly fit the KGB definition. He did not conceal his meetings with Soviet officials (though he did not advertise them either) and since he was a public figure these were impossible to arrange clandestinely. He was an 'opinion-creator', and therefore more an agent of influence (a term of art) than an agent (a specific term of espionage). Foot would not have known that the KGB classified him as an agent, an internal definition. He retained his intellectual independence. He leaked no state secrets (and at that time had no access to any). He doubtless believed he was serving progressive politics and the cause of peace in accepting Soviet largesse in support of *Tribune*. He may even have been unaware that his interlocutors were KGB officers, feeding him information, and passing whatever he revealed back to Moscow. If so, he was stunningly naïve.

In 1968, the BOOT case changed gear. Foot was intensely critical of Moscow in the wake of the Prague Spring. At a protest rally in Hyde Park he declared: 'The actions of the Russians confirm that one of the worst threats to socialism comes from within the Kremlin itself.' No more money changed hands. BOOT was downgraded from 'agent' to 'confidential contact'. The meetings became less frequent, and by the time Foot was running for the Labour leadership they had ceased entirely. But, from the KGB perspective in 1981, the case remained open, and might yet be revived.

The BOOT file left Gordievsky in no doubt: 'The KGB regarded Michael Foot as an actual agent until 1968. He took cash directly from us, which meant we could regard him in good conscience as an agent. If an agent takes money it is very good – a reinforcing element in the relationship.'

Foot had not broken the law. He was not a Soviet spy. He had not betrayed his country. But he had taken direction and secretly accepted money from, while providing information to, an enemy power, a totalitarian dictatorship. If his relationship with the KGB were discovered by his political rivals (inside as well as outside his own party), it would destroy his career in a moment, decapitate the Labour Party, and ignite a scandal that would rewrite British politics. At the very least, Foot would be sure to lose the next election.

Lenin is often credited with coining the term 'useful idiot', *poleznyi durak* in Russian, meaning one who can be used to spread propaganda without being aware of it, or subscribing to the goals intended by the manipulator.

Michael Foot had been useful to the KGB, and completely idiotic.

Gordievsky read the BOOT files in December 1981. The following month he read them again, committing as much as he could to memory.

Dmitri Svetanko, the deputy department head, was surprised to find Gordievsky still buried in the British case histories, particularly when he had told him not to bother.

'What are you doing?' he asked abruptly.

'I am reading the files,' said Gordievsky, trying to sound matter of fact.

'Do you really need to?'

'I thought I should be thoroughly prepared.'

Svetanko was unimpressed. 'Why don't you write some useful

paper rather than wasting time reading those files?' he snapped, and left the office.

On 2 April 1982, Argentina invaded the Falkland Islands, Britain's outpost in the South Atlantic. Even Michael Foot, Leader of the Opposition and apostle of peace, called for 'action not words' in response to Argentine aggression. Margaret Thatcher dispatched a task force to repel the invaders. In Moscow Centre, the Falklands War provoked a violent upsurge of anti-British feeling. Thatcher was already a hate-figure in the Soviet Union; the Falklands conflict was yet another example of British imperialist arrogance. The 'hostility of the KGB was almost hysterical', Gordievsky recalled. His colleagues were convinced Britain would be defeated by plucky little Argentina.

Britain was at war. Gordievsky, alone within the KGB, was on Britain's side. He wondered if he would ever reach the country to which he had sworn secret allegiance.

Finally the KGB's Fifth Department gave Gordievsky the all-clear to travel to Britain. On 28 June 1982, he boarded the Aeroflot flight to London, with Leila and their daughters, now aged two and nine months. He was relieved to be on his way, anxious to re-establish contact with MI6, but the future remained murky. If his work for Britain succeeded, he would eventually have to defect, and might never return to Russia. He might never again see his mother or younger sister. If he was exposed, he might well come back, but under KGB guard, to face interrogation and execution. As the plane took off, Gordievsky's mind was heavy with the accumulated mental baggage from four months of tense secret study in the KGB archives. Making notes of what he had uncovered would have been far too dangerous. Instead, in his head, he carried the names of every PR Line agent in Britain, and every KGB spy in the Soviet embassy in London; he brought evidence of the identity of 'the Fifth Man', the activities in exile of Kim Philby, and further proof that the Norwegian Arne Treholt was a spy for Moscow. And, most important of all, he brought memorized details of the BOOT files, the KGB dossier on Michael Foot – a surprise gift for British intelligence, and an exceptionally volatile lump of political explosive.

# PART TWO

# 7.    The Safe House

On the outside Aldrich Ames was just an averagely unhappy CIA officer. He drank too much. His marriage was collapsing in a slow and unspectacular slither. He never had enough money. His job, trying to recruit Soviet spies in Mexico City on the fringes of the Cold War, was surprisingly dull, and just unproductive enough to ensure a steady stream of chivvying demands from CIA headquarters in Langley, Virginia. Ames felt underappreciated, underpaid and undersexed. He had recently received a number of reprimands: for getting plastered at a Christmas party, forgetting to lock a safe, and leaving a briefcase, containing photos of a Soviet agent, on a train. But there was nothing in his work record to indicate he was anything other than uniformly mediocre, reliably second-rate and inconspicuously idle. Tall and spare, with thick spectacles and a moustache that never seemed fully confident of itself, he was hard to spot in a group, and invisible in a crowd. There was nothing special about Ames – and that, perhaps, was the problem.

Deep inside Rick Ames was a canker of cynicism, hard and inflamed, growing so slowly that no one had noticed it, least of all Ames himself.

Ames had once harboured big dreams. Born in River Falls, Wisconsin, in 1941, he had a 1950s childhood that looked like the sort of idyllic suburban dream depicted on the cereal packets, concealing its share of depression, alcoholism and quiet despair. His father had started life as an academic, and ended up working for the CIA in Burma, passing money to Burmese publications secretly bankrolled by the US government. As a boy, Ames read Leslie Charteris's thrillers featuring Simon Templar, 'the Saint', and imagined himself as a 'dashing, debonair British adventurer'. He wore a trench coat to look like a spy, and practised magic tricks. He liked fooling people.

Ames was intelligent and imaginative, but reality never seemed to measure up to his hopes, or furnish him with what he considered his just deserts. He flunked out of the University of Chicago, and worked for a while as a part-time actor. He resented authority. 'If asked to do something he didn't want to do, he didn't argue: he just didn't do it.' He finally scraped a degree, and drifted into the CIA, on his father's suggestion. 'Lying is wrong, son, but if it serves a greater good, it's OK,' said his father, through an increasingly thick fug of bourbon.

The CIA's Junior Officer Training course was intended to inspire patriotic devotion to duty in the complex and demanding world of intelligence-gathering. But it could have other effects. Ames learned: that morality can be malleable; the laws of the US overrode those of other countries; a greedy spy was worth more than an ideological one, because 'once you had the money hooks in, it was easier to hold them and play them'. Agent recruitment, Ames came to believe, depended on 'the ability to assess a person's vulnerability'. Once you knew a man's weakness, you could snare and manipulate him. Disloyalty was not a sin, but an operational tool. 'The essence of espionage is betrayal of trust,' Ames declared. He was wrong: the essence of successful agent-running is the *maintenance* of trust, the supplanting of one allegiance by another, higher, loyalty.

Ames was posted to Turkey, a centre for the espionage war between East and West, and began putting his training into practice by recruiting Soviet agents in Ankara. Ames decided he was a natural spymaster, with 'the ability to focus on a target, establish a relationship, [and] manipulate myself and him into the situation I aimed for'. His bosses, however, considered his performance no more than 'satisfactory'. After the Prague Spring, he was instructed to paste up hundreds of posters at night with the slogan: 'Remember '68' – to give the impression that the Turkish population was outraged by the Soviet invasion. He dumped the posters in a bin, and went for a drink.

Returning to Washington in 1972, Ames took a training course in Russian, and spent the next four years working in the Soviet–East European Department. The ship he joined was not a happy one. The revelation that Richard Nixon had used the CIA to try to obstruct a federal investigation into the Watergate burglary in 1972 triggered a crisis within the agency, and a series of investigations into its activities over the preceding twenty years. The resulting reports, known as the 'Family Jewels', identified a damning litany of illegal actions far outside the CIA's charter, including wiretapping of journalists, burglaries, assassination plots, experimentation on humans, collusion with the Mafia and systematic domestic surveillance of civilians. James Angleton, the CIA's cadaverous, orchid-collecting counter-intelligence chief, had almost destroyed the CIA with his internal mole-hunts, based on the obsessive and erroneous belief that Kim Philby was orchestrating the mass penetration of Western intelligence. Angleton was finally forced to retire in 1974, leaving behind a legacy of profound paranoia. The CIA was also falling behind in the spy war: 'Thanks to the excessive zeal of Angleton and his counter-intelligence staff, we had very few Soviet agents inside the USSR worthy of the name,' said Robert M. Gates, who was recruited at around the same time as Ames and went on to head the CIA. The agency would undergo wholesale reform over the next decade, but Ames had joined when it was at its lowest ebb: demoralized, disorganized and widely distrusted.

In 1976 he was moved to New York to try to recruit Soviet agents, and then posted on to Mexico City in 1981. The CIA noted his drinking, as well as a tendency to procrastinate and complain, but there was never any suggestion he should be fired. After nearly twenty years in the CIA he understood the workings of the agency, but his career was stagnating, for which he blamed everybody else. His attempts to recruit agents in Mexico yielded little, and he regarded most of his colleagues, and all of his superiors, as idiots. 'Much of what I was doing was for nothing,' he admitted. Ames had married a fellow intelligence officer, Nancy Segebarth, swiftly and with too little thought. His marriage, like that of Gordievsky, turned out to be chilly and childless. Nan did not come with him to Mexico City. He had a number of unsatisfying affairs with women he did not much like.

By mid-1982 Ames was slipping into a rut: disgruntled, lonely, peevish and unfulfilled, but too lazy and boozy to do anything to arrest the slide. Then Rosario came into his life, and the lights came on.

Maria de Rosario Casas Dupuy was the cultural attaché at the

Colombian embassy. Born into an impoverished aristocratic Colombian family of French origin, Rosario was twenty-nine, well read, flirtatious and vivacious, with curly dark hair and a flashing smile. 'She was like a breath of fresh air entering a room stale with cigar smoke,' said one State Department employee in Mexico City. She was also immature, needy and greedy. Her family had once owned large country estates. She had been educated at the finest private schools, and had studied in Europe and the US. She was a member of the Colombian elite. But the family was broke. 'I grew up around people with wealth,' she once said. 'But we never had it.' Rosario intended to rectify that.

She met Rick Ames at a diplomatic dinner party. They sat on the floor eagerly discussing modern literature, and then went back to his flat. Rosario thought Ames was a regular American diplomat, and therefore probably reasonably rich. Rick found her 'brilliant and beautiful', and swiftly decided he was in love. 'Sex between us was fantastic,' he said.

Rosario's enthusiasm may have dimmed a little when she discovered that her new American lover was already married, impecunious and a CIA spy. 'What are you doing with these creeps?' she demanded. 'Why are you wasting your time, your talents?' Ames promised he would divorce Nan as soon as possible, and marry Rosario. Then they would start a new life together back in the US, and 'live happily ever after'. For a man on a paltry CIA salary, this was a costly promise: divorcing Nan was likely to be expensive, and taking on Rosario, with her extravagant tastes, could be ruinous. He told Rosario he would quit the CIA and start another career, but at the age of forty-one he had neither the inclination nor the energy to do so. Instead, somewhere in Rick Ames's unquiet mind, a plan was forming to make his underpaid and unsatisfying job at the CIA a lot more lucrative.

While Aldrich Ames was making plans for a profitable new future, on the other side of the world a stocky man in a peaked leather cap slipped out of the Soviet embassy at Number 13, Kensington Palace Gardens, in London, and headed west towards Notting Hill Gate. After a few hundred yards he doubled back, turned right down one road and swiftly left down another before entering a pub and, a minute later, walking out through a side door. Finally, in a side street, he entered a red telephone box, closed the heavy door, and dialled the number he had been given in Copenhagen four years earlier.

'Hello! Welcome to London,' said the recorded voice of Geoffrey Guscott, in Russian. 'Thank you so much for calling. We look forward to seeing you. Meanwhile take a few days to relax and settle in. Let's be in touch at the beginning of July.' The recording invited him to call back on the evening of 4 July. The sound of Guscott's voice was 'immensely reassuring'.

MI6 had been running Oleg Gordievsky for eight years; it now had an eager, experienced spy implanted inside the KGB's London station, and it was not going to blow the case by moving too fast.

Oleg and his family had settled quickly into their two-bedroom flat in a building entirely occupied by Soviet embassy staff on Kensington High Street. Leila was entranced by her unfamiliar new surroundings, but Gordievsky felt an unexpected twinge of disappointment. Britain had been his goal ever since his recruitment by Richard Bromhead, and the place had taken on an aura of glamour and sophistication in his imagination it could never match in reality. London was a lot dirtier than Copenhagen, and not much cleaner than Moscow. 'I had imagined that everything would be much tidier and more attractive.' Still, he reflected, simply getting to the UK was 'a mighty victory, for British intelligence and for me'. MI6 would undoubtedly know he had arrived, but he waited a few days before making contact, just in case he was under KGB surveillance.

The morning after his arrival, Gordievsky walked the quarter-mile to the Soviet embassy, presented his brand-new pass to the doorman, and was escorted to the KGB *rezidentura*: a cramped, smoky, fortified enclave on the top floor, rigid with mistrust and ruled over by an obsessively suspicious chief who went by the blunt and unmusical name of Guk.

General Arkadi Vasilyevich Guk, nominally First Secretary at the Soviet embassy but in reality the KGB *rezident*, had arrived in Britain two years earlier, and made a point of refusing to assimilate. Fiercely ignorant, brutally ambitious and frequently drunk, he dismissed any form of cultural interest as intellectual pretension, and entirely rejected all books, films, plays, art and music. Guk had come to prominence in the KGB's counter-intelligence (KR) directorate, by liquidating nationalist opposition to Soviet rule in the Baltic states. He was an advocate and connoisseur of assassination, and liked to boast that he had offered to liquidate a number of renegades who had fled to the West, including Stalin's daughter and the chairman of the Jewish Defense League in New York. He ate only Russian food, in vast amounts, and barely spoke any English. Before coming to London, he had been head of the municipal KGB station in Moscow city. In contrast to Mikhail Lyubimov, he hated Britain and the British. But most of all he loathed the Soviet ambassador, Viktor Popov, an educated, slightly foppish diplomat who represented everything Guk despised. The KGB chief spent much of his time closeted in his office, drinking vodka and chain-smoking, bitching about Popov and trying to think of new ways to undermine him. Much of the information he sent back to Moscow was pure invention, cleverly framed to feed Moscow's rampant conspiracy theories – such as the idea that the centre-left Social Democratic Party (SDP), the new grouping formed in March 1981, had been created by the CIA. Gordievsky summed up his new boss as 'a huge, bloated lump of a man, with a mediocre brain and a large reserve of low cunning'.

Rather more intelligent, but also more menacing, was Leonid Yefremovitch Nikitenko, the head of counter-intelligence, Guk's principal confidant. He was handsome, charming when he felt like it, and cold-blooded. He had deep-set, yellowish eyes, which missed very little. Early on, Nikitenko had decided that the way to get ahead in London was to pander to Guk, but he was a skilled counter-intelligence officer, methodical and devious, and after three years' experience in London he had learned much about the ways of British intelligence. 'There is no business like it,' Nikitenko declared, reflecting on his work combating MI5 and MI6. 'We are politicians. We are soldiers. And, above all, we are actors on a wonderful stage. I cannot think of a better business than the intelligence business.' If anyone was going to make problems for Gordievsky, it was Nikitenko.

The head of the PR Line, Gordievsky's immediate superior, was Igor Fyodorovich Titov (no relation to Gennadi), a balding, chain-smoking martinet with an insatiable taste for Western pornographic magazines, which he bought in Soho and sent to Moscow in the diplomatic bag as gifts for his KGB cronies. Titov was not officially on the embassy diplomatic staff, but worked under journalistic cover, as a correspondent for the Russian weekly *New Times*. Gordievsky had got to know Titov in Moscow, and considered him 'a truly evil man'.

The three bosses were waiting for Gordievsky in the *rezident*'s office. Their handshakes were tepid, the greetings formulaic. Guk immediately took against the newcomer on the grounds that he appeared cultured. Nikitenko eyed him with the reserve of a man trained to trust nobody. And Titov saw his new subordinate as a potential rival. The KGB was an intensely tribal community: both Guk and Nikitenko were products of the KR Line, with an ingrained counter-intelligence mindset, and therefore instinctively regarded the newcomer as a threat, who had 'elbowed his way' into a job for which he was barely qualified.

Paranoia is born of propaganda, ignorance, secrecy and fear. The KGB's London station in 1982 was one of the most profoundly paranoid places on earth, an organization imbued with a siege mentality largely based on fantasy. Since the KGB devoted enormous time and effort to spying on foreign diplomats in Moscow, it assumed MI5 and MI6 must be doing the same in London. In reality, although the Security Service certainly monitored and shadowed suspected KGB operatives, the surveillance was nothing like as intensive as the Russians imagined.

The KGB, however, was convinced that the entire Soviet embassy was the target of a gigantic and sustained eavesdropping campaign, and the fact that this snooping was invisible confirmed that the British must be very good at it. The Nepalese and Egyptian embassies next door were assumed to be 'listening posts', and officers were banned from speaking near the adjoining walls; unseen spies with telephoto lenses were thought to be tracking everyone entering or leaving the building; the British, it was said, had built a special tunnel under Kensington Palace Gardens in order to install bugging equipment beneath the embassy; electric typewriters were banned, on the grounds that the sound of tapping might be picked up and deciphered, and even manual typewriters were discouraged in case the keystrokes gave something away; there were notices on every wall warning: 'DON'T SAY NAMES OR DATES OUT LOUD'; the windows were all bricked up, except in Guk's office, where miniature radio speakers pumped canned Russian music into the space between the panes of the double glazing, emitting a peculiar muffled warble that added to the surreal atmosphere. All secret conversations took place in a metal-lined, windowless room in the basement, which was dank all year round and roasting in summer. Ambassador Popov, with his offices on the middle floor, believed (probably rightly) that the KGB had inserted bugging devices through his ceiling to listen in on his conversations. Guk's personal obsession was the London Underground system, which he never entered since he was convinced that certain advertising panels in Tube stations contained two-way mirrors, through which MI5 was tracking the KGB's every move. Guk went everywhere in his ivory-coloured Mercedes.

Gordievsky now found himself working inside a miniature Stalinist state, sealed off from the rest of London, an enclosed world of roiling distrust, petty jealousies and backbiting. 'The envy, the vicious thinking, the underhand attacks, the intrigues, the denunciations, all these were on a scale that made the Centre in Moscow seem like a girls' school.'

The KGB station was a truly nasty place to work. But then the KGB, in Gordievsky's mind, was no longer his primary employer.

On 4 July 1982, Gordievsky called the MI6 number again, from a different phone box. The switchboard, alerted in advance, immediately routed the call to a desk on the twelfth floor. This time Geoffrey Guscott answered in person. Their conversation was joyful, but brisk and practical: a proposed rendezvous at 3 p.m. the following afternoon in a place where, it was calculated, Russian spies were most unlikely to be lurking.

The Holiday Inn on Sloane Street had a good claim to be London's most boring hotel. Its sole distinction was to host the annual Slimmer of the Year competition.

At the appointed hour, Gordievsky entered the swing doors and immediately spotted Guscott across the lobby. Beside him sat an elegant woman in her early fifties with neat blonde hair and sensible shoes. Veronica Price had worked on the case for five years, but had only ever seen Gordievsky in blurred photographs and passport snaps. She nudged Guscott, and whispered: 'There he is!' Guscott thought the 43-year-old Gordievsky had aged in the intervening years, but he appeared fit. A 'slight smile' crossed the Russian's face as he spotted his English handler. Guscott and Price rose to their feet and, without making eye contact, made their way down the corridor leading to the back of the hotel. As agreed, Gordievsky followed them out through the back door, across the tarmac and up one flight of stairs to the first floor of the hotel car park. A beaming Guscott was waiting beside a car, with the back door open. Price had parked it the night before for a quick getaway, beside the stairway door but near the exit ramp. The car was a Ford, specially purchased for the purposes of the pickup, with a number plate untraceable back to MI6.

Only when the spy was safely inside did they exchange greetings. Guscott and Gordievsky sat in the back, speaking rapid Russian, two old friends catching up on family news, while Price drove, steering confidently through the light traffic. Guscott explained that he had returned to London from abroad in order to welcome Gordievsky, make plans for the future, and arrange his handover to a new case officer. The Russian nodded. They passed Harrods and the Victoria and Albert Museum, crossed Hyde Park, turned into the forecourt of a new block of flats in Bayswater, and drove into the underground car park.

Veronica had spent weeks scouting west London with oblivious estate agents before finding the right safe house. The one-bedroom flat on the third floor of a modern block was screened from the street by a line of trees. The exit from the underground car park led directly into the building: anyone attempting to follow Gordievsky might see his car drive in, but would be unable to tell which flat he had entered. A gate from the rear garden led into a side street, offering an emergency escape route through the back of the building and into Kensington Palace Gardens. The flat was sufficiently far from the Soviet embassy to make it unlikely that Gordievsky would be randomly spotted by other KGB officers, but near enough for him to drive there, park, meet his case officers, and return to Kensington Palace Gardens – all within two hours. A nearby delicatessen could supply gastronomic back-up. Price insisted: 'The flat had to have a nice atmosphere, a certain status. Some shabby place in Brixton wouldn't do.' It was furnished with tasteful modern furniture. It was also bugged.

Once they were seated in the sitting room, Price bustled around, laying out tea. Female case officers were virtually unknown in the KGB, and Gordievsky had never met a woman quite like Price. 'He took to her at once,' Guscott observed. 'Oleg had an eye for the women.' This was also his first experience of a formal English tea. Like many people of her age and class, Price regarded tea as a sacred patriotic ritual. Guscott introduced her as 'Jean'. Her face, Gordievsky reflected, 'seemed to embody all the traditional British qualities of decency and honour'.

Guscott outlined the operational plan. If Oleg agreed, he would meet his MI6 case officers, at lunchtime, once a month, in this flat. The KGB station emptied out during the lunch hour, when the officers went to wine and dine their contacts (or, more precisely, themselves). Gordievsky's absence would not be noticed.

Guscott now handed him a key to a house between Kensington High Street and Holland Park. This was his bolthole, a place where he could go to ground, with or without his family, the moment he sensed danger. If he wanted to cancel a meeting, needed to see an MI6 officer at short notice, or required emergency help of any sort, he should call the telephone number he had dialled on arrival. The switchboard was manned twenty-four hours a day, and an operator would direct the call to whichever of the team was on duty.

Guscott offered one more, crucial, reassurance. The escape plan from Moscow, Operation PIMLICO, would be kept in readiness while he was in London. The KGB was generous in its holiday entitlement, and officers tended to return on annual leave for four weeks in the winter and up to six weeks in the summer. He might also be summoned back at short notice. Whenever he was in Moscow, MI6 officers would continue to check the signal sites at the bread shop on Kutuzovsky Prospekt and the Central Market, looking out for a man with a Safeway bag. They would even do so when the spy was not in the country. The KGB closely watched all British diplomats in Moscow, and bugged their apartments, while surveillance posts monitored their movements from the top of the Hotel Ukraine and the roof of the foreigners' apartment block. Any deviation from routine might be noticed; if they regularly walked past the bread shop when Gordievsky was in Moscow, stopped doing so when he was absent, and started again when he returned, the pattern might just be detected. For several weeks either side of his visits, MI6 would continue to monitor the site. Strict tradecraft required that the procedure for Operation PIMLICO be maintained for months, or years.

The case had entered a new phase and was given a new codename: SUNBEAM became NOCTON (a village in Lincolnshire).

MI6 had never run a KGB spy based in London before, and the situation raised novel challenges, not least the threat posed by its sister service, MI5. The Security Service was responsible for monitoring the movements of all suspected KGB officers in London. If Section A4, the MI5 surveillance team known as the 'Watchers', spotted Gordievsky attending a clandestine meeting at a suspicious location in Bayswater, they would undoubtedly investigate. But issuing a blanket order *not* to put Gordievsky under surveillance would clearly indicate that he was being protected. Either way, the security of the case could be fatally compromised. No case of this importance could have been run in Britain without informing the Security Service. A decision was therefore taken to run the case jointly with MI5, and 'indoctrinate' a handful of senior MI5 officers, including the Director General: that way MI6 could be informed of the times when Gordievsky was under surveillance, and thus ensure that meetings took place without the Watchers observing.

This collaboration between MI5 and MI6 was unprecedented. The two branches of British intelligence had not always seen eye to eye — perhaps unsurprisingly, since the task of catching spies and the job of running them are not necessarily compatible, sometimes overlapping and occasionally in conflict. The two intelligence organizations had distinct traditions, codes of behaviour and techniques. The rivalry was deep, and often counterproductive. Historically, some in MI6 had tended to look down on the domestic Security Service as little more than a police outfit, lacking in imagination and verve; MI5, in turn, tended to view foreign-intelligence officers as flaky public school adventurers. Each regarded the other as 'leaky'. The long investigation by MI5 into the MI6 officer Kim Philby had deepened the mutual suspicion into outright hostility. But for the purposes of NOCTON they would be working in tandem: MI6 would run Gordievsky day to day; a chosen few in MI5 would be kept abreast of developments and handle the security aspects of the case. The decision to widen the circle of secrecy outside MI6 represented a remarkable break with tradition, and a gamble. Information shared between MI6 and MI5 relating to Gordievsky was given the codename LAMPAD (an underworld nymph in Greek mythology). A tiny handful within MI6 knew of NOCTON; an even smaller number within MI5 knew of LAMPAD; the intersecting Venn diagram of MI6 and MI5 personnel who were privy to both numbered no more than a dozen people.

With the terms of engagement agreed, and the tea cleared away, Gordievsky leaned forward and started to unload four years of accumulated secrets, a great tumbling screed of information gathered and committed to memory in Moscow: names, dates, places, plans, agents and illegals. Guscott scribbled notes, and only occasionally interrupted to clarify some point. But Gordievsky needed little prompting. He steadily ran through his prodigious reservoir of memorized fact, step after step, lap after lap. The first meeting only skimmed the surface of Gordievsky's memory, but as time passed, and he relaxed, the secrets poured out of him, in a controlled, cathartic cascade.

Everyone rehearses their recollections, believing that the more often an event is remembered, the closer we come to its reality. This is not always true. Most people tell a version of the past, and then either stick to or embellish it. Gordievsky's powers of recall were different. He was not just consistent, but progressive and accreting. 'He added more and more details, at every meeting, gradually building up what we knew,' said Veronica Price. A photographic memory records a single, precise black-and-white image; Gordievsky's memory was pointillist, a series of dots which, when joined up and filled in, created a massive canvas of vivid colour. 'Oleg had a great gift for remembering conversations. He recalled timing, context, wording . . . he wouldn't be steered.' He had even memorized his conversations with other officers when he was assigned to night duty. As a highly trained intelligence officer, he knew what was likely to be of interest, and what was surplus. The information came ready-packaged, and analysed. 'He had keen insights, a very good understanding of what it meant, which set him apart.'

The meetings followed a set pattern, at first once a month, then fortnightly, then every week. Whenever the Russian arrived at the safe flat, Guscott and Price would be waiting with a warm welcome and a light lunch. 'He was still suffering from culture shock, and working in a KGB station that was essentially hostile,' Guscott recalled. 'He had piles of knowledge stored up. Our main aim was to ensure there was no withdrawal. We were very anxious to reassure him.'

On 1 September 1982, Gordievsky arrived at the flat to find a third person waiting alongside Guscott and Price, a dapper, intense-looking young man with dark receding hair. Guscott introduced him, in Russian, as 'Jack'. Gordievsky and James Spooner shook hands for the first time. Their rapport was immediate.

James Spooner's fluent Russian and operational skills made him the natural candidate to run the case when Guscott returned to Stockholm. He had been due to take up a new posting in Germany, when he was asked to run NOCTON instead. 'It took me about two minutes to say yes.' The agent and agent-runner quietly appraised one another.

'I had been carefully briefed, and he was exactly what I had expected,' said Spooner. 'Young, vigorous, on the ball, disciplined, focused.' These were words that might have been used to describe Spooner himself. Both men had been steeped in intelligence throughout their adult lives; both viewed spycraft through the prism of history; they spoke the same language, figuratively and actually.

'I never had any suspicion of him. Not a squeak,' said Spooner. 'It's hard to explain, but you just know what to trust and what not to trust. You exercise your judgement. Oleg was completely reliable, honest and driven by the right motivations.'

Gordievsky immediately recognized Spooner as a 'first-class

intelligence officer, but also truly kind, full of emotion and sensitivity, honest both personally and in his ethical principles'. He would later describe him as 'the best minder I have ever had'.

To Gordievsky, Britain still seemed 'alien and unfamiliar', but, as one meeting followed another, the routine of regular contact with MI6 fell into a pattern. The Bayswater flat provided a haven, a refuge from the brutal infighting and paranoid antagonisms inside Guk's KGB *rezidentura*. Veronica would prepare a meal from the local deli, usually picnic food, including occasional Russian delicacies such as pickled herring and beetroot, and a bottle of beer or two. Spooner always placed a tape recorder on the coffee table, back-up in case the hidden eavesdropping technology failed, but also a statement of professionalism, a focus. The meetings lasted up to two hours, and at the end of each they made an arrangement for the next. Then Spooner would transcribe and translate their exchanges, and write up a full report. He often worked late into the night, and from home to avoid drawing attention inside Century House: to disguise from MI6 colleagues what he was really up to, Spooner was said to be working on a case abroad, requiring foreign travel. His transcript would then become the quarry from which to mine individual reports for the various 'customers' – each one, as was standard MI6 practice, dealing with only one subject area. One meeting might produce twenty reports, some as short as a single sentence. Responsibility for collating, analysing, dividing, disguising and distributing the NOCTON product fell to a special cell within MI6, led by a talented Cold War specialist.

Gordievsky systematically excavated his memory, remembering, refining and accumulating. After three months of debriefing, he had scoured his recollections for every detail: the result was the single largest 'operational download' in MI6 history, an astonishingly meticulous and comprehensive insight into the KGB: its past, present and future plans.

One by one, Gordievsky exorcised the demons of MI6 history. Kim Philby was still working for the KGB, he explained, but as a part-time analyst, and certainly not the all-seeing mastermind imagined by the CIA's James Angleton. For years, the British establishment had wondered if another spy like Philby lurked within its ranks, while the tabloids relentlessly hunted for the so-called 'Fifth Man', identifying numerous candidates and wrecking several careers and lives in the process. Peter Wright, the renegade MI5 officer and author of *Spycatcher*, had been obsessed with the theory that Roger Hollis, the former chief of MI5, was a Soviet mole, prompting a series of highly damaging internal investigations. Gordievsky laid that conspiracy theory to rest, definitively clearing Hollis's name. The Fifth Man, he confirmed, was John Cairncross, a former MI6 officer who had confessed to being a Soviet agent back in 1964. The spectacle of the British tying themselves in knots over a fantasy provoked much baffled amusement in the Centre, Gordievsky reported, and seemed so bizarre that the KGB suspected a plot. He described how Gennadi Titov himself, on reading yet another British newspaper account of the witch-hunt, had asked: 'Why is it they are speaking about Roger Hollis? Such nonsense, can't understand it, it must be some special British trick directed against us.' The twenty-year mole-hunt had been a fabulously destructive waste of time.

Gordievsky's research in the KGB archives unlocked other mysteries. A Soviet spy discovered back in 1946, codenamed ELLI but never formally identified, was actually Leo Long, another former intelligence officer recruited to the communist cause at Cambridge University before the war. The Italian nuclear physicist Bruno Pontecorvo, who worked on Britain's wartime atomic bomb research, had volunteered his services to the KGB seven years before he defected to the USSR in 1950. Gordievsky was also able to reveal that Arne Treholt, the Norwegian spy, was still active. Treholt had been part of Norway's delegation to the UN in New York, and was now back in Norway, studying at the Joint Staff College with access to plenty of sensitive material – which he passed on to the KGB. The Norwegian security service had been monitoring Treholt ever since Gordievsky's first tip-off in 1974, but had not yet pounced – partly at British urging, since it was feared that arresting him might direct suspicion onto their source, who had not been identified to the Norwegians. Now the noose began to tighten around Treholt.

*

A small group of senior MI6 officers gathered in Century House to hear the initial results of the debriefing from the NOCTON case officers. These were not demonstrative and emotional people, but there was an air of 'excitement and anticipation' in the room. The grandees had expected to learn of a vast network of KGB agents in Britain, communist spies like the Cambridge Five who had wormed their way into the establishment in order to destroy it from within. It was assumed that the KGB in 1982 must be as potent as ever. Gordievsky proved it was not.

The discovery that the KGB had only a small handful of agents, contacts and illegals in Britain, none seriously threatening, came as both a relief and a disappointment. Gordievsky had revealed how the KGB archives contained active files on Jack Jones, the trade union leader, and Bob Edwards, the Labour MP. He identified sympathetic 'contacts' who had accepted KGB money or entertainment, such as Richard Gott, the *Guardian* journalist, and the elderly peace activist Fenner Brockway. But the spy-hunters found they had little in the way of big game worth pursuing. There was one particular source of concern: Gordievsky had apparently never heard of Geoffrey Prime, an analyst at GCHQ, the branch of British intelligence dealing with communications and signals intelligence, who had just been arrested as a Soviet spy. If Gordievsky had seen all the files, why was there not one on Prime, who began spying for the USSR in 1968? The answer was simple: Prime had been run by KGB counter-intelligence rather than the British–Scandinavian section.

Gordievsky's detailed depiction of the KGB operations in London, Scandinavia and Moscow proved that the Soviet adversary was not the ten-foot giant of myth, but flawed, clumsy and inefficient. The KGB of the 1970s was clearly not what it had been a generation earlier. The ideological fervour of the 1930s, which had seen the recruitment of so many committed agents, had been replaced by a terrified conformity, which produced a very different sort of spy. It remained vast, well funded and ruthless, and it could still call on some of the brightest and best recruits. But its ranks now also included many time-servers and boot-lickers, lazy careerists with little imagination. The KGB was still a dangerous antagonist, but its vulnerabilities and deficiencies were now exposed. At the same time as the KGB was entering a period of decline, new life and ambition were beginning to animate Western intelligence. MI6 was emerging from the defensive crouch it had adopted during the debilitating spy scandals of the 1950s and 1960s.

A tremor of confidence and excitement ran through the organization. This KGB could be beaten.

But there was one aspect of the Gordievsky trove that made the top brass of British intelligence and security sit up and swallow, hard.

Michael Foot's dalliance with the KGB lay in the distant past. Gordievsky had been careful not to exaggerate the importance of Agent BOOT, and Geoffrey Guscott was clear in his assessment of the case: Foot had been used only for 'disinformation purposes', a long time ago; he was not a spy, or 'conscious agent' in the accepted sense. But since 1980 he had been Leader of the Labour Opposition, challenging Margaret Thatcher for leadership of the country. He might become Prime Minister at the next general election, to be held at the latest by 1984. If his previous financial relationship with the KGB was revealed, it would destroy Foot's credibility, end his chances of winning power, and possibly change the course of history. Many already considered him dangerously left-wing, but his contacts with the KGB would lend his ideological position an altogether more sinister tint. The truth was sufficiently damning to make Foot appear naïve and foolish in the extreme. But in the heat of an election he could be made to look like a full-blown, paid-up KGB spy.

'We were worried about the sensitivity of this knowledge and the need to avoid it being used for party-political reasons,' said Spooner. 'There was a deep ideological division in the country, but we knew we had to keep this information out of the political mainstream. We were sitting on information that was massively open to misinterpretation.'

The revelations about Foot had serious implications for national security. MI6 passed the evidence to John Jones, Director General of MI5. The Security Service would have to decide the next move. 'It was their call.'

As Cabinet Secretary, Sir Robert Armstrong was the head of the

Civil Service, the senior policy adviser to the Prime Minister and the official responsible for overseeing the intelligence services and their relationship to government. Politically neutral, the living embodiment of Whitehall probity, Armstrong had served as Principal Private Secretary under both Harold Wilson and Edward Heath. He was among Thatcher's most trusted advisers. But that did not mean he told her everything.

The Director General of MI5 told Armstrong that Michael Foot had once been Agent BOOT, a paid contact of the KGB. They agreed that the information was far too politically incendiary to be passed on to the Prime Minister.

When asked about this episode, many years later, Armstrong was deliberate and opaque, in the finest government tradition: 'I knew that Michael Foot was thought to have had contacts with the KGB before he became Leader of the Labour Party and that *Tribune* was believed to have received financial support from Moscow, probably from the KGB . . . Gordievsky confirmed this. I do not know how much of that was disclosed to the Foreign Secretary or to the Prime Minister.'

Armstrong would later find himself the key witness in the 'Spy-catcher trial', the British government's failed attempt to block the publication of Peter Wright's revelatory memoir. He coined the phrase 'economical with the truth'. He certainly appears to have been most economical in distributing the truth about Michael Foot. He did not tell Margaret Thatcher or her other top advisers; he did not tell anyone in the Civil Service, the Conservative Party or the Labour Party. He did not tell the Americans, or any other of Britain's allies. He did not tell a soul.

Having been passed the unexploded bomb, the Cabinet Secretary put it in his pocket, and kept it there, in the hope that Foot would lose, and the problem would defuse itself. Veronica Price was blunt: 'We buried it.' Even so, within MI6 there were discussions about the constitutional implications if Michael Foot won the election: it was agreed that should a politician with a KGB history become Prime Minister of Britain, then the Queen would have to be informed.

There was one additional element in Gordievsky's download that was even more dangerous than the BOOT files, a KGB secret with the potential not just to change the world, but to destroy it.

In 1982 the Cold War was heating up again to the point where nuclear war seemed a genuine possibility. Gordievsky revealed that the Kremlin believed, wrongly but completely seriously, that the West was about to press the nuclear button.

# 8.   Operation RYAN

In May 1981, Yuri Andropov, Chairman of the KGB, gathered his senior officers in a secret conclave to issue a startling announcement: America was planning to launch a nuclear first strike, and obliterate the Soviet Union.

For more than twenty years, a nuclear war between East and West had been held at bay by the threat of mutually assured destruction, the promise that both sides would be annihilated in any such conflict, regardless of who started it. But by the end of the 1970s the West had begun to pull ahead in the nuclear arms race, and tense détente was giving way to a different sort of psychological confrontation, in which the Kremlin feared it could be destroyed and defeated by a pre-emptive nuclear attack. Early in 1981, the KGB carried out an analysis of the geopolitical situation, using a newly developed computer program, and concluded that 'the correlation of world forces' was moving in favour of the West. Soviet intervention in Afghanistan was proving costly, Cuba was draining Soviet funds, the CIA was launching aggressive covert action against the USSR, and the US was undergoing a major military build-up: the Soviet Union seemed to be losing the Cold War, and, like a boxer exhausted by long years of sparring, the Kremlin feared a single, brutal sucker punch could end the contest.

The KGB chief's conviction that the USSR was vulnerable to a surprise nuclear attack probably had more to do with Andropov's personal experience than rational geopolitical analysis. As Soviet ambassador to Hungary in 1956, he had witnessed how quickly an apparently powerful regime might be toppled. He had played a key role in suppressing the Hungarian Uprising. A dozen years later, Andropov again urged 'extreme measures' to put down the Prague Spring. The 'Butcher of Budapest' was a firm believer in armed force and KGB repression. The head of the Romanian secret police described him as 'the man who substituted the KGB for the Communist Party in governing the USSR'. The confident and bullish stance of the newly installed Reagan administration seemed to underscore the impending threat.

And so, like every genuine paranoiac, Andropov set out to find the evidence to confirm his fears.

Operation RYAN (an acronym for *Raketno-Yadernoye Napadeniye*, Russian for Nuclear Missile Attack) was the biggest peacetime Soviet intelligence operation ever launched. To his stunned KGB audience, with the Soviet leader, Leonid Brezhnev, alongside him, Andropov announced that the US and NATO were 'actively preparing for nuclear war'. The task of the KGB was to find signs that this attack might be imminent and provide early warning, so that the Soviet Union was not taken by surprise. By implication, if proof of an impending attack could be found, then the Soviet Union could itself launch a pre-emptive strike. Andropov's experience in suppressing liberty in Soviet satellite states had convinced him that the best method of defence was attack. Fear of a first strike threatened to provoke a first strike.

Operation RYAN was born in Andropov's fevered imagination. It grew steadily, metastasizing into an intelligence obsession within the KGB and GRU (military intelligence), consuming thousands of man-hours and helping to ratchet up tension between the superpowers to terrifying levels. RYAN even had its own imperative motto: '*Ne Prozerot!* – Don't Miss It!' In November 1981 the first RYAN directives were dispatched to KGB field stations in the US, Western Europe, Japan and Third World countries. In early 1982 all *rezidenturas* were instructed to make RYAN a top priority. By the time Gordievsky arrived in London, the operation had already acquired a self-propelling momentum. But it was based on a profound misapprehension. America was not preparing a first strike. The KGB hunted high and low for evidence of the planned attack, but as MI5's authorized history observes: 'No such plans existed.'

In launching Operation RYAN, Andropov broke the first rule of intelligence: never ask for confirmation of something you already believe. Hitler had been certain that the D-Day invasion force would land at Calais, so that is what his spies (with help from Allied double agents) told him, ensuring the success of the Normandy landings. Tony Blair and George W. Bush were convinced that Saddam Hussein possessed weapons of mass destruction, and that is what their intelligence services duly concluded. Yuri Andropov, pedantic and autocratic, was utterly convinced that his KGB minions would find evidence of a looming nuclear assault. So that is what they did.

Gordievsky had been briefed on Operation RYAN before leaving Moscow. When this far-reaching KGB policy initiative was revealed to MI6, the Soviet experts in Century House at first treated the report with scepticism. Did the geriatrics of the Kremlin really misunderstand Western morality so completely as to believe America and NATO could attack first? Surely this was just alarmist nonsense from a veteran KGB crank? Or perhaps, even more sinister, a deliberate misinformation ploy intended to persuade the West to back off and scale down the military build-up? The intelligence community was dubious. James Spooner wondered: could the Centre really be 'so out of touch with the real world'?

But, in November 1982, Andropov succeeded Leonid Brezhnev as Soviet leader, becoming the first KGB chief to be elected General Secretary of the Communist Party. Soon after, *rezidentura*s were informed that RYAN was 'now of particularly grave importance' and had 'acquired an especial degree of urgency'. A telegram duly arrived at the KGB's London station, addressed to Arkadi Guk (under his alias, 'Yermakov'), labelled 'strictly personal' and 'top secret'. Gordievsky smuggled it out of the embassy in his pocket, and handed it to Spooner.

Entitled 'Permanent operational assignment to uncover NATO preparations for a nuclear-missile attack on the USSR', this was the RYAN blueprint, chapter and verse on the various indicators that should alert the KGB to preparations for an attack by the West. The document was proof that Soviet fears of a first strike were genuine, deeply held and growing. It stated: 'The objective of the assignment is to see that the *rezidentura* works systematically to uncover any plans in preparation by the main adversary [USA] for RYAN, and to organize continual watch to be kept for indications of a decision being

taken to use nuclear weapons against the USSR or immediate preparations being made for a nuclear-missile attack.' The document
listed twenty indications of a potential attack, ranging from the
logical to the ridiculous. KGB officers were instructed to carry out
close surveillance of 'key nuclear decision-makers', including,
bizarrely, Church leaders and top bankers. Buildings where such a
decision might be taken should be closely watched, as well as nuclear
depots, military installations, evacuation routes and bomb shelters.
Agents should be recruited as a matter of urgency within government, military, intelligence and civil-defence organizations. Officers
were even encouraged to count how many lights were switched on at
night in key government buildings, since officials would be burning
the midnight oil preparatory to a strike. The number of cars in government car parks should also be counted: a sudden demand for
parking spaces in the Ministry of Defence, for example, might indicate preparations for an attack. Hospitals should also be watched,
since the enemy would expect retaliation for its first strike, and make
provision for multiple casualties. A similarly close eye should be kept
on slaughterhouses: if the number of cattle killed at abattoirs increased
sharply, that might indicate that the West was stockpiling ham-
burgers prior to Armageddon.

The oddest injunction was to monitor 'the level of blood held in
blood banks', and report if the government began buying up blood
supplies and stockpiling plasma. 'One important sign that preparations are beginning for RYAN could be increased purchases of
blood from donors and the prices paid for it . . . discover the location
of the several thousand blood donor reception centres and the price of
blood, and record any changes . . . if there is an unexpectedly sharp
increase in the number of blood donor centres and the prices paid,
report at once to the Centre.'

In the West, of course, blood is donated by members of the public.
The only payment is a biscuit, and sometimes a cup of tea. The Kremlin, however, assuming that capitalism penetrated every aspect of
Western life, believed that a 'blood bank' was, in fact, a bank, where
blood could be bought and sold. No one in the KGB outstations
dared to draw attention to this elemental misunderstanding. In a

craven and hierarchical organization, the only thing more dangerous than revealing your own ignorance is to draw attention to the stupidity of the boss.

Gordievsky and his colleagues were initially dismissive of this peculiar shopping list of demands, seeing Operation RYAN as just another example of pointless, ill-informed make-work by the Centre. The more perceptive and experienced KGB officers knew there was no appetite for nuclear war in the West, let alone a surprise attack launched by NATO and the US. Guk himself only 'paid lip-service to the Centre's demands', which he considered 'ridiculous'. But obedience was more powerful than common sense in the world of Soviet intelligence, and KGB stations across the world dutifully began searching for evidence of hostile plans. And, inevitably, finding them. Almost any human behaviour, if scrutinized sufficiently intensely, can begin to seem suspicious: a light left on in the Foreign Office, a parking shortage at the Ministry of Defence, a potentially bellicose bishop. As the 'evidence' of the non-existent plan to attack the USSR accumulated, it seemed to confirm what the Kremlin already feared, increasing paranoia in the Centre and prompting fresh demands for proof. Thus do myths self-perpetuate. Gordievsky called it 'a vicious spiral of intelligence-gathering and evaluation, with foreign stations feeling obliged to report alarming information even if they did not believe it'.

Over the following months, Operation RYAN became the single dominant preoccupation of the KGB. Meanwhile the rhetoric of the Reagan administration reinforced the Kremlin's conviction that America was on an aggressive path to lopsided nuclear war. Early in 1983, Reagan denounced the Soviet Union as the 'evil empire'. The impending deployment of Pershing II intermediate-range ballistic missiles in West Germany added to Soviet fears. These weapons had a 'super-sudden first-strike capability', and could hit hard Soviet targets, including missile silos, without warning, in as little as four minutes. The flight time to Moscow was estimated to be around six minutes. If the KGB gave sufficient warning of an attack, this would allow Moscow 'a period of anticipation essential . . . to take retaliatory measures': in other words, to strike first. In March, Ronald

Reagan made a public announcement that threatened to neuter any such pre-emptive retaliation anyway: America's Strategic Defense Initiative, immediately known as 'Star Wars', envisaged the use of satellites and space-based weapons to create a shield able to shoot down incoming Soviet nuclear missiles. It could render the West invulnerable, and enable the US to launch an attack without fear of retaliation. Andropov furiously accused Washington of 'inventing new plans on how to unleash a nuclear war in the best way, with the hope of winning it . . . Washington's actions are putting the entire world in jeopardy.' The RYAN programme was expanded: for Andropov and his obedient KGB underlings, this was a matter of Soviet survival.

At first, MI6 interpreted RYAN as encouraging additional evidence of KGB incompetence: an organization devoted to searching for a phantom plot would have little time for more effective espionage. But as time passed, and the angry rhetoric escalated on both sides, it became clear that the Kremlin's fears could not be dismissed as mere time-wasting fantasy. A state that feared imminent conflict was increasingly likely to lash out first. RYAN demonstrated, in the most emphatic way, just how unstable the Cold War confrontation had become.

Washington's hawkish stance was feeding into a Soviet narrative that could end in nuclear Armageddon. American foreign-policy analysts, however, tended to dismiss Soviet expressions of alarm as deliberate exaggerations for the sake of propaganda, part of the long-running game of bluff and counter-bluff. But Andropov was serious when he insisted the US was planning to unleash nuclear war; and, thanks to the Russian spy, the British knew it.

America would have to be told that the Kremlin's fears, though founded on ignorance and paranoia, were sincere.

The relationship between the British and American intelligence agencies is a little like that between older and younger siblings: close but competitive, friendly but jealous, mutually supportive but prone to spats. Both Britain and America had suffered high-level penetration by communist agents in the past, and both nursed the lingering suspicion that the other might be unreliable. Under established agreements, intercepted signals intelligence was pooled, but information gathered from human sources was shared more sparingly. America had spies Britain knew nothing about, and vice versa. The 'product' from those sources was proffered on a 'need to know' basis, and the definition of necessity was variable.

Gordievsky's revelations about Operation RYAN were passed to the CIA in a way that was helpful, but economical with the truth. Hitherto, NOCTON material had been distributed exclusively to 'indoctrinated' intelligence readers within MI6 and MI5 and, on an *ad hoc* basis, to PET, as well as the Prime Minister's Office, the Cabinet Office and the Foreign Office. The decision to widen the circle of distribution to include the US intelligence community marked a critical juncture in the case. MI6 did not say which part of the world the material came from, nor who had supplied it. The source was carefully camouflaged and underplayed, the intelligence packaged in such a way that its origin was obscured. 'The decision was taken to pass filleted, edited material as normal CX [an intelligence report]. We had to disguise the provenance. We said it came from a middle-ranking official, not in London. We had to make it look as bland as possible.' But the Americans were in no doubt about the authenticity and reliability of what they were hearing: this was information of the highest grade, trustworthy and valuable. MI6 did not tell the CIA that the intelligence came from within the KGB. But it probably did not need to.

So began one of the most important intelligence-sharing operations of the twentieth century.

Slowly, carefully, with quiet pride and subdued fanfare, MI6 began drip-feeding America with Gordievsky's secrets. British intelligence has long prided itself on running human agents. America might have the money and technological muscle, but the Brits understood people, or liked to believe so. The Gordievsky case compensated, in some measure, for the lasting embarrassments of the Philby years, and it was presented with a slight British swagger. The American intelligence establishment was impressed, intrigued, grateful and very slightly irked to be patronized by its smaller sibling. The CIA is not used to other agencies deciding what it needs, and does not need, to know.

Eventually, as Gordievsky's espionage haul grew in volume and detail, the intelligence would find its way to the highest levels of the American government, influencing policy within the Oval Office itself. But only a tiny handful of American intelligence officers ever knew that the Brits had a highly placed Soviet mole: one of these was Aldrich Ames.

Ames's CIA career had picked up since his return from Mexico. He and Rosario set up home in Falls Church, Virginia, in the Washington suburbs, and in 1983, despite his patchy work record, he was promoted to head the counter-intelligence branch of the CIA's Soviet operations wing. Ames was still climbing the CIA ladder, but not fast enough to arrest his growing professional dissatisfaction. Rosario had agreed to marry him, but his divorce was going to be ruinously expensive. Ames took out a new credit card, and immediately ran up a debt of $5,000, buying new furniture. Rosario was disappointed and plaintive, and frequently phoned home to Colombia. The telephone bills alone cost $400 a month. The flat was cramped. Ames drove a dilapidated old Volvo.

To Ames's way of thinking, a salary of just $45,000 a year was measly in the extreme, given the value of the secrets he handled every day. Under Bill Casey, Reagan's energetic new CIA Director, the Soviet division had taken on new life, and was now running some twenty spies behind the Iron Curtain. Ames knew the identities of all of them. He knew that the CIA was tapping a cable outside Moscow and sucking out vast amounts of intelligence. He knew that the boys in the technical department had adapted a shipping container to pick up information from passing trains carrying nuclear warheads on the Trans-Siberian Railway. Eventually he was let into the secret that MI6 had a highly placed agent, probably inside the KGB, whose identity the Brits were concealing. Ames knew these secrets, and many more. But as he sat nursing his bourbon at various Washington bars, he knew this above all: he was broke. And he wanted a new car.

After six months in Britain, Gordievsky's double life had settled into a pleasant routine. Leila was happy exploring her new home, entirely unaware of her husband's clandestine activities. His daughters seemed to become little British girls overnight, talking to their dolls in English. He loved London's parks and pubs, the little Middle Eastern restaurants of Kensington with their exotic, spicy smells. In contrast to Yelena, Leila loved to cook, and never ceased to report, with wonder, on the vast array of ingredients available in British shops. The household chores and childrearing were left entirely to Leila: far from complaining, she frequently remarked on her good fortune to be able to live abroad for a time. She missed her family and friends back in Moscow, but she knew they would be returning home soon enough since Soviet diplomatic postings were seldom extended beyond three years. Whenever Leila grew homesick, Oleg tried to change the subject. One day, he knew, he would have to tell her that he was a spy for Britain, and they were never going back. But why expose her to the stress and danger now? Leila was a good Russian wife, he told himself, and when the time came to reveal his deception, though she might be shocked and unhappy for a while, she would accept it. But she would have to learn the truth sooner or later. Later seemed the preferable option.

They immersed themselves in the artistic life of the British capital, attending classical-music concerts, gallery openings and theatrical performances. His spying for the West was, he believed, the act of a cultural dissident, not a turncoat: 'Just as Shostakovich, the composer, fought back with music, and Solzhenitsyn, the writer, fought back with words, so I, the KGB man, could only operate through my own intelligence world.' He fought back with secrets.

Every morning, he would run in Holland Park. And every week or so, on a different, prearranged day, when MI5's Watchers were known to be elsewhere, he would tell colleagues he was meeting a contact for lunch, climb into his car and drive to the safe house in Bayswater. In the underground car park, he pulled a plastic cover over his car, to conceal the diplomatic plates.

The Centre no longer sent its instructions on microfilm, so Gordievsky found himself smuggling out physical documents before each meeting, sometimes in batches. He would wait until the office emptied out before discreetly tucking the papers into a pocket. There was plenty to choose from. The different departments in the Centre competed in making demands on the London *rezidentura*'s numerous personnel: twenty-three KGB officers within the embassy, another eight working undercover at the Soviet trade delegation, four more posing as journalists, as well as illegals and a separate posse of fifteen military-intelligence officers deployed by the GRU. 'The Centre churned out an immense volume of information, any of which I was at liberty to pass on.'

Once Gordievsky was inside the flat, Spooner debriefed him while Veronica Price made lunch and Sarah Page, an MI6 secretary of gentle charm and extreme efficiency, photographed any documents in the bedroom. After completing the excavation of Gordievsky's memory, the focus shifted to current operations. 'Quite quickly we were into live stuff,' said Spooner. 'He would bring us up to date on everything that had happened in the intervening period: events, instructions, visits, local activity, conversations with *rezidentura* colleagues.' A trained observer, Oleg made mental notes of anything and everything that might be of use: instructions from the Centre, the latest RYAN requests and reports, the activity of illegals and clues to their identities, targets of cultivation, agent recruitment and staff changes. But he also brought gossip and rumour, titbits revealing what his colleagues were thinking, plotting and doing out of hours, how much they were drinking, who they were sleeping with, who they wanted to sleep with. 'You are an extra member of the KGB *rezidentura*,' Gordievsky told Spooner.

From time to time, Veronica Price would go over the details of Operation PIMLICO, in case he was suddenly recalled to Moscow and needed to escape. The exfiltration plan had undergone some important modifications since it was first conceived. Gordievsky was now a married man with two young children. MI6 would therefore provide not one escape car, but two; one adult and one child would be hidden in each boot, and the girls would be injected with a strong soporific drug to make them sleep and reduce the trauma. To prepare for the moment when he might have to drug his own daughters at the moment of exfiltration, Veronica Price produced a syringe and an orange for him to practise administering injections. Every few months, he would weigh his daughters, the weights would be reported to the MI6 station in Moscow, and the dosage in the waiting syringes would be adjusted accordingly.

The case developed its own rhythm, yet the tension was relentless. After one meeting at the safe flat, Oleg went to retrieve his car from nearby Connaught Street (for once he had decided not to park in the underground car park). As he was about to step off the pavement he saw, to his horror, Guk's ivory Mercedes, gliding towards him down the road with the fat *rezident* at the wheel. Thinking he had been spotted, Gordievsky broke into a sweat and immediately began inventing reasons to explain what he was doing in a residential neighbourhood away from the embassy. But Guk, it seems, had not seen him.

Only three politicians were brought into the circle of trust. Margaret Thatcher was indoctrinated into the NOCTON case on 23 December 1982, fully six months after Gordievsky's arrival in Britain. The raw intelligence was placed in a special red folder, known as a 'red jacket', and placed inside a locked blue box to which only the Prime Minister, her foreign adviser and her Private Secretary had the key. Thatcher was informed that MI6 had an agent within the KGB's London station. She did not know his name. William Whitelaw, her Home Secretary, was informed a month later. The only other Cabinet minister in the know was the Foreign Secretary. The NOCTON material, most notably Operation RYAN, made a 'powerful impression' on Geoffrey Howe when he took up that post: 'the Soviet leadership really did believe the bulk of their own propaganda. They did have a genuine fear that "the West" was plotting their overthrow — and might, just might, go to any lengths to achieve it.'

But while Gordievsky's espionage for MI6 prospered mightily, his work for the KGB was running into the sand. Guk and Nikitenko, the *rezident* and his deputy, were openly hostile. Igor Titov, his immediate boss, was consistently unfriendly. But not all of his colleagues were paranoid philistines. Some were highly perceptive. Maksim Parshikov, a fellow PR Line officer in his thirties, was the son of a Leningrad artist who shared many of Gordievsky's cultural tastes. They listened to classical music on Radio 3 while working at adjacent desks in the political section. Parshikov found his colleague 'agreeable and intelligent, with an education and a level of culture that set him apart'. When Parshikov caught a cold, Gordievsky introduced him to the nasal decongestant Otrivin, which he had recently discovered in a British pharmacy. 'We were united in our love of classical music, and Otrivin,' Parshikov wrote. Yet he sensed Gordievsky's internal anxiety: 'For me and others who were close to Oleg during his first months in London, it was obvious that something serious and uneasy was happening in his life – he seemed extremely nervous and under pressure.' There was something different about the new man, a tense reserve. As Parshikov said:

> The leadership of the *rezidentura* disliked him from the start. He did not drink in the usual way, he was too intellectual, he was not 'one of us'. Imagine a typical party, to mark a Soviet holiday, in a small central room of the residency. Everything is as it should be: on the table are sandwiches and fruit, vodka and whisky for the men, a bottle of wine for the few ladies. Toasts are drunk, one by one, starting with the *rezident*. Gordievsky voluntarily assumes the role of butler, obligingly filling every empty glass, except his own, which contains only red wine. He never really fraternized. Some found it weird. But I thought: what the hell, you come across different people in our ranks. The wife of one officer could not stand Gordievsky. She could not explain the reason for her dislike, but she thought Oleg somehow 'wrong', 'unnatural', with 'two faces'.

Parshikov paid little attention to the bad-mouthing. 'I was too lazy to get involved with slandering my nice colleague in the *rezidentura*.' Gordievsky's main problem, Parshikov reflected, was his failing job performance. His English was still poor. He seemed to head off to lunch with some regularity, but came back with little new information. Within months of his arrival, a whispering campaign had begun in the gossip-soaked *rezidentura* to the effect that Oleg was not up to the job.

Gordievsky knew he was floundering. He had inherited a number of contacts from his predecessor in the PR Line, but these provided no useful intelligence. He contacted a European diplomat identified by the Centre as an agent, and found that 'although he was prepared to eat large meals, he never told me anything of the slightest interest'. Another individual identified for possible recruitment was Ron Brown, the Labour MP for Edinburgh Leith, a former trade union organizer who had attracted the KGB's attention by his vocal support for communist regimes in Afghanistan, Albania and North Korea. He was frequently in trouble with the parliamentary authorities for rowdy behaviour, and would eventually be expelled from the Labour Party after stealing his mistress's underwear and wrecking her flat. Born in Leith, Brown had a Scottish accent as thick as porridge. He was colourful, convivial and, to Russian ears, almost completely incomprehensible. Gordievsky, who had difficulty enough following the Received English pronunciation of the BBC, took Brown out to lunch on several occasions, and sat nodding intelligently, grasping one word in ten, while the Scotsman burbled away in his native brogue. 'For all I understood, he could have been talking Arabic or Japanese.' Back at the *rezidentura*, Gordievsky wrote up a report that was pure fabrication, based on what he thought the Scot might have said. Brown may have been leaking top-grade secrets; but, equally, he might have been talking about football. Brown's guilt, or innocence, remains a historical mystery, hidden for ever behind his impenetrable Scottish accent.

Reviving and consolidating old contacts was as frustrating as trying to find new ones. Bob Edwards was nearly eighty, the oldest sitting MP, an unrepentant friend of the KGB who was happy to chat about the old days, but had very little to reveal about the new ones. Gordievsky also re-established contact with Jack Jones, the former trade union leader, and met him in his council flat. Long retired, Jones was delighted to accept lunch, and occasional disbursements of cash, but as an informant he was 'absolutely useless'. The Centre frequently identified prominent 'progressives', such as the CND campaigner Joan Ruddock and the broadcaster Melvyn Bragg, in the belief that with the right approach these might spy for the Soviets. In this, as in so much else, the KGB was mistaken. For weeks, Gordievsky floated around the fringes of the Labour Party, the peace movement, the British Communist Party and the trade unions, trying and failing to cultivate new contacts. After six months, he had little to show for his efforts.

The *rezidentura*'s chief analyst, another of Guk's cronies, was scathing about Gordievsky's work, and began complaining that the new man was an incompetent dud. Gordievsky confided to Parshikov that he was afraid to return to Moscow on annual leave, fearing 'he might be criticized for his poor performance'. The Centre was unsympathetic: 'Stop panicking and keep working.'

Gordievsky was in trouble: disliked by the *rezident*, unpopular within the embassy, and struggling to make an impression in a new post, a new language and a new city. He was also so busy gathering information for the British there was insufficient time to devote to his KGB day job.

Gordievsky's problems in his day job presented MI6 with an unexpected and alarming dilemma. If he was sent home, the West's most important spy case would come to a halt just as it was beginning to produce intelligence of world-changing importance. The case depended on Gordievsky's professional progress, because the more he succeeded in the eyes of the KGB, the better his promotion prospects, and the wider his access to useful material. His KGB career needed a boost. MI6 decided to bring this about in two, unprecedented ways: by doing the spy's homework for him, and by disposing of those who stood in his way.

Martin Shawford, a young MI6 officer in the NOCTON cell within the Soviet branch, was assigned the task of making Gordievsky look good in the eyes of his peers and bosses. Speaking Russian and newly returned from a posting in Moscow, Shawford handled political reporting from the case. He began to pull together information that Gordievsky could pass off as his own and feed back to the KGB: enough to convince the Centre that he was an expert in gathering political intelligence, but not so good that it might actually prove useful to the Soviets. In spy jargon such information is known as 'chickenfeed', genuine but not seriously damaging information that can be given to an enemy to establish an agent's bona fides, bulky, filling, but lacking in any real nutritional value. British intelligence had become expert in manufacturing chickenfeed during the Second World War, passing vast quantities of carefully monitored information through double agents to their German handlers: some true, some half true, and some false but undetectably so. Shawford combed open-source information such as magazines and newspapers for nuggets of information Gordievsky could have gleaned from contacts or other sources: summaries of the situation in apartheid South Africa, the state of the Anglo-American relationship, or internal gossip from the Conservative Party gathered on the fringes of party conferences. With some imagination, these could be made to seem like gathered intelligence. 'We needed material he could feed back into the *rezidentura* to justify his absences, his meetings and so on. It was important to build up his credibility and justify his movements. We knew what sort of chitchat he might be picking up from the sort of people he knew.' MI6's demands for releasable material were such that K6, the MI5 department responsible for the case, struggled to keep up. 'This caused almost the only friction between the Services in the history of the Gordievsky case.' Shawford would type up a three-quarter-page summary every week, which Gordievsky took back to the *rezidentura*, translated into KGB language, added a few details of his own, and handed to the bosses. The original MI6 crib sheet he tore into shreds and washed down the toilet.

But feeding Oleg chickenfeed was only one way of fattening up his career prospects. In order to convince his superiors that he was working well, Gordievsky needed to meet real people who could supply him with genuine, though valueless, information. Simply offering reams of information without a named source would eventually invite suspicion. Gordievsky needed his own 'confidential contacts'. So MI6 gave him some.

Within MI5, Department K4 handled counter-espionage against Soviet targets, identifying, monitoring, tailing and whenever possible neutralizing spies active in Britain – KGB and GRU officers, their recruits and illegals. This frequently involved the use of 'access agents', people in civilian life who could make contact with a suspected spy, gain his confidence, draw him out, extract information, and pretend to be sympathetic and available for recruitment. If the spy revealed himself, he could be arrested if illegal, or expelled if he was in Britain under diplomatic cover. But the ultimate aim of any such operation was to lure a spy into complicity, and then persuade him, by inducement or threat, to spy *against* the Soviet Union. These access agents, also known as 'controlled contacts', were ordinary men and women, secretly recruited by K4 to lend a hand in the unseen espionage battle. They were, in effect, dangles; they were also, by definition, the sorts of people a Soviet intelligence officer might want to recruit. In the early 1980s, K4 was simultaneously running dozens of cases against Soviet targets, using scores of undercover access agents.

The striking, tall, dark-haired figure of Rosemary Spencer was a familiar sight in Conservative Central Office, the nerve centre of the Tory Party based at 32 Smith Square, in the heart of Westminster. Miss Spencer, forty-two years old, worked in the international section of the research department, and had helped to draw up the Franks Report into the Falklands War. People said, rather unkindly, that she was married to the party. She was convivial, clever, possibly rather lonely, and just the kind of well-informed member of the political establishment that the KGB encouraged its officers to recruit. Her Conservative colleagues would have been staggered to discover that the jolly single woman in the research department was really an undercover agent for MI5.

Gordievsky first encountered Rosemary Spencer at a party in Westminster. Their meeting was not accidental. He had been told to look out for a vivacious Tory researcher. She had been warned that she might be approached by a KGB officer posing as a Russian diplomat, and if so she should encourage the relationship. They met for lunch. Gordievsky was at his most charming. He knew she was an MI5 access agent. She knew he was KGB. She did not know he was actually working for MI6. They lunched again. And then again. Rosemary's MI5 handler advised her on what information she might pass over, nothing too sensitive, but items of interest from her work, snippets of insider Tory gossip, morsels of chickenfeed. These Gordievsky typed up into a report, which included not just what Rosemary *had* told him, but other information, supplied by MI6, that a well-connected member of the Conservative Party *might* have told him. The KGB was duly impressed: Gordievsky was cultivating an important new source inside Conservative Central Office, who might eventually develop into a confidential contact, or even an agent.

The relationship between Gordievsky and Spencer became a solid friendship, but it was also one of deception. She believed she was deceiving him; and he was deceiving her by allowing her to think that. He was using her to improve his standing with the KGB. She thought she was striking a blow against the Soviet Union. Here was another example of the combined trickery and tenderness inherent in espionage: a friendship between a British Tory researcher and a Russian Soviet diplomat, both of whom were secret spies. They were lying to each other, with genuine affection.

Within the KGB *rezidentura*, Gordievsky's stock rose rapidly. Even Guk seemed to be warming to him. Reports to the Centre were signed by the *rezident*, and Gordievsky's work was beginning to make Guk look good. Parshikov noticed a marked change in Gordievsky's demeanour. 'He began to get used to the team, to build relationships with people.' He seemed more confident and relaxed. One person who did not appreciate Gordievsky's success was his immediate superior, Igor Titov. The head of the PR Line had always regarded his subordinate as a threat, and Gordievsky's knowledgeable reports and new raft of sources redoubled his determination to stymie his underling's chances of promotion. Gordievsky was on the way up. But Titov was in the way. So MI6 removed him.

In March 1983, Igor Titov was declared *persona non grata* in the UK, and ordered to leave the country immediately. Gordievsky was informed in advance of the plan to throw out his boss. To deflect suspicion, two GRU officers were simultaneously expelled, for 'activities incompatible with their diplomatic status', the accepted euphemism for espionage. Titov was enraged. 'I am no spy,' he lied to reporters. Few in the KGB station were sorry to see him go, and fewer were surprised. The preceding months had seen a flurry of spy expulsions in Western countries, and there was ample evidence to indicate Titov was an active KGB officer.

With Titov eliminated, Gordievsky was the obvious candidate to succeed him as head of political intelligence. He was promoted to the rank of lieutenant-colonel.

MI6's ruse to bump their spy up the KGB ranks worked perfectly. By the middle of 1983, he had been transformed from an unpopular failure in danger of losing his job into the rising star of the *rezidentura*, with a burgeoning reputation for recruiting agents and gathering intelligence. And his manufactured promotion had been achieved without raising a flicker of suspicion. As Parshikov observed: 'It all seemed quite natural.'

As chief of political intelligence in the *rezidentura*, Gordievsky now had access to the PR Line files and was able to confirm what MI6 already suspected: Soviet penetration of the British establishment was pitiful, with just half a dozen people classed as 'recruited agents' (mostly very old) and perhaps a dozen 'confidential contacts' (mostly very minor). Many were merely 'paper agents', who were 'kept on the books in order to make officers look busy to Moscow'. There was no new Philby hidden in the woodwork. More positively, Gordievsky's new position gave him increased insight into the workings of other departments, or lines: Line X (scientific and technical), Line N (illegals) and Line KR (counter-intelligence and security). Piece by piece, Gordievsky was cracking open the secrets of the KGB and passing them on to MI6.

Yet another source of information became available when Leila joined the KGB station as a part-time employee. Arkadi Guk needed another secretary. Leila was a fast and efficient typist. She was told to put her children into morning nursery, and report for work at the *rezidentura*. Henceforth, she would be typing Guk's reports. Leila was in awe of the *rezident*. 'He was a peacock. To be a KGB general, that was really something. I never asked questions, just typed what I was told to type.' She did not notice how closely her husband was listening when, over dinner, she would describe her day, the reports she had typed up for the boss, and gossip among the secretaries.

Parshikov noted how happy his newly elevated boss seemed, and how generous. 'Guys, spend money on entertainment expenses,' Gordievsky told his subordinates. 'This year we spent very little on entertainment and gifts for contacts. If you don't, next year the allowance will be cut.' It was a call to fiddle their expenses, and some of his colleagues needed no second invitation.

Gordievsky had every reason to feel contented and confident. He was rising up the ranks. His position was secure. His intelligence haul was landing, regularly, on the desk of the British Prime Minister, and he was attacking, from within, the communist system he loathed. What could go wrong?

On 3 April 1983, Easter Sunday, Arkadi Guk returned to his flat in 42 Holland Park, and found an envelope had been pushed through the letterbox. It contained a top-secret document: the MI5 legal brief outlining the case for expelling Titov and the two GRU men the previous month, including details of how all three had been identified as Soviet intelligence officers. In an accompanying note, the writer offered to provide more secrets, and gave elaborate instructions on how to contact him. It was signed 'Koba', one of Stalin's early nicknames.

Someone inside British intelligence was offering to spy for the Soviet Union.

# 9.  Koba

Arkadi Guk detected threats and conspiracies everywhere: the KGB *rezident* in London saw them in the minds of his Soviet colleagues, behind the hoardings in the London Underground, and in the invisible machinations of British intelligence.

The letter from 'Koba' sent his suspicious mind into a frenzy. The instructions it contained were detailed and explicit: Guk should indicate his willingness to cooperate by putting a single drawing pin at the top of the right-hand bannister of the stairs from platforms three and four of the Piccadilly line at Piccadilly Underground station; Koba would acknowledge receipt of the signal by wrapping a piece of blue adhesive tape around the telephone cable of the middle telephone box of a row of five on Adam and Eve Court, off Oxford Street; he would then make the dead drop, a canister of film containing secret information, taped under the lid of the cistern of the gents' lavatory in the Academy Cinema, Oxford Street.

Guk had until 25 April to accept the offer, twenty-two days hence.

The *rezident* took one look at the extraordinary letter and decided it must be a plant, a 'dangle' by MI5, a deliberate provocation designed to trap him, embarrass the KGB, and then have him expelled. So he ignored it.

Guk assumed, rightly, that his home must be under MI5 surveillance. A genuine spy inside British intelligence would surely know this, and would therefore not take the risk of being spotted delivering a packet to his front door. It did not occur to him that Koba could have access to MI5's surveillance schedules, and might therefore have chosen to make his delivery after midnight on Easter Sunday, when he knew there were no Watchers on duty.

Guk filed the package away, congratulating himself on having foiled so obvious a ruse.

But Koba refused to be ignored. After two months of silence, on 12

June a second packet plopped through Guk's letterbox in the middle of the night. This one was even more intriguing: it contained a two-page MI5 document, a complete list of every Soviet intelligence officer in London; each spy was graded as 'fully identified', 'more or less identified' or 'under suspicion of belonging to the KGB station'. Once again, the accompanying note offered to supply further classified material, and suggested a new signalling system and a dead-letter box: if Guk wanted to make contact, he should park his ivory Mercedes during lunchtime on 2 or 4 July at the parking meters on the north side of Hanover Square. If he received the signal, on 23 July the writer would leave a green Carlsberg beer can containing film at the foot of a broken lamp post without a shade and leaning to one side, on the footpath running parallel to Horsenden Lane in Greenford, West London. Guk should acknowledge receipt of the can and its contents by placing a piece of orange peel at the foot of the right-hand gatepost of the first entrance to St James's Gardens in Melton Street, by Euston Station. Again, the message was signed by Koba.

Guk summoned Leonid Nikitenko, his counter-intelligence chief, and behind closed doors in the embassy attic, over vodka and cigarettes, they picked over the mystery. Guk still insisted the approach was a clumsy plot. A spy who volunteers his services is known as a 'walk-in', and is immediately more suspect than one who has been picked out for recruitment. The document revealed only what the KGB already knew, information that was correct but unhelpful: in other words, chickenfeed. Once again, it does not seem to have occurred to him that Koba was demonstrating his bona fides by deliberately furnishing information that Guk could verify. Nikitenko was less convinced this was an MI5 provocation. The document seemed authentic, a complete chart of the *rezidentura*'s 'order of battle', drawn up by the Security Service. It was certainly accurate. The spycraft of signal sites and dead-letter boxes was sufficiently complex to indicate someone who did not wish to be caught. To Nikitenko's yellow eyes, the offer looked genuine; but he was far too canny and ambitious to contradict his boss. The Centre was consulted, and the order came back: do nothing, and see what transpires.

Gordievsky sensed that 'something unusual was brewing in the station'. Guk and Nikitenko kept disappearing into a private huddle and sending urgent telegrams to Moscow. The *rezident* wore his most conspiratorial look. For a man steeped in paranoid secrecy, Guk could be surprisingly indiscreet. He was also a braggart. On the morning of 17 June, he called Gordievsky into his office, closed the door and asked portentously: 'Would you like to see something exceptional?'

Guk then pushed the two photocopied pages across his desk. '*Bozhe Moi!*' Gordievsky muttered softly. 'My God! Where did these come from?'

He scanned the list of KGB officers, and came to his own name. He was graded as 'more or less identified'. He immediately grasped the implications: whoever had compiled the list did not know, for certain, that he was a KGB agent; and whoever had passed it on could not know that he was secretly spying for Britain, because if he did he would have betrayed him to Guk to protect himself from exposure. Koba clearly had access to secrets, but he did not know Gordievsky was a double agent. Yet.

'It's pretty accurate,' he said, handing back the document.

'Yes,' said Guk. 'They've done well.'

Gordievsky got a closer look at the document when the deputy reports officer, Slava Mishustin, asked for help in translating it. Mishustin marvelled that the British had been able to gather 'such precise information' on the KGB personnel. Gordievsky had a pretty good idea where that information had come from.

But he was more puzzled than alarmed. He tended to agree with Guk that the midnight deliveries to 42 Holland Park seemed more like a provocation than a genuine offer. British intelligence must be up to something. But if the Brits were attempting a dangle, why had Spooner not warned him? And would MI5 really want the KGB to know that it had correctly identified all its officers working in Britain?

He slipped out at lunchtime and called the emergency number. Veronica Price answered immediately. 'What is going on?' asked Gordievsky, before describing the mysterious deliveries to Guk's flat and the documents he had seen. For a moment, Veronica was silent. Then she said: 'Oleg, we need to meet.'

James Spooner and Veronica Price were waiting at the safe house when Gordievsky appeared an hour later.

'I know *you* wouldn't do this, but someone is messing us around,' he said.

Then he saw the look on Spooner's face. 'Oh my God! You don't mean it's real?'

Veronica spoke: 'As far as we know, there is no provocation operation underway.'

Gordievsky later described the MI6 reaction as 'classically calm'. In reality, the revelation that someone in British intelligence was volunteering to spy for the Soviets provoked consternation among the few made aware of it, accompanied by a horrible flood of déjà vu. As with Philby, Hollis and other spy scandals of the past, British intelligence would now have to launch an internal mole-hunt, and try to dig out the traitor. If the mole got wind of the investigation, he might realize that someone inside the KGB *rezidentura* had tipped off the British, and Gordievsky himself would be in danger. The 'walk-in' was clearly well placed, with access to classified material and a knowledge of spycraft. He or she had to be stopped before more damaging secrets were passed to the Soviets. Several thousand people worked for MI5 and MI6. Koba was among them.

But in the feverish hunt that now ensued, British intelligence had one overriding advantage.

The spy, whoever it was, did not know that Gordievsky was a British agent. If Koba had been part of the NOCTON team, he would never have made such an approach, knowing this would immediately be reported back to MI6 by Gordievsky – as had now happened. His first move would have been to expose Gordievsky to Guk, and ensure his own safety. This had not happened. The search for the traitor should therefore be carried out exclusively by those officers who knew the Gordievsky secret, and could be trusted completely. The mole-hunt was codenamed ELMEN (a municipality in the Austrian Tyrol).

The handful of MI5 personnel indoctrinated into the Gordievsky case would be responsible for finding the internal mole, under the leadership of John Deverell, Director of K, MI5's counter-intelligence branch. Working out of Deverell's office, they were sealed off from the rest of MI5 while they dug, a secret cell within a secret department of a secret organization. 'Nobody outside the team noticed anything out of the ordinary.' The ELMEN team nicknamed themselves 'the Nadgers'. This slang term is obscure, but appears to have been coined by Spike Milligan on *The Goon Show* in the 1950s, to mean a non-specific affliction, disease or illness. As in 'Oo-er, I've got a nasty dose of the nadgers.' Nadgers is also slang for testicles.

Eliza Manningham-Buller had joined the Security Service in 1974 after being recruited at a party. The work was already in her DNA: her father, the former Attorney-General, had prosecuted earlier spies, including George Blake, the MI6 double agent; during the Second World War, her mother trained carrier pigeons which were dropped into occupied France and used by the Resistance to send messages back to Britain. Picked out as utterly reliable and discreet, she had been indoctrinated into the Gordievsky case early on and brought into the tiny LAMPAD team, analysing his output from Denmark and liaising with MI6. By 1983, she was in MI5's personnel department, and ideally placed to search for the spy.

Manningham-Buller would become Director General of MI5 in 2002, rising to the pinnacle of a competitive world dominated by men. Her 'jolly hockey sticks' manner was deceptive: she was direct, self-confident and extremely clever. Despite the sexism and prejudice inside MI5, she was intensely loyal to the organization she called 'my lot', and greatly shocked by the discovery of yet another traitor inside British intelligence. 'It was one of the nastiest times in my career, particularly in the early days when you didn't know who it was, because you would get in the lift and look round and wonder.' To avoid arousing suspicion among their colleagues, the Nadgers frequently met, after hours, in the Inner Temple flat belonging to Manningham-Buller's mother. One of the team was heavily pregnant. Her unborn child was nicknamed 'Little Nadger'.

For an intelligence service, there is no process more painful and debilitating than an internal hunt for an unidentified traitor. The damage Philby did to MI6's self-confidence was far greater and more enduring than anything he inflicted by spying for the KGB. A mole does not just foment mistrust. Like a heretic, he undermines the coherence of faith itself.

Manningham-Buller and her fellow Nadgers called up the personnel files, and began whittling down the list of potential traitors. The MI5 document outlining the case for expelling the three Soviet spies had been distributed in the Foreign Office, Home Office and 10 Downing Street. The chart listing all the Soviet intelligence officers had been drawn up by K4, MI5's Soviet counter-intelligence branch, and fifty copies sent to various departments of the secret world. The mole-hunters began by identifying everyone who might have had access to both documents.

The investigation was running at full tilt in late June when Oleg Gordievsky and his family flew back to Moscow. He was hardly in holiday mood, but turning down his annual leave would have raised immediate suspicions. The risk was huge. Koba was still at large; at any moment, he might discover Gordievsky's activities, and expose him to Guk. If that happened while he was in Moscow, Gordievsky might well not be coming back. The MI6 station in Moscow was placed on alert in case he needed to make contact or fly the escape signal.

Meanwhile, the Nadgers were closing in on a man whose presence inside British intelligence seemed, in retrospect, like an unfunny joke.

Michael John Bettaney was a loner, unhappy and unstable. At Oxford University he goose-stepped around his college quad and played Hitler's speeches loudly on a gramophone. He wore tweeds and brogues, and smoked a pipe. 'He dressed like a bank manager and dreamt of being a storm trooper,' said one fellow undergraduate. He once set fire to himself after a party, and briefly grew a toothbrush moustache, which girls did not find attractive. He changed his northern accent to an upper-class drawl. A later investigation described him as 'a man with a considerable sense of inferiority and insecurity'. Raging insecurity is not an ideal quality in an officer of the Security Service, yet he was tapped up as a recruit while still at Oxford, and joined MI5 in 1975.

After a formal induction course, he was plunged into the deep end, combating terrorism in Northern Ireland. Bettaney himself questioned whether, as a Catholic, he was suitable for the job. His doubts were overruled. This was grim work, complex and extremely dangerous: running agents inside the IRA, tapping telephones, talking to unpleasant people in very unfriendly pubs, in the knowledge that a wrong move could mean a bullet in the head in a Belfast backstreet. Bettaney was traumatized by the work, and not very good at it. His father died in 1977, and his mother a year later. Despite the double bereavement, Bettaney's tour of duty in Belfast was extended. Looking back over his file, Eliza Manningham-Buller was appalled: 'We made Bettaney what he became. He never recovered from Northern Ireland.' He was a man with an accent, wardrobe and image that was not his own, without family, friends, love or settled convictions, looking for a cause and doing a job to which he was utterly unsuited. 'He was not authentic,' said Manningham-Buller. The peculiar stress and secrecy of intelligence work may have pushed him ever further from reality. Bettaney would probably have lived a contented and uneventful life if only he had chosen some other line of work.

Back in London, he spent two years in the training department before being transferred, in December 1982, to K4, the MI5 section analysing and combating Soviet espionage in the UK, including the running of access agents. He lived alone, with a large plastic figurine of the Madonna, a number of Russian icons, a drawer of Nazi war medals and an extensive collection of pornography. Withdrawn and isolated, he repeatedly tried to persuade the female staff at MI5 to sleep with him, without success. He was occasionally overheard at parties drunkenly shouting: 'I'm working for the wrong side' and 'Come and see me in my dacha when I retire.' Six months before the first delivery to Guk, Bettaney had been found sitting on a pavement in London's West End, too inebriated to stand. When taken into custody for being drunk in a public place, he shouted at police: 'You can't arrest me, I'm a spy.' He was fined £10. MI5 did not accept his offer of resignation. This was an error.

Michael Bettaney should not have been allowed within a mile of a state secret, yet, by the age of thirty-two, he had been in the Security Service for eight years, and had risen to become a middle-ranking officer in MI5's Soviet counter-espionage section.

Obvious signs that he was heading off the rails had been noted, but ignored. His Catholic faith suddenly evaporated. By 1983 he was drinking a bottle of spirits a day, and was given some 'friendly advice' by a supervisor to cut down his alcohol consumption. No further action was taken.

Bettaney, meanwhile, was taking action of his own. He began memorizing the contents of secret documents and taking longhand notes, later typing them up in his semi-detached house in the southern suburbs of London, and photographing them. Whenever he was on night duty, he took a camera into MI5, and photographed whatever files he could lay his hands on. No one searched him. His colleagues called him Smiley, after John le Carré's fictional spymaster, but they also noted 'an air of superiority [and] bumptiousness'. Like many spies, Bettaney wanted to know, and conceal, a bigger secret than the spy sitting alongside him.

There were four officers in K4. Two of these were indoctrinated into the Gordievsky case. Bettaney was not, but, both literally and metaphorically, he was sitting right next to the biggest secret in the organization: an MI6 spy inside the KGB's London *rezidentura*.

Bettaney later claimed to have converted to Marxism in 1982, and insisted his desire to work for the KGB sprang from pure ideological conviction. In a long, self-justifying treatise, he painted his actions in the bright colours of political martyrdom, a strange confection of resentment, conspiracy theory and righteous outrage. He accused the Thatcher government of 'slavish adherence to the aggressive and maverick policy of the Reagan administration' and deliberately increasing unemployment to bring 'greater wealth to those who already have too much'. He claimed to be acting in pursuit of world peace, and attacked MI5 for using 'sinister and immoral methods . . . not merely to remove the Soviet Government and Party, but also to destroy the entire fabric of society in the USSR'. He adopted the high-flown rhetoric of the revolutionary: 'I call on comrades everywhere to renew their determination and redouble their efforts in pursuit of a victory which is historically inevitable.'

Bettaney's Marxist politics were as artificial as his fruity accent. He was never a committed communist in the Philby mould. There is little evidence he felt any particular affinity for the Soviet Union, the ineluctable march of communism or the oppressed proletariat. In one, unguarded moment, he gave himself away: 'I felt I needed radically to influence events.' Bettaney did not want money, revolution or world peace; he wanted attention.

Which made it all the more hurtful when the KGB took no notice of him.

Bettaney was extremely surprised when his first delivery to Guk's letterbox elicited no response. He returned to Piccadilly Station several times, and when no drawing pin appeared in the bannister, he concluded his choice of dead-letter box and signal site must have been too close to the Soviet embassy. His second set of instructions identified sites outside central London, suggested a signal date several weeks ahead, and provided one of the most secret recent documents in K4. Bettaney waited, wondered and drank.

With hindsight, Bettaney should have been identified as a risk years earlier. But the three most powerful spy agencies in the world – the CIA, MI6 and KGB – were all, at different times, vulnerable to betrayal from within by people who seemed, on closer inspection, to stand out as highly suspicious. Intelligence agencies have a reputation for brilliant insight and cool efficiency, but despite close vetting of candidates they are just as likely to hire and retain the wrong sorts of people as any other large organization. This was a business that involved heavy drinking, on both sides of the Cold War, and officers and agents frequently took refuge from the stress in booze, and the blurring of reality that alcohol can bring. The peculiarly demanding relationship between agent and agent-runner is often oiled by the convivial, disinhibiting effects of drink. Unlike other branches of government, secret services tend to recruit imaginative people who have what Winston Churchill called 'corkscrew minds'. If the marks of potential treachery are being clever, eccentric and inclined to have a few too many drinks, then half the wartime and post-war spies in Britain and America would have been suspect. But in this respect the KGB was different, since it officially frowned on both inebriation and individuality. Gordievsky's betrayal was invisible because he was sober and outwardly conformist; Bettaney went undetected because he was not.

The Nadger team, meanwhile, had narrowed down the mole-hunt to three suspects, with Bettaney at the top of the list. But putting him under surveillance posed problems. Bettaney knew the A4 surveillance teams well, and had been trained to spot when he was being followed – if he recognized one of the Watchers, the game would be up. Moreover, the Watchers knew Bettaney, and might be unable to resist leaking to others in MI5 that their colleague was being monitored. Instead of using the professionals of MI5, therefore, it was decided to deploy the MI6 NOCTON team, none of whom were known to Bettaney. The Director General of MI5 explicitly vetoed the use of MI6 officers in an MI5 operation. Deverell ignored the order. The MI6 officers in the Gordievsky case would shadow Bettaney, and try to catch him in the act of treachery.

Bettaney was given the codename PUCK, an unpopular choice among the Nadgers. 'The Shakespearean connection was deemed highly inappropriate by all members of the team and the word itself was too close to a well-known Anglo-Saxon expletive for comfort.'

On the morning of 4 July, a dishevelled couple in tattered clothes could be seen lounging aimlessly at the end of Victoria Road, Coulsdon, in the South London suburbs. One was Simon Brown, of P5, MI6's head of Soviet bloc operations; the other was Veronica Price, the architect of Gordievsky's escape plan. A Home Counties creature from her pearls to her twinset, Price was not suited to this sort of subterfuge. 'I've borrowed the char's hat,' she announced, as they climbed into their disguises.

At 8.05, Michael Bettaney emerged from Number 5, paused at the front gate of his home, and looked up and down the street. 'That moment, I knew it was him,' said Brown. 'No one does that unless they are guilty, and looking for signs of surveillance.' Bettaney did not give the down-and-outs a second glance. Nor did he spot the pregnant woman a little way down the carriage, on the 8.36 train from Coulsdon Town; nor the balding man who tailed him on the ten-minute walk from Victoria Station to the MI5 building in Curzon Street. That day Bettaney took a two-hour lunch break, but at some point he was lost in the lunchtime crowds. MI5 could not be sure whether he had gone to Hanover Square to check if the *rezident* had finally signalled a willingness to play ball by parking his car on the north side – which Guk had not.

Frustrated and increasingly anxious, Bettaney resolved to make one more effort to coax the KGB into cooperation. After midnight on 10 July, he dropped a third letter through Guk's letterbox: this asked for an indication of whether the earlier packages had been received, and what the Soviet response might be. He proposed to call the Soviet embassy switchboard on 11 July, at 8.05 a.m., and ask for Guk by name. The *resident* should answer and indicate, by a specific form of words, whether or not he was interested in Koba's trove of secrets.

Why MI5 did not have Guk's property under tight surveillance, and thus spot the spy making his third delivery, remains a mystery. Gordievsky was now in Moscow, and not in a position to tip off his British friends to this latest approach. But, in any case, Bettaney was incriminating himself in various ways suggestive of intense mental strain, and possibly some sort of breakdown: on 7 July he discussed Guk with colleagues in a manner that struck them as 'obsessional', and suggested the KGB *rezident* should be recruited by MI5; the next day he remarked that even if the KGB was offered a 'peach' of a source, they would reject it; he began asking odd questions about specific KGB officers, and showing an interest in files outside his immediate remit. He spoke at length about the motivations of spies from the past, including Kim Philby.

On the morning of 11 July, he called the Soviet embassy from a public telephone, identified himself as 'Mr Koba', and asked to speak to Guk; the KGB station chief declined to pick up the phone. Three times, Bettaney had presented the KGB chief with a valuable gift horse; each time, Guk had looked it squarely in the mouth. Intelligence history offers few comparable examples of such an opportunity squandered.

Three days later, Bettaney asked an MI5 colleague: 'How do you think Guk would respond if a British intelligence officer put a letter through the door of his house?' This was the clincher: Koba was Michael Bettaney.

But the evidence against Bettaney was circumstantial. His telephone had been tapped, without producing any result. His house was subjected to a cursory search, without uncovering anything incriminating. Bettaney was covering his tracks with professional efficiency. For a successful prosecution MI5 needed to catch him in the act of treachery, or secure a confession.

The Gordievsky family returned from their holiday on 10 August. At the first meeting in the Bayswater safe house since his return, Gordievsky was told that while there was now a definite suspect, the spy in MI5 had not yet been arrested. Back at the KGB *rezidentura*, he made casual inquiries as to whether the dangle by the mysterious Koba had progressed in his absence, but learned nothing new. He attempted to resume his normal routine, cultivating contacts for the KGB and gathering intelligence for MI6, but it was hard to focus knowing that there was still a spy at liberty, somewhere inside British intelligence. Clearly this person had been unaware that Gordievsky was spying for Britain when he first posted his letter to Guk. But that was now more than four months ago. Had Koba discovered the truth in the interim? Had Guk agreed to take him on, and were his KGB colleagues even now watching him, waiting for him to make a slip? Every day that the spy remained uncaught, the threat increased. He picked up the girls from school, took Leila out to dinner, listened to Bach and read his books, trying to appear unperturbed, as the anxiety steadily mounted: would his friends in MI6 catch the nameless spy, before the spy caught him?

Bettaney, meanwhile, apparently tired of waiting for Guk to respond, had decided to take his illicit wares elsewhere. At the office, he let slip that he was thinking of taking a holiday in Vienna, a centre of Cold War espionage with a large KGB *rezidentura*. A search of his cupboard at work turned up documents referring to a KGB officer expelled from the UK in Operation FOOT, who was now living in Austria. Bettaney, it seemed, was about to fly the coop.

MI5 decided to haul him in, and attempt to extract a confession. It was a huge gamble. If Bettaney denied everything, and resigned from the Service, he could not be legally prevented from leaving the country. The plan to confront Bettaney, codenamed COE, might backfire. 'We could not guarantee success,' MI6 warned, pointing out that if Bettaney played his cards right, he might 'walk away at the end of the day free to do what he wants'. Above all, the interception of Bettaney must not be traceable to Gordievsky.

On 15 September, Bettaney was summoned to a meeting at MI5's Gower Street headquarters to discuss an urgent counter-intelligence case that had arisen. Instead, on arrival, he was taken to a flat on the top floor, and the evidence against him was laid out by John Deverell and Eliza Manningham-Buller – including a photograph of Guk's front door, intended to imply that he had been seen making his deliveries, which he had not. Bettaney was shocked and 'visibly nervous', but in control. He spoke hypothetically about what this theoretical spy was supposed to have done, without ever indicating that he had done anything at all. He noted that it would not be in his interest to confess, an implicit admission, but hardly a confession. Even if he had acknowledged his guilt, the evidence would not have been admissible, since he had not been arrested and no lawyer was present. MI5 wanted him to tell all, then arrest him, and get him to confess again under caution. But he did not.

Bugs relayed the conversation to the monitoring room below, where a bank of senior MI5 and MI6 officers craned to catch every word: 'Listening to his attempts to avoid admitting anything was an excruciating experience,' said one. Bettaney might be unstable, but he was not stupid. 'We had a very real fear that Bettaney would succeed in bluffing it out.' By evening, everyone was exhausted, and no nearer a breakthrough. Bettaney agreed to spend the night in the flat, though MI5 had no legal right to detain him. He had refused to eat lunch, and now declined dinner. He demanded a bottle of whisky, which he drank steadily. Manningham-Buller and two other minders listened sympathetically, 'occasionally asking disingenuous questions', as he expressed his admiration for the 'battery of evidence' MI5 had gathered, without admitting its truth. At one point he began referring to the British as 'you' and the Russians as 'us'. He admitted that he had wanted to warn the KGB officers they were under surveillance. But he did not confess. At 3 a.m. he finally collapsed into bed.

The next morning, Manningham-Buller cooked him breakfast, which he did not eat. Sleepless, hungover, hungry and exceptionally ill-tempered, Bettaney announced he had no intention of confessing.

But then he suddenly abandoned the hypothetical form of speech, and switched to the first person. He began referring sympathetically to 'Kim [Philby] and George [Blake]', the earlier Cold War spies.

Deverell was out of the room when Bettaney turned to the interrogators, at 11.42, and declared: 'I think I ought to make a clean breast of it. Tell Director K I wish to make a confession.' It was entirely in character for the impulsive Bettaney to hold out adamantly for so long, and then suddenly buckle. Within the hour, he was in Rochester Row police station, making a full confession.

A more intensive search of 5 Victoria Road revealed proof of his espionage: in a Philips electric-shaver box were details of KGB officers he intended to contact in Vienna; photographic equipment was discovered under rubble in the coal cellar; the laundry cupboard contained undeveloped film of classified material; in a cardboard box, under a layer of glasses, were handwritten notes on top-secret material; typed notes were sewn into a cushion. Bettaney was strangely contrite: 'I have put the Service in a bloody position – it wasn't my intention.'

The uncovering of yet another mole inside the British spy establishment was portrayed as a triumph for the Security Service. Margaret Thatcher congratulated MI5's Director General on 'how well the case had been handled'. The Nadgers sent a personal message to Gordievsky, emphasizing 'how warmly we feel about him'. And Gordievsky sent a message back, through Spooner, saying that he hoped one day to thank the officers of MI5 in person: 'I don't know whether such a day will come or not – maybe not. Nevertheless I would like this idea to be recorded somewhere: they have underlined my belief that they are the real defenders of democracy in the most direct sense of the word.'

Margaret Thatcher was the only member of the Cabinet aware of Gordievsky's role in catching the British spy. Inside British intelligence, only the Nadgers knew what had really happened. With the press in a frenzy, some judicious disinformation was spread suggesting that the tip-off about Bettaney's treachery had come from 'signals intelligence' (i.e. wiretaps), or that the Russians themselves had told the Security Service about the spy in its midst. One newspaper reported, wrongly: 'The Russians in London grew tired of Bettaney's approaches to them and, believing that he was a classic *agent provocateur*, told MI5 that Bettaney was wasting his time. It was then that MI5 began investigating Bettaney.' In case there might be another spy within, and to divert attention away from the real source, MI5 faked up a report for the files suggesting that the leak about Bettaney's approach had come from a regular diplomat in the Soviet embassy. The Soviets denied everything, and insisted that the talk of KGB espionage was cynically fabricated propaganda, 'aimed at damaging the normal development of Soviet–British relations'. Inside the KGB station, Guk clung to his belief that the whole charade had been orchestrated by MI5 to embarrass him. (To do otherwise would have been to admit a blunder of staggering proportions.) Gordievsky detected no hint of suspicion as to the real source of Bettaney's exposure: 'I do not think Guk or Nikitenko ever connected me with "Koba".'

Amid all the speculation, and the reams of newsprint devoted to the sensational Bettaney case, the truth never once broke the surface: that the man in Brixton Prison awaiting trial on ten counts of violating the Official Secrets Act had been put there by Oleg Gordievsky.

## 10.   Mr Collins and Mrs Thatcher

The Iron Lady had developed a soft spot for her Russian spy.

Margaret Thatcher had never met Oleg Gordievsky. She did not know his name, and referred to him, inexplicably and insistently, as 'Mr Collins'. She knew he spied from within the Russian embassy, worried about the personal strain he was under, and reflected that he might 'jump at any time', and defect. If that moment came, the Prime Minister insisted, he and his family must be properly cared for. The Russian agent was no mere 'intelligence egg layer', she said, but a heroic, half-imagined figure, working for freedom under conditions of extreme peril. His reports were conveyed by her Private Secretary, numbered and marked 'Top Secret and Personal' and 'UK Eyes A', meaning they were not to be shared with other countries. The Prime Minister consumed them avidly: 'She would read, word for word, annotate, pose questions, and the papers came back with her marks over them, underlinings, exclamation marks and comments.' In the words of her biographer, Charles Moore, Thatcher was 'not above being excited by secrecy in itself and by the romance of espionage', but she was also conscious that the Russian was furnishing uniquely precious political insight: 'Gordievsky's despatches . . . conveyed to her, as no other information had done, how the Soviet leadership reacted to Western phenomena and, indeed, to her.' The spy opened up a window into Kremlin thinking, which she peered through with fascination and gratitude. 'Probably no British Prime Minister has ever followed the case of a British agent with as much personal attention as Mrs Thatcher devoted to Gordievsky.'

While British intelligence had been hunting for Koba, the KGB was working hard to try to ensure that Thatcher lost the 1983 general election. In the eyes of the Kremlin, Thatcher was 'the Iron Lady' – a nickname intended as an insult by the Soviet army newspaper that coined it, but one in which she revelled – and the KGB had been organizing 'active measures' to undermine her ever since she came to power in 1979, including the placing of negative articles with sympathetic left-wing journalists. The KGB still had contacts on the left, and Moscow clung to the illusion that it might be able to influence the election in favour of the Labour Party, whose leader, after all, was still listed in KGB files as a 'confidential contact'. In an intriguing harbinger of modern times, Moscow was prepared to use dirty tricks and hidden interference to swing a democratic election in favour of its chosen candidate.

Had Labour won, Gordievsky would have found himself in a truly bizarre position: passing KGB secrets to a government whose Prime Minister had once been the willing recipient of KGB cash. In the end, Michael Foot's earlier incarnation as Agent BOOT remained a closely held secret; KGB efforts to swing the election had no impact whatever, and on 9 June Margaret Thatcher won by a landslide, boosted by victory in the Falklands the year before. Armed with a new mandate, secretly equipped with Gordievsky's insights into Kremlin psychology, Thatcher turned her sights to the Cold War. What she saw was deeply alarming.

In the latter half of 1983, East and West seemed to be heading into armed and perhaps terminal conflict, propelled by a 'potentially lethal combination of Reaganite rhetoric and Soviet paranoia'. Speaking to the Houses of Parliament, the American President promised to 'leave Marxism–Leninism on the ash heap of history'. The US military build-up continued apace, accompanied by a range of Psyops (psychological operations), including penetrations into Soviet airspace and clandestine naval operations demonstrating how close NATO could get to Russian military bases. These were designed to stoke Russian anxiety, and they succeeded: the RYAN programme moved up a gear, as KGB stations were bombarded with orders to find evidence that the US and NATO were preparing a surprise nuclear attack. In August a personal telegram from the head of the First Chief Directorate (later the KGB's chief), Vladimir Kryuchkov, instructed *rezidenturas* to monitor preparations for war, such as the 'secret infiltration of sabotage teams with nuclear, bacteriological and chemical weapons' into the Soviet Union. KGB stations that dutifully reported suspicious activity were praised; those that did not were sharply criticized, and told to do better. Guk was forced to admit 'shortcomings' in his efforts to uncover 'specific American and NATO plans for the preparation of surprise nuclear-missile attack against the USSR'. Gordievsky dismissed Operation RYAN as 'farcical', but his reports to MI6 left no room for doubt: the Soviet leadership was genuinely fearful, braced for combat, and panicky enough to believe that its survival might depend on pre-emptive action, a situation that grew dramatically worse following a tragic accident over the Sea of Japan.

In the early hours of 1 September 1983, a Soviet interceptor aircraft shot down a Korean Air Lines 747 that had strayed into Soviet airspace, killing all 269 passengers and crew. The shooting down of Flight KAL 007 sent East–West relations plummeting to a dangerous new low. Moscow initially denied any role in the shoot-down, but then claimed the airliner was a spy-plane that had violated Soviet airspace in a deliberate provocation by the US. Ronald Reagan condemned the 'Korean airline massacre' as 'an act of barbarism . . . [and] inhuman brutality', stoking domestic and international outrage and luxuriating in what one US official later called 'the joy of total self-righteousness'. Congress agreed to a further increase in defence spending. Moscow, in turn, interpreted Western anger over KAL 007 as manufactured moral hysteria, preparatory to an attack. Instead of an apology, the Kremlin accused the CIA of a 'criminal, provocative act'. A volley of most urgent 'flash' telegrams arrived at the London KGB station, with instructions to protect Soviet assets and citizens against possible attack, pin the blame on America, and collect information to bolster Moscow's conspiracy theories. The London KGB station was later commended by the Centre for its 'efforts to counteract the anti-Soviet campaign over the South Korean airliner'. Ailing and bedridden with what would prove to be his final illness, Andropov lashed out at what he called America's 'outrageous militarist psychosis'. Gordievsky smuggled the telegrams out of the embassy and passed them to MI6.

The downing of KAL 007 was the consequence of basic human incompetence on the part of two pilots, one Korean and one Russian. But Gordievsky's reporting to MI6 clearly showed how, under the pressure of escalating tension and mutual incomprehension, an ordinary tragedy had exacerbated an extraordinarily dangerous political situation.

Into this stew of ferocious mistrust, misunderstanding and aggression came an event that took the Cold War to the brink of actual war.

'ABLE ARCHER 83' was the codename for a NATO war game, held from 2 to 11 November 1983, intended to simulate an escalating conflict, culminating in a nuclear attack. This sort of military dress rehearsal had been held many times in the past, by both sides. ABLE ARCHER involved 40,000 US and other NATO troops in Western Europe, deployed and coordinated through encrypted communications. The command post training exercise imagined a situation in which the Blue Forces (NATO) defended its allies after Orange Forces (Warsaw Pact countries) sent troops into Yugoslavia, before invading Finland, Norway and eventually Greece. As the make-believe conflict intensified, a conventional war would seem to escalate into one involving chemical and nuclear weapons, enabling NATO to practise nuclear release procedures. No real weapons were deployed. This was a dummy run, but in the febrile atmosphere following the KAL 007 incident, Kremlin alarmists saw something much more sinister: a ruse intended to cover up preparations for the real thing: a nuclear first strike of the sort that Andropov had been predicting, and Operation RYAN had been seeking, for more than three years. NATO began to simulate a realistic nuclear assault at the very moment the KGB was attempting to detect one. Various unprecedented features of ABLE ARCHER reinforced Soviet suspicions that this was more than a game: a burst of secret communications between the US and UK a month earlier (in fact a response to the US invasion of Grenada); the initial participation of Western leaders; and different patterns of officer movements at US bases in Europe. The Cabinet Secretary, Sir Robert Armstrong, later briefed Mrs Thatcher that the Soviets had responded with such deep alarm because the exercise 'took place over a major Soviet holiday [and] had the form of actual military activity and alerts, not just war-gaming'.

On 5 November the London *rezidentura* received a telegram from the Centre warning that once the US and NATO decided to launch a first strike, their missiles would be airborne in seven to ten days. Guk was ordered to carry out urgent surveillance to detect any 'unusual activity' in key locations: nuclear bases, communications centres, government bunkers and, above all, 10 Downing Street, where officials would be working frantically to prepare for war, 'without informing the press'. In an instruction that says much about its own priorities, the KGB instructed its officers to monitor evidence that members of the 'political, economic and military elite' were evacuating their own families from London.

The telegram, passed by Gordievsky to MI6, was the first indication received by the West that the Soviets were responding to the exercise in an unusual and deeply alarming way. Two (or perhaps three) days later, a second flash telegram was sent to KGB *rezidenturas* reporting, erroneously, that American bases had been placed on alert. The Centre offered various explanations, 'one of which was that the countdown to a nuclear first strike had begun under the cover of ABLE ARCHER'. (In fact, the bases were merely tightening security, following the terrorist attack on American service personnel in Beirut.) The intelligence from Gordievsky came too late for the West to stop the exercise. By this point, the Soviet Union had begun preparing its own nuclear arsenal: aircraft in East Germany and Poland were fitted with nuclear weapons, around seventy SS-20 missiles targeted on Western Europe were placed on heightened alert, and Soviet submarines carrying nuclear ballistic missiles were deployed under the Arctic ice to avoid detection. The CIA reported military activity in the Baltic states and Czechoslovakia. Some analysts believe that the Soviet Union actually readied its ICBM silos, preparatory to launch, but held back from doing so at the last moment.

On 11 November, ABLE ARCHER wound down on schedule, the two sides slowly lowered their guns, and a terrifying Mexican standoff, unnecessary and unnoticed by the general public, came to an end.

Historians disagree on just how close the world had come to war. The authorized history of MI5 describes ABLE ARCHER as the 'most dangerous moment since the Cuban Missile Crisis of 1962'. Others argue that Moscow knew all along this was merely an exercise, and that Soviet nuclear-war preparations were merely shadow-boxing of a familiar sort. Gordievsky himself was phlegmatic: 'I felt that this was a further and disturbing reflection of the increasing paranoia in Moscow, not a cause of urgent concern in the absence of other indications.'

But within the British government those who read Gordievsky's reports and the stream of telegrams from Moscow believed nuclear catastrophe had been narrowly averted. In the words of Geoffrey Howe, Britain's Foreign Secretary: 'Gordievsky left us in no doubt of the extraordinary but genuine Russian fear of a real-life nuclear strike. NATO deliberately changed some aspects of the exercise so as to leave the Soviets in no doubt that it was only an exercise.' In fact, by departing from standard practice, NATO may have compounded the impression of sinister intent. A subsequent report by the Joint Intelligence Committee (JIC) concluded: 'we cannot discount the possibility that at least some Soviet officials/officers may have misinterpreted ABLE ARCHER . . . as posing a real threat'.

Margaret Thatcher was deeply worried. The combination of Soviet fears and Reaganite rhetoric might have ended in nuclear war, but America was not fully aware of a situation it had partly created. Something must be done, she ordered, 'to remove the danger that, by miscalculating Western intentions, the Soviet Union would over-react'. The Foreign Office must 'urgently consider how to approach the Americans on the question of possible Soviet misapprehensions about a surprise NATO attack'. MI6 agreed to 'share Gordievsky's revelations with the Americans'. The distribution of NOCTON material moved up another gear: MI6 specifically told the CIA that the KGB thought a war game had been a deliberate prelude to the outbreak of war.

'I don't see how they could believe that,' said Ronald Reagan, when told that the Kremlin had genuinely feared a nuclear attack during ABLE ARCHER, 'but it's something to think about.'

In fact the US President had already given considerable thought to the prospect of nuclear apocalypse. A month earlier, he was 'greatly depressed' after watching *The Day After*, a film about an American Midwestern city destroyed in a nuclear attack. Shortly after ABLE ARCHER, he attended a Pentagon briefing depicting the 'fantastic-ally horrible' impact of a nuclear war. Even if America 'won' such a conflict, 150 million American lives would probably be lost. Reagan described the briefing as 'a most sobering experience'. That night he noted in his diary: 'I feel the Soviets are . . . so paranoid about being attacked that . . . we ought to tell them no one here has any intention of doing anything like that.'

Both Reagan and Thatcher understood the Cold War in terms of a communist threat to peaceful Western democracy: thanks to Gordievsky, they were now aware that Soviet anxiety might represent a greater danger to the world than Soviet aggression. In his memoirs, Reagan wrote: 'Three years had taught me something surprising about the Russians: Many people at the top of the Soviet hierarchy were genuinely afraid of America and Americans . . . I began to realize that many Soviet officials feared us not only as adversaries but as potential aggressors who might hurl nuclear weapons at them in a first strike.'

ABLE ARCHER marked a turning point, a moment of terrifying Cold War confrontation, undetected by the Western media and public, that triggered a slow but perceptible thaw. The Reagan administration began to moderate its anti-Soviet rhetoric. Thatcher resolved to reach out to Moscow. 'She felt the time had come to move beyond the rhetoric of the "evil empire" and think how the West could bring the Cold War to an end.' Kremlin paranoia started to abate, particularly after the death of Andropov in February 1984, and though KGB officers were told to remain alert for signs of nuclear preparation, the momentum of Operation RYAN began to wane.

Gordievsky was partly responsible. Hitherto, his secrets had been doled out to the US in small, highly selective bits and pieces; from now on, his intelligence haul would be shared with the CIA in ever larger chunks, though still carefully camouflaged. The information about Soviet alarm during ABLE ARCHER was said to have come from 'a Czechoslovak intelligence officer . . . tasked with monitoring major NATO exercises'. Gordievsky was happy for MI6 to share his intelligence with the CIA. 'Oleg wanted it,' said one of his British handlers. 'He wanted to make an impact.' And he did.

The CIA had several spies in the USSR, but no source able to provide this kind of 'real insight into Soviet psychology', and supply original 'documents which betrayed a genuine nervousness that a pre-emptive strike could take place at any time'. Robert Gates, Deputy Director of Intelligence at the CIA, read the reports based on Gordievsky's intelligence, and realized the agency had missed a trick: 'My first reaction to the reporting was not only that we might have had a major intelligence failure, but further that the most terrifying thing about ABLE ARCHER was that we may have been at the brink of nuclear war and not even known it.' According to a secret internal CIA summary of the ABLE ARCHER scare, written several years later, 'Gordievsky's information was an epiphany for President Reagan . . . only Gordievsky's timely warning to Washington via MI6 kept things from going too far.'

From ABLE ARCHER onwards, the essence of Gordievsky's political reporting was passed to Ronald Reagan in the form of a regular summary, clearly flowing from a single agent. Gates wrote with hindsight: 'Our sources in the Soviet Union tended to be those who provided us with information about their military and military R&D. What Gordievsky was giving us was information about the thinking of the leadership – and that kind of information was for us as scarce as hens' teeth.' Reagan was 'very moved' by what he read, knowing that it came from an individual risking his life from somewhere deep within the Soviet system. The information from MI6 was 'treated as the holy of holies in the CIA, seen only by a small group who read it in hard copy under strict conditions', before being repackaged and sent to the Oval Office. Gordievsky's intelligence underpinned 'Reagan's conviction that a greater effort had to be made not just to reduce tension, but to end the Cold War'. The CIA was appreciative but frustrated, deeply curious as to where this steady stream of secrets could be coming from.

Spies tend to make extravagant claims for their craft, but the reality of espionage is that it frequently makes little lasting difference. Politicians treasure classified information because it is secret, which does not necessarily render it more reliable than openly accessible information, and frequently makes it less so. If the enemy has spies in your camp, and you have spies in his, the world may be a little safer, but essentially you end up where you started, somewhere on the arcane and unquantifiable spectrum of 'I know that you know that I know . . .'

Yet very occasionally spies have a profound impact on history. The breaking of the Enigma code shortened the Second World War by at least a year. Successful espionage and strategic deception underpinned the Allied invasion of Sicily and the D-Day landings. The Soviet penetration of Western intelligence in the 1930s and 1940s gave Stalin a crucial advantage in his dealings with the West.

The pantheon of world-changing spies is small and select, and Oleg Gordievsky is in it: he opened up the inner workings of the KGB at a pivotal juncture in history, revealing not just what Soviet intelligence was doing (and not doing), but what the Kremlin was thinking and planning, and in so doing transformed the way the West thought about the Soviet Union. He risked his life to betray his country, and made the world a little safer. As a classified internal CIA review put it, the ABLE ARCHER scare was 'the last paroxysm of the Cold War'.

Thousands of people filled Red Square for the funeral of Yuri Andropov on 14 February 1984. Among the international dignitaries in attendance was Margaret Thatcher, clad in elegant mourning dress and looking slightly stouter than usual thanks to a hot-water bottle tucked beneath her coat to ward off the Moscow chill. The funeral, she had told Vice-President George Bush, was 'a Godsend' for East–West relations. She put on a bravura show. While other Western leaders 'chattered inattentively' during the funeral, and even sniggered when Andropov's coffin was dropped by bearers, she remained 'suitably solemn' throughout. A burly British bodyguard, his pockets bulging with what the KGB assumed to be weaponry, followed her back to the reception at the Kremlin, and then whipped out a pair of high-heeled shoes for the Prime Minister to change into. She spent forty minutes talking to Andropov's successor, the elderly and ailing Konstantin Chernenko, and told him 'they had a chance, perhaps the last chance, of securing fundamental disarmament agreements'. Chernenko struck her as astonishingly ancient, a living fossil of the communist past. 'For heaven's sake try and find me a young Russian,' she told aides in the plane on the way home. In fact, officials had already identified someone who might fit the bill as an interlocutor on the Soviet side, a rising star in the Politburo named Mikhail Gorbachev.

Thatcher had played her role perfectly, following a script that had been written, in part, by Gordievsky. Before the funeral, James Spooner asked him for tips on how Thatcher should aim to present herself: Gordievsky urged decorum and friendliness, but warned that the Russians were touchy and defensive. 'Oleg provided a full briefing on how she should conduct herself,' said the MI6 officer responsible for analysing and distributing the 'product' from the case. 'On the rostrum she wore a black dress and a fur hat, and looked very serious. It was a seductive performance. She had an insight into their psychology. Without Oleg she would have been much tougher. Because of Oleg she knew how best to play her hand. They noticed.'

Back at the Soviet embassy in London, Ambassador Popov told a meeting of embassy staff, including the KGB contingent, that Mrs Thatcher's attendance at the funeral had gone down extremely well in Moscow. 'The Prime Minister's sensitivity to the occasion and formidable political brain has made a deep impression,' Popov reported. 'Mrs Thatcher had gone out of her way to charm her hosts.'

Here was a perfect intelligence cycle: Gordievsky was briefing the Prime Minister on how to respond to the Soviets, and then reporting back the Soviet reaction to that behaviour. Spies usually furnish facts, leaving the recipient to analyse them; with his unique perspective, Gordievsky was able to interpret, for the West, what the KGB was thinking, hoping and fearing. 'That is the essence of Oleg's contribution,' said the MI6 analyst. 'Getting inside the minds of others, getting into their logic, their rationality.'

Gordievsky's espionage was both positive and negative: in its positive form, it supplied important secrets, advance warnings and insight; in its negative, but equally useful form, it offered reassurance that the KGB station in Britain was, by and large, hopeless, as lumbering, inefficient and mendacious as the man who ran it. Arkadi Guk scorned his bosses back at the Centre, but rushed to fulfil their demands, however ludicrous. When he heard on the BBC that a cruise missile exercise had taken place at Greenham Common, the *rezident* hastened to manufacture a report indicating that he had known about the test beforehand. When mass anti-nuclear demonstrations took place in Britain, Guk claimed credit by insisting, falsely, that the KGB's 'active measures' had prompted the protests. Two suicides of Soviet citizens in London, one in the trade delegation and the other the wife of an official, thrust Guk's suspicions into overdrive. He sent the bodies back to Moscow, with orders to establish whether they had been poisoned, which the KGB scientists obediently confirmed – even though one had hanged himself and the other had thrown herself off a balcony. Here, thought Gordievsky, was 'yet another sign of how Soviet paranoia was feeding off its own neuroses'. The KGB *rezident* carefully covered up his own incompetence over the Bettaney case, assuring Moscow that it was all an elaborate ruse cooked up by British intelligence.

Guk jealously guarded his secrets, yet Gordievsky was able to pick up an astonishing quantity of useful information, ranging from embassy gossip to information of political and national significance. The KGB ran a number of illegals in Britain, and although Line N operated semi-independently within the *rezidentura*, Gordievsky tipped off MI5 whenever he picked up information about the underground spy network. At the height of the miners' strike in 1984–5, Gordievsky learned that the National Union of Mineworkers (NUM) had contacted Moscow to request financial support. The KGB opposed funding the miners. Gordievsky himself told KGB colleagues that it would be 'undesirable and unproductive' for Moscow to be seen bankrolling industrial action. But the Central Committee of the Soviet Communist Party thought otherwise, and approved the transfer of more than $1m from the Soviet Foreign Trade Bank (in the end, the Swiss receiving bank became suspicious, and the transfer never happened). Thatcher vilified the miners as 'the enemy within' – a prejudice no doubt reinforced by the discovery that the enemy without was prepared to finance their strike.

Gordievsky's espionage radar was able to pick up other enemies, far from Moscow. On 17 April 1984 a woman police officer named Yvonne Fletcher was killed by machine-gun fire from the Libyan People's Bureau in St James's Square in central London. The next day the KGB *rezidentura* received a telegram from the Centre relaying 'reliable information that the shooting had been personally ordered by Gaddafi' and reporting that 'an experienced hitman from the Libyan intelligence station in East Berlin had been flown to London to oversee the shooting'. Gordievsky immediately passed the telegram to MI6 – reinforcing the argument for a strong response. The Thatcher government broke off diplomatic relations with Libya, expelled Gaddafi's thugs and effectively expunged Libyan terrorism from Britain.

Intelligence sometimes matures slowly. Gordievsky had first alerted MI6 to the espionage activities of Arne Treholt back in 1974, but it took the Norwegian security service a decade to act, partly to protect the source. In the meantime, the glamorous star of the Norwegian left had risen to become head of the press section at the Norwegian Foreign Ministry. Early in 1984, Gordievsky was told that the Norwegians were ready to swoop, and asked if he objected; since he had provided the first tip-off, his security might be compromised if Treholt was apprehended. Gordievsky did not hesitate: 'Of course. He is a traitor to NATO and Norway, so of course you must arrest him as soon as possible.'

Treholt was detained at Oslo airport on 20 January 1984, by the chief of Norwegian counter-intelligence. He was believed to be heading for Vienna to meet Gennadi 'the Crocodile' Titov, his KGB handler and lunch partner for the previous thirteen years. Some sixty-five classified documents were found in his briefcase. Another 800 documents were found in his home. Initially he denied spying, but when shown a photograph of himself with Titov, he vomited violently and then said: 'What can I say?'

Titov was also intercepted by the Norwegian intelligence service, and offered a deal: if he agreed to change sides or defected to the West, he would be paid half a million US dollars. He refused, and was thrown out of the country.

At his trial, Treholt was accused of inflicting 'irreparable damage' on Norway by passing secrets to Soviet and Iraqi agents in Oslo, Vienna, Helsinki, New York and Athens. He was accused of receiving $81,000 from the KGB. Newspapers described him as the 'greatest traitor to Norway since Quisling', the wartime Nazi collaborator whose name became an English noun meaning traitor. The judge observed that he harboured 'unrealistic and exaggerated opinions about his own importance'. He was found guilty of treason, and sentenced to twenty years in prison.

In the late summer of 1984, James Spooner moved to another posting, and was succeeded as case officer by Simon Brown, the Russian-speaking former head of the Soviet section, P5, who had tailed Bettaney disguised as a tramp. Brown had been inducted into the NOCTON case back in 1979 when, as station chief in Moscow, he had been responsible for monitoring the signal sites for PIM-LICO, the escape operation. There was not the same immediate personal chemistry Gordievsky had enjoyed with Spooner. During their first encounter Veronica provided celery for lunch, and put the kettle on. Brown was nervous. 'I thought: if I don't speak fluent Russian he's going to think I'm an idiot. Then, when I played back the tape, to my horror all I could hear was the rising whoosh from a boiling kettle and the crunch of a man eating celery.' The MI6 secretary Sarah Page was always present at such meetings, quietly unflappable and reassuring: 'Her calming presence did much to humanize and gently soothe the somewhat fraught atmospherics.'

Meanwhile Gordievsky continued with his day job, the cultivation of political contacts, some of them genuine Soviet sympathizers and some, like Rosemary Spencer, providing useful chickenfeed. The researcher at Conservative Central Office was not the only controlled-access agent, unaware that Gordievsky was really a double agent working for British intelligence, being used by MI5 to feed him information. Neville Beale, a Tory member of the Greater London Council for Finchley and former chairman of the Chelsea Conservative Association, was another. He provided Gordievsky with council documents which were non-confidential and quite boring, but further evidence of his skill in extracting official information.

The Centre frequently came up with suggestions for possible recruits, most of them entirely impractical and unlikely. In 1984 a personal telegram arrived from the Centre, instructing Gordievsky to reconnect with Michael Foot, the former Agent BOOT. After his crushing election defeat, Foot had stepped down as Labour leader, but he remained an MP, and a leading figure of the Left. The telegram noted that although Foot had had no interaction with the KGB since the late 1960s, 'it might be useful to re-establish contact'. If it emerged that a spy run by MI6 was actively trying to recruit one of Britain's most senior political figures, the fallout would be spectacular. 'Drag your feet,' MI6 advised. 'Get out of it if you can.' Gordievsky sent a message back to the Centre, saying he would contrive to speak to Foot at a party, 'gently' reveal a knowledge of his past contacts, and sound out his sympathies. Then he did nothing at all, and hoped the Centre would forget about the idea – which it did, for a time.

In the first two years, the NOCTON case produced thousands of separate intelligence and counter-intelligence reports, some only a few sentences long, others running to many pages. These were further divided up and parcelled out – to MI5, Margaret Thatcher, parts of Whitehall and the Foreign Office, and, increasingly, the CIA. Other selected allies received occasional counter-intelligence leads, but only when important interests were at stake. The CIA was in a special, 'favoured nation' category.

MI6 was mightily pleased with Gordievsky, and so was the KGB. The bosses in Moscow were impressed by the steady stream of information he was producing as head of the PR Line; MI6 was providing him with enough interesting information among the chickenfeed to keep the KGB fat and satisfied; even Guk was happy with him, unaware that his successful underling was about to bring his own espionage career to an ignominious end.

The trial of Michael Bettaney opened at the Old Bailey on 11 April 1984, under the tightest possible security, with court windows masked, a large police presence and a scrambler-telephone link to MI5 headquarters should consultation be necessary during proceedings. The evidence was so secret that most of the trial took place in camera, without public or reporters present. Bettaney wore a pinstriped suit and a spotted tie. He insisted that his motivation had been 'pure and ideological – he was not a homosexual, not being blackmailed, and not working for profit'.

After five days of testimony, Bettaney was sentenced to twenty-three years in prison.

'You have made treachery your course of action,' said Lord Lane, the Lord Chief Justice, pronouncing sentence. 'It is quite plain to me that in many ways you are puerile. It is also clear to me that you are both opinionated and dangerous. You would not have hesitated to disclose names to the Russians which would almost certainly have led to death for more than one person.'

The press accepted Bettaney's self-description as a communist spy, because it was easier to understand a man who had undergone a 'gradual but eventually overwhelming political conversion'. The newspapers saw in Bettaney what they wanted to see: 'Tweedy twit became a wicked traitor,' shouted the *Sun*. 'The intelligence cold war never diminishes,' said *The Times*. The *Daily Telegraph* tied itself in homophobic knots trying to imply he was gay, and therefore implicitly untrustworthy. 'Bettaney appeared to have enjoyed the company of the arty, homosexual college community.' The left-leaning *Guardian* was the most sympathetic: 'In his own mind he was using his position in MI5 to try to stop Britain and the Western Alliance tottering into a new world war.' In Washington, the American establishment fretted (and quietly sniggered) at the way British intelligence had yet again fallen prey to internal espionage. 'The President is truly alarmed,' said a White House spokesman. One CIA source told the *Daily Express*: 'We have to wonder again about security in the British intelligence community.' A subsequent inquiry by the Security Commission was damning of MI5's failure to detect the danger posed by the unstable Bettaney. *The Times* even wondered whether the time had come to merge MI5 and MI6 into a single intelligence agency: 'After all, the KGB operates both at home and abroad.'

What none of the newspapers guessed was that MI5's first convicted traitor had been exposed by an MI6 spy inside the KGB. Gordievsky had saved Britain from an intelligence catastrophe, and once again paved the way for his own professional advancement.

Arkadi Guk was identified in court testimony as the KGB's head of station. The portly Russian general was photographed leaving his Kensington home with a wife in winged spectacles. His picture was splashed over the front pages beneath the headline 'Guk the Spook', the blundering Soviet spy chief who had 'turned down the KGB's first opportunity since the Second World War to recruit a penetration agent inside the Security Service'. Guk actually seemed to be enjoying the attention, and was 'parading around like a film star'.

Here was the perfect opportunity to get rid of him, and clear the way for Gordievsky to rise further up the KGB pecking order, and increase his access to secret material. MI6 requested Guk's immediate expulsion. Whitehall had little appetite for another diplomatic row. There would be no second opportunity to get rid of the *resident*, pointed out Christopher Curwen, the new Director of Counter-Intelligence and Security (DCIS) at MI6: 'Guk has always been most careful not to become directly involved in KGB agent running operations and is likely to be even more careful in the future.' Some in MI5 also argued against the move, pointing out that a new Post Security Officer had just been deployed to Moscow who would certainly be thrown out in a tit-for-tat expulsion if Guk was given his marching orders. But that, MI6 insisted, was a price worth paying. With Guk out of the way and Nikitenko nearing the end of his posting, Gordievsky might eventually take over as KGB *resident* in London. 'The stakes are very high,' argued one senior official. 'Nothing less than the chance of access to all, or practically all, the KGB operations against this country.' A letter was drafted for Mrs Thatcher to send to the Foreign Office, stating that since Guk had been identified publicly, he must be ejected. In a clever little detail, Guk was spelled 'Gouk' in the letter. That was how the *Daily Telegraph*, uniquely among British newspapers, spelled it. Mrs Thatcher was a *Telegraph* reader. The hint to the Foreign Office was implicit: the Prime Minister had read about the Russian spy chief in her morning newspaper and wanted him out, so if the Foreign Office continued to block the expulsion, she would take it personally. The ploy worked.

On 14 May 1984, Guk was declared *persona non grata* for 'activities incompatible with his diplomatic status', and given a week to pack his bags and leave Britain. As expected, the Soviets immediately responded by kicking MI5's new appointee out of Moscow.

A leaving party was held at the Soviet embassy on the evening before Guk's departure, with lashings of food and drink, and a succession of speeches in honour of the departing *rezident*. When it was Gordievsky's turn to speak, he ladled on the flattery. 'I must have sounded just a touch too smooth, and very slightly insincere.' Guk lurched up afterwards and muttered, 'You've learned a lot from the ambassador', whose talent for hypocritical speechifying was a running joke in the embassy. Although already quite drunk, Guk sensed that his underling was happy to see him depart. The next day, General Guk flew back to Moscow, and vanished into complete obscurity. He had embarrassed the KGB by drawing attention to himself. That, far more than his extraordinary incompetence, was unforgiveable.

Leonid Nikitenko was named acting *rezident*, and immediately began manoeuvring to make the appointment permanent. Gordievsky became his deputy, with increased access to the KGB station telegrams and files. MI6 was suddenly inundated with fresh intelligence. The ultimate prize was now within reach: if he could manoeuvre his way into the *rezident*'s office, the station's entire trove of secrets would be his for the taking. Only Nikitenko stood in the way.

Leonid Nikitenko was one of the cleverest men in the KGB, and one of the few who saw his job as a vocation. He would go on to head Directorate K, the KGB's counter-intelligence branch. One CIA officer who met him described 'a barrel-chested bear of a man, full of life . . . he loved the drama of the spy game, and there was no question he was good at it. He was at home in this secret universe and relished every moment, an actor on a stage that he had set for himself, playing a role that he had scripted.' After more than four years in the UK, the yellow-eyed counter-intelligence officer was overdue to be rotated back to Moscow, but Nikitenko had his sights set on the coveted role of *rezident*. A KGB job abroad usually lasted three years but the Centre was sometimes prepared to extend a posting, so he now launched a vigorous campaign to demonstrate that he was the best man for the job; or, more accurately, to show that Gordievsky was not. The two men had never liked one another: a war over the succession to Guk now began, all the more intense for being undeclared.

MI6 wondered whether to intervene yet again and declare

Nikitenko *persona non grata*, leaving Gordievsky a clear route to the top. The knock-on effect was working: in a pun on the codename for the case, the case officers called it the 'NOCTON effect'. The strategy was tempting. If Gordievsky could be levered into the top position, then his time in London would yield maximum results, and at the end of his posting he could defect. But, after some debate, it was decided that expelling Nikitenko would be a step too far, and 'possibly counterproductive'. Kicking out two KGB officers in quick succession was par for the course given the febrile atmosphere of the times; removing all three of Gordievsky's immediate bosses might look like a pattern.

Maksim Parshikov, Gordievsky's closest colleague, noticed that his friend now 'seemed to get into his stride. From the moment he was promoted to deputy *rezident* Oleg seemed softened, liberated, and behaved more calmly and naturally.' Some thought he was getting above himself. Mikhail Lyubimov, his friend and former colleague, was back in Moscow trying to make a new career as a writer after his sacking. 'He and I exchanged letters, and I was upset when he didn't reply promptly, sometimes sending only one letter to two of mine – power spoils people, and the deputy *rezident* in London is a big shot.' Lyubimov had no idea how busy his old friend was, doing two secret jobs at once, while scheming for another promotion.

The family had settled happily in London. The girls were growing up fast, speaking fluent English and attending a Church of England school. A century earlier, Karl Marx himself had been astonished how quickly his own children adapted to life in Britain: 'The idea of leaving the country of their precious Shakespeare appals them; they've become English to the marrow,' said Mrs Marx. Gordievsky was similarly surprised, and delighted, to find himself the father of two little English girls. Leila was also enjoying British life more and more. Her English improved, but it was hard to make English friends as wives were forbidden to see British citizens unaccompanied. Unlike Gordievsky, permanently on edge among his colleagues, she mixed easily with others in the KGB fraternity, drinking tea and gossiping happily with the wives of other embassy staff. 'I grew up in a family of KGB officers,' she once said. 'My dad was a KGB officer, my mother was a KGB officer.

Almost everyone in our district, where I spent my youth, was employed by the KGB. The fathers of all of my friends and classmates were KGB officers. Therefore, I never considered the KGB to be monstrous, or associated with anything horrible. It was my whole life, my everyday life.' She was proud of her husband's rapid promotion, and encouraged his ambition to take over as *rezident*. He often seemed preoccupied and occasionally stared intensely into the distance, as if locked on to another world. He bit his nails constantly. Some days he seemed particularly excited, wired taut with nervous stress. She put that down to the pressure of his important job.

Gordievsky loved Leila's lack of inhibition, her vitality and dedication to family life. Her naïve sweetness, her very lack of worldly suspicion, was an antidote to the contortions of subterfuge he was living through. He had never felt so close to her, despite the falsehood, known only to him, that kept them apart. 'I was so happily married,' he reflected. From time to time, he wondered whether he could let her in on his secret, and draw her into a complicity that would make their union truthful, and complete. She would find out eventually, when and if he finally defected to Britain. When MI6 gently probed him on how his wife might react when that moment came, he was adamant: 'She will accept it. She is a good wife.'

From time to time, he openly criticized Moscow in front of Leila. On one occasion, a little carried away, he described the communist regime as 'bad, wrong, criminal'.

'Oh stop yakking,' Leila snapped at him. 'It's just chat, you can't do anything about it so what point is there in talking about it?'

Nettled, Gordievsky shot back. 'Maybe I *can* do something. Maybe one day you will see that I *was* able to do something about it.'

Just in time, he reined himself in. 'I stopped. I knew if I had continued I would have told her more, or given her a hint.'

Later he reflected: 'She would not have understood. Nobody would have understood. Nobody. I never told anyone else. It was impossible. Strictly impossible. It was lonely. It was very lonely.' There was a hidden solitude in the heart of his marriage.

Gordievsky adored his wife, but he could not trust her with the truth. Leila was still KGB. And he was not.

On holiday back in Moscow that summer, Oleg was summoned to the First Chief Directorate headquarters for 'high-level discussions' about his future. Nikolai Gribin, the guitar-playing whiz kid he had got to know in Denmark who now headed the British–Scandinavian department, was 'friendliness itself', and dangled two possible promotions: the role of deputy department head back in Moscow and that of *rezident* in London. Gordievsky politely but firmly indicated his preference for the latter job. Gribin advised patience: 'The closer anyone moves to the position of head of station, the greater the danger, the more intense the intrigues.' But he pledged to give Gordievsky his full backing.

The conversation moved on to politics, and Gribin spoke warmly about a bright new star in the communist firmament named Mikhail Gorbachev. The son of a combine harvester operator, Gorbachev had risen swiftly within the communist hierarchy, becoming a full Politburo member before the age of fifty. He was widely tipped as the likely successor to the moribund Chernenko. The KGB, Gribin revealed, had 'come to the conclusion that Gorbachev was the best bet for the future'.

Margaret Thatcher had reached the same conclusion.

Gorbachev had been identified as the energetic Russian leader she was hoping for: a reformist, a man of vision who had travelled outside the Soviet bloc, in contrast to the narrow-minded Soviet gerontocracy. The Foreign Office had put out feelers, and in the summer of 1984 Gorbachev accepted an invitation to visit Britain the following December. Charles Powell, Mrs Thatcher's Private Secretary, told her the visit presented 'a unique opportunity to try and get inside the minds of the next generation of Soviet leaders'.

It was also an opportunity for Gordievsky. As head of political intelligence in the *rezidentura*, he would be responsible for briefing Moscow on what Gorbachev should expect; as a British agent, he would also be briefing MI6 on Russian preparations for the visit. Uniquely in intelligence history, a spy was in a position to shape, even choreograph, a meeting between two world leaders, by spying for, and reporting to, both sides: Gordievsky could advise Gorbachev on what to say to Thatcher, while simultaneously suggesting what Thatcher might say to Gorbachev. And if the meeting went well, it would improve Gordievsky's chances of securing the post of *rezident* – and the intelligence windfall that would bring.

The news that the Soviet leader-in-waiting was coming to London plunged the London KGB station into a ferment of preparations. Instructions from Moscow flooded in, demanding detailed information on every aspect of British life: political, military, technological and economic. The continuing miners' strike was of particular interest: Would they win? How were they financed? Strikes, of course, were forbidden in the Soviet Union. The Centre wanted chapter and verse on what Gorbachev should expect from his British hosts, and what British intelligence might be planning by way of unpleasant surprises. When Khrushchev had visited London in 1956, MI6 bugged his hotel, monitored his telephone calls and even sent a frogman to inspect the hull of the Soviet cruiser on which he had arrived.

The legacy of mistrust ran deep on both sides. Gorbachev was a dedicated Party member, a creation of the Soviet system; Thatcher was a strident opponent of communism, a philosophy she condemned as immoral and oppressive. 'Is there conscience in the Kremlin?' she had asked a year earlier in a speech to the Winston Churchill Foundation in the US. 'Do they ever ask themselves what is the purpose of life? What is it all for? . . . No. Their creed is barren of conscience, immune to the promptings of good and evil.' History has framed Gorbachev as a liberal progressive. The future architect of *glasnost* (openness) and *perestroika* (restructuring) would transform the Soviet Union, setting in motion forces that would dismantle it. But little of that was visible in 1984. Thatcher and Gorbachev stood on opposite sides of a vast political and cultural gulf. A successful meeting was by no means guaranteed; rapprochement would require some delicate diplomacy, and surreptitious engineering.

The KGB saw the visit to Britain as an opportunity to strengthen Gorbachev's hand. 'Send us the best possible briefing,' Gribin told Gordievsky. 'That way, it will look as though he has a superior intellect.'

Gordievsky and his team set to work. 'We really rolled up our sleeves,' recalled Maksim Parshikov, 'producing in-depth memoranda on all fundamentally important aspects of British policy and details on all the British participants.' Everything Gordievsky gathered for Nikitenko to pass to the KGB in Moscow, he also handed over to MI6. More than that, British intelligence fed Gordievsky with information to introduce into his reports to Moscow: subjects for discussion, possible points of agreement and disagreement such as the miners' strike, tips on how to interact with the personalities involved. Britain's intelligence service was effectively setting the agenda for the upcoming meetings, and briefing both sides.

Mikhail and Raisa Gorbachev arrived in London on 15 December 1984, on a visit that would last eight days. There was time for shopping and sightseeing, including a devout pilgrimage to the seat in the British Library where Marx wrote *Das Kapital*, but the visit was in essence an extended diplomatic démarche, as the Cold War adversaries cautiously sounded one another out in a series of meetings at Chequers, the Prime Minister's country residence. Every evening, Gorbachev demanded a detailed memorandum of three or four pages, with a 'forecast of the line the next day's meeting would take'. The KGB did not have that information. But MI6 did. Here was a perfect opportunity to ensure the two teams were on the same page, while demonstrating Gordievsky's value to his Moscow bosses. MI6 obtained the Foreign Office briefing document drawn up for Geoffrey Howe, the Foreign Secretary, listing the points he would be raising with Gorbachev and his team. This was then handed over to Gordievsky, who dashed back to the KGB station, hurriedly typed it up into Russian and handed it over to the reports officer to put into the daily memorandum. 'Yes!' said Nikitenko, when he read it. 'This is just what we need.'

Geoffrey Howe's Foreign Office briefing had become Mikhail Gorbachev's KGB briefing. 'In it went, verbatim.'

Gorbachev's visit to Britain was a resounding success. For all their ideological differences, Thatcher and Gorbachev appeared to be on the same wavelength. Of course, there were moments of strain: Thatcher lectured her visitor on the merits of free enterprise and competition; Gorbachev insisted 'the Soviet system was superior' and invited her to see for herself how 'joyfully' the Soviet peoples lived their lives. They sparred over the fate of dissidents, including the physicist Andrei Sakharov, and the arms race. In a particularly tense exchange, Thatcher accused the USSR of funding the miners. Gorbachev denied it. 'The Soviet Union had transferred no funds to the NUM,' he said, before shooting a sideways glance at his propaganda chief, a member of the Soviet delegation, and adding: 'As far as I know.' That was a lie, and Mrs Thatcher knew it. Back in October, Gorbachev himself had personally signed off on a plan to provide the striking miners with $1.4 million.

But, for all the verbal jousting, the two leaders got on well. It was almost as if they were working from the same script, which, in a way, they were. The daily KGB briefing for Gorbachev came back 'with passages underlined to show gratitude or satisfaction'. He was reading it closely. 'Both sides were being briefed by us,' said the MI6 analyst. 'We were doing something new – really trying to use the information, not distort it, to manage relations and open up new possibilities. We were a handful of people working amazing hours on the cusp of history.'

Observers noted the 'palpable human chemistry at work'. At the end of their discussions, Gorbachev pronounced himself 'very satisfied indeed'. Thatcher felt the same: 'His personality could not have been more different from the wooden ventriloquism of the average Soviet apparatchik.' Gordievsky reported the 'enthusiastic Moscow feedback' to MI6.

In a note to Reagan, Mrs Thatcher wrote: 'I certainly found him a man one could do business with. I actually rather liked him – there is no doubt that he is completely loyal to the Soviet system, but he is prepared to listen and have a genuine dialogue and make up his own mind.' That expression became the catchphrase of the visit, shorthand for the more vigorous leadership that would emerge when Chernenko died and was finally succeeded, in March 1985, by Gorbachev: 'A man one could do business with.'

The business breakthrough had been made possible, in part, by Gordievsky.

The Centre was pleased. Gorbachev, the KGB's preferred candidate for the leadership, had demonstrated statesmanlike qualities, and the London *rezidentura* had excelled itself. Nikitenko received a special commendation 'for handling the trip so well'. But much of the credit redounded to Gordievsky, the capable head of political intelligence who had produced such detailed and knowledgeable briefings, based on information gathered from his many British sources. Gordievsky was now the front-runner for the job of *rezident*.

And yet, amid the satisfaction of a job well done for both the KGB and MI6, a sharp little shard of anxiety lodged itself in Gordievsky's mind.

In the midst of the Gorbachev visit, Nikitenko had summoned his deputy. On the desk before him, the acting *rezident* had laid out the memoranda sent to Gorbachev, complete with his jottings.

The KGB's counter-intelligence specialist fixed Gordievsky with an unwavering yellow gaze. 'Hmm. Very good report about Geoffrey Howe,' said Nikitenko, and then paused for a beat. 'It sounds like a Foreign Office document.'

## 11.  Russian Roulette

Burton Gerber, chief of the CIA's Soviet section, was an expert on the KGB, with wide operational experience of the espionage war with the Soviet Union. A lanky Ohio native, assertive and single-minded, he was one of a new generation of American intelligence officers, unscathed by the paranoia of the past. He established the so-called 'Gerber Rules', which held that every offer to spy for the West should be taken seriously, every lead pursued. One of his odder hobbies was the study of wolves, and there was something distinctly vulpine about the way Gerber hunted his KGB prey. Posted to Moscow in 1980 as the CIA's station chief, he had returned to Washington early in 1983 to take over the agency's most important division: running spies behind the Iron Curtain. There were plenty of them. The uncertainty of the previous decade had given way, under the Director of the CIA, Bill Casey, to a period of intense activity and considerable achievement, particularly in the military sphere. Within the Soviet Union, the agency had more than 100 covert operations underway, and at least twenty active spies, more than ever before: inside the GRU, the Kremlin, the military establishment and scientific institutes. The CIA's spy network included several KGB officers, but none of the calibre of the mysterious agent supplying first-hand, high-grade material to MI6.

What Burton Gerber didn't know about spying on the USSR wasn't worth knowing, with one important exception: he didn't know the identity of Britain's KGB spy. And that bugged him.

Gerber had seen the material being supplied by MI6, and he was both impressed and intrigued. The psychological gratification of all intelligence work lies in knowing more than your adversaries, but also more than your allies. In the all-embracing, global view from Langley, the CIA had a right to know anything and everything it wanted to know.

The Anglo-American intelligence relationship was close and mutually supportive, but unequal. With its vast resources and worldwide network of agents, the CIA was rivalled only by the KGB in its intelligence-gathering capability. When it served America's interests to do so, the CIA shared information with its allies, although, like all intelligence agencies, sources were rigorously protected. Intelligence sharing was a two-way street, but in the opinion of some CIA officers America had a right to know everything. MI6 was providing intelligence of the highest quality, but no matter how often the CIA hinted that it would like to know where it was coming from, the British refused to say, with infuriating and obdurate politeness.

The hints became less subtle. At a Christmas party, Bill Graver, the CIA's station chief in London, came sidewinding up to the MI6 Sovbloc controller. 'He grabbed me and pinned me up against the wall and said: "Can you tell me more about this source? We need to have some guarantee that this info is reliable, because it's really shit hot."'

The British officer shook his head. 'I'm not going to tell you who it is, but you can be reassured that we have full confidence in him, and that he has the authority to authenticate this intelligence.' Graver backed off.

At around the same time, MI6 asked the CIA for a favour. For years, senior officers in British intelligence had been lobbying the technical department at Hanslope to develop an effective secret camera, but the MI6 board had always vetoed this on the grounds of expense. MI6 was still using the old-fashioned Minox camera. The CIA, however, was known to have recruited a Swiss watchmaker to develop an ingenious miniature camera hidden inside an ordinary Bic cigarette lighter, which could take perfect photographs when used in conjunction with a length of thread, 11¼ inches long, and a pin. Using a piece of chewing gum, the thread was stuck to the bottom of the lighter; when the pin at the end lay flat on a document, that measured the ideal focal length, and the button on top of the lighter could be pressed to click the shutter. The pin and thread could be hidden behind a lapel. The lighter looked entirely innocent. It even lit cigarettes. This would be the ideal camera for Gordievsky. When the time came for him to defect, he could take it into the residency and then, photographically speaking, 'empty out the safe'. In a decision that went all the way up to Bill Casey, the CIA finally agreed to provide MI6 with one of the cameras, but before it was handed over an intriguing exchange took place between the CIA and MI6.

CIA: 'Do you want this for any particular purpose?'

MI6: 'We have someone on the inside.'

CIA: 'Would we get the intelligence?'

MI6: 'Not necessarily. That can't be guaranteed.'

MI6 was not responding to demands, coaxing or bribery, and Gerber was frustrated. The British had someone very good and they were hiding him. As the subsequent secret CIA assessment of the ABLE ARCHER scare put it: 'the information reaching [the CIA] . . . came primarily from British intelligence and was fragmentary, incomplete, and ambiguous. Moreover, the British protected the identity of the source . . . and his bona fides could not be independently established.' This intelligence was being passed up all the way to the President: not knowing where it came from was just embarrassing.

And so, with approval from above, Gerber launched a discreet spy-hunt. Early in 1985, he instructed a CIA investigator to set about uncovering the identity of the British superspy. MI6 should on no account discover what was going on. Gerber did not see this as a betrayal of trust, and still less as spying on an ally; more a tying up of loose ends, prudent and legitimate cross-checking.

Aldrich Ames was the CIA's chief of Soviet counter-intelligence. Milton Bearden, a CIA officer who eventually took over the Soviet division, wrote: 'Burton Gerber was determined to identify the British source and assigned the Soviet and East European Division's chief of counter-intelligence, Aldrich Ames, to puzzle it out.' Gerber later claimed that he had not asked Ames himself to do the detective work, but another, unnamed officer who was 'gifted in doing that kind of checking'. That officer would have been working alongside Ames, the counter-intelligence chief.

Ames's job title sounded impressive, but the section of the Soviet department responsible for rooting out spies and assessing which operations were vulnerable to penetration was considered a backroom job in Casey's CIA, 'a dumping ground for vaguely talented misfits'.

Ames was forty-three years old, a grey government bureaucrat with bad teeth, a drink problem and a very expensive fiancée. Every day, he left his small rented apartment in Falls Church, struggled through the commuter traffic to Langley, and then sat at his desk, 'brooding, and thinking dark thoughts about the future'. Ames was in debt to the tune of $47,000. He fantasized about robbing a bank. An internal assessment noted his 'inattention to matters of personal hygiene'. Lunch was almost always liquid, and long. Rosario spent 'her ample free time spending Rick's money', and complaining that there was not enough of it. His career had stalled. This would be his last promotion. The CIA had let him down. He was also resentful of his boss, Burton Gerber, who had reprimanded him for taking Rosario to New York at agency expense. Perhaps the agency should have spotted Ames was going bad, but, as with Bettaney in MI5, mere oddity of behaviour, alcoholic excess and a patchy work record were not in themselves grounds for suspicion. Ames was part of the furniture at the CIA, tatty but familiar.

Ames's position and seniority gave him access to the files on all operations aimed at Moscow. But there was one Soviet spy, sending valuable intelligence to the CIA at one remove, whose identity he did not know: a high-grade agent handled by the British.

Identifying a single spy within the vast Soviet government apparatus was a daunting task. In the words of Sherlock Holmes: 'Once you eliminate the impossible, whatever remains, no matter how improbable, must be the truth.' That is what the CIA now set about trying to do. Elementary, it wasn't, but every spy leaves clues. The CIA sleuths began combing through the information supplied by the mysterious British agent over the previous three years, and trying to pinpoint him (or, conceivably, her) by a process of elimination and triangulation.

The inquiry probably went something like this.

The details about Operation RYAN supplied by MI6 indicated that the source was a KGB officer, and although the material was said to come from a middle-ranking official, the quality suggested someone in a senior position. The regularity of the reporting implied that the individual was meeting MI6 frequently, which in turn would indicate he was probably located outside the Soviet Union, and possibly in the UK itself – a hunch reinforced by the fact that he seemed to be 'privy to information about England'. An individual spy may be pinpointed by what he produces, but also by what he does not. The intelligence being passed on by the Brits contained little technical or military information, but a great deal of high-grade political intelligence. The probability, therefore, was that he was working in the PR Line of the First Chief Directorate. An agent inside the KGB would undoubtedly have fingered a number of Western spies working for the Soviets. So where had the Soviets recently lost agents? Haavik and Treholt in Norway. Bergling in Sweden. But the most dramatic exposure of a Soviet spy in recent times had taken place in Britain, with the much-publicized arrest and trial of Michael Bettaney.

The CIA understood the structure of the KGB intimately. The Third Department of the FCD lumped together Scandinavia and Britain. The pattern seemed to point at someone in that department.

A trawl of the CIA database of known and suspected KGB agents would have established that only one such individual had been in Scandinavia when Haavik and Bergling were nabbed, and in Britain when Treholt and Bettaney were caught: a 46-year-old Soviet diplomat, who had appeared on the radar in Denmark back in the early 1970s. A cross-reference would have located Oleg Gordievsky's name in the CIA file on Standa Kaplan. A closer look would reveal that the Danes had identified this man as a probable KGB officer, but the British had granted him a visa as a *bona fide* diplomat in 1981, in direct contravention of their own rules. The Brits had also recently expelled a number of KGB officers, including the *rezident*, Arkadi Guk. Were they deliberately clearing an upward path for their own spy? Finally, a search of the CIA records from Denmark in the 1970s revealed that 'a Danish intelligence officer had once let slip that MI6 had recruited a KGB officer in 1974 while he was stationed in Copenhagen'. A cable to the CIA station in London established that Oleg Gordievsky fitted the profile.

By March, Burton Gerber was sure he knew the identity of the spy Britain had concealed for so long.

The CIA had won a small but satisfying professional victory over MI6. The Brits thought they knew something the Americans did not know; but now the CIA knew something that MI6 did not know they knew. That is how the game is played. Oleg Gordievsky was assigned the random CIA codename TICKLE, a neutral-sounding label to go with a little harmless international rivalry.

Back in London, Gordievsky awaited word from Moscow with mounting excitement, tinged with a queasy unease. He was in pole position to take over as *rezident*, but the Centre, as usual, was taking its time. Nikitenko's sinister remarks about Gordievsky's unusually well-informed briefings during the Gorbachev visit continued to haunt him, and he privately berated himself for failing to disguise his hand sufficiently.

In January, he was instructed to fly back to Moscow for a 'high-level briefing'.

Within British intelligence, the summons triggered a debate. Given Nikitenko's veiled threat, some feared a trap. Should this be the moment to bring Oleg in from the cold, and arrange his defection? The spy had already acquitted himself nobly. A few argued that the risk of letting him return to Russia was too great. 'There was a potential bonanza here. But if it went wrong, we would not just lose a highly placed agent. We were sitting on a treasure trove of information that so far had had only limited circulation because it could not be fully exploited and shared without potentially compromising Oleg.'

But the prize was now within reach, and Gordievsky himself was confident. There were no danger signals from Moscow. The summons was probably evidence that he had won his power struggle with Nikitenko. 'We were not too concerned, and nor was he,' Simon Brown recalled. 'The slowness in getting him confirmed was a worry, but his view was that he was probably OK.'

Even so, Gordievsky was offered the opportunity to quit. 'We said to him – and we meant it – if you want to step off now, you can. It would have been a bitter disappointment if he had. He was as keen as we were. He didn't see any great hazard.'

At their last meeting before his departure, Veronica Price carefully rehearsed Operation PIMLICO, step by step.

On his arrival at FCD headquarters in Moscow Gordievsky was welcomed heartily by Nikolai Gribin, the department head, and told that he 'had been chosen as the best candidate to succeed Guk'. The official announcement would not be made until later in the year. A few days later he was introduced at an internal KGB conference as 'the *rezident* designate in London, Comrade Gordievsky'. Gribin was furious that the appointment had been prematurely revealed to their KGB colleagues, but Gordievsky was relieved and delighted: word of the promotion was out.

His satisfaction was only slightly dented by learning of the fate of a colleague, Vladimir Vetrov, a KGB colonel in Line X, the department devoted to technical and technological espionage. After working in Paris for several years, Vetrov had begun spying for the French intelligence service. Codenamed FAREWELL, he provided more than 4,000 documents and information that led to the expulsion of forty-seven KGB officers from France. Back in Moscow in 1982, Vetrov got into a violent argument with his girlfriend in a parked car. When an auxiliary policeman heard the commotion and knocked on the window, Vetrov, thinking he was about to be arrested for spying, stabbed and killed him. While in prison, he carelessly revealed that he had been involved in 'something big' before his arrest. Subsequent investigation revealed the extent of his treachery. The unfortunately named FAREWELL was executed on 23 January, a few days before Gordievsky flew back to London. Vetrov was a murderous maniac who had brought about his own destruction, but his execution was a reminder of what happened to KGB traitors caught spying for the West.

When Gordievsky returned to London at the end of January 1985 with news of his appointment, the rejoicing in MI6 was unconstrained – or would have been, had it not also been utterly secret. In the Bayswater safe house, the meetings took on new urgency and excitement. Here was an unprecedented coup: their spy would soon be taking over the KGB station in London, with access to every single secret therein. After this, he would surely rise further. There were hints that he was about to be promoted again, and might end up a KGB general.

Thirty-six years before, Kim Philby had risen to become MI6's station chief in Washington DC, a KGB spy at the heart of Western power. Now MI6 was doing to the KGB what the KGB had once done to it. The wheel had turned. The possibilities seemed limitless.

Gordievsky awaited formal confirmation of his appointment in a euphoric daze. One change in his friend's behaviour struck Maksim Parshikov as distinctly odd: 'His sparse, greying hair suddenly acquired a yellow-red colour.' Overnight, Gordievsky's hairdo changed from Soviet-salt-and-pepper to punk-exotic. His colleagues sniggered privately. 'Had a young mistress appeared on the scene? Or, God forbid, five minutes before taking over as KGB *rezident* in London, had Oleg unexpectedly turned gay?' When Parshikov cautiously inquired what had happened to his hair, Oleg explained, with some embarrassment, that he had accidentally used his wife's hair dye instead of shampoo, a most unconvincing explanation since Leila's dark locks were quite different in colour to the startling ochre hue of Gordievsky's new dye-job. 'When the "mistake with the shampoo" took on a regular character, we stopped asking.' Parshikov concluded: 'Everyone has a right to their own strangeness.'

Nikitenko was instructed to prepare for his return to Moscow. He was furious at being leapfrogged by an underling with just three years' experience in Britain, and elaborately insincere in his congratulations. Gordievsky would not officially take over as *rezident* until the end of April; in the interim, Nikitenko went out of his way to be as uncooperative and unpleasant as possible, dripping poison into the ears of his superiors and disparaging the new appointee to anyone who would listen. More worryingly, he refused to hand over telegrams which the *rezident*-in-waiting had a right to see. Perhaps this was merely petty revenge, Gordievsky told himself, but there was something about Nikitenko's attitude that smelled of something nastier than just sour grapes.

For Gordievsky and the NOCTON team, the case entered a peculiar limbo. When Nikitenko finally departed, to take up his new job at KGB headquarters in the counter-intelligence department, Gordievsky would have the keys to the KGB safe, and MI6 would surely reap a bumper harvest.

Twelve days before Gordievsky was due to take over as *rezident*, Aldrich Ames offered his services to the KGB.

Ames was truculent. His breath smelled and his job stank. He felt underappreciated by the CIA. But he would later offer a simpler explanation for his actions: 'I did it for the money.' He needed to pay for Rosario's shopping trips to Neiman Marcus and dinners at The Palm restaurant. He wanted to move out of his one-bedroom apartment, pay off his ex-wife, hold an expensive wedding and own his car outright.

Ames chose to sell out America to the KGB in order to buy the American Dream he felt he deserved. Gordievsky had never been interested in the money. Ames was interested in nothing else.

Early in April, Ames telephoned an official at the Soviet embassy named Sergey Dmitriyevich Chuvakhin, and suggested they meet. Chuvakhin was not one of the forty KGB officers working in the embassy. He was an arms control specialist and a 'person of interest' to the CIA, considered a legitimate target for cultivation. Ames told colleagues he was sounding out the Russian official as a possible contact. The meeting was 'sanctioned' by both the CIA and FBI. Chuvakhin agreed to meet Ames for drinks at 4 p.m. on 16 April, at the bar of the Mayflower Hotel, not far from the Soviet embassy on 16th Street.

Ames was nervous. Waiting at the Mayflower bar, he drank a vodka martini, and then another two. When, after an hour, Chuvakhin had still not appeared, Ames decided to 'improvise', as he put it: he walked, rather unsteadily, up Connecticut Avenue to the Soviet embassy, handed the package he had intended for Chuvakhin to the receptionist, and left.

The small parcel was addressed to the KGB *rezident* in Washington, General Stanislav Androsov. Inside was another envelope, addressed to Androsov under his operational alias, 'Kronin'. A handwritten note read: 'I am H. Aldrich Ames and my job is branch chief of Soviet counter-intelligence at the CIA. I served in New York where I used the alias Andy Robinson. I need $50,000 and in exchange for the money, here is information about three agents we are developing in the Soviet Union right now.' The names he listed were all individuals the Soviets had 'dangled' at the CIA, posing as potential recruits but in reality KGB plants. 'These weren't real traitors,' Ames later said. By revealing them, he told himself, he was not harming anyone, or damaging a CIA operation. The envelope also contained a page torn from the CIA internal telephone directory, with Ames's name underlined in yellow felt pen.

Ames had carefully engineered his approach to include four distinct elements that would establish his seriousness: information about current operations that no mere provocateur would have revealed; an earlier alias that would be known to the KGB from his time in New York; knowledge of the *resident*'s secret codename; and proof of his own identity and CIA job. That would surely grab the Soviets' attention, and get the money rolling in.

Knowing how the KGB worked, Ames did not expect an immediate response: the 'walk-in' would be referred back to Moscow, inquiries would be made, the possibility of a provocation explored, and eventually the Centre would take up his offer. 'I was sure they would respond positively,' he later wrote. 'And they did.'

Two weeks later, on 28 April 1985, Oleg Gordievsky became London *resident*, the most senior KGB officer in London. The handover from Nikitenko was peculiar. By tradition, the departing KGB station chief left behind a locked briefcase containing important secret documents. With Nikitenko safely on the plane to Moscow, Oleg opened the case, to find just one brown envelope containing two sheets of paper: photocopies of the letters Michael Bettaney had pushed through Guk's letterbox two years earlier, the contents of which had already been reported in every British newspaper. Was this a joke? A souvenir hinting at Guk's incompetence? A warning? Or was Nikitenko sending some ominous message? 'Was it because he did not trust me, and felt he could not leave anything that was still secret?' But if that was the case, why leave a veiled tip-off? Most likely, Nikitenko was simply trying to destabilize the rival who had got the job he coveted.

MI6 was also puzzled: 'We were expecting the crown jewels and didn't get them. We had wondered whether we would learn that members of the Cabinet were long-standing KGB agents, or discover more Bettaneys, and we didn't. That was a relief, but mixed with disappointment.' Gordievsky began reading through the *rezidentura* files, and gathering for MI6 what would surely prove to be a bonanza of fresh intelligence.

As Ames predicted, the KGB took time to respond to his overtures, but then did so with enthusiasm. In early May, Chuvakhin called Ames, and casually suggested they 'get together for a drink at the Soviet embassy on May 15, and then proceed to lunch at a local restaurant'. In fact Chuvakhin was neither enthusiastic nor casual. He was a genuine arms control expert, and had no desire to be dragged into some dodgy and dangerous spy game. 'Let one of your boys do this dirty work,' he said, when instructed to contact Ames and arrange the meeting. The KGB swiftly set him straight: Ames had singled him out, and Chuvakhin would be playing the game whether or not he wanted to.

The KGB had been busy over the previous three weeks. Ames's letter was passed immediately to Colonel Viktor Cherkashin, chief of counter-intelligence at the Soviet embassy. Realizing its importance, Cherkashin dispatched a densely encoded 'burst' transmission to Kryuchkov, head of the First Chief Directorate, who went to see Viktor Chebrikov, Chairman of the KGB, who immediately authorized the withdrawal of $50,000 in cash from the Military Industrial Commission. The KGB was a cumbersome beast, but it could move fast when it needed to.

On Wednesday, 15 May, Ames reappeared, as bidden, at the Soviet embassy, having informed the CIA and FBI he was following up his earlier efforts to cultivate the military specialist. 'I knew what I was doing. I was determined to make it work.' Chuvakhin met Ames in the embassy lobby and introduced him to the KGB officer Cherkashin, who then led him to a small conference room in the basement. Not a word was exchanged. Indicating by gestures that the room might be bugged, the smiling Cherkashin handed Ames a note: 'We accept your offer and are very pleased to do so. We would like you to use Chuvakhin as the cut-out, the go-between for our discussions. He will be able to give you the money and be available to lunch with you.' On the back of the note Ames wrote: 'Okay. Thank you very much.'

But that was not all.

There is one question every case officer is bound to ask of a newly recruited spy: Do you know of any penetration of our service? Does your side have a spy inside our organization who could give you away? Gordievsky had been asked this question the moment he agreed to spy for Britain. Cherkashin was highly trained. It is inconceivable that he would have failed to ask whether Ames was aware of any spies inside the KGB who might discover that he was offering to swap sides, and report this back to the CIA. Ames in turn would have been expecting the question. He knew of more than a dozen such agents, including two inside the Soviet embassy itself; and one, the most senior of all, being run by the British.

Ames later claimed that he did not, at this stage, identify Gordievsky by name. His systematic betrayal of every Soviet agent on the CIA's books would not take place for another month. In memoirs published in 2005, Cherkashin claimed the crucial tip-off about Gordievsky came not from Ames, but from a shadowy informant, 'a Washington-based British journalist'. The CIA dismisses this as disinformation designed to reflect well on the KGB, with 'all the earmarks [sic] of being a false lead'.

Most intelligence analysts who have studied the Gordievsky case agree that, at some point during his initial contact with the Russians, Ames revealed that there was a top-level mole inside the KGB working for British intelligence. He may not have been aware of Gordievsky's name by this point, particularly if he was not personally conducting the investigation. But he surely knew that the investigation into the identity of an MI6 spy codenamed TICKLE was underway, and it is highly likely he passed this on during the wordless meeting in the basement of the Soviet embassy, in a warning message scribbled on a piece of paper. Even if he did not yet divulge a name, this would have been enough to unleash the hunting dogs of K Directorate.

When Ames emerged from his subterranean meeting, Chuvakhin was waiting in the lobby. 'Let's go for lunch,' he said.

The two men sat at a corner table in Joe and Mo's restaurant, and began to talk, and drink. Uncertainty surrounds exactly what was said during that 'long, boozy' lunch. Ames later claimed, implausibly, that they spent the time discussing arms control. It is possible that, somewhere between the third and fourth martinis, Ames confirmed the existence of a British-run spy in the KGB. But he later admitted: 'My memory is sort of a blur.'

At the end of the meal, Chuvakhin, who had drunk considerably less than Ames, handed him a plastic carrier bag filled with papers. 'Here are some press releases I think you will find interesting,' he said, just in case the FBI might be listening on a directional microphone. The men shook hands, and the Russian hastened back to the embassy. Despite the alcohol sloshing through his system, Ames climbed into his car, and headed homewards. On the George Washington Parkway, he parked in a scenic lay-by overlooking the Potomac and opened the shopping bag: at the bottom, under assorted embassy bumf was a wrapped rectangular parcel, the size of a small brick. He tore off a corner. Ames was 'totally exhilarated'. Inside was a wad of 500 $100 bills.

While the American was counting his money, back at the Soviet embassy Chuvakhin briefed Cherkashin, and the KGB officer composed another encrypted 'burst' cable, marked for the attention of Chebrikov himself.

By the time Ames got home, one of the biggest manhunts in KGB history was underway.

On Thursday, 16 May, the day after Ames's first meeting with Cherkashin, an urgent telegram from Moscow landed on the desk of the newly appointed KGB *rezident* in London.

As he read it, Oleg Gordievsky felt a cold prickle of apprehension.

'In order to confirm your appointment as *rezident*, please come to Moscow urgently in two days' time for important discussions with Comrades Mikhailov and Alyoshin.' These were the operational aliases for Viktor Chebrikov and Vladimir Kryuchkov, the KGB Chairman and the head of the First Chief Directorate. The summons came from the summit of the KGB.

Gordievsky told his secretary he had an appointment, rushed to the nearest telephone box, and called an emergency meeting with his MI6 handler.

Simon Brown was waiting at the Bayswater safe house when he arrived a few hours later. 'He looked worried,' Brown recalled. 'Obviously concerned, but not panicked.'

Over the next forty-eight hours, MI6 and Gordievsky would have to decide whether he should answer the summons and return to Moscow, or wrap up the case and move him and his family into hiding.

'Oleg started rehearsing the pros and cons: his immediate rationale was that it was unusual, but not so unusual as to be immediately and necessarily suspicious. There could be all sorts of logical reasons for the recall.'

Moscow had been oddly silent since his appointment. Gordievsky had expected at least a note of congratulation from Gribin, and more worryingly he had not yet received the all-important telegram containing the *rezidentura*'s cipher communication codes. On the other hand, his KGB colleagues exhibited no trace of suspicion, and seemed anxious to please.

Gordievsky wondered if he was worrying unnecessarily: perhaps, along with Guk's job, he had inherited his predecessor's paranoia.

More than one MI6 officer compared the situation to a gambler's dilemma. 'You have built up a big pile of chips. Do you stake it all on one last spin of the roulette wheel? Or do you gather up your winnings, and leave the table?' Calculating the odds was no easy matter, and the stakes were now astronomically high: a win could yield untold riches, with access to the KGB's innermost secrets; but a losing bet could mean Gordievsky would be lost for ever, or he might simply disappear with no confirmation for months as to his fate. None of his store of intelligence could be used and more widely disseminated meanwhile. And for Gordievsky himself it would mean, ultimately, his destruction.

There was something odd about the tone of the message, at once peremptory and polite. According to KGB tradition, the Chairman himself appointed *rezidents*, particularly in target countries as important as the UK. Chebrikov had been away from Moscow in January when Oleg was awarded the job, and so this might be no more than formal confirmation, a ceremonial 'laying on of hands' by the KGB supremo. Perhaps the fact that he had yet to be fully 'anointed' by the

KGB explained the lack of information left by Nikitenko and the failure to send the cipher codes. If the KGB suspected him of treachery, why did they not call him home immediately, rather than in two days' time? Perhaps they were trying not to spook him with an immediate recall. But if they knew he was a spy, why had they not sent in the thugs of the Thirteenth Department, specialists in kidnapping, to drag him back to Russia? And if this was just business as usual, why the lack of forewarning? Gordievsky had been fully briefed on his new role just three months earlier. What further discussions were necessary? And what made these so vital and urgent that their import could not be revealed in a telegram? The summons came from the head of the KGB: that was either alarming, or a sign of the esteem in which Gordievsky was now held.

Brown tried to put himself into the mind of the KGB. 'If they had known, 100 per cent, they would not have behaved that way, and taken the risk of giving him time to escape. They would have bided their time, played it longer, fed him chickenfeed and waited. They could have brought him back in a more professional way. They could have faked his mother's death or something.'

The meeting ended without reaching a firm conclusion. Gordievsky agreed to meet again at the safe house the following evening, Friday, 17 May. In the meantime, he would book a ticket on the Sunday flight to Moscow, and give no hint that anything might be amiss.

Maksim Parshikov was driving out of the embassy car park to a lunch appointment when, to his surprise, Gordievsky 'threw himself across the path of the car and excitedly spoke through the open window: "I have been summoned to Moscow. Come after the lunch break, and we will talk."' Two hours later, Parshikov found the new *rezident* 'nervously pacing back and forth' in his office. Gordievsky explained that he had been called back to receive Chebrikov's final blessing. That was not abnormal in itself, but the way it had been done was strange: 'No one had sent any personal letters to alert me beforehand. But there is nothing for it: I will go for a few days, and find out what's going on. You will be deputy in my absence. Sit tight, and don't do anything until I return.'

Back at Century House a 'convocation of the chief and grandees' gathered in 'C''s office to discuss the situation: Chris Curwen, the newly appointed chief, John Deverell from MI5, the controller of the Sovbloc section and Brown, Gordievsky's case officer. There was no sense of alarm. Some in MI6 later claimed to have harboured serious concerns, but then spies, like everyone else, tend to claim 20-20 vision with hindsight. The case was on the cusp of triumph, and Veronica Price and Simon Brown, the officers closest to the case, could see no clear reason to pull the plug. Deverell reported that MI5 had picked up no indication the KGB had rumbled their spy. 'We took the decision that we really couldn't tell whether it was safe for him to go back,' said the Sovbloc controller. It was agreed that the final choice should be left to Gordievsky himself. He would not be forced to return to Moscow, but neither would he be encouraged to throw in the towel. 'This was a cop-out,' one MI6 officer insisted with hindsight. 'His life was at stake and we should have protected him.'

The key to successful gambling is intuition, the sixth sense that enables a player to predict events and read an opponent's mind. What, if anything, did the KGB know?

In reality, Moscow knew very little.

Colonel Viktor Budanov of K Directorate, the counter-intelligence branch, was by general agreement the 'most dangerous man in the KGB'. In the 1980s he had served in East Germany, where one of the KGB officers under his command was the young Vladimir Putin. Within K Directorate, his role was to investigate 'abnormal developments', maintain security within the various intelligence branches of the First Chief Directorate, eliminate corruption in the ranks, and root out spies. A dedicated communist, spare and desiccated, he had the face of a fox and the mind of a highly trained lawyer. His approach to his work was methodical, and fastidious. He saw himself as a detective, working to uphold the rules, not an agent of retribution. 'We always strictly followed the letter of the law, at least during my time with counter-intelligence and intelligence divisions of the KGB of the Soviet Union. I never had to launch an operation that could have broken the law effective in the territory of the Soviet Union.' He would catch the spy by evidence and deduction.

Budanov had been informed by his superiors that there was a senior mole in the KGB. He did not yet have a name, but he had a place. If the traitor was being run by British intelligence, then he might be someone inside the London *rezidentura*. Before leaving London, Leonid Nikitenko, an experienced counter-intelligence officer, had sent a series of critical reports questioning Gordievsky's reliability. Ames's tip-off, combined with Nikitenko's unverified suspicions, might have pointed to the new *rezident*. Gordievsky was a suspect, but he was not the only one. Nikitenko himself was another. Parshikov a third, though he was not yet recalled. And there were others. The reach of MI6 was global, and the mole could be anywhere. Budanov did not know for certain that Gordievsky was the traitor; but he certainly knew that once the man was back in Moscow his guilt or innocence could be ascertained without the risk of his absconding.

The next morning, Friday the 17th, brought a second urgent telegram from the Centre addressed to Gordievsky, and a measure of reassurance. 'As to your Moscow trip, please remember that you will have to speak about Britain and British problems, so prepare well for specific discussions, with plenty of facts.' That sounded more like a regular meeting, with the usual excessive demands for information. Gorbachev, in power for just three months, was taking a keen interest in Britain after his successful visit the previous year. Chebrikov was known to be a stickler for protocol. Perhaps there was nothing to worry about.

That evening, Gordievsky and his handlers gathered once more in the safe flat. Veronica Price provided smoked salmon and granary bread. The tape recorder was running.

Simon Brown laid out the situation. No intelligence had been picked up by MI6 to suggest that Oleg's recall was anything other than routine. But if Gordievsky wanted to defect now, he was free to do so, and he and his family would be protected and looked after for the rest of their lives. If he decided to carry on, Britain would be eternally in his debt. The case was at a crossroads. Quit now, and they would scoop up the enormous winnings already made, and head to the bank. But if he returned from Moscow having been personally blessed as *rezident* by the head of the KGB, then they would hit an even bigger jackpot.

Brown later reflected: 'If he decided not to go, he wasn't going to be dissuaded, and nor would we have tried. I think he realized we were genuine. I tried as much as possible to be impartial.'

The case officer ended with a declaration: 'If you think this looks bad, stop now. Ultimately it has to be your decision. But if you do go back and things go wrong, then we will execute the exfiltration plan.'

It is perfectly possible for two people to listen to the same words, and hear entirely different things. This was one of those moments. Brown thought he was offering Oleg a way out, while reminding him that this might waste a golden opportunity. Gordievsky believed he was being instructed to return to Moscow. He was hoping to hear his case officer say that he had done enough, and he should now stand down with honour. But Brown, as instructed, gave no such direction. The decision was Gordievsky's.

For long minutes, hunched and still, the Russian sat utterly silent, apparently lost in thought. Then he spoke: 'We're on the brink, to stop now would be a dereliction of duty and everything I've done. There is a risk, but it's a controlled risk, and one I'm prepared to take. I will go back.'

As one MI6 officer puts it: 'Oleg knew we wanted him to carry on and he bravely went along with this, in the absence of any clear signs of danger.'

Veronica Price, architect of the escape plan, was now all business.

Once more, she walked Gordievsky through all the arrangements for Operation PIMLICO. Yet again, Gordievsky studied the photographs of the rendezvous site. These had been taken in winter, when the large rock at the entrance to the lay-by stood out against the snow. He wondered if he would be able to recognize it with the trees in foliage.

Throughout Gordievsky's time in Britain, the escape plan had remained primed and ready. Every new MI6 officer deployed to Moscow was scrupulously briefed on the details, shown a photograph of the spy named PIMLICO (though never told his name), and coached on the procedures for the brush contact, pickup point and exfiltration: the complex pantomime of the escape and recognition signals. Before leaving Britain, the officers, and their spouses, were taken to a wood near Guildford, and practised climbing in and out of the boot of a car, in order to appreciate exactly what might be involved in rescuing this nameless spy and his family. At the start of a posting, each officer was instructed to drive to Russia from Britain, via Finland, in order to familiarize himself with the route, the rendezvous point and the border crossing. When Simon Brown drove through the border post for the first time in 1979 he counted seven magpies perched on the barrier post, and was immediately put in mind of the old nursery rhyme about counting magpies: 'Seven for a secret never to be told.'

Whenever Gordievsky was in Moscow, and for several weeks before he arrived and after he left, the MI6 team was instructed to monitor the signal site on Kutuzovsky Prospekt not just weekly, but every evening. A Tuesday night was the optimal time to fly the signal, since the exfiltration team would then be able to reach the rendezvous in just four days, the following Saturday afternoon. But in an emergency the team could go into action on any day: a signal on Friday, for example, would mean exfiltration would have to take place the following Thursday, due to the restricted opening times of the garage providing the number plates. One officer left a vivid account of the extra burden this placed on the British spies: 'Each night for about eighteen not wholly foreseeable weeks a year, we had to check the bread shop, near the combined bus and concert timetable, where we expected – and always dreaded – that PIMLICO would appear. The winters were the worst: too dark and foggy to check by any means other than walking; the snow scraped off the sidewalks piled so high that you could barely identify someone from more than thirty yards away. And how many times a week can a wife plead that she'd forgotten to buy any bread that day, and "Would you be so kind as to pop out in minus twenty-five degrees for the last, stale consignment of buns"?'

Preparing for Operation PIMLICO was one of the most important tasks of the MI6 station: a dedicated escape plan to save a spy who frequently wasn't there, in readiness for a time when he might be. Every MI6 officer kept on hand, in his flat, a pair of grey trousers, a green Harrods bag, and a stock of KitKats and Mars bars.

One additional refinement was added to the plan. If, after getting to Moscow, Gordievsky discovered he was in trouble, he could alert London: he should make a telephone call to Leila, on their London home number, and inquire how the children were doing at school. The phone was being tapped, and MI5 would be listening. If the warning call came through, MI6 would be told, and the Moscow team would be placed on full alert.

Finally Veronica Price handed him two small packets. One contained pills. 'These may help you to stay alert,' she said. The other was a small pouch of snuff from James J. Fox, tobacconist of St James's. If he sprinkled it over himself as he climbed into the car boot, it might put the sniffer dogs at the border off his scent and perhaps disguise the smell of any chemical the KGB might have sprayed on his clothes or shoes. A team of London-based MI6 officers would be waiting at a secluded rendezvous point on the Finnish side of the border to spirit Oleg to Britain. If that moment ever came, said Veronica, she would be there in person to greet him.

That evening, Gordievsky told Leila he was flying back to Moscow for 'top-level discussions' and would return to London in a few days. He seemed nervous and eager. 'He was going to be confirmed as *rezident*. I was excited too.' She noticed that his fingernails were bitten down to the quick.

Saturday, 18 May 1985 was a day of intense espionage, in three capitals.

In Washington, Aldrich Ames deposited $9,000 in cash in his bank account. He told Rosario the money was a loan from an old friend. The exhilaration of his treachery was starting to wear off, and reality was setting in: any one of the CIA's spies might get wind of his approach to the KGB, and expose him.

In Moscow, the KGB prepared for Gordievsky's arrival.

Viktor Budanov had the flat on Leninsky Prospekt thoroughly searched, but nothing incriminating was found, save a lot of questionable Western literature. The handsome edition of Shakespeare's sonnets attracted no special attention. The apartment was invisibly bugged, including the telephone, by the technicians of K Directorate. Cameras were concealed in the light fittings. On the way out, the KGB locksmith carefully locked the apartment's front door.

Budanov, meanwhile, was combing through Gordievsky's personnel file. Save for a divorce, on the surface his record was blemish-free: the son and brother of distinguished KGB officers, married to the daughter of a KGB general, a dedicated Party member who had worked his way to the top through diligence and flair. Yet a closer look would have revealed another side to Comrade Gordievsky. The KGB investigation dossier will never be released, so it is impossible to say exactly what the investigators knew, and when.

But there was plenty for Budanov to chew on: Gordievsky's close friendship at university with a Czech defector; his interest in Western culture, including banned literature; his ex-wife's assertion that he was a two-faced fraud; the way he had taken out and read every British file in the archive before his posting to London; and the suspicious speed with which his British visa had been issued.

Like the CIA before him, Budanov looked for patterns. The KGB had lost a number of valuable assets in Scandinavia: Haavik, Bergling and Treholt. Had Gordievsky, in Denmark, got wind of those agents, and informed Western intelligence? Then there was Michael Bettaney. Nikitenko could confirm that Gordievsky had been made aware of the Englishman's bizarre offer to spy for the KGB. The British had caught Bettaney with remarkable dispatch.

On inspection, Gordievsky's work record would also have thrown up some interesting traces. In the first few months of his posting to Britain, he had performed so badly there was talk of sending him home, but then the range of his contacts had markedly improved, as had the depth and quality of his intelligence reports. The decision by the British government to expel Igor Titov and Arkadi Guk in quick succession had seemed unremarkable at the time, but no longer. Budanov may also have learned of Nikitenko's earlier suspicions, notably the way that Gordievsky had produced reports during Gorbachev's visit that read as if they had been copied directly from Foreign Office briefings.

Deep in the files was another potential lead. Back in 1973, during his second posting to Denmark, Gordievsky had had direct contact with British intelligence. A known MI6 officer, Richard Bromhead, had approached him, and invited him to lunch. Gordievsky had gone through the correct procedure, informing his *rezident* and gaining formal permission before meeting the Englishman at a Copenhagen hotel. His reports from the time indicated that the contact had come to nothing. But had it? Had Bromhead recruited Gordievsky eleven years earlier?

The circumstantial evidence was certainly damaging, but not yet conclusively damning. Budanov would later boast in an interview with *Pravda* that Gordievsky was 'identified by me personally among hundreds of officers serving with the First Chief Directorate of the KGB'. But at this stage he still lacked hard proof: his punctilious legal mind would only be satisfied by catching the spy red-handed, or a complete confession, preferably in that order.

In London, the NOCTON team on the twelfth floor of Century House was excited, and nervous.

'There was anxiety, and a great weight of responsibility,' said Simon Brown. 'We might be acquiescing in him going back to his death. I thought it was the right decision, otherwise I would have tried to persuade him not to go along with it. It felt like a calculated risk, a controlled gamble. But then we'd been taking risks from the start. That is in the nature of it.'

Before leaving, Gordievsky had a task to complete for the KGB: a dead drop for an illegal agent, newly arrived in Britain and operating under the codename DARIO. A Line N officer in the *rezidentura* usually performed illegals operations in Britain, but this one was considered important enough for the new station chief to carry out in person.

In March, Moscow had sent £8,000 in untraceable £20 notes, with orders to transfer the money to DARIO.

The cash could simply have been handed over to the illegal on arrival, but the KGB never opted for simplicity when something more elaborate could be devised. Operation GROUND was an object lesson in over-complication.

First, the *rezidentura* technical department fashioned a hollow artificial brick, in which to conceal the money. DARIO would signal that he was ready for the pickup by leaving a blue chalk mark on a lamp post on the south side of Audley Square, near the American embassy. Gordievsky was instructed to deposit the money-brick, inside a plastic bag, on a verge between a path and a high fence on the north side of Coram's Fields, a park in Bloomsbury. DARIO would acknowledge safe receipt by leaving a lump of chewing gum on top of a concrete post near the Ballot Box pub in Sudbury Hill.

Gordievsky described the operational details to Brown, who passed them on to MI5.

On the evening of Saturday, 18 May, Gordievsky took his daughters to play in Coram's Fields. At 7.45 p.m., he dropped the brick and bag. The only people in the vicinity were a woman wheeling her baby in a pram, and a cyclist fiddling with his bike chain. The woman was one of MI5's top surveillance experts. Her pram contained a concealed camera. The cyclist was John Deverell, the head of K Section. A few minutes later a man appeared, walking fast. He stooped to scoop up the bag, pausing just long enough for the hidden camera to catch an image of his face. Deverell followed as he hurried northwards, but then he ducked into the Tube station at King's Cross. Deverell hurriedly chained up his bicycle and dashed down the escalator, but he was too late: the man had been swallowed up by the crowds. MI5 also failed to spot whoever stuck a plug of chewing gum on a concrete post outside a nondescript pub in north-west London. DARIO was well trained. Gordievsky sent a cable to Moscow reporting the successful completion of Operation GROUND. The mere fact that he had been allowed to carry out such a sensitive mission was, in itself, reason to think that he was still trusted.

There was still time to pull out. Instead, on Sunday afternoon, he kissed his wife and daughters. He knew he might never see any of them again. He tried not to show it, but he kissed Leila a little longer, and hugged Anna and Maria a little closer. Then he climbed into a taxi, and headed for Heathrow.

At 4 p.m. on 19 May, in an act of stupendous bravery, Oleg Gordievsky boarded the Aeroflot flight to Moscow.

# PART THREE

# 12. Cat and Mouse

In Moscow, Gordievsky checked the locks again, praying he might be mistaken. But no, the third lock, the flat-bolt he never used and had no key for, had been turned. The KGB was on to him. 'This is it,' he thought, as a trickle of fear-sweat ran down his back. 'I will soon be a dead man.' At a time of the KGB's choosing, he would be arrested, interrogated until the last secret had been wrung out of him, and then killed, the 'ultimate punishment', an executioner's bullet in the head and an unmarked grave.

But as his horrified thoughts raced and skidded, Gordievsky's training began to kick in. He knew how the KGB worked. If K Directorate had uncovered the full extent of his espionage, he would never have reached his own front door: he would have been arrested at the airport, and would now be in the basement cells of the Lubyanka. The KGB spied on everyone. Perhaps the break-in to his flat was just routine snooping. Clearly, if he was under suspicion, the investigators did not yet have sufficient evidence to nail him.

Paradoxically, given its lack of moral restraint, the KGB was an intensely legalistic organization. Gordievsky was now a KGB colonel. He could not simply be detained on suspicion of treachery. There were strict rules about torturing colonels. The shadow of the Purges of 1936–8, when so many innocents had perished, still lingered. In 1985 evidence needed to be gathered, a trial held, and sentence duly passed. The KGB investigator Viktor Budanov was doing exactly what MI5 had done with Michael Bettaney, and what every effective counter-intelligence agency does: watching the suspect, listening, waiting for him to make a mistake or contact his handler, before pouncing. The difference was this: Bettaney did not know he was under surveillance, and Gordievsky did. Or thought he did.

But he still needed to get into the flat. One of the other residents of the block was a KGB locksmith with a set of tools, and happy to help a neighbour and fellow officer who had lost his key. Once inside the apartment, Gordievsky discreetly checked for any other evidence of a KGB visit. Doubtless, the place was now bugged. If the technicians had planted cameras, they would be watching his behaviour carefully for suspicious signs, such as searching for bugs. From now on, he must assume that his every word was being heard, his every move watched, his every telephone call recorded. He must behave as if nothing was out of the ordinary. He must appear calm, casual and confident; everything, in fact, that he was not. The flat seemed tidy. In the medicine cupboard he found a box of wet-wipe tissues, sealed with a foil top. Someone had pushed a finger through the seal. 'It could have been Leila,' he told himself. 'The hole could have been there for years.' Or it could have been a KGB searcher, poking around for clues. In a box under his bed were books by authors that the Soviet censors would consider seditious: Orwell, Solzhenitsyn, Maximov. Lyubimov had once advised him that displaying these on open shelves was a risk. The box appeared undisturbed. Gordievsky cast an eye along the bookshelf, and noted that the OUP edition of Shakespeare's sonnets was still in place, apparently intact.

When he called his boss at home, Gordievsky thought Nikolai Gribin sounded odd. 'There was no warmth or enthusiasm in his voice.'

He barely slept that night, fears and questions swirling. 'Who had betrayed me? How much did the KGB know?'

The next morning he made his way to the Centre. He did not detect any surveillance, which by itself meant nothing. Gribin met him at the Third Department. His manner seemed almost normal, but not quite. 'You'd better start preparing,' Gribin remarked. 'The two big bosses are going to summon you for a discussion.' They spoke desultorily of what Chebrikov and Kryuchkov might be expecting to learn from the new London *rezident*. Gordievsky said he had brought extensive notes, as instructed: on Britain's economy, relations with the US, and developments in science and technology. Gribin nodded.

An hour later he was summoned to the office of Viktor Grushko, now deputy head of the First Chief Directorate. Usually so affable, the Ukrainian seemed tense, and 'relentlessly inquisitive'.

'What about Michael Bettaney?' he asked. 'It looks as though he was a real man after all, and seriously wanted to cooperate with us. He could have become a second Philby.'

'Of course he was real,' Gordievsky replied. 'And he would have been far better than Philby, *much* more valuable.' (A wild exaggeration.)

'But how did we make such a mistake?' Grushko pressed him. 'Was he genuine from the start?'

'I thought so. I can't imagine why comrade Guk didn't agree.'

A pause, before Grushko continued:

'Guk was expelled. But he hadn't done anything about Bettaney. He hadn't even made contact. So why did they sack [i.e. expel] him?'

Something in Grushko's expression made Gordievsky's stomach lurch.

'I think his mistake was to behave too much like a KGB man, always driving around in his Mercedes, boasting about the KGB and playing the general. The Brits didn't like that.'

The subject was dropped.

A few minutes later, the officer appointed to greet Gordievsky at the airport was summoned by Grushko and loudly upbraided for his inefficiency. 'What happened? You were supposed to meet Gordievsky and bring him home. Where were you?' The man stammered that he had gone to the wrong part of the airport. The scene seemed stage-managed. Had the KGB deliberately failed to send anyone to greet him, in order to follow his movements on arrival?

Gordievsky returned to his office, fiddled with his notes, and waited for the summons from the KGB boss that would indicate he was safe, or the tap on his shoulder from the counter-intelligence section that would mean the end. Neither came. He went home, to spend another evening of wondering, another night of fearful imagining. The next day was the same. Gordievsky might have been bored, had it not been for the dread inside. On the third day Gribin said he was leaving work early, and offered a lift in his car.

'What if a summons comes, and I've gone?' asked Gordievsky.

'There's no chance of them sending for you tonight,' replied Gribin.

As they crawled through the traffic in the rain, Gordievsky remarked, as casually as he could, that important work needed to be done in London.

'If there is nothing to detain me in Moscow, I would like to get back to deal with it. There is an important NATO meeting coming up, and the parliamentary year is ending. Some of my people need guidance with running contacts . . .'

Gribin waved his hand, a little too airily. 'Oh, nonsense! People are often away for months at a time. Nobody's indispensable.'

The next day was played out with the same mixture of inner turmoil and external charade; and the next. A strange deceptive dance was underway, with both Gordievsky and the KGB pretending to be in step, while waiting for the other to trip up. The strain was unremitting, and unshared. He could detect no surveillance, yet a sixth sense told him eyes and ears were everywhere, on every corner, in every shadow. Big Brother was watching him; or, more precisely, the man at the bus stop was watching him, the neighbour on the street, the babushka with her samovar in the lobby. Or perhaps not. As the days passed without incident, Gordievsky began to wonder if his fears were imaginary. Then came proof they were not.

In a corridor of the Third Department, he bumped into a colleague from Directorate S (responsible for the illegals network) called Boris Bocharov, who hailed him: 'Oleg, what is happening in Britain? Why have all the illegals been pulled out?' Oleg struggled to disguise his shock. The order to stand down the deep-cover spies could only mean one thing: the KGB knew it had been compromised in the UK and was urgently dismantling its illegals network. DARIO, the recipient of the cash-filled brick, had lasted less than a week as an undercover spy in London. He has never been identified.

A strange parcel was waiting on Gordievsky's desk, addressed for 'Mr Grushko's eyes only'. It had arrived in the diplomatic bag from the London *rezidentura*, and since Gordievsky was now the London *rezident*, the clerks had assumed he was the logical first recipient. Hands trembling, he shook the parcel and heard a dry rattle and the tinkle of a buckle from within. This was surely his own satchel, which he had left on his desk in London, containing a number of important papers. The KGB was gathering evidence. Keep calm, he told himself. Behave normally. He passed the parcel to Grushko's office, and returned to his desk.

'People say that when soldiers hear the artillery start, they go into a sort of panic. That is what happened to me. I could not even remember the escape plan. But then I thought: "The plan is unreliable anyway. I should forget about it, and just look forward to the bullet in the back of the neck." I was paralysed.'

That evening he placed a call to the Kensington flat. Leila answered. Recording devices in both London and Moscow clicked on.

'How are the children doing at school?' he asked, enunciating clearly.

Leila, detecting nothing unusual, replied that the girls were doing fine. They chatted for a few minutes and then Gordievsky rang off.

Gribin, all bogus bonhomie, invited Gordievsky to stay in his dacha for the weekend. Clearly he was under instructions to stick closely to his underling in case he let anything slip. Gordievsky politely declined the invitation, explaining that he had not yet visited his mother and sister, Marina, since his return to Moscow. Gribin was insistent they meet, and announced that he and his wife would visit Gordievsky at home. For several hours, sitting around a fake-marble-topped coffee table, they talked of life in London, how the girls were growing, and speaking English as a first language. His daughter Maria had even learned the Lord's Prayer in English. To a casual listener, Gordievsky might have been a proud father describing the pleasures of a foreign posting to an old and close colleague over a friendly cup of tea. In reality, a brutal, unacknowledged psychological fist-fight was taking place.

By Monday morning, 27 May, Gordievsky was ragged from sleeplessness and strain. Before leaving home, he swallowed one of Veronica Price's pep pills, a non-prescription caffeine-based booster often used by students trying to stay alert during all-night study sessions. By the time he reached the Centre, Gordievsky was feeling better, the edge taken off his exhaustion.

He had been seated at his desk only a few minutes when the phone rang, the dedicated line from the office of the department head.

Gordievsky felt a small surge of hope. Perhaps the long-awaited meeting with the KGB chiefs was at hand. 'Is it the bosses?' he asked when Viktor Grushko came on the line.

'Not yet,' said Grushko blandly. 'There are two people who want to discuss high-level agent penetration in Britain with you.' The meeting place, he added, would be outside the building. Grushko would be coming too. This was all highly unusual.

Apprehension rising, Gordievsky left his briefcase on the desk and headed down to the lobby. Grushko appeared a moment later, and ushered him into a car parked at the kerbside. The driver swung out of the rear gates, and after less than a mile stopped beside a high-walled compound used to house the visitors and guests of the First Chief Directorate. Chatting amiably, Grushko led Gordievsky to a small bungalow, a benign-looking building surrounded by a low picket fence and apparently unguarded. The day was already muggy and hot, but inside it felt cool and airy. Bedrooms led off a long central room, sparsely but elegantly furnished with new furniture. At the door stood two stewards, a man in his fifties and a younger woman. Both greeted Gordievsky with extreme deference, as if he were a visiting foreign dignitary.

When they were seated, Grushko produced a bottle. 'Look, I've got some Armenian brandy,' he said cheerfully, and poured out two glasses. They drank. The servants laid out plates and a platter of sandwiches, cheese, ham and red salmon caviar.

At this moment, two men entered the room. Gordievsky did not recognize either of them. The older, in a dark suit, had the lined and leathery face of a heavy drinker and smoker. The younger man was taller, with a long face and pointed features. Neither smiled. Grushko made no introductions, other than to say that the two men 'want to talk to you about how to run a very important agent in Britain'. Gordievsky's anxiety rose another notch: 'I thought: "This is nonsense. There is no important agent in Britain. There is some other reason for all this."' Grushko carried on blithely. 'Let's eat first,' he said, as if hosting a convivial working lunch. The male servant poured more brandy. The men drained their glasses, and Gordievsky followed suit. Another bottle appeared. Another round was poured, and drunk. The strangers made the smallest of small talk. The older man chain-smoked.

Then, with shocking suddenness, Gordievsky felt his reality lurch into a hallucinatory dream world, in which he seemed to be observing himself, only half-conscious, from far away, through a refracting, warping lens.

Gordievsky's brandy had been spiked with some sort of truth serum, probably a psychotropic drug manufactured by the KGB known as SP-117, a form of sodium thiopental containing a fast-acting barbiturate-anaesthetic, without smell, taste or colour, a chemical cocktail designed to erode the inhibitions and loosen the tongue. While the attendant had poured the other three men drinks from the first bottle, Gordievsky's glass had been surreptitiously filled from a different one.

The older man was General Sergei Golubev, the head of Directorate K, the KGB branch in charge of internal counter-intelligence. The other was Colonel Viktor Budanov, the KGB's top investigator.

They began to ask questions, and Gordievsky found himself answering them, only dimly aware of what he was saying. Yet some part of his brain was still self-aware and defensive. 'Stay alert,' he told himself. Gordievsky was now fighting for his life, in a miasma of sweat and fear, through a haze of drugged brandy. He had heard the KGB sometimes used drugs to extract secrets rather than physical torture, but was wholly unprepared for this sudden chemical assault on his nervous system.

Gordievsky could never explain exactly what happened over the next five hours. Yet he later recalled scraps, like the half-remembered shards of some shattering nightmare, assembled through a pharmacological fog: suddenly vivid scenes, snatches of words and phrases, the looming faces of his interrogators.

Of all people Kim Philby, the elderly British spy still living in Moscow exile, came to his aid. 'Never confess,' Philby had advised his KGB students. As the psychoactive drug took a grip, Philby's words came back: 'Like Philby, I was denying everything. Deny, deny, deny. It was instinctive.'

Budanov and Golubev seemed to want to talk about literature, Orwell and Solzhenitsyn. 'Why do you have all these anti-Soviet volumes?' they demanded. 'You deliberately used your diplomatic status to import things you knew were illegal.'

'No, no,' Gordievsky heard himself say. 'As a political-intelligence officer I needed to read books like that, they gave me essential background.'

Suddenly here at his side was Grushko, all smiles. 'Well done, Oleg! You're having an excellent conversation. Carry on! Tell them everything.' Then he was gone again, and the two interrogators were leaning over him once more.

'We know you are a British agent. We have irrefutable evidence of your guilt. Confess! *Priznaysya!*'

'No! I've nothing to confess.' Slumped and soaked in sweat, he felt himself slip in and out of consciousness.

Budanov, with the soothing voice one might use to a recalcitrant child: 'You confessed very well a few minutes ago. Now please go through it again, and confirm what you said. Confess again!'

'I've done nothing,' he pleaded, clinging to his lie like a drowning man.

At some point he recalled lurching to his feet, rushing to the bathroom and vomiting violently into the basin. The two attendants seemed to stare at him nastily from a corner of the room, all deference gone. He asked for water, and drank greedily, spilling it down his shirtfront. Grushko was there one moment, and gone the next. The interrogators seemed alternately consoling and accusatory. Sometimes gently admonishing him: 'How can you, a communist, be proud of your daughter being able to say the Lord's Prayer?' The next trying to trap him, reeling off the names of spies and defectors by their code-names. 'What about Vladimir Vetrov?' Budanov demanded, referring to the KGB officer executed a year earlier for collaborating with French intelligence. 'What do you think of him?'

'I don't know what you're talking about,' said Gordievsky.

Then Golubev played his trump card. 'We know who recruited you in Copenhagen,' he growled. 'It was Richard Bromhead.'

'Nonsense! That's not true.'

'But you wrote a report about him.'

'Of course, I met him once, and I wrote a report of the meeting. But he never focused on me particularly. He used to talk to everybody . . .'

Budanov tried another tack: 'We know that your telephone call to your wife was a signal to the British intelligence service. Just admit it.'

'No,' he insisted. 'That is not true.' Deny, deny, deny.

The two interrogators refused to let up. 'Confess!' they said. 'You've done it once already. Confess again!'

Sensing his willpower waning, Gordievsky summoned up a spark of defiance, and told the two KGB questioners they were no better than Stalin's secret police, extracting false confessions from the innocent.

Five hours after the first sip of brandy, the light in the room seemed to fade suddenly. Gordievsky felt a deathly fatigue engulf him, his head tipped back, and the spy slipped into the black.

Gordievsky awoke in a clean bed, with morning sunlight streaming through the window, dressed only in vest and underpants. His mouth was dust-dry, and his head ached with a savage intensity he had never experienced before. For a moment he had no idea where he was, or what had happened: but then slowly, in fragments, with growing horror, some of the events of the previous day began to filter back. A wave of nausea struck as he levered himself upright in bed. 'I'm finished,' he thought. 'They know everything.'

But set against that conclusion was one self-evident fact suggesting the KGB might not know quite everything: he was still alive.

The male attendant, obsequious once more, arrived with coffee. Gordievsky drank cup after cup. Head still throbbing, he climbed into his suit, hung neatly by the door. He was tying his shoes when the two interrogators reappeared. Gordievsky braced himself. Had the coffee been drugged? Was he about to descend back into that chemical fog? But no. His misted brain seemed clearer by the moment.

The two men looked at him quizzically.

'You've been very rude to us, Comrade Gordievsky,' said the younger man. 'You accused us of reviving the spirit of 1937, the Great Terror.'

Budanov's manner was sullenly resentful. Gordievsky's accusation that he was no better than a Stalinist butcher had offended his sense

of legal propriety. He considered himself an investigator, an upholder
of the rules, a seeker after truth, an inquirer not an inquisitor, dealing
in facts not falsehoods. 'What you said wasn't true, Comrade Gordievsky, and I'll prove it.'

Gordievsky was stunned. He had expected his interrogators to display the triumphant swagger of hunters who had trapped their quarry
and would now go in for the kill. Instead they seemed aggrieved and
frustrated. Through his befuddlement, Gordievsky experienced a sudden clarity, and with it a little surge of hope: the two interrogators, he
realized, had not got what they wanted.

'If I have been rude, I apologize,' he stammered. 'I don't remember.'

There was an awkward silence. Then Budanov spoke again. 'A car
is coming to take you home.'

An hour later, dishevelled and bemused, Gordievsky found himself outside the apartment on Leninsky Prospekt; once again he was
locked out, having left his keys on his office desk, so once again the
locksmith neighbour had to let him in. It was now mid-morning.
Gordievsky collapsed in a chair, more conscious than ever of being
watched, and tried to recall the events of the night before.

His interrogators seemed to know about Richard Bromhead. They
also seemed to have realized that his call to Leila was a tip-off to British intelligence. But they clearly did not, yet, know the full magnitude
of his espionage. He was certain that, despite their angry demands for
a confession of guilt, he had stuck to his denials. The truth serum had
not worked properly. Perhaps the single pep pill he had swallowed
that morning had been enough to counteract the full effects of the
sodium thiopental, a fortuitous side-effect that Veronica Price had
never envisaged when she gave them to him. Even so, any lingering
hope that he was still above suspicion had now evaporated. The KGB
was on his trail. The interrogators would be back.

As the after-effects of the drugs ebbed, the nausea was replaced by
a steadily rising panic. By the middle of the afternoon, he could take
the tension no longer. He called Grushko at the office, and tried to
sound normal.

'I'm sorry if I was rude to those fellows, but they were very
strange,' he said.

'No, no,' said Grushko. 'They're excellent chaps.'

Next he called Gribin, his department head.

'Something extraordinary has happened, and I'm very worried,' said Gordievsky. He described being taken to the little bungalow, meeting the two strangers, and then passing out. He pretended to remember nothing of the interrogation.

'Don't worry, old chap,' said Gribin, lying silkily. 'I'm sure it's nothing important.'

Back in London, Leila was beginning to wonder why her husband had not called again. Then came the explanation. On the morning of 28 May, an official from the embassy arrived unannounced at the flat. Oleg had been taken ill, he explained, a minor heart problem. 'It's nothing too serious, but you will have to go back to Moscow immediately with the girls. The embassy chauffeur will be coming to collect you. As the wife of the *rezident*, you will be flying First Class. Take only hand luggage, as you will all be returning to London very soon.' Leila packed hurriedly, while the official waited in the hall. 'I was worried for Oleg, of course. Why had he not called himself to reassure me that he was OK? That was odd.' Perhaps the heart problem was more serious than the official was letting on. The girls were excited to be going on a surprise holiday to Moscow. They were all waiting at the front door when the embassy car pulled up.

After an almost sleepless night, Gordievsky dressed, took two more pep pills, and headed for the Centre, pretending this was just another working day, knowing it might be his last. He had been seated at his desk just a few minutes when the phone rang and he was summoned, once more, to Grushko's office.

There, ranged behind a massive desk, a KGB tribunal was waiting. On either side of Grushko sat Gribin, stone-faced, and Golubev, the chief of K Directorate. Gordievsky was not invited to sit.

A remarkable piece of espionage theatre now ensued.

'We know very well you've been deceiving us for years,' declared Grushko, like a judge passing sentence. 'Yet we've decided that you may stay in the KGB. Your job in London is terminated. You'll have

to move to a non-operational department. You should take any holiday you are owed. The anti-Soviet literature in your home must be
delivered to the library of the First Chief Directorate. Remember, in
the next few days, and for ever, *no telephone calls to London.*'

Grushko paused, and then added in a tone that was almost conspiratorial: 'If only you knew what an unusual source we heard about
you from.'

Gordievsky was stunned, and momentarily speechless. The very
oddity of the scene seemed to call for some dramatic performance on
his part. Adopting an air of bafflement that was only half feigned, he
said: 'I'm terribly sorry about what happened on Monday. I think
there was something wrong with the drink, or with the food . . . I
was in a bad way. I felt awful.'

Golubev the interrogator seemed to wake up at this point, and
asserted, surreally: 'Nonsense. There was nothing wrong with the
food. It was delicious. The sandwiches with the salmon roe were excellent, and so were the ones with ham.'

Gordievsky wondered if he might be hallucinating again. Here he
was being accused of treason, and the chief investigator was defend-
ing the quality of KGB sandwiches.

Gordievsky addressed Grushko: 'Viktor Fyodorovich, as to what
you say about my deceiving you for a long time, I really don't know
what you're talking about. But whatever your decision, I'll accept it
like an officer and gentleman.'

And then, radiating injured innocence and soldierly honour, he
turned and marched out.

Back at his desk, Gordievsky felt his head spinning. He had been
accused of working for an enemy intelligence service. KGB officers
had been shot for doing far less. Yet they were keeping him on the
payroll and telling him to take a holiday.

A moment later, Gribin entered his office. During the weird scene
in Grushko's office, he had not uttered a word. Now he looked sadly
at Gordievsky.

'What can I say to you, old chap?'

Gordievsky sensed a trap.

'Kolya, I don't know exactly what this is all about, but I suspect

I've been overheard saying something critical about the Party leaders, and now there's a big intrigue going on.'

'If only it was that,' said Gribin. 'If only it was a question of some indiscretion recorded by the microphones. But I'm afraid it's far, far worse than that.'

Gordievsky adopted a look of fresh bewilderment: 'What can I say?'

Gribin looked at him hard: 'Try to take it all philosophically.' It sounded like a death sentence.

Back at the flat, Gordievsky tried to make sense out of what had taken place. The KGB did not go in for clemency. If they knew even a fraction of the truth, he was doomed. But the fact that he was not yet in the Lubyanka basement could only mean that the investigators still lacked decisive proof of his guilt. 'For the moment I could not tell what the KGB had or had not found out; but it was clear that I was, in effect, under sentence of death, even if that sentence was suspended pending further investigations.' The KGB was running a long game. 'They've decided to play with me,' he thought. 'Like a cat with a mouse.' Eventually the cat gets bored with the game, and either frightens the mouse to death, or kills it.

Viktor Budanov had a point to prove. Gordievsky believed Veronica's pep pill had saved him. But, in fact, it might have been his defiant remark in mid-interrogation, comparing the investigators to Stalin's killers, that explained why he was still alive. Budanov had been nettled by that suggestion. He wanted proof. He would let Gordievsky think he was safe but keep him under surveillance until he cracked, confessed or tried to contact MI6, at which point Budanov would swoop. There was no reason for haste, since there was nowhere for the man to run to. No suspected spy had ever escaped from the Soviet Union while under KGB surveillance. Normally, the Seventh Directorate would have used its own surveillance personnel to follow a suspect, but in this case it was agreed to use a team from the FCD. Grushko had been insistent: since this was his department's problem, his department would solve it, and the fewer people outside the directorate who knew what was happening the better (for Grushko's career, among other things). The surveillants could not be people Gordievsky might recognize, and so a surveillance team from the

Chinese department was seconded for the job: they were not told exactly who the suspect was, or what he was suspected of doing; they were merely told to follow him, report his movements, and not let him out of their sight. Once Gordievsky's family was back in Moscow, there was even less chance he might try to abscond. Leila and the two girls would be held as unconscious hostages. A second, day-time break-in was staged at Gordievsky's flat and his shoes and clothes were sprayed again with radioactive dust, invisible to the naked eye but that could be seen with special glasses and tracked using an adapted Geiger counter. Wherever he went, Gordievsky would now be leaving a radioactive trail.

Budanov was disappointed that the truth drug had not worked properly, though it seemed that Gordievsky had no memory of what had been said during the interrogation. The investigation was proceeding as planned.

In London, the NOCTON team was by now deeply alarmed. 'It was a very long two weeks,' said Simon Brown. MI5 reported that Gordievsky had called his wife from Moscow, but the conversation had not been fully recorded, and the eavesdroppers had failed to note whether Gordievsky had made the all-important reference to his daughters' schooling. Had Gordievsky signalled that he was in trouble? 'There was not enough evidence to draw a firm conclusion.' When the senior MI6 officer liaising with the MI5 eavesdropping team was asked how the alarm raised by Gordievsky could possibly have been missed, he offered a quotation from Horace: *Indignor quandoque bonus dormitat Homerus*, often translated as 'Even Homer nods.' The most highly trained experts can still be caught napping.

Then came the hammer blow. The Security Service reported that Leila Gordievsky and her two children were booked on a flight to Moscow. 'When I heard that, my blood turned cold,' recalled Brown. The sudden recall of Gordievsky's family could mean only one thing: he was in the hands of the KGB, and it was impossible to intervene. 'Stopping them travelling would have been a death sentence for him.'

An urgent cable was dispatched to the MI6 Moscow station with instructions to be on high alert for the activation of Operation

PIMLICO. But within the London team there was deep pessimism, and a widespread assumption that the case was over. 'Once the family was brought back to Moscow, it seemed certain that Gordievsky had already been arrested. Escape seemed exceptionally unlikely.' The spy had been found out. But how? What had gone wrong?

Brown recalled: 'It was an awful time. The whole NOCTON team was in shock. I stopped going into the office, because everyone was walking around like zombies.

'As time went on, I convinced myself we'd got it hopelessly wrong, and Oleg was dead.'

Of all the MI6 officers, Veronica Price was emotionally the closest to Gordievsky. Ever since 1978, protecting him had been her most pressing duty, a daily preoccupation. Her manner remained brisk and businesslike, but she was deeply concerned. 'I thought we had done all we could with the plans,' she said. 'Now it was up to the Moscow people to take over.' Price did not hold with hand-wringing. Her ward, her special responsibility, had been lost, but she was confident he would be found, and saved.

Price had been told that the mosquitoes could be fierce on the Russian–Finnish border in early summer. So she bought some mosquito repellent.

Viscount Roy Ascot, later to become an earl, was MI6 station chief in Moscow, and possibly the most blue-blooded spy Britain has ever produced. His great-grandfather had been Britain's Prime Minister. His paternal grandfather, after whom he was named, was a scholar and lawyer, one of the most brilliant of his generation, who was killed in the First World War. His father, the second earl, had been a colonial administrator. People tend to either fawn over aristocracy or dismiss it. Being posh is quite a good cover for spying, and Viscount Ascot was an exceptionally good spy. After joining MI6 in 1980, he learned Russian and was posted to Moscow in 1983 at the age of thirty-one.

Before leaving Britain, Ascot and his wife, Caroline, had been briefed on PIMLICO. Spouses of serving officers were treated as additional, unpaid adjuncts to the MI6 station, and entrusted with high-grade secrets when necessary. The daughter of an architect, Caroline, Viscountess Ascot, was scholarly, imaginative and unshakably discreet. The Ascots were shown a photograph of Gordievsky, and drilled on the plans for making the brush contact and exfiltration. Veronica Price personally described Gordievsky to them, without ever revealing his name, where he might be, or what he did. Everyone referred to him as PIMLICO. 'Veronica was straight out of John le Carré. In her face, manner and bearing, she described the man as quite simply a hero. She completely admired him and thought there was something unique about him. She told us: "PIMLICO is an absolutely remarkable person." '

Over the previous two years of their Moscow posting, the Ascots had travelled by car to and from Helsinki several times, to familiarize themselves with the escape route and the rendezvous point. Just five people in Moscow knew of the escape plan: Ascot and his wife; his deputy, Arthur Gee, an experienced officer who was soon due to take over from Ascot as head of station, and his wife, Rachel; and the MI6 secretary, Violet Chapman. All five lived in the expatriate compound on Kutuzovsky Prospekt. Every month, one of the officers headed off to the Central Market to look out for a man with a Safeway bag. Whenever Gordievsky had returned home on leave, and for several weeks before and after, one of them had checked the signal site outside the bread shop on the other side of the avenue, every evening, rain or shine. The rota was deliberately irregular. Violet could actually see the site from the stairwell outside her flat. When it was their turn, Ascot and Gee monitored the site on foot, or when driving home. 'We had to ring the changes quite imaginatively so a pattern didn't build up that could be spotted by those who we knew were watching us and listening. You can imagine the number of artificially cultivated and artificially broken conversations necessary to the timing of this manoeuvre.' The team kept a stock of chocolate on hand, ready to give the recognition signal. 'Large numbers of stale, uneaten chocolate bars used to accumulate in our coat pockets, handbags and glove compartments.' Ascot acquired a lifelong aversion to KitKats.

Ascot knew the escape plan by heart, and did not think much of it. 'It was a complex plan, and we knew how flimsy the whole thing was. It seemed so unlikely it would happen.' Operation PIMLICO provided for the exfiltration of up to four people, two adults and two little girls. Ascot had three children of his own under six years old: getting them to sit quietly on the back seat of his car was hard enough. How they would react to being stuffed in a trunk did not bear thinking about. Even if the spy managed to throw off the surveillance for long enough to reach the border, which seemed unlikely, the chances of the MI6 officers evading the KGB and reaching the rendezvous without being intercepted were, he calculated, almost exactly nil.

'The KGB was absolutely all over us.' The flats of the diplomats were bugged, as were their cars and telephones. The KGB occupied the floor above: 'Every evening you would see them carrying out their tapes in Red Cross boxes having sat upstairs listening to us.' They strongly suspected the presence of hidden cameras. Whenever Caroline went shopping, she had a three-car convoy of KGB cars in attendance. Ascot himself was sometimes accompanied by no fewer than five. The cars of suspected MI6 officers were sprayed with the same radioactive dust put on Gordievsky's shoes and clothes. If the dust turned up on the clothes of someone they suspected of spying for Britain, that would be proof of contact. In addition, the KGB sometimes sprayed the footwear of suspected spies with a chemical odour imperceptible to humans, but easily traced by sniffer dogs. Each MI6 officer kept two pairs of identical shoes, so that he could slip on an uncontaminated pair if necessary. Another pair was kept inside the station at the embassy, sealed in a plastic bag. These were known as 'doggy-proof' shoes. The only way husband and wife could communicate at home was by passing notes, in bed, under the sheets. Usually these were written in fountain pen with soluble ink on toilet paper that could then be flushed down the loo. 'We were under constant watch. There was almost no privacy, ever, anywhere. It was exhausting, and quite stressful.' Even in the embassy, the only place to be sure a conversation was not overheard was the 'safe-speech room' in the basement, 'a sort of Portakabin surrounded by noise within an empty space'.

The first sign of a change of tempo had come on Monday, 20 May, with a cable warning that PIMLICO was now on high alert. 'We sensed something was wrong,' wrote Ascot. 'We tried to resist this sense, but in contrast to the many weeks of the previous three years, we felt each night could be for real.' A fortnight later, following the departure of Leila and the girls, a message from London urged that the signal site be monitored with even greater vigilance. 'The telegrams said: "Nothing to worry about,"' recalled Ascot, 'so there was clearly something to worry about.'

Gordievsky was waiting at the airport when his wife and children arrived back in Moscow. So was the KGB. Leila was in good spirits. An official from Aeroflot had accompanied Leila and the girls onto the plane in London, and another had greeted them at Moscow and escorted them from the first-class cabin. They were whisked to the front of the passport queue. Being the wife of the *rezident* had its perks. She was relieved to see Gordievsky waiting at the arrivals barrier. 'Great. He's all right,' she thought.

One look at Gordievsky's haggard face and haunted expression changed that. 'He looked terrible, stressed and tense.' In the car, he explained: 'I'm in big trouble. We can't go back to England.'

Leila was astonished. 'Why on earth not?'

Gordievsky took a deep breath, and lied.

'There is a plot against me, and tongues are wagging, but I'm innocent. Some conspiracy against me is brewing behind the scenes. Because I have been appointed *rezident*, a good position with lots of applicants, certain people are out to get me. I'm in a very difficult position. Don't believe what you may hear about me. I'm not guilty of anything. I'm an honest officer, I'm a Soviet citizen, and I'm loyal.'

Leila had been brought up within the KGB, and was familiar with the malicious gossip and intrigue that gusted around the Centre. Her husband had risen far and fast within the organization, so of course his devious and jealous colleagues would be out to get him. After the initial shock, Leila's natural optimism resurfaced. 'I am practical, pragmatic, down to earth. Naïve, maybe sometimes. I just accepted it. I was his wife.' The plotting against him would subside, and his career would get back on track, as it had done before. He should try to relax, and wait for the crisis to blow over. Everything would turn out all right.

31 (top) Leila and her two daughters, soon after arriving in London in 1982, at a cafe outside the National Gallery on Trafalgar Square.

32 (bottom) The Soviet Embassy at Number 13, Kensington Palace Gardens. The KGB's London station, or *rezidentura* was located on the top floor, and was one of the most profoundly paranoid places on earth.

33 Gordievsky's daughters, Maria and Anna. The family had settled happily in London, and the girls grew up speaking fluent English and attending a Church of England school.

34 (top) Michael Bettaney, the MI5 officer who approached the KGB in London and offered to spy for the Soviets, using the codename 'Koba', one of Stalin's nicknames.

35 (bottom) Eliza Manningham-Buller, a key member of the secret MI5/MI6 task force nicknamed 'The Nadgers' set up to try to identify the spy inside the British Security Service. She would go on to become Director-General of MI5 in 2002.

36 (top) General Arkadi Guk (right), the KGB *rezident* with his wife and bodyguard. Gordievsky described him as 'a lump of a man, with a mediocre brain and a large reserve of low cunning'.

37 (bottom left) Guk's home at 42 Holland Park. On 3 April 1983, Bettaney pushed a package through the letterbox containing a top-secret MI5 document and an offer to divulge more intelligence to the KGB. Guk dismissed this as an MI5 'provocation'.

38 (bottom right) Century House, MI6's London headquarters until 1994; an unremarkable building but the most secret premises in London.

ČESKOSLOVENSKO

39 (top left) Michael Foot, Labour MP, future leader of the party, and a KGB contact codenamed BOOT.

40 (top right) Jack Jones, described by a British Prime Minister, Gordon Brown, as 'one of the world's greatest trade union leaders'. He was also a KGB agent.

41 (bottom) Oleg Gordievsky with Ron Brown, Labour MP for Edinburgh (centre), and Jan Sarkocy, a Czechoslovakian spy who also met Jeremy Corbyn, the future party leader. Gordievsky attempted to recruit Brown to the KGB on several occasions, but found his Scottish accent completely incomprehensible.

42 (top) The downing of KAL flight 007 in September 1983 by a Soviet fighter prompted widespread protests and brought Cold War tensions to new levels of intensity.

43 (bottom) Margaret Thatcher attends the funeral of the Soviet leader Yuri Andropov in Moscow on 14 February 1984. Britain's Prime Minister played a 'suitably solemn' role following a script written, in part, by Gordievsky.

44 (top) The future Soviet leader Mikhail Gorbachev meets Thatcher at Chequers in December 1984. She later described him as 'a man one could do business with'.

45 (bottom left) Mikhail Lyubimov, the Anglophile, tweed-wearing, pipe-smoking KGB officer nicknamed 'Smiley Mike' by MI5, which tried to recruit him as a double agent.

46 (bottom right) The Cabinet Secretary, Sir Robert Armstrong, responsible for overseeing the intelligence services. He decided not to inform Thatcher that Michael Foot, her Labour opponent, had once been a paid KGB contact.

47 **The signal site on Kutuzovsky Prospekt, as seen from the front of the Ukraine Hotel. The bread shop can be glimpsed through the trees on the left of the picture.**

**Safeway Shopping is... QUALITY AT LOW PRICES**

48 (top) St Basil's Cathedral in Red Square, where Oleg Gordievsky attempted to pass a message to MI6 requesting that the escape plan, Operation PIMLICO, be activated immediately. The 'brush contact' failed.

49 (bottom left) A Safeway supermarket bag, the escape signal flown by Gordievsky at 7.30pm on Tuesday, 16 July 1985, at the Kutuzovsky Prospekt signal site.

50 (bottom right) To indicate that the signal had been received, an MI6 officer would walk past Gordievsky, make brief eye contact, and eat a Mars bar.

**PICK-UP SITE**
(Km Post 836)

North

FOREST

Military access Track

Hiding place in ditch

TRACK

Picnic Area

Rock

TRACK

FOREST

TREES AND BUSHES

Km Post 836

**VYBORG**
16 miles

**LENINGRAD**
99.5 miles

FOREST

FOREST

51 (top) The rendezvous site south of Vyborg where the MI6 escape team would attempt to pick up Gordievsky, and take him across the Finnish border.

52 (bottom) One of the escape cars, a Saab driven by the MI6 officer Viscount Roy Ascot.

53 (top) The road to freedom: a reconnaissance photo taken on the escape route heading north.

54 (bottom) The MI6 exfiltration team pauses for a souvenir photograph
en route to Norway, a few hours after the fugitive spy crossed into Finland.
From left to right: Gordievsky, MI6 officers Simon Brown and Veronica
Price, and Danish intelligence officer Jens Eriksen.

55 (top) One of the three military border barriers at the
Vyborg frontier between Russia and Finland.

56 (bottom) The view through the car windscreen of one of the MI6 officers expelled from Russia
in the aftermath of PIMLICO. The British cars, accompanied by a convoy of KGB vehicles, are
passing the rendezvous point where Gordievsky had been picked up three months earlier.

57 (top) The arrest of Aldrich Ames on 21 February 1994, a decade after he began spying for the KGB. 'You're making a big mistake!' he insisted. 'You must have the wrong man!'

58 (bottom) Arrest photographs of Rosario and Rick Ames. She was released after completing her sentence but Ames, Prisoner 40087-083, is currently imprisoned at the Federal Correctional Institution in Terre Haute, Indiana.

59 (top) Gordievsky greets his family as they arrive by helicopter in the UK, following six years of enforced separation.

60 (bottom) The reunited Gordievskys pose for pictures in London, but the marriage swiftly disintegrated.

61 (top left) Gordievsky with Ronald Reagan in the Oval Office in 1987. 'We know you,' said Reagan. 'We appreciate what you've done for the West.'

62 (bottom left) In the 2007 Queen's birthday honours, Gordievsky was appointed Companion of the Most Distinguished Order of St Michael and St George (CMG), for 'services to the security of the United Kingdom'.

63 (bottom right) The CIA chief, Bill Casey, who flew to the UK for a meeting with Gordievsky a few weeks after his escape.

64 **The retired spy. Oleg Gordievsky still lives, under an assumed name, in the safe house on a nondescript suburban street in England that he moved into soon after his escape from Russia.**

Leila did not notice the KGB car tailing them back from the airport. Gordievsky did not point it out.

He did not tell his wife that he had been ordered to surrender his diplomatic passport, and that he was now on leave, indefinitely. Nor did he reveal that his box of Western books had been confiscated, and he had been instructed to sign a document admitting possession of anti-Soviet literature. For the hidden microphones, and Leila's benefit, he kept up the charade, loudly complaining of the injustice and the baseless plot against him: 'It's an outrage to treat a KGB colonel like this.' She did not know that his colleagues no longer met his eye, and that he sat at an empty desk all day. He did not tell her that their flat was bugged, nor that they were under twenty-four-hour KGB surveillance. He told her nothing, and she believed him.

But Leila could see her husband was under intense psychological strain. He looked terrible, with hollow, bloodshot eyes. He had begun drinking Cuban rum, anaesthetizing himself into sleep every night. He even took up smoking, trying to calm his raging nerves. In two weeks he had lost a stone. She made him see a doctor, a family friend, who was shocked at what she heard through the stethoscope. 'What's wrong with you?' the doctor demanded. 'Your heartbeat's irregular. You're frightened. What are you so scared of?' She prescribed sedatives. 'He was like a beast in a cage,' Leila recalled. 'My role was to calm him down. "I am your rock," I said. "Don't worry. Drink if you want to. I don't mind."'

At night, rum-sodden and panic-stricken, Gordievsky chewed over his limited options. Should he tell Leila? Should he try to make contact with MI6? Could he activate his escape plan, and attempt to flee? But if he did so, should he take Leila and the girls too? On the other hand, he had survived the drugged interrogation, and he had not been arrested. Was the KGB genuinely backing off? If they still did not have the evidence to haul him in, then an escape attempt would be foolish and premature. He would wake exhausted, no nearer a decision, head pounding and heart fluttering.

It was his mother who persuaded him that he needed to take a break. The many perks of KGB membership included access to various health spas and holiday centres. One of the most exclusive of these was the sanatorium at Semyonovskoye, about sixty miles south of Moscow, built by the Chairman of the KGB, Andropov, in 1971 for 'the rest and cure of leaders of the Communist Party and Soviet Government'. Still acting on the pretence that all was as it should be, the KGB authorities granted Gordievsky permission for a two-week stay at the spa.

Before leaving, he called his old friend Mikhail Lyubimov, the former KGB *rezident* in Copenhagen now trying to make a living as a writer. 'I'm back. It seems permanently,' said Gordievsky, in an 'uneven voice'. They agreed to meet. 'I was completely staggered by his appearance,' wrote Lyubimov. 'Pale as death, nervy, with fussy movements and confused speech. He explained his problems by saying that some books by Solzhenitsyn and other émigrés had been spotted in his London home, this had been reported by his enemies in the *rezidentura*, and in Moscow it had been blown up into a serious issue.' Lyubimov, ever buoyant, tried to cheer him up: 'Forget it, man. Why not leave the KGB and write a book? You were always keen on history and you have a good brain.' But Gordievsky seemed inconsolable, drinking glass after glass of vodka. ('A new phenomenon,' Lyubimov noted. 'I always thought he was one of the few people in the KGB who didn't drink.') Gordievsky said that he was going to a health farm to 'repair his nervous system', and then staggered off into the Moscow night. Lyubimov was worried enough about his old friend's state of mind to call Nikolai Gribin, with whom he remained on good terms. 'What's wrong with Oleg? He's not the man he was. What has happened to bring him to this point?' Gribin 'muttered something about the KGB resort in Semyonovskoye, where an unsuccessful *rezident* could be cured' and added: 'He will be there soon.' Then he rang off.

As the date of his departure approached, Gordievsky reached a decision. Before leaving for the sanatorium, he would fly the signal at the Central Market indicating that he needed to pass on a message. On his return, three Sundays later, he would go to the brush contact site at St Basil's. He had not yet decided what message to send to MI6. He only knew he needed to make contact, before he went mad.

Meanwhile, the KGB investigators watched and probed, combing the files, interviewing everyone Gordievsky had worked with, searching out the clues that would prove his guilt and seal his fate.

Budanov was prepared to be patient. He did not have to wait long.

On 13 June 1985, Aldrich Ames committed one of the most spectacular acts of treason in the history of espionage: he named no fewer than twenty-five individuals spying for Western intelligence against the Soviet Union.

In the month since his first payment from the KGB, Ames had arrived at a brutally logical conclusion. Any of the CIA's numerous spies inside Soviet intelligence could get wind of what he was up to, and expose him. The only way to protect himself, therefore, was to reveal to the KGB any and every asset who could betray him, so the Russians could sweep them up, and execute the lot: 'Then they would pose no threat.' Ames knew he was issuing a death warrant for every person he named but that, he reasoned, was the only way to ensure that he would be safe, and rich.

'All of the people on my June 13 list knew the risks they were taking. If one of them learned about me, he would have told the CIA and I would have been arrested and thrown in jail . . . It wasn't personal. It was simply how the game was played.'

That afternoon, Ames met Sergey Chuvakhin in Chadwick's, a popular Georgetown restaurant, and handed him seven pounds of intelligence reports in a shopping bag, a vast trove of secrets he had amassed over the preceding weeks that would later become known, unromantically, as 'the big dump': classified cables, internal memos and agent reports, an 'espionage encyclopaedia, a Who's Who that revealed the identity of every important Soviet intelligence officer working for the United States'. And one working for the UK, to whom he had almost certainly alluded on their first meeting. And he provided a name: the MI6 spy the CIA had pinpointed three months earlier and codenamed TICKLE was Oleg Gordievsky. Burton Gerber claimed Ames had discovered the name 'coincidentally'. Milton Bearden, soon to become Gerber's deputy in the Soviet section, alleges that Ames had done the detective work himself.

Ames's intelligence bonanza was swiftly passed on to Moscow, and an enormous mopping-up operation began. At least ten spies identified by Ames would perish at the hands of the KGB, and more than 100 intelligence operations were compromised. Soon after the big dump, Ames received a message, via Chuvakhin, from Moscow: 'Congratulations, you are now a millionaire!'

This was the evidence Budanov had been waiting for, proof positive of Gordievsky's treachery, straight from the CIA. Yet still the KGB did not pounce. Quite why has never been fully established, but a combination of complacency, inattention and over-ambition seems the most likely explanation: the counter-intelligence directorate was preoccupied with rounding up the two dozen spies identified by Ames; Budanov still wanted to catch Gordievsky *in flagrante* with MI6, to cause Britain maximum embarrassment.

And anyway, under constant surveillance, Gordievsky could not possibly escape.

On the morning of 15 June 1985, the third Saturday of the month, Gordievsky emerged from the flat, carrying a Safeway bag, and wearing the grey leather cap he had brought back from Denmark and a pair of grey trousers. He walked 500 metres to the nearest shopping precinct, careful not to look behind for his tail, the first rule of evading surveillance. The lessons he had learned at School 101, twenty-three years earlier, were coming back. He entered a chemist's, and casually looked through the window, while appearing to search the shelves. Then to a savings bank on a first floor, which afforded a view of the street from the stair; then a busy food shop. Next he walked up a long narrow alleyway between two blocks of flats, turned the corner, and ducked into one of the blocks, climbed two flights of the communal stairs, and surveyed the street. No sign of surveillance, which did not mean it was not there. He walked on, rode a bus for a few stops, got off again, hailed a taxi, took a roundabout route to the apartment block where his younger sister Marina lived with her new husband. He climbed up the main stairs, passed the door of her apartment without knocking and then went down the back staircase, sauntered into the Metro and headed east, changed trains, alighted, crossed the platform, and headed west again. Finally, he reached the Central Market.

At 11 a.m., he took up his post beneath the clock, and pretended to be waiting for a friend. The place was thronged with Saturday morning shoppers, but he saw no one carrying a Harrods bag. After ten minutes he left. Had MI6 spotted his signal indicating he needed to make a brush contact at St Basil's three Sundays hence? He would have to wait another two weeks before finding out if the signal had been picked up.

Two days later, Gordievsky found himself in a spacious room overlooking the Lopasnaya River, in one of Russia's most luxurious official resorts. But he also discovered he had a roommate, a man in his mid-sixties who followed him everywhere. Many of the guests were clearly spies and stool pigeons, planted to watch and listen. Gordievsky had packed the Safeway bag in his luggage. Partly this was out of superstition, an unwillingness to be parted from his escape signal, but it was also a practical measure: he might need to get to the signal site in a hurry. One afternoon he found his roommate inspecting the treasured shopping bag. 'Why have you got a foreign plastic bag?' the man asked. Gordievsky snatched it from his hand. 'You never know when there might be something in the shops worth buying,' he snapped.

The next day, jogging in the woods, he spotted surveillance officers lurking in the undergrowth, who hurriedly turned their backs and pretended to be urinating. Semyonovskoye sanatorium was, in reality, an extremely comfortable prison, where the KGB could keep a close eye on Gordievsky, and wait for him to drop his guard.

The sanatorium had a good library, containing a number of map books. Surreptitiously, he studied the border region between Russia and Finland, trying to memorize its contours. He ran every day, building up his fitness. The more he thought about the escape, the less impractical it seemed. Slowly, through the paralysing fog of fear, he was inching towards a decision: 'There's no alternative. If I don't get out I'm going to die. I'm as good as a dead man on holiday.'

## 13.   The Dry-Cleaner

Gordievsky returned from the Semyonovskoye sanatorium refreshed, apprehensive, but also, for the first time since his return to Russia, resolute: he must escape. He would first alert his British friends that the KGB was on to him by passing a written message at the brush contact site in St Basil's, then fly the PIMLICO escape signal, and flee. The chances of success were vanishingly small. If he had been betrayed by a mole inside MI6, then the KGB would be lying in wait. Perhaps they were expecting him to make exactly this move, and preparing a trap. But at least he would die trying, no longer ensnared in the hellish web of surveillance and suspicion, waiting for the investigators to move in.

Risking his own life was the easier part of that decision. What about his family? Should he try to take Leila and his daughters with him, or leave them behind? During a decade of spying he had made many hard choices, but nothing remotely as agonizing as this: a decision pitting loyalty against prudence, a choice between survival and love.

He found himself intently studying his daughters, now aged five and three, and trying to imprint them on his memory: Maria, now known as Masha, so active and bright, a natural athlete like her father; plump little Anna, fascinated by animals and insects. At night he heard the girls talking in their beds, in English: 'I don't like it here,' Masha told her younger sister. 'Let's go back to London.' Did he dare to take them with him when he tried to escape? Sensing her husband's inner turmoil but ignorant of its real cause, Leila told her mother-in-law that she feared Oleg was having some sort of crisis, triggered by trouble at work. Ever practical, Olga Gordievsky advised her to distract him with small projects, odd jobs around the house and fixing the car. Leila did not press him for explanations, or reprimand him for his drinking, though it alarmed her deeply. Her gentle solicitude, her instinctive sense that the man she loved was going through some private inner hell he could not share, made the looming decision all the harder to bear.

Including Leila and the girls in the escape plan would radically increase the probability of failure. Gordievsky was trained to evade surveillance, whereas they were not. A family of four was far more conspicuous than a single man travelling alone. However heavily sedated, his daughters might wake up in the car boots; they might cry, or suffocate; they would certainly be terrified. If they were caught, innocent Leila would be considered complicit in his espionage, and treated accordingly. She would be interrogated, imprisoned, or worse, and certainly ostracized. His daughters would be pariahs. He had chosen this path, and they had not. What right did he have to expose them to such danger? Gordievsky was a gruff father and a demanding husband, but a doting one. The thought of abandoning his family caused him such anguish that he found himself gasping, doubled up in physical pain. If he did manage to get away, perhaps the British could eventually persuade the Kremlin to release his family to the West. Spy swaps were part of the established Cold War arithmetic. But that could take years, if it ever happened at all. He might never see his family again. Perhaps it was better to take the chance and try to escape together, as a family, whatever the outcome, regardless of the danger. At least they would succeed, or fail, together.

But into that thought wriggled a worm of doubt. Spies trade in trust. Over a lifetime of espionage, Gordievsky had developed a knack for detecting loyalty, suspicion, conviction and faith. He loved Leila, but he did not entirely trust her; and, in one part of his heart, he feared her.

The daughter of a KGB general, steeped in propaganda from childhood, Leila was a loyal and unquestioning Soviet citizen. She had enjoyed her exposure to Western life, but never fully immersed herself in it as he had. Would she put her political responsibility above marital loyalty? In all totalitarian cultures, the individual is encouraged to consider the interests of society before personal welfare: from Nazi Germany to communist Russia to Cambodia under the Khmer Rouge and North Korea today, a willingness to betray those nearest to you for the greater good was the ultimate mark of committed citizenship and ideological purity. If he revealed himself to Leila, would she renounce him? If he told her of the escape plan and asked her to join him, would she refuse? Would she denounce him? It is a mark of how far ideology and politics had corrupted human instinct that Gordievsky could not be sure whether his wife's love was stronger than her communism, or vice versa. He attempted a litmus test.

One evening, on the balcony of their apartment, out of reach of the microphones, he attempted to sound out the loyalties of his own wife, in a classic KGB 'dangle'.

'You enjoyed London, didn't you?' he said.

Leila agreed that their life in Britain had been magical. She already missed the Middle Eastern cafés on Edgware Road, the parks and the music.

He pressed on: 'You know how you said you wanted the girls to go to English schools?'

Leila nodded, wondering where this was going.

'I have enemies here. We are never going to be sent back to London. But I have an idea: we could go to Azerbaijan, on holiday to visit your family there, and then slip over the mountains into Turkey. We could escape, and go back to Britain. What do you think, Leila? Shall we run away?'

There was a narrow, heavily militarized eleven-mile border between Azerbaijan and Turkey. Gordievsky, of course, had no real intention of trying to get across it. This was a test. 'I wanted to gauge her reaction to the idea.' If she agreed, it would be a sign that she was willing, at some level, to defy Soviet law and run away with him. He could then introduce her to the PIMLICO plan, and reveal the real reason he needed to escape. If she refused, and was interrogated after his disappearance, she might lay a false clue to his escape route and send the hunters haring to the Azeri–Turkish border.

Leila looked at him as if he was raving. 'Don't be idiotic.'

He quickly dropped the subject. And deep inside him a dreadful conviction took root. 'My heart was aching so much that I could hardly bear to think about it.' His wife's loyalty could not be relied upon, and he must continue to deceive her.

That conclusion may have been wrong. Many years later Leila was asked whether, if she had known of the escape plan, she would have told the authorities. 'I would have let him escape,' she said. 'Oleg had made his moral choice and for that, at least, he deserves respect. Whether considered bad or good, the man made his choice in life, he did it because he considered it necessary. Knowing the mortal danger he was in, my soul could not have carried the sin of sending him to his death.' She did not, however, say whether she would have been prepared to join him in the escape attempt. Still on the balcony, he told her again: 'There is a conspiracy, people are very jealous of my appointment as *rezident*. But if something happens to me, don't believe anything anyone tells you, I'm a proud officer, a Russian officer, and I did nothing wrong.' She believed him.

Gordievsky was not given to introspection, but at night, with Leila sleeping peacefully alongside him, he wondered what kind of person he had become, and whether his double life had 'drastically inhibited [his] emotional development'. He had never told Leila who he really was. 'Inevitably this meant that we had never come as close as we might have in normal circumstances: always I had withheld the central feature of my existence from her. Is intellectual deception of one's partner more or less cruel than physical deception? Who can say?'

But his mind was made up. 'My overriding priority was to save my skin.' He would attempt to escape alone. At least that way, he reflected, Leila would be able to tell the KGB, honestly, that she had known nothing.

The decision to leave his family behind was either an act of monumental self-sacrifice, or one of selfish self-preservation, or both. He told himself he had no choice, which is what we all tell ourselves when forced to make a terrible choice.

Leila's father, the elderly KGB general, had a dacha in Azerbaijan on the shores of Lake Caspian, where Leila had spent her childhood holidays. It was agreed that she and the girls would join her Azeri family there for a long summer holiday. Masha and Anna were excited at the prospect of spending a month at their grandfather's dacha, swimming and playing in the sun.

Gordievsky's parting from his family was an agony, not least because Leila and the girls had no inkling of its significance. The saddest moment of his life took place in a humdrum rush, in a bustling supermarket doorway. Leila was distracted, rushing to buy clothes and other last-minute supplies for the train journey south. The girls had already vanished into the shop before he could embrace them. Leila gave him a swift kiss on the cheek, and a cheerful wave. 'That could have been a bit more tender,' he said, half to himself, the reproach of a man about to commit an act of desertion that would end in indefinite separation at best, and at worst his own arrest, disgrace and execution. Leila did not hear him. She vanished into the crowded shop in pursuit of their daughters without a backward glance. And part of his heart broke.

On Sunday, 30 June, after three hours of dry-cleaning, exhausted and rigid with tension, Gordievsky arrived at Red Square, which was packed with Russian tourists.

At the Lenin Museum, he headed to the basement lavatories, locked himself in a cubicle, and took a Biro and envelope out of his pocket. Opening up the envelope, hands quivering, he wrote, in block capitals:

AM UNDER STRONG SUSPICION AND IN BAD TROUBLE, NEED EXFILTRATION SOONEST. BEWARE OF RADIOACTIVE DUST AND CAR ACCIDENTS

Gordievsky suspected he had been sprayed with spy dust. He knew the KGB had a nasty technique of ramming cars that might be involved in an espionage operation, to force the actors into the open.

As a last act of evasion, he entered GUM, the vast department store running along the side of Red Square, and moved swiftly from one department to another, up and down stairs, along one aisle and down another. Anyone observing him would have assumed he was an overexcited but hopelessly indecisive shopper; or that he was trying to shake off a tail.

It was only now that he spotted a flaw in the brush contact plan. He was supposed to be recognized by his cap, but men were not allowed to wear hats in St Basil's. (Religion was banned in communist Russia, but marks of religious respect, oddly, were still observed.)

That hiccup paled to irrelevance a moment later, when he entered the vast cathedral a few minutes before 3 p.m., headed for the stairs, and found the way barred by a large sign: UPPER FLOORS CLOSED FOR REDECORATION.

The staircase, on which he was supposed to pass his message, was sealed off with tape. Stumped, his shirt soaked with the sweat of adrenalin and fear, he looked around, pretending to admire the cathedral interior, wondering if the lady in grey might still be lingering. There was no one fitting that description among the crowds. People seemed to be staring back at him. On the Metro, he carefully tore the envelope to pieces inside his pocket, chewed each fragment to pulp, and spat them out, one by one. Close to despair, he arrived home three hours after he had left, wondering when, or even if, the KGB surveillance team had lost and found him again.

The brush contact had failed. The MI6 team in Moscow had not picked up the signal flown at the Central Market on 15 June.

The reason was simple. MI6 already knew that the top floor of St Basil's was closed for renovation. 'We had to work on the assumption that before flying the Central Market signal, he would have checked the St Basil's location and realized this was a non-starter.'

Many years later Ascot looked back on the missed signal as a blessing: 'Thank God. Red Square was a terrible place for a brush contact, stuffed with KGB. I tried to ban that meeting place. We would have been caught.'

The KGB waited and watched.

In London, MI6 tried to imagine what had happened to their spy, hope ebbing.

MI6 continued to monitor the escape signal site. Every evening at 7.30, Ascot, Gee or the secretary, Violet, headed to the pavement outside the bread shop, sometimes by car (the signal time had been chosen to coincide with a convenient moment when they would normally be returning from work), or on foot. They were buying far more bread than they could eat. It was agreed that if one of them spotted the man with the Safeway bag, he or she would call Ascot and leave a message about tennis: that would be the signal between them that PIMLICO was underway.

And on the other side of the city Gordievsky wondered how his life had come to this: an enemy of the people, about to desert his family, drinking too much and guzzling prescription sedatives, trying to summon up the courage to activate a plan that was probably suicidal. He paid another visit to Mikhail Lyubimov, who was struck once more by the change in Gordievsky's behaviour. 'He looked even worse than before, nervously pulled out of his briefcase an open bottle of export Stolichnaya, and poured himself a drink with a shaking hand.' Lyubimov, touched and saddened, invited him to come and stay at his dacha in Zvenigorod. 'We can chat and relax.' Lyubimov came away thinking that his old friend might be close to suicide.

Back at the flat, questions ricocheted around Gordievsky's exhausted, pickled mind. Why had the brush contact failed? Had MI6 abandoned him? Why was the KGB still toying with him? Who had betrayed him? Could he get away?

William Shakespeare has an answer for most of life's questions. In *Hamlet*, the greatest writer in the English language pondered the nature of fate and courage, when life's challenges seem overwhelming. 'When sorrows come, they come not single spies, but in battalions.'

On Monday, 15 July 1985, Oleg Gordievsky reached for his copy of Shakespeare's *Sonnets*.

He had left a pile of clothes to soak in the kitchen sink, and now deftly slipped the book under them and into the soapy water. After ten minutes the book was sodden.

The only place in the flat he could be sure of being unseen by any hidden cameras was a small box room off the corridor. Inside, by the light of a candle, Gordievsky peeled back the wet endpaper, extracted the thin cellophane sheet inside, and read the escape instructions: the train from 'Paris' to 'Marseilles', the distances, and Kilometre Post 836. If he flew the signal the next day, Tuesday, and it was acknowledged, he could be picked up on Saturday. The very familiarity of the instructions was reassuring. He dropped the soaked copy of the *Sonnets* down the rubbish chute. That night he slept with the instructions in a tin tray on the bedside table, under a newspaper, with a box of matches alongside. If the KGB raided in the night, he would probably have time to destroy the damning evidence.

The next morning, Tuesday, 16 July, he read the escape plan for the last time in the dark box room, and then watched the cellophane sheet flare up with an acrid flash. The telephone rang. It was Leila's father, Ali Aliyev, the retired KGB general. The old man knew that his son-in-law was having problems at work, and had been asked by his daughter to look after Gordievsky while the family was away at the dacha. 'Come for supper at seven tonight,' said Aliyev. 'I'll cook a nice chicken in garlic.'

Gordievsky thought fast. The invitation for 7 p.m. clashed with the escape signal timing. The KGB eavesdroppers listening in on the bugged telephone would be suspicious if he turned it down; and if he accepted, they would be expecting him at his father-in-law's home at Davitkova, on the city outskirts, at the very moment when, with luck, he would be free of surveillance at the signal site on Kutuzovsky Prospekt. 'Thank you,' he said, 'I'll look forward to it.'

Gordievsky wanted to look smart for his rendezvous with MI6, even if the KGB was waiting. He dressed in suit and tie, put on shoes that were probably radioactive, and picked up his Danish leather cap. Then he took the Safeway plastic bag, with its distinctive bright red logo, from the drawer of his desk.

The phone rang again. It was Mikhail Lyubimov, urging him to come and stay at his dacha for a few days the following week. Gordievsky, again thinking quickly, accepted the invitation. He would come on Monday, he said, catch the train arriving at Zvenigorod at 11.13, and travel in the last carriage. On the notebook by his telephone he wrote: 'Zvenigorod 11.13'. Here was another false trail for the KGB. By the following Monday, he would be either in prison, or in Britain, or dead.

At 4 p.m., he left the flat, and for the next two hours and forty-five minutes carried out the most rigorous dry-cleaning operation so far: shops, buses, Metro trains, in and out of apartment blocks, pausing to buy some provisions to bulk up the Safeway bag, methodically brushing off his tail and moving just fast and erratically enough to make it all but impossible to keep up with him, but not so swift as to make that obvious. Only the most skilled trackers could have followed him through this artificial maze. At 6.45 he emerged from Kievsky Metro station. He could not detect anyone following him. He had gone 'black', or so he fervently hoped.

Tuesday, 16 July, was a glorious summer evening, clear and bright. He walked slowly towards the bread shop, and killed time by buying a packet of cigarettes. Ten minutes early for the 7.30 signal, he took up the position on the edge of the pavement, outside the bread shop. The heavy traffic on the avenue included numerous official limousines, carrying home members of the Politburo and KGB officials. He lit a cigarette. The edge of the pavement suddenly seemed an idiotically conspicuous place to stand. There were too many people milling about, reading the notice boards and bus timetables, or pretending to. The place seemed suspiciously crowded. A black Volga, a favoured vehicle of the KGB, pulled out of the traffic and mounted the pavement. Two men in dark suits jumped out. He flinched. The driver seemed to be staring at him. The two men entered the shops and re-emerged with a strongbox: a routine cash collection. He tried to breathe again. He lit another cigarette.

It was Arthur Gee's turn to monitor the signal site, but the traffic was slow.

Roy and Caroline Ascot were going out to dinner with a Russian acquaintance, a former diplomat. As they pulled onto Kutuzovsky Prospekt in their Saab and headed east, a surveillance car slotted in behind as usual. It was easy to spot the KGB vehicles: the brushes of the KGB carwash, for reasons unknown, could not quite reach a spot in the middle of the bonnet, so each car had a telltale triangle of dirt on the front. Ascot glanced across the wide avenue, and froze: a man was standing in front of the bread shop, holding a carrier bag with a distinctive red pattern 'like a beacon among the drab Soviet shopping bags'. The time was 7.40. Gordievsky's instructions were to remain at the site no longer than half an hour.

'Arthur's missed him,' thought Ascot, swearing under his breath. 'My heart went straight to my toes.' He poked Caroline in the ribs, pointed across the road, and drew on the dashboard the shape of the letter P, for PIMLICO. Caroline resisted the urge to swivel in her seat and stare: 'I knew exactly what he meant.'

Ascot had ten seconds to decide if he should swing the car around, and perform the recognition signal. There were KitKat bars in the glove compartment. But the KGB was already tight on his bumper, and any change of behaviour would instantly arouse suspicion. The KGB would know, from bugging the telephone, that they were going out to dinner: suddenly performing a U-turn, jumping out of the car and eating a chocolate bar while walking down the pavement would lead the KGB straight to PIMLICO. 'I drove on, feeling as if the world had fallen in and I had done the wrong thing, for the right reasons.' The dinner party was hellish. Their host was an unreconstructed communist apparatchik, who spent the whole evening 'talking about how great Stalin was'. All Ascot could think about was the spy with the Safeway bag, waiting in vain for a man with a chocolate bar.

In fact, while Ascot had been driving east on Kutuzovsky, Arthur Gee passed the bread shop in his Ford Sierra, slowed a little, and scanned the pavement. There seemed to be lots of people milling around, noticeably more than usual for a weekday evening. And there, on the edge of the pavement, he was almost certain, was a man wearing a peaked cap, holding an unusual carrier bag. Whether it was adorned with a large red S, he could not be quite sure.

Gee drove on, adrenalin racing, performed a U-turn at the end of the avenue, entered the compound and parked in the car park. Trying to appear unhurried, he took the lift to the flat, dropped his briefcase, and called loudly to Rachel: 'I need to get some bread.'

She immediately knew what was happening. 'We had absolutely tons of bread already.'

Gee swiftly changed into his grey trousers, picked up the Harrods bag, and grabbed a Mars bar from the kitchen drawer. The time was 7.45.

The lift took an eternity. He walked to the underpass, fighting the urge to run. The man had gone. He wondered if he would recognize him anyway, since he had only ever seen one grainy photograph of PIMLICO standing outside a butcher's shop in a Danish suburb. 'I was so convinced I had seen someone,' Gee recalled. He queued at the bread shop, keeping one eye on the street, which seemed even more crowded than before. Gee decided to make another pass, one hand on the Harrods bag in his pocket. Then he saw him.

A man of medium height, holding a Safeway bag, standing in the shadow of a shop. He was smoking a cigarette. For a moment Gee hesitated. Veronica had never described PIMLICO as a smoker, and it was not the sort of detail she would have omitted.

Gordievsky spotted Gee at the same moment. On the point of leaving, he had drawn back from the pavement edge. It was not the man's grey trousers that first caught his attention, nor the way he drew a green bag from his pocket, took out a bar of chocolate and tore off the black wrapper. It was his demeanour. To Gordievsky's famished eyes, the man walking towards him, chewing, looked wholly, unmistakably British.

Their eyes locked for less than a second. Gordievsky heard himself 'silently shouting', at the top of his voice: 'Yes! It's me!' Gee took another, deliberate bite of the Mars bar, slowly looked away, and walked on.

Both men knew, with crystal conviction, that the signal had been flown, and it had been acknowledged.

General Aliyev was annoyed when Gordievsky finally arrived at his flat, sweaty and apologetic, nearly two hours late. His special garlic chicken was overcooked. Yet his son-in-law seemed strangely 'elated', and devoured the burned meal with gusto.

Roy and Caroline Ascot returned from their excruciating dinner party around midnight, accompanied by five surveillance cars. Beside the telephone was a note from the nanny, saying that Arthur Gee had called and left a message.

The German tennis player Boris Becker had won Wimbledon for the first time, at the age of seventeen. The message read: 'Would you like to come and watch a video of the tennis later in the week?'

Grinning, Ascot showed the message to his wife. Gee had picked up the escape signal after all. 'I was relieved that he'd seen it. But it was like the coming of Armageddon.'

PIMLICO had been triggered.

The KGB surveillance team had already lost Gordievsky twice. On both occasions he soon popped up again, but he knew that they would be more attentive from now on, if they were any good at their jobs. Which, oddly, they were not.

The decision to use a surveillance team from within the First Chief Directorate, rather than the experienced professionals of the Seventh Directorate, had been taken for reasons of internal office politics. Viktor Grushko did not want the story of Gordievsky's treachery gaining wider currency. The deputy head of the FCD was determined to solve this embarrassing, and possibly damaging, problem in-house. But the team allocated to follow the suspect were used to trailing around after Chinese diplomats, a boring job requiring little imagination or expertise. They did not know who Gordievsky was, or what he had done; they had no idea they were tailing a trained spy and dangerous traitor. And so, when Gordievsky lost them, they assumed it was accidental. Admitting to failure was not a career-enhancing move in the KGB. So instead of reporting that their quarry had vanished, twice, they were merely relieved when he turned up again, and kept their mouths shut.

On Wednesday morning, 17 July, Gordievsky left the flat, and headed, using every trick in the anti-surveillance manual, towards Leningrad Station on Komsomolskaya Square, to buy a train ticket. At the bank, he took out 300 roubles in cash, wondering if the KGB was monitoring his account. He trailed through a shopping centre, and then headed for a nearby housing estate, where a narrow footpath passed between high apartment buildings, arranged in two blocks of three. He turned the corner at the end of the path, and sprinted thirty yards, into the nearest staircase, and up one flight. From the landing window, he saw an overweight man in a jacket and tie burst into view at a fast jog, and then stop and look up and down the pathway, clearly flustered. Gordievsky shrank into the shadow. The man spoke into a lapel microphone, and ran on. A moment later a beige Lada, another vehicle favoured by the KGB, came rattling up the footpath at a brisk pace: the man and woman in the front seat were both speaking into a microphone. Gordievsky choked down a fresh squall of terror. He had known the KGB was tailing him. But this was the first time he had flushed them out into the open. They were probably following the classic KGB surveillance pattern: one car out front, two others nearby in support, two officers in each, linked by radio, one to follow on foot whenever necessary, the other by road. He waited five minutes, then descended, walked briskly to the main road, caught a bus, then a taxi, then a Metro train, and finally reached Leningrad Station. There, under a false name, he booked a fourth-class ticket for the 5.30 p.m. overnight train to Leningrad, leaving on Friday, 19 July, and paid in cash. When he got home, he spotted the beige Lada, parked a little way down the street.

Simon Brown was on leave. Gordievsky's case officer was still coming to terms with the grim situation: one of the most effective agents ever recruited by British intelligence had been sent back to Moscow, and apparently straight into a KGB ambush. Inevitably, questions were being asked: how had Gordievsky been found out? Was there another mole inside MI6? The familiar, leaden fear of internal betrayal gnawed once more. As for Gordievsky, he was now surely languishing in a KGB cell, if he was not already dead. The relationship between an agent and case officer is a peculiar amalgam of the professional and the emotional. A good agent-runner provides psychological stability, financial support, encouragement, hope and a strange species of love; but also the promise of protection. Recruiting and running a spy carries a duty of care, the implicit commitment that the spy's safety will always come first, and the risks will not outweigh the rewards. Every case officer feels the burden of that pact, and Brown, a sensitive man, felt it more acutely than most. He had done everything right, but the case had gone wrong, and the responsibility was ultimately his. Brown tried not to dwell on what Gordievsky must be going through, but could think of little else. Losing an agent can feel like an act of intimate betrayal.

P5, the head of the Soviet operational section, was in his Century House office at 7.30 a.m. on Wednesday, 17 July, when the phone rang. A double-encrypted telegram had been sent overnight by the Moscow office, hidden among the regular flow of Foreign Office wireless traffic. It read: 'PIMLICO FLOWN. HEAVY SV [Surveillance]. EXFILTRATION UNDERWAY. ADVISE.' P5 dashed downstairs to 'C'’s office. Christopher Curwen had been fully briefed on the case, but seemed momentarily fazed.

'Do we have a plan?' he said.

'Yes, sir,' said P5. 'We do.'

Brown was in the garden, trying to distract himself by reading a book in the sunshine, when the call came through from P5: 'I think it would be useful if you popped in.' The voice was neutral.

A minute after he put the telephone down, Brown clicked. 'It was Wednesday. That meant something had happened on the Tuesday. It must be the escape signal. Hope suddenly leaped.' Gordievsky might still be alive.

The train from Guildford to London seemed to take for ever. Brown arrived on the twelfth floor to find the team in a scramble of feverish preparations.

'Suddenly, it was non-stop,' Brown recalled.

After a series of hurried meetings, Martin Shawford flew to Copenhagen to alert the Danish intelligence service and coordinate plans, before flying on to Helsinki to prepare the groundwork, contact the MI6 station there, hire vehicles, and reconnoitre the rendezvous point near the Finnish border.

Assuming Gordievsky and his family were successfully smuggled across the Russian border, a second phase of the escape plan would begin, because reaching Finland would not mean that Gordievsky was safe. As Ascot observed: 'The Finns had an agreement with the Russians to turn over to the KGB any fugitives from the Soviet Union that fell into their hands.' The term 'Finlandization' had come to mean any small state cowed into submission by a much more powerful neighbour, retaining theoretical sovereignty but effectively in thrall. Finland was officially neutral in the Cold War, but the Soviet Union retained many of the conditions of control in the country: Finland could not join NATO, or allow Western troops or weapons systems on its territory; anti-Soviet books and films were banned. The Finns deeply resented the term Finlandization, but it accurately represented the situation of a country forced to look both ways, keen to be seen as Western but unwilling and unable to alienate the Soviet Union. The Finnish cartoonist Kari Suomalainen once described his country's uncomfortable position as 'The art of bowing to the East without mooning the West.'

A few months before, the MI6 Sovbloc controller had paid a visit to Finland to meet up with Seppo Tiitinen, the chief of the Finnish Security Intelligence Service (known as SUPO). The MI6 visitor posed a hypothetical question: 'If we had a defector that we needed to bring through Finland, I imagine that you would rather we got him out without involving you?' Tiitinen replied: 'Quite right. Tell us about it afterwards.'

The Finns did not want to know anything in advance, and if Gordievsky was intercepted in Finland by the Finnish authorities, he would almost certainly be returned to the Soviet Union. If he was not, and the Soviets discovered he was there, the Finns would come under intense pressure to seize him. And if they did not, the KGB was perfectly capable of sending a Spetsnaz special forces squad to do the job. The Soviets were known to monitor Finnish airports, so simply flying the family out of Helsinki was not an option.

Instead, two cars would transport the escapers 800 miles to the far north of Finland: one car would be driven by Veronica and Simon, the other by two Danish intelligence officers: Jens Eriksen, the officer known as 'Asterix' who had worked with Richard Bromhead a decade earlier, and his partner, Björn Larsen. South-east of Tromsø, at the remote Karigasniemi border crossing, they would enter Norway, and NATO territory. The team debated whether to deploy a military C-130 Hercules to pick them up, but instead decided that a scheduled flight from Norway would attract less attention. From Hammerfest, the northernmost city in Europe, inside the Arctic Circle, they would be flown to Oslo, and connect with another commercial flight to London. The Danes had been integral to the case from the start, and the two PET officers would drive the other escape car and accompany the exfiltration team all the way to Hammerfest. 'It was partly courtesy, but we also might need Danish cover to get into Norway: local Scandinavian help in case we hit some snag.'

Veronica Price retrieved the shoebox marked PIMLICO, containing four false Danish passports for Gordievsky and his family, in the name Hanssen. She packed mosquito repellent, clean clothes and a shaving kit. Gordievsky would certainly need a shave. She hoped the Moscow team would remember to bring additional spare tyres, in good condition, in case of punctures. That, too, was in the escape plan.

For nearly two months, the NOCTON team (now renamed PIMLICO) had waited, grim, inactive and anxious. Now they were excited, and suddenly operating at a hectic pace.

'There was a complete change of tone,' Brown recalled. 'It was a surreal feeling. This was something we'd been practising for years. Now we were all thinking: My God, we have to do this for real . . . Will it ever work?'

In the safe-speech room of the British embassy in Moscow, the personnel of the MI6 station gathered to rehearse an amateur dramatic performance.

The trip to Finland, in two diplomatic cars, required a cover story that the listening KGB would believe. To make matters even more complicated, a new British ambassador, Sir Bryan Cartledge, would be arriving in Moscow on Thursday, and a drinks reception was to be held in his honour at the embassy the following evening. The two cars needed to be at the rendezvous point south of the Finnish border at exactly 2.30 on Saturday, but KGB suspicions would immediately be raised if Ascot and Gee, nominally two of Cartledge's senior diplomats, were not present to toast his arrival. They needed a believable emergency. Before leaving home, Gee had passed his wife a note, written on loo paper: 'You're going to have to get ill', it read.

The story would go like this: Rachel Gee would suddenly develop an extremely painful back. Although a woman of considerable vitality, she had suffered from asthma and other health problems in the past, a fact that would be known to the all-hearing KGB. She and her husband would agree to drive to Helsinki to see a specialist. Caroline Ascot, her close friend, would suggest that she and her husband come too, and 'make a weekend of it'. The two couples would drive in two separate cars, and agree to do some shopping in the Finnish capital at the same time. The Ascots would bring along their fifteen-month-old daughter, Florence, leaving their two other children with the nanny. 'We decided it was better cover if we took the baby.' They would attend the ambassador's drinks party on Friday, set off immediately afterwards, drive overnight to Leningrad, and then on across the Finnish border to make the doctor's appointment in Helsinki late on Saturday afternoon.

The performance started that afternoon, with each of the four actors playing a part. In the flat, Rachel Gee started complaining, for the hidden KGB microphones, of a searing pain in her lower back. The complaints grew steadily louder as the day wore on. 'I gave it the works,' she said. Her friend Caroline Ascot came around to see if she could help. 'There was a great deal of groaning from me, and poor you-ing from Caroline,' Rachel recalled. Her imitation of a woman in pain was so convincing that her mother-in-law, who happened to be staying, became alarmed. Gee took his mother for a walk, away from the microphones, to explain that Rachel was not really unwell at all. 'Rachel was a wonderful actress,' said Ascot. Arthur Gee called a doctor friend in Finland, on the bugged telephone, to ask for medical advice. He also telephoned a number of airlines to inquire about flights, but rejected these on the grounds of cost. 'Why don't we come too?' said Caroline, when Rachel told her she was going to have to drive to Finland. The scene now shifted to the Ascots' flat. When Caroline told her husband that he would be driving overnight to Finland, with their baby, to take poor Rachel to a doctor and do some shopping, Ascot put on a show of extreme reluctance – 'Oh God, What a bore. Do we really have to? The new ambassador is arriving. I have lots of work to do . . .' – before finally agreeing to the trip.

Somewhere in the Russian archives is a set of eavesdropping transcripts that together add up to a small, strange melodrama, staged by MI6 entirely for the benefit of the KGB.

Ascot and Gee wondered whether the whole charade was a waste of time, and the escape plan doomed to failure. 'Something doesn't smell right,' said Gee. Both had spotted what seemed to be unusually high levels of activity at the signal site on Tuesday evening, with large numbers of cars and milling pedestrians, possibly indicating increased surveillance. If the KGB kept them under close watch all the way to the Finnish border, it would be impossible to slip into the lay-by and pick up the escapees without being spotted, and the operation would fail. Gee was not even sure that the man with the Safeway bag was really PIMLICO. Perhaps the KGB had uncovered the escape plan, and sent a stand-in while the real PIMLICO was already in custody.

Surveillance also seemed heavier around the embassy and

diplomatic compound. 'My fear was that it was all a set-up,' said Gee. The KGB might be putting on its own performance: drawing MI6 into a trap that would lead to exposure, expulsion of both officers for 'activities incompatible', and a violent diplomatic explosion that would embarrass the British government and set back Anglo-Soviet relations at a vital moment. 'Even if we were heading into an ambush, I knew we had no choice but to press ahead anyway. The escape signal had been flown.' Ascot still did not know PIMLICO's identity, but London now decided to reveal what he was: a KGB colonel, a long-term agent, and a person for whom it was worth taking this monumental risk. 'It was a boost to morale,' wrote Ascot.

The MI6 station kept Century House abreast of preparations, although the number of cables passing between London and Moscow was kept to a minimum, in case the KGB spotted the increased activity and became suspicious.

In London, too, there was disquiet within the tiny circle made aware that PIMLICO was underway. 'There were voices saying this is too dangerous. If it goes wrong, this will completely upend Anglo-Soviet relations.' Several senior Foreign Office mandarins were extremely dubious about the escape plan, including the Foreign Secretary, Geoffrey Howe, and Sir Bryan Cartledge, Britain's newly appointed ambassador to Moscow.

Cartledge was due to arrive in Russia on Thursday, 18 July. He had been briefed on PIMLICO two months before, but told it was highly unlikely to be implemented. Now he was informed that MI6 planned, two days after his arrival, to smuggle a senior KGB officer out of Russia in the boot of a car. The exfiltration had been meticulously planned and rehearsed, MI6 explained, but it was also highly risky, and, whether or not it succeeded, there would be major diplomatic repercussions. A career diplomat with an academic pedigree, Sir Bryan had already served in Sweden, Iran and Russia, before taking up his first ambassadorial post in Hungary. His appointment as ambassador in Moscow was the high point of his career. He was not happy. 'Poor Bryan Cartledge,' Ascot recalled. 'He had just started a new job and he had this smoking bomb handed to him . . . He saw his last ambassadorship going down the tubes.' If the escape team was caught in the act, there was a possibility that the new ambassador might even be declared *persona non grata* before he had presented his credentials to the Kremlin, a humiliating diplomatic first. The new ambassador registered a strong objection, and argued that the operation be called off.

A meeting was called at the Foreign Office. Present were the MI6 delegation, consisting of the Chief, Christopher Curwen, his deputy, P5, and the Sovbloc controller, and various Foreign Office officials, including Bryan Cartledge and David Goodall, the Deputy Under-Secretary. Goodall, according to one of those present, 'got into a frightful flap', and kept repeating: 'What are we going to do?' Cartledge was still fuming: 'It's an absolute bloody disaster. I've got to leave for Moscow tomorrow, and in a week I'll be back again.' The deputy head of MI6 was adamant: 'If we don't go ahead with this the Service will never be able to hold its head up again.'

At this moment, the meeting was joined by Sir Robert Armstrong, the Cabinet Secretary, who had crossed the road from Downing Street. He loudly plonked his leather briefcase on the table: 'I am quite certain that the Prime Minister will feel we have an overwhelming moral duty to save this man.' That ended the debate. Sir Bryan Cartledge looked 'like a man going to the gallows' as the Foreign Office contingent headed off to inform the Foreign Secretary, who had just returned from a memorial service. Howe remained hesitant. 'What if it goes wrong?' he asked. 'What if the car is searched?' To his credit, the new ambassador now spoke up: 'We'll say it's a gross provocation. We'll say they shoved the fellow in the boot of the car.'

'Hmmm,' said Howe, dubiously. 'I suppose so . . .'

Operation PIMLICO still required authorization at the highest level. Mrs Thatcher would have to give her personal stamp of approval for the escape plan. But the Prime Minister was in Scotland, with the Queen.

Gordievsky made his preparations, appearing to do the sorts of things a man who was about to escape would not do. Attention to detail helped keep the dread at bay. He was now on a mission, no longer mere quarry, but a professional again. His fate was now back in his own hands.

Much of Thursday was spent with his younger sister, Marina, and her family in their Moscow apartment. A sweet and unquestioning soul, Marina would have been utterly horrified to learn that her only surviving brother was a spy. He also visited his widowed mother. Olga was now seventy-eight, and frail. Throughout his childhood she had represented a spirit of quiet resistance, in contrast to his father's timidity and conformity. Of all his family members, Gordievsky's widowed mother was the one most likely to understand his actions. She would never have denounced him, but like any mother, she would also have tried to dissuade him from the path he was about to take. He embraced her and said nothing, knowing that, whether the escape succeeded or failed, he would probably never see her again. Once home, he called Marina to arrange another get-together early the following week: a false trail laid, maintaining the pretence that he would still be in Moscow beyond the weekend. The more arrangements and appointments he made for the future, the better his chances of diverting KGB attention from what he was about to do. It felt manipulative to be using his family and friends as diversions, but they would surely understand, even if they never forgave him.

Then Gordievsky did something exceptionally foolhardy, and very funny.

He called Mikhail Lyubimov and confirmed that he was coming to stay at his dacha the following week. Lyubimov said he was looking forward to it. His new girlfriend, Tanya, would be staying. They would meet Gordievsky at 11.13 on Monday at Zvenigorod Station.

Gordievsky switched subject.

'Have you read "Mr Harrington's Washing" by Somerset Maugham?'

This was one of the short stories in the Ashenden series. Lyubimov had introduced him to the works of Maugham a decade earlier, when both were in Denmark. Gordievsky knew that his friend owned the complete works.

'It's very good. You should read it again,' said Gordievsky. 'It's in Volume Four. Look it up, and you'll see what I mean.'

After some more chat, they rang off.

Gordievsky had just planted a coded farewell to Lyubimov, and an unambiguous literary clue: 'Mr Harrington's Washing' is the tale of a British spy who escapes from revolutionary Russia through Finland.

In Maugham's short story, set in 1917, the British secret agent Ashenden travels on the Trans-Siberian Express on a mission to Russia. During the journey, he shares a carriage with an American businessman, Mr Harrington, endearingly loquacious but infuriatingly fastidious. As revolution engulfs the country, Ashenden urges Harrington to take the train north before the revolutionary forces close in, but the American refuses to leave without his clothing, which has not been returned by the hotel laundry. Harrington is shot dead in the street by the revolutionary mob, having just retrieved his washing. The story is about risk – 'man has always found it easier to sacrifice his life than to learn the multiplication table' – and getting out in time. Ashenden takes the train, and escapes through Finland.

It was highly unlikely that the KGB's eavesdroppers were versed in early-twentieth-century English literature, and even more improbable that they would be able to decipher the clue in less than twenty-four hours. But it was a hostage to fortune nonetheless.

His rebellion had always been, in part, a cultural one, a defiance of the philistinism of Soviet Russia. Leaving an obscure hint from Western literature was his parting shot, a demonstration of his own cultural superiority. Whether or not he escaped, the KGB would comb through the transcripts of his telephone conversations afterwards, and realize they had been mocked: they would hate him all the more, but perhaps admire him too.

Her annual visit to stay with the Queen in Balmoral was one of the prime ministerial duties Margaret Thatcher liked least. The tradition by which prime ministers spend a few days every summer as a guest in the royal Scottish castle was, Thatcher declared, a 'tedious waste of time'. The Queen did not have much time for Thatcher either, mocking her middle-class accent as 'Royal Shakespeare received pronunciation from circa 1950'. Rather than stay in the main castle, Thatcher was housed in a bothy in the grounds, where she spent her days with her red boxes and a lone secretary, as far as possible from the royal world of bagpipes, wellingtons and corgis.

On Thursday, 18 July, Christopher Curwen made an urgent appointment to see Thatcher's Private Secretary, Charles Powell, at 10 Downing Street. There, in a private meeting room, 'C' explained that Operation PIMLICO had been activated, and now required the personal authorization of the Prime Minister.

Charles Powell was Thatcher's most trusted adviser, privy to the innermost secrets of her government. One of the handful of officials who had been briefed on the NOCTON case, he later described the escape attempt as 'the single most secret thing I ever heard about'. Neither he, nor Thatcher, had been told the real name of the man she called 'Mr Collins'. Powell was sure she would give her approval, but the escape plan was 'far too sensitive for the telephone'. She would have to give clearance in person, and only Powell could ask her. 'I couldn't tell anyone in Number 10 what I was doing.'

That afternoon, Powell left Downing Street without saying where he was going, caught a train to Heathrow, and boarded a flight, which he had booked himself, to Aberdeen. ('It was so secret I later had a problem getting my expenses reimbursed.') There, he hired a rental car, and headed west, in the pouring rain. Balmoral Castle, the royal family's summer residence since 1852, is a vast granite pile, adorned with turrets and set in 50,000 acres of Scottish moors; on a gloomy and damp Scottish evening, it was quite hard to find. The clock was running, and Powell was exhausted and anxious by the time he eventually drew up at the massive gates to the castle in his small hire car.

The equerry in the gatehouse was on the telephone, conducting a high-level discussion on a matter of considerable royal concern: the Queen wanted to borrow the Queen Mother's videotape recorder in order to watch *Dad's Army*. This was proving hard to arrange.

Powell tried to interrupt the conversation, but was silenced with a cold look. Cold looks are taught at equerry school.

For the next twenty minutes, while Powell tapped his foot and looked at his watch, the equerry continued to discuss the royal videotape recorder, its precise whereabouts and the need to move it from one room in the castle to another. Finally the problem was solved. Powell explained who he was and that he needed to see the Prime Minister urgently. After another long delay, he was ushered into the presence of the Queen's Private Secretary, Sir Philip Moore, later Baron Moore of Wolvercote, GCB, GCVO, CMG, QSO and PC, and chief keeper of the Queen's secrets. Moore was a courtier of ingrained caution and immoveable protocol. On retirement, he would become a Permanent Lord-in-Waiting. He did not like to be hurried.

'Why do you want to see Mrs Thatcher?' he asked.

'I can't tell you,' said Powell. 'It's secret.'

Moore's sense of propriety was piqued. 'We can't have people wandering around the Balmoral estate without knowing why they are here.'

'Well, you're going to have to, because I need to see the Prime Minister. Now.'

'Why do you need to see her?'

'I can't tell you that.'

'You have to tell me.'

'I don't.'

'Whatever you tell the Prime Minister she will tell the Queen and Her Majesty will tell me. So please tell me your business.'

'No. If the Prime Minister wishes to tell the Queen and the Queen wishes to tell you, that is for them to decide. But I am not able to tell you.'

The royal courtier fumed. If you are a Private Secretary, there is nothing more galling than another Private Secretary being more private than you are.

Powell got to his feet. 'I am going to go and look for the Prime Minister.'

With the injured air of a man who has witnessed an intolerable display of bad manners, Moore summoned a footman who led Powell out of a side door, into the damp garden, and down a path to what appeared to be a 'sort of garden shed'.

Margaret Thatcher was propped up in bed, surrounded by papers. 'She was *very* surprised to see me.'

It took Powell just a few minutes to explain the situation, and an even shorter time for Thatcher to authorize Operation PIMLICO. The unnamed spy had played a vital part in her premiership, at great personal risk. 'We have to honour our promises to our agent,' she said.

Powell later commented: 'She admired him hugely even though it cut against some of her principles – she hated traitors. But he was different. In a different league. She had huge respect for those who stood up to the regime.'

'Mr Collins', whoever he was, had done the West a great service, and now that he was in danger, Britain must do everything in its power to save him, whatever the diplomatic repercussions.

What Mrs Thatcher did not know – and never discovered – was that she had authorized an operation that was already underway. Had she declined to approve the escape attempt, there was no way to inform Gordievsky that there would be no one waiting for him at the rendezvous. He would have been abandoned.

PIMLICO was unstoppable.

## 14.  Friday, 19 July

As the hour of departure approached, Roy Ascot's mounting excitement competed with a rising dread. He had spent much of the night praying. 'I was pretty certain that, however we prepared ourselves, only prayer would see us through the operation.' MI6 had never attempted to smuggle anyone across the Russian border before. If PIMLICO arrived at the rendezvous alone it would be hard enough, but if, as expected, he brought his wife and two children, the chance of success was infinitesimal. 'I thought: this man will be shot. The plan could not work. We all knew how flimsy the whole thing was. We were fulfilling a promise, and we had to do it, even though we were walking into something that wasn't going to work. I put the chances at 20 per cent or lower.'

A telegram arrived from Century House. The bosses in London 'detected signs of wobbliness' on the part of the embassy management, and had composed a message 'to stiffen the sinews'. It read: 'The Prime Minister has personally approved this operation and expressed her complete confidence in your ability to carry it out. We all here join in standing 100% behind you and are confident you will succeed.' Ascot showed it to Cartledge, to demonstrate the 'continuing top-level clearance in London'.

Then another potentially lethal snag emerged. In order to leave the Soviet Union by car, foreign diplomats needed formal permission and special number plates. The official garage doing the plating closed at midday on Fridays. Gee's Ford was re-plated without a hitch, but Ascot's Saab was sent back with the message: 'Sorry. We can't plate this because your wife hasn't got a driving licence.' Caroline's handbag containing her Soviet licence had been stolen the month before, and, to obtain a new one, she had sent in her British licence to the consular authorities. This had not yet been returned and a new Soviet licence issued. Diplomats were not permitted to drive alone; without a co-driver with a valid Soviet licence Ascot could not get the official plates; without these plates they could not leave the Soviet Union. PIMLICO was about to founder on a tiny but immoveable rock of Russian bureaucracy. At 11 a.m., an hour before the traffic authorities shut for the weekend, Ascot was still racking his brains for a solution, when a package arrived from the Soviet Foreign Ministry containing Caroline's British licence and a new Soviet one. 'We had an hour to get our car plated in time. I couldn't believe it, this incredible stroke of luck.' But, on second thoughts, Ascot wondered if the unexpected and timely return of the licence really was serendipity, or part of the KGB set-up: 'We had cleared the last obstacle to travel, but it all looked very pat.'

### 11 a.m. Leninsky Prospekt, Moscow

Gordievsky spent the morning cleaning the flat from top to bottom. In a very short time, the KGB would tear it apart, rip up the floorboards, demolish his library page by page and dismantle every stick of furniture. But some odd pride made him determined that his home should look 'shipshape' when they arrived to destroy it: he did the washing up, arranged the crockery, washed his clothes in the sink and hung them out to dry. On the counter, he left money for Leila, 220 roubles, enough to cover household expenses for a few days. It was a small gesture . . . but of what? His continuing care? Apology? Regret? The money would probably never reach her. The KGB would surely confiscate or steal it. Yet, like the meticulous cleaning of the flat, he was sending a message that said more about him, perhaps, than he realized: Gordievsky wanted to be thought of as a good man; he wanted the KGB, which he had deceived so comprehensively, to respect him. He left no note of self-justification, no explanation for having betrayed the Soviet Union. If they caught him, the KGB would extract all that, and this time with nothing so gentle as a truth drug. He left a spotless flat, and a lot of clean laundry. Like Mr Harrington, he would not flee without doing his washing.

Then Gordievsky prepared to throw off the KGB surveillance

squad for a fourth and final time. The timing was crucial. If he left the flat and evaded his watchers too early, they might finally spot what was afoot, and raise the alarm. But if he left it too late, he might not be able to complete his dry-cleaning, and would reach the railway station with the KGB still on his tail.

He did his packing, meagre enough, in an ordinary plastic bag: a light jacket, his Danish leather cap, sedatives and a small, Soviet-printed road atlas that covered the Finnish border region, doubtless inaccurate since the area was militarily sensitive.

He forgot to pack the snuff.

### 11 a.m. Vaalimaa Motel, Finland

The Finnish end of Operation PIMLICO was running according to schedule. The team assembled at a small motel, about ten miles from the border. Veronica Price and Simon Brown, travelling under false passports, had arrived in Helsinki the previous evening, and spent the night in an airport hotel. Martin Shawford, the young MI6 officer in charge of coordinating matters in Finland, was already waiting when they drew up in the motel car park, followed a few minutes later by the two Danish PET officers, Eriksen and Larsen. Coincidentally, the cars had all been booked through the same rental company at the airport, and to Shawford's horror three identical cars were now parked in the car park: three bright-red, brand-new Volvos, with sequential number plates. 'We looked like a convention. It could hardly have been more conspicuous.' At least one car would have to be changed before the next day.

The rendezvous point on the Finnish side of the border had been selected when Veronica Price first formulated the plan. Five miles north-west of the border crossing, a forestry track turned off to the right and led into the woods. About a mile along it on the left was a small clearing, where the logging lorries turned, surrounded by trees and invisible from the main road: the spot was close enough to the frontier to ensure Oleg and his family would not remain cramped in the car boots a moment longer than necessary, but far enough away to be well clear of the border security zone.

The combined MI6–PET team thoroughly reconnoitred the area around the rendezvous point. The Finnish pine forest stretched away unbroken on every side. There were no houses in sight. Here they would meet the getaway team, swiftly move the escapers from the MI6 cars into the Finnish hire cars, and then split up into two groups. The Finnish team would reassemble at a second rendezvous point in the woods about ten miles further on, where they could check the escapers' health, change their clothing and speak freely without fear of being overheard through the bugged diplomatic cars. Meanwhile, the Moscow team would take the road towards Helsinki, and wait at the first petrol station. The escape team would begin the long journey north to the Finnish–Norwegian border: Leila and one child would travel in the Danes' car, Gordievsky and the other girl with Brown and Price. Shawford would rejoin the MI6 Moscow team at the petrol station, debrief Ascot and Gee, and make an important call from the public telephone kiosk in the forecourt.

The call would be automatically routed through to the Sovbloc controller, waiting with the P5 team in Century House. The petrol station telephone might be monitored by the KGB or Finnish intelligence, so the outcome of PIMLICO would have to be reported in veiled language. If Gordievsky and his family were out and safe, Shawford would say that his fishing holiday had been successful. If, however, the escape had failed, he would report that he had caught nothing.

Having thoroughly checked the rendezvous area, the team drove back to Helsinki, swapped one of their fleet of bright-red Volvos for another model, and dispersed to separate hotels.

### 12 p.m. Kutuzovsky Prospekt, Moscow

In the diplomatic flats, Caroline Ascot and Rachel Gee did the packing. They could take no personal clothing, since all the space in the car boots was needed to accommodate PIMLICO and his family. Instead, they assembled a number of empty holdalls that looked realistically bulky when stuffed with cushions, but could be folded flat when emptied. The escape kit, first assembled seven years earlier, was retrieved from the British embassy safe: water bottles and children's plastic 'sippy cups' (which were easier for the girls to drink from in the cramped boots), two large empty bottles to urinate into and four 'space blankets' made of heat-reflective thin plastic sheeting, of the sort to reduce heat loss in cases of hypothermia or exertion. Heat sensors and infrared cameras at the Soviet border were believed to be capable of picking up a concealed body, but no one in MI6 was sure how the technology worked, or whether it really existed. The escapers would have to strip to their underwear before pulling the blankets over themselves; it would be hot inside the boots, and the lower their body temperatures, the less the likelihood of attracting the sniffer dogs.

Caroline put together a picnic – hamper, rugs, sandwiches and potato crisps – which they could spread out at the lay-by as a form of camouflage. The escapers might take time to emerge from hiding. They might be late reaching the rendezvous. There could be others in the lay-by, who might become suspicious if four foreigners simply appeared on the scene with no obvious purpose. The two couples needed to have an innocent explanation for turning off the road, and an English picnic would provide perfect cover. Caroline also prepared a travel bag for Florence, with clothes, baby food and spare nappies. Rachel Gee took her two small children and mother-in-law to the park. Every so often, she would stop and clutch her back as if in pain. Her performance was so convincing that Gee's mother asked him: 'Are you sure she's not ill? She doesn't look a bit well to me, you know.'

### 3 p.m. British embassy, Moscow

The assistant naval attaché, one of several military experts at the embassy, arrived back in Moscow, following a trip to Finland, having inadvertently thrown a very large spanner in the works: he reported that he had been challenged by the KGB border guards at Vyborg, both on leaving and again on re-entering the Soviet Union. Against all the diplomatic rules, the guards had demanded to search his car, and the attaché had not objected. 'The stupid man had let them put a dog through it,' fumed Ascot. If the border authorities were flouting convention and using sniffer dogs to search British diplomatic vehicles, the escape plan was sunk. Four hot people crammed into the boots of two cars give off a powerful scent. The attaché had unknowingly set a dangerous precedent, at the worst possible moment.

Ascot hurriedly forged a formal diplomatic note of protest from the ambassador to the Ministry of Foreign Affairs complaining that the attaché's car had been searched and insisting that British diplomatic immunity had been violated. The note was not sent, but Ascot took a copy indicating that it had, along with a translation, into Russian, of the relevant clauses of the Vienna Convention. If the KGB tried to search the cars at the border, he would brandish the fake letter. But there was no guarantee this would work: if the border guards wanted to see what was inside the car boots, no amount of official protest would stop them.

There was one final bit of paperwork. Violet, the MI6 secretary, typed up a copy of the escape instructions on soluble paper. If the KGB arrested them, the *aide-mémoire* 'could be dissolved in water or, most uncomfortably, in one's mouth'. In an extreme emergency, the MI6 team could eat Operation PIMLICO.

### 4 p.m. Leninsky Prospekt, Moscow

Gordievsky dressed in a thin green sweater, faded green corduroy trousers and old brown shoes, selected from the back of the cupboard in the hope that they might have escaped contamination by radioactive dust or the other chemical, used to alert sniffer dogs. The outfit was probably sufficiently similar to his green tracksuit for the concierge (and KGB watchers) to assume he was going for a run. He locked the front door of his flat. The KGB would be opening it again in a few hours. 'I was closing it not only on my home and my possessions, but on my family and my life.' He took no souvenir photographs with him or other emotional mementoes. He made no farewell calls to his mother or sister, although he knew he would probably never see either of them again. He left no note of explanation or justification. He did nothing that might seem out of the ordinary, on the most extraordinary day of his life. The concierge did not look up as he passed through the lobby. He had exactly one and a half hours to make the journey across Moscow to Leningrad Station, and lose his tail for the last time.

On his earlier dry-cleaning runs, he had made for the nearby shopping precinct. This time, he crossed over the avenue and into a wooded area on the other side that ran the length of the avenue. Once out of sight of the road, he broke into a jog, and steadily increased his speed, until he was almost sprinting. The fat KGB surveillance officer would never keep up. At the end of the park, he crossed over the road, doubled back, and then entered the shops from the opposite side. Plastic bags were rare enough to be distinctive, so he bought a cheap artificial leather valise, stuffed his few items into it, and left by the rear entrance. Then he ran through the full surveillance-evasion menu, methodically and meticulously: jumping on a Metro train as the door closed, alighting after two stops, waiting for the next train to arrive and then making certain every passenger on the platform had boarded before letting the doors close and catching a train in the opposite direction; ducking down one street, doubling back and up another, into a shop by one entrance and then out of the back.

Leningrad Station was awash with people, and police. By chance, 26,000 young leftists from 157 countries were pouring into Moscow for the 12th World Festival of Youth and Students, starting the following week, billed as a celebration of 'anti-imperialist solidarity, peace and friendship'. At a mass rally, Gorbachev would tell them: 'Here, in the homeland of the great Lenin, you can directly feel how deeply our young people are devoted to the noble ideals of humanity, peace and socialism.' Most festival-goers had come not for Lenin, but for the music: among the performers would be Dean Reed, the pro-Soviet American-born singer who had settled behind the Iron Curtain, the British pop duo Everything But the Girl, and Bob Dylan – who had been invited by the Soviet poet Andrei Voznesensky. Many of the youth delegates were arriving from Scandinavia, via Finland. Gordievsky was alarmed to see riot police patrolling the station, but then tried to reassure himself: with so many people crossing the northern border, the guards might be too preoccupied to pay much attention to diplomatic cars passing in the other direction. He bought bread and sausage at a stall. As far as he could tell, no one was following him.

The overnight train to Leningrad consisted largely of fourth-class sleeper carriages, with six bunks to each compartment, open onto a corridor. Gordievsky found he was in the topmost bunk. He collected clean sheets and made up his bed. The female conductor, a student earning money during her vacation, did not seem to pay him particular attention. At 5.30 precisely the train pulled out. For a few hours, Gordievsky lay on the bunk, chewing his scanty supper and trying to remain calm, while beneath him his fellow passengers did the crossword together. He took two sedative pills, and in a few moments fell into a deep sleep, compounded of mental exhaustion, fear and chemicals.

### 7 p.m. British embassy, Moscow

The ambassador's inaugural drinks party was a great success. Sir Bryan Cartledge, who had arrived the night before, gave a brief speech, of which the MI6 party could remember not a single word. Rachel stayed at home, moaning for the hidden microphones, and occasionally emitting 'the odd sob'. After an hour of diplomatic chitchat beneath the chandeliers, the two intelligence officers made their excuses, explaining that they had to drive overnight to Leningrad to take Rachel to a doctor in Finland. Of those at the party, only the ambassador, the Minister, David Ratford, and the MI6 secretary, Violet Chapman, knew the real purpose of their journey. At the end of the party, Violet retrieved the PIMLICO 'medicine package' from the MI6 safe in the embassy, and handed it to Ascot: tranquillizer pills for the adults, and a pair of syringes for sedating two terrified little girls.

Back at Kutuzovsky Prospekt, while the men loaded up the cars, Rachel went into the bedroom where her children were sleeping, and kissed them goodnight. She wondered when she would see them again. 'If we get caught,' she reflected, 'we're going to be stuck for a very long time.' Gee walked his stiff-backed and hobbling wife to the Ford Sierra, and settled her in the front seat.

At about 11.15 p.m., the two-car convoy pulled into the wide avenue and headed north, with Gee taking the lead in the Ford, while Ascot followed in his Saab. Both couples had brought a plentiful stock of music cassettes for the long journey to Helsinki.

A single KGB surveillance car escorted them to Sokol on the city outskirts, and then peeled off. As they hit the wide highway, Ascot and Gee could detect no obvious surveillance cars following them. This was not necessarily reassuring. A tail-car was not the KGB's only method of vehicle surveillance. Along every main road State Automobile Inspection Posts (GAI posts) were stationed at regular intervals, which would note when a car under observation passed by, radio ahead to alert the next post, and if necessary maintain contact with any surveillance cars that might be deployed out of sight.

Inside the cars the atmosphere was otherworldly and tense. Since the vehicles were assumed to be bugged, recording or relaying sound to an unseen radio car, there could be no let-up in the play-acting. The performance was entering its second, mobile act. Rachel complained of her painful back. Ascot grumbled about having to drive hundreds of miles with a small baby, just as the new ambassador had arrived. No one mentioned the escape, or the man who was even now, they all hoped, in a train rumbling towards Leningrad.

'This has got to be a set-up,' Gee mused, as Rachel fell asleep. 'We can't possibly get away with this.'


## Saturday, 20 July

### 3.30 a.m. Moscow to Leningrad train

Gordievsky woke up on the bottom bunk, with a splitting headache and, for a long and unreal moment, no idea where he was. A young man was looking down on him from the upper bunk, with an odd expression: 'You fell out,' he said. The sedatives had plunged Gordievsky into such profound slumber that when the train braked suddenly he had rolled off the bunk and landed on the floor, cutting his temple as he fell. His jersey was covered in blood. He staggered into the corridor for some air. In the next compartment, a group of young women from Kazakhstan were talking animatedly. He opened his mouth to join in the conversation, but as he did so one of the women recoiled in horror: 'If you speak one word to me, I'll scream.' Only then did he realize what he must look like: dishevelled, blood-spattered and unsteady on his feet. He backed away, grabbed his bag, and retreated to the end of the corridor. There was still more than an hour to go before the train reached Leningrad. Would the other passengers report him for being drunk? He went to find the guard, handed her a five-rouble note, and said: 'Thank you for your help', though she had done nothing but supply his bedsheets. She gave him a quizzical look, with what seemed to be a hint of reproach. But she pocketed the money anyway. The train rattled on through the lifting darkness.

### 4 a.m. Moscow to Leningrad highway

About halfway to Leningrad, in the Valday Hills, the escape team drove into a spectacular dawn that moved Ascot to lyricism: 'A thick mist had risen from the lakes and rivers, extending into long belts beside the hills and through the trees and villages. The land slowly coalesced into substantial forms out of these foaming banks of violet and rose. Three very bright planets shone out in perfect symmetry, one to the left, one to the right, and one straight ahead. We passed solitary figures already scything hay, picking herbs or taking cows to pasture along the slopes and gullies of common land. It was a stunning sight, an idyllic moment. It was difficult to believe that any harm could come out of a day of such beginnings.'

Florence slept happily in her car seat on the back seat.

A devout Catholic and a spiritual man, Ascot thought: 'We are on a line and we are committed to it – there is only one line and that's the one we've got to go on.'

In the second car, Arthur and Rachel Gee were experiencing their own transcendent moment, as the sun emerged over the horizon and light flooded the mist-cloaked Russian uplands.

The Dire Straits album *Brothers in Arms* was playing on the cassette deck, with Mark Knopfler's virtuoso guitar seeming to fill the dawn.

*These mist covered mountains*
*Are a home now for me*
*But my home is the lowlands*
*And always will be*
*Someday you'll return to*
*Your valleys and your farms*
*And you'll no longer burn*
*To be brothers in arms*

*Through these fields of destruction*
*Baptisms of fire*
*I've watched all your suffering*
*As the battles raged higher*
*And though they did hurt me so bad*
*In the fear and alarm*
*You did not desert me*
*My brothers in arms*

'For the first time I thought: this is going to come out all right,' Rachel recalled.

At that moment, a snub-nosed brown Soviet-made Fiat known as a Zhiguli, the standard-issue KGB surveillance car, slotted in behind the convoy at a distance of about 200 feet. 'We were being followed.'

*5 a.m. Main railway station, Leningrad*

Gordievsky was among the first passengers to alight when the train pulled in. He walked swiftly to the exit, not daring to look behind to see if the guard was already talking to station staff and pointing out the strange man who had fallen out of his berth and then overtipped her. There were no taxis outside the station. But a number of private cars were milling around, their drivers touting for fares. Gordievsky climbed into one: 'To the Finland Station,' he said.

Gordievsky arrived at the Finland Station at 5.45. The almost deserted square in front was dominated by a vast statue of Lenin, commemorating the moment in 1917 when the great theorist of revolution arrived from Switzerland to take charge of the Bolsheviks. In communist lore, the Finland Station is symbolic of revolutionary liberty and the birth of the Soviet Union; to Gordievsky it also represented the route to freedom, but in the opposite direction, in every sense, to Lenin.

The first train towards the border left at 7.05. It would take him as far as Zelenogorsk, thirty miles north-west of Leningrad and just over a third of the way to the Finnish border. From there he could catch a bus that would take him along the main road towards Vyborg. Gordievsky climbed aboard, and pretended to fall asleep. The train was excruciatingly slow.

### 7 a.m. KGB headquarters, Moscow Centre

It is not clear exactly when the KGB spotted that Gordievsky had gone. But by dawn on 20 July the surveillance team from the First Chief Directorate (Chinese department) must have been seriously worried. He had last been seen on Friday afternoon, jogging into the woods on Leninsky Prospekt, carrying a plastic bag. On the previous three occasions that he had gone missing, Gordievsky reappeared within a few hours. This time, he had not returned to the flat. He was not with his sister, his father-in-law or his friend Lyubimov, or at any other known address.

At this moment, the most sensible action would have been to raise the alarm. The KGB could then have launched an immediate manhunt, stripped Gordievsky's flat for clues to his whereabouts, pulled in for questioning every friend and relative, redoubled surveillance of British diplomatic personnel, and then shut down every avenue of escape, by air, sea and land. There is no evidence, however, that the surveillance team did this on the morning of 20 July. Instead, they seem to have done what time-servers do in every autocracy that punishes honest failure: they did nothing at all, and hoped the problem would go away.

### 7.30 a.m. Leningrad

The MI6 exfiltration team parked outside Leningrad's Astoriya hotel. The brown KGB surveillance car had followed them all the way to central Leningrad, before disappearing. 'I assumed we had a new tail,' wrote Ascot. They opened the car boots and 'ostentatiously rummaged inside, to show the surveillance we had nothing to hide and our boots were genuinely full of luggage'. While Gee and the two women went inside, to feed the baby and have breakfast ('disgusting hard-boiled eggs and wooden bread'), Ascot remained in his car, pretending to be asleep. 'The KGB was sniffing around and I didn't want people to look inside.' Two different men approached the car and peered through the window; on both occasions, Ascot pretended to wake up with a start, and glared at them.

The 100-mile drive north to the lay-by, he estimated, would take about two hours. So they would need to leave Leningrad at 11.45 to get there in plenty of time for the rendezvous at 2.30. The car that had shadowed them into Leningrad, and now the inquisitive types hanging around the car, suggested a worrying degree of KGB interest. 'At that point I knew they were going to follow us to the border, and that took the enthusiasm out of me.' The powerful Western cars might be able to outrun a single Soviet-made KGB car and get far enough ahead to swerve into the rendezvous lay-by without being seen. But what if the KGB also put a surveillance car in front, as they sometimes did? If PIMLICO had been unable to shake off surveillance, they could be driving into an ambush. 'I feared most of all that two sets of KGB surveillance would plan on meeting in a pincer movement at the rendezvous itself. My remaining optimism was evaporating fast.'

With two hours to kill, Ascot suggested they use up the time by making an ironic pilgrimage to the Smolny Institute and Convent, one of communism's most venerated sites. Originally the Smolny Institute for Noble Maidens, one of the first schools in Russia to educate women (aristocrats only), the great Palladian edifice was used by Lenin as his headquarters during the October Revolution, and became the seat of the Bolshevik government until this was moved to the Kremlin in Moscow. It was filled with what Ascot called 'Leniniana'.

In the gardens of the Smolny, the foursome sat on a bench, and ostensibly huddled over a guidebook. 'It was a last council of war, rehearsing everything,' said Ascot. If they successfully reached the rendezvous site, the contents of the car boots would need to be rearranged to accommodate the passengers. Rachel would lay out the picnic while the men cleared the luggage from the boots. Caroline, meanwhile, would walk to the entrance to the lay-by with Florence in her arms, and look up and down the road. 'If anything seemed amiss, she would remove her headscarf.' But if the coast was clear Gee would open the bonnet of his car to signal to PIMLICO that it was safe to emerge. Any microphones would overhear the conversation, so the pickup should be conducted wordlessly. If he was the only escapee, he would be hidden in the boot of Gee's car. The Ford suspension was higher than that of the Saab, and the extra weight of the body would be slightly less noticeable. 'Arthur would lead the way out of the RV site,' wrote Ascot. 'And I would protect from behind, against any attempt to ram the boot.'

Lenin's revolutionary headquarters seemed an appropriate place to be plotting. 'It was two fingers to the KGB, really.'

Before climbing back into their cars for the last leg, they wandered down to the banks of the Neva, and watched the river flowing past an abandoned wharf, 'now strewn with rusting, wheel-less buses and torn bales of cellophane floating into the river weed'. Ascot suggested this might be a good opportunity for a brief communication with the Almighty. 'All four of us had a moment of reflection. We felt very connected to something beyond – and we really needed to.'

On the outskirts of Leningrad, they passed a large GAI police post with a watchtower. Moments later, a blue Lada Zhiguli, with two male passengers and a tall radio aerial, tucked in behind them. 'This was a depressing sight,' wrote Ascot. 'But worse was to follow.'

### 8.25 a.m. Zelenogorsk

Gordievsky climbed down off the train and looked around. The town of Zelenogorsk, known until 1948 by its Finnish name, Teri-joki, was waking up, and the station was busy. It seemed impossible that he could have been followed here, but back in Moscow the sur-veillance team must have raised the alarm by now. The border post at Vyborg, fifty miles to the north-west, might already be on alert. The escape plan called for him to catch a bus the rest of the way, and get off at the 836 marker post, 836 kilometres from Moscow and sixteen miles short of the border town. At the bus station he bought a ticket to Vyborg.

The ancient bus was half full, and as it wheezed out of Zelenogorsk, Gordievsky tried to make himself comfortable on the hard seat, and closed his eyes. A young couple took the seat in front of him. They were talkative and friendly. They were also, in a way that is almost unique to Russia, stupendously drunk at nine o'clock in the morning. 'Where are you going?' they hiccupped. 'Where are you from?' Gordievsky gave a mumbled reply. As is the habit of drunks seeking conversation, they asked the same question, louder. He said he was visiting friends in a village near Vyborg, dredging up a name from his study of the mini-atlas. Even to his own ears, that sounded like a flat lie. But it seemed to satisfy the couple, who burbled on inconsequentially and then, after about twenty minutes, lurched to their feet and alighted, waving cheerily.

Dense woods lined either side of the road, conifers mixed with scrub birch and aspen, broken by the occasional clearing with picnic tables. It would be an easy place to get lost in, but also a good place to hide. Tourist buses streamed in the opposite direction, bringing Scandinavian youths to the music festival. Gordievsky noted a large number of military vehicles, including armoured personnel carriers. The border area was heavily militarized, and some sort of training exercise was underway.

The road curved to the right, and suddenly the photographs Veronica Price had shown him so often seemed to come alive. He had not spotted the marker post, but felt certain this was the place. Jumping to his feet, he peered out of the window. The bus was almost empty now, and the driver was looking at him quizzically in his mirror. He brought the bus to a stop. Gordievsky hesitated. The bus started to move again. Gordievsky hurried up the aisle, one hand over his mouth. 'Sorry, I'm feeling sick. Can you let me off?' Irritated, the driver stopped once again and opened the door. As the bus pulled away, Gordievsky bent over the roadside ditch, pretending to retch. He was making himself far too conspicuous. At least half a dozen people would now remember him clearly: the train guard, the man who had found him blacked out on the floor of the compartment, the drunk couple and the bus driver, who would surely recall a sick passenger who seemed not to know where he was going.

The entrance to the lay-by was 300 yards ahead, marked by the distinctive rock. It turned off in a wide D-shaped loop 100 yards in length, with a screen of trees on the roadside and thick undergrowth of bracken and scrub. A military track at the widest point of the D led deeper into the woods on the right. The dirt surface of the lay-by was dusty, but the ground around it was boggy, with pools of semi-stagnant water. It was beginning to get warm, and the earth gave off a pungent, foetid aroma. He heard the whine of a mosquito, and felt the first bite. Then another. The forest seemed echoingly quiet. It was still only 10.30. The MI6 getaway cars would not arrive for another four hours, if they came at all.

Fear and adrenalin can have a strange effect on the mind, and the appetite. Gordievsky should have remained hidden in the undergrowth. He should have pulled his jacket over his head, and allowed the mosquitoes to do their worst. He should have waited. Instead he did something that was, with hindsight, very nearly insane.

He decided he would go into Vyborg, and have a drink.

### 12 p.m. Leningrad to Vyborg highway

The two MI6 cars were leaving the outskirts of Leningrad, with the blue KGB Zhiguli following, when a Soviet police car pulled out ahead of Ascot's Saab, and positioned itself at the head of the little convoy. A few moments later, a second police car passed in the opposite direction, then signalled and performed a U-turn, and slotted in behind the KGB car. A fourth car, a mustard-coloured Zhiguli, joined the rear of the column. 'We were bracketed,' said Ascot. He exchanged an anxious look with Caroline but said nothing.

Some fifteen minutes later, the police car in front suddenly pulled ahead. At the same moment, the KGB car also accelerated, overtook the two British cars, and assumed the front position. A mile ahead, the first police car was waiting in a side road. Once the convoy had passed, it pulled out and took up the rear position. The convoy was bracketed again, but now with the KGB in front, and the two police cars behind. A classic Soviet power play had just taken place, coordinated by radio and performed as a bizarre motorized dance: 'The KGB had said to the police: "You can stay, but we're going to run this operation." '

Whatever order they might choose to drive in, this was intense surveillance, with no effort made to disguise it. Ascot drove on gloomily. 'At that point I thought we were in a pincer movement. I saw us turning into the place and meeting a reception committee, a whole lot of uniformed people coming out of the bushes.'

The kilometre marker posts were counting down. 'I had no plan formulated to deal with such a situation: I hadn't quite imagined that we might be moving towards the rendezvous with the KGB a few yards ahead and just behind us.' With one car in front and three in the rear, it would be impossible to pull into the lay-by. 'If they are still with us at the rendezvous point,' thought Ascot, 'we are going to have to abort.' PIMLICO – and his family, if he had brought them – would be left high and dry. Assuming, that is, that he had ever left Moscow.

### 12.15 a.m. A café south of Vyborg

The first car on the road going in the direction of Vyborg had been a Lada, which obligingly stopped the moment Gordievsky stuck out his thumb. Hitchhiking, known as *Avtostop*, was common in Russia, and encouraged by the Soviet authorities. Even in a military zone, a lone hitchhiker was not necessarily suspicious. The young driver was smartly dressed in civilian clothes. Possibly military or KGB, Gordievsky reflected, but if so he was remarkably incurious, asked not a single question, and played loud Western pop music all the way to the edge of the town. When Gordievsky proffered three roubles for the short journey, the man accepted the money wordlessly, and drove away without looking back. A few minutes later Gordievsky was sitting down to his fine lunch: two bottles of beer and a plate of fried chicken.

The first bottle of beer slipped down, and Gordievsky began to feel a delicious drowsiness as the adrenalin subsided. The chicken leg was one of the tastiest things he had ever eaten. The empty cafeteria on the outskirts of Vyborg seemed utterly nondescript, a glass and plastic bubble. The waitress had barely glanced at him as she took his order. He began to feel, not safe exactly, but oddly calm, and suddenly exhausted.

Vyborg had changed nationality repeatedly down the centuries, from Sweden to Finland to Russia, then the Soviet Union, back to Finland, and finally Soviet again. In 1917, Lenin had passed through the town at the head of his contingent of Bolsheviks. Before the Second World War its population of 80,000, though the majority were Finnish, also included Swedes, Germans, Russians, Gypsies, Tatars and Jews. During the Winter War between Finland and the Soviet Union (1939–40), virtually the entire population was evacuated, and more than half the buildings were destroyed. After bitter fighting, it was occupied by the Red Army, and annexed by the Soviet Union in 1944 when the last Finns were expelled, and replaced by Soviet citizens. It had the stark, inert atmosphere of every town that has been demolished, ethnically cleansed, and rebuilt swiftly and cheaply. It felt utterly unreal. But the café was warm.

Gordievsky came to with a jolt. Had he been asleep? Suddenly it was 1 p.m. Three men had entered the cafeteria, and were staring at him, Gordievsky thought, with suspicion. They were well dressed. Trying to appear unhurried, he picked up the second bottle of beer, put it in the bag, left money on the table, and walked out. Steeling himself, he walked casually south; after 400 yards, he dared to look back. The men were still inside the café. But where had the time gone? The road was now deserted. With the arrival of lunchtime, the traffic had melted away. He began to run. The sweat was pouring off him after just a few hundred yards, but he picked up speed. Gordievsky was still an accomplished runner. Despite the trials of the last two months, he remained fit. He could feel his heart pumping, from fright and exertion, as he got into his stride. A hitchhiker might be unremarkable, but a man sprinting along an empty road would surely excite curiosity. At least he was running *away* from the border. He ran faster. Why had he not remained at the rendezvous? Could he possibly cover the sixteen miles back to the lay-by in an hour and twenty minutes? Almost certainly not. But he ran anyway, as fast as he could. Gordievsky ran for his life.

### 1 p.m. Two miles north of Vaalimaa village, Finland

On the Finnish side of the border, the MI6 reception team got into position early. They knew Ascot and Gee had set off from Moscow on time the previous evening, but had heard nothing since. Price and Brown parked their red Volvo off the track, on the edge of the clearing. Shawford and the Danes took up positions on either side of the road. If the two cars arrived with the KGB in hot pursuit, Eriksen and Larsen would use their vehicle to try to block or ram the pursuers. They seemed most cheerful at the possibility. It was hot and quiet, oddly peaceful after the frenetic activity of the previous four days.

'I felt an extraordinary period of stillness at the centre of the turning world,' Simon Brown recalled. He had brought along *Hotel du Lac*, the Booker Prize-winning novel by Anita Brookner. 'I thought if I took a long book it would be tempting fate, so I took a short book.' The Danes dozed. Veronica Price made a mental checklist of everything on the escape plan. Brown read as slowly as he could, and 'tried not to think of the minutes ticking by'. Dark forebodings kept intruding: 'I wondered whether we had killed the kids by injecting drugs into them.'

### 1.30 p.m. Leningrad to Vyborg highway

Russia's road-building authorities were proud of the highway running from Leningrad to the Finnish border, the main gateway between Scandinavia and the Soviet Union. It was a show road, wide and properly asphalted and cambered, with neat signs and road markings. The little convoy was making good progress, cruising at 120 kph, with the KGB car in front, the MI6 cars corralled in the middle, and two police vehicles and a second KGB car following a little way behind. It was all far too easy for the KGB; so Ascot decided to make it more difficult.

'I had been under surveillance for years, and we had got to know the way the KGB Seventh Directorate thought. While they often knew that *you* knew they were around, what really offended and embarrassed them was when someone deliberately indicated that he had spotted them: psychologically, no surveillance team likes to be shown up by its target as obvious and incompetent. They hate you putting two fingers up, and saying in effect: "We know you are there and we know what you're up to." ' On principle, Ascot always ignored surveillance, however overt. Now, for the first time, he broke his own rule.

The Viscount-spy reduced speed until he was travelling at just 55 kph. The rest of the convoy did likewise. At Kilometre Post 800, Ascot slowed again, until they were crawling along at barely 45 kph. The KGB car in front decelerated and waited for the British cars to catch up. Other cars began to stack up behind the convoy.

The KGB driver did not like it. The British were mocking him, deliberately impeding progress. 'Finally, the nerve of the driver in front broke, and he shot off at top speed. He didn't like being shown up.' A few miles further on, the blue KGB Zhiguli was waiting in a side road leading to the village of Kaimovo. It tucked in behind the other surveillance cars. Ascot's Saab was once again in the lead.

Gradually, he increased speed. So did Gee, maintaining a distance of just fifty feet between his car and the Saab in front. The three following cars began to fall behind. The road ahead was straight and clear. Ascot accelerated again. They were now speeding at around 140 kph. A gap of more than 800 yards had opened up between Gee and the Russian cars. Kilometre Post 826 shot past. The rendezvous point was just ten kilometres ahead.

Ascot swung round a bend, and hit the brakes.

An army column was crossing the road, from left to right: tanks, howitzers, rocket launchers, armoured personnel carriers. A bread van was already stopped ahead, waiting for the convoy to pass. Ascot drew to a halt behind the van. Gee pulled up behind him. The surveillance cars caught up, and bunched up behind. The Russian soldiers on top of the tanks spotted the foreign cars, and raised clenched fists and shouted, an ironic Cold War salutation.

'That's it,' thought Ascot. 'We are done.'

*2.00 p.m. Leningrad highway, ten miles south-east of Vyborg*

Gordievsky heard the truck rumbling up behind him before he saw it, and stuck out his thumb. The driver beckoned the hitchhiker aboard. 'What do you want to go there for? There's nothing there,' he said when Gordievsky, panting, explained that he would like to be dropped off at Kilometre Post 836.

Gordievsky shot him what he hoped was a conspiratorial look. 'There are some dachas in the woods. I've got a nice lady waiting for me in one of them.' The truck driver gave a snort of approval, and grinned in complicity.

'You lovely man,' thought Gordievsky, when the driver dropped him, ten minutes later, at the rendezvous point, and drove away with a lascivious wink and three roubles in his pocket. 'You lovely, Russian man.'

At the lay-by, he crawled into the undergrowth. The mosquitoes hungrily welcomed him back. A bus carrying women to the military base turned into the lay-by and down the track; Gordievsky flattened himself on the damp earth, wondering if he had been spotted. Silence fell, save for the whining mosquitoes, and his thumping heart. Dehydrated, he drank the second bottle of beer. 2.30 passed. Then 2.35.

At 2.40, another moment of madness gripped him, and he got to his feet and walked into the road, heading in the direction the MI6 getaway cars should be coming from. Perhaps he could save a few minutes by meeting them on the road itself. But after a few steps, sanity returned. If the cars had a KGB escort, they would all be caught in the open. He ran back to the lay-by and dived into the concealing bracken once more.

'Wait,' he told himself. 'Control yourself.'

*2.40 p.m. Kilometre Post 826, Leningrad to Vyborg highway*

The last vehicle of the military convoy finally trundled across the road. Ascot gunned the engine of the Saab, shot around the stationary bread van, and accelerated hard, with Gee just a few yards behind him. They were 100 yards ahead before the KGB car had started its engine. The road ahead was clear. Ascot put his foot to the floor. Handel's *Messiah* was playing on the tape deck. Caroline turned it up to full volume. 'The people that walked in darkness have seen a great light; and they that dwell in the land of the shadow of death, upon them hath the light shined.' Ascot thought grimly: 'If only . . .'

The MI6 officers had driven the route several times before, and both knew that the turning was just a few miles ahead. In moments they were back up to 140 kph, and the escort cars were already 500 yards behind, the gap steadily increasing. Just before the 836 Marker Post, the road straightened and dipped for about half a mile, and then rose again before a sharp bend to the right. The turning was on the right, about 200 yards further on. Would the lay-by be full of Russian picnickers? Caroline Ascot still did not know whether her husband was going to attempt the pickup, or drive on past the lay-by. Nor did Gee. Nor, in fact, did Ascot.

At the brow of the dip, as Ascot turned into the curve, Gee glanced in his rearview mirror, to see the blue Zhiguli just coming into view on the straight, half a mile behind, a gap of half a minute, perhaps less.

The rock loomed into view, and almost before he knew he had done it, Ascot slammed on the brakes, shot into the lay-by, and came to a screeching stop, with Gee just a few yards behind, their skidding tyres kicking up a cloud of dust. They were screened from the road by the trees and the rock. The place was deserted. The time was 2.47. 'Please God, don't let them see the dust,' thought Rachel. As they clambered out of the cars, they heard the sound of three Lada engines, screaming in protest, hurtle past on the main road, less than fifty feet away on the other side of the trees. 'If just one of them looks in his rear mirror now,' thought Ascot, 'he will see us.' The sound of the engines faded. The dust settled. Caroline tied on her headscarf, picked up Florence and headed to the lookout point at the lay-by entrance. Rachel, following the script, took out the hamper and laid out the picnic rug. Ascot set about transferring luggage from the boots to the back seats, and Gee moved to the front of the Saab, preparing to open the bonnet as soon as Caroline gave the all-clear signal.

At that second, a tramp erupted from the undergrowth, unshaven and unkempt, covered in mud, ferns and dust, dried blood in his hair, a cheap brown bag clutched in one hand, and a wild expression on his face. 'He looked absolutely nothing like the photograph,' thought Rachel. 'Any fantasies we had of meeting a suave spy disappeared on the spot.' Ascot thought the figure looked like 'some forest troll or woodman in Grimms' *Fairy Tales*'.

Gordievsky recognized Gee as the man with the Mars bar. Gee had barely glimpsed him outside the bread shop, and momentarily wondered if this scruffy apparition could be the same person. For a beat, on a dusty track in a Russian forest, the spy and the people sent to rescue him stared at one another in indecision. The MI6 team had prepared for four people, including two small children, but PIM-LICO was evidently alone. Gordievsky was expecting to be picked up by two intelligence officers. Veronica had said nothing about any women, let alone women who seemed to be laying out some sort of formal English picnic, complete with teacups. And was that a child? Could MI6 really have brought along a baby on a dangerous escape operation?

Gordievsky looked from one man to the other, and then grunted, in English: 'Which car?'

## 15.   Finlandia

Ascot pointed to the open boot of Gee's car. Caroline hurried back from the lay-by entrance with the baby. Rachel took Gordievsky's mud-caked, malodorous and possibly radioactive shoes, tied them in a plastic bag and threw them under the front seat of the car. Gordievsky climbed into the boot of the Sierra and lay down. Gee handed him water, the medical pack and the empty bottle, and indicated by signs that he should undress in the boot. The aluminium blanket was laid on top of him. The women bundled the picnic into the back seats. Gee gently closed the car boot, and Gordievsky disappeared into darkness. With Ascot in the lead, the two cars rejoined the main road, and accelerated.

The entire pickup had taken eighty seconds.

At Kilometre Post 852, the next GIA observation post loomed into view, and with it a memorable tableau. The mustard-coloured Zhiguli and the two police cars were parked up, doors open, on the right side of the road. The KGB man in plainclothes was in earnest conversation with five militiamen. 'They all turned swiftly to look at us as we appeared,' and stared, open-mouthed, as the two British cars drove by, their faces registering a mixture of confusion and relief. 'The driver ran back to his car as soon as we were past,' wrote Ascot. 'He had such a puzzled and incredulous look on his face that I expected to be stopped and at least questioned about our movements.' But the sur-veillance cars slotted in behind, just as before. Had they radioed ahead to the border, warning the guards to look out for a party of foreign diplomats? Did they file a report admitting that they had lost the Brit-ish diplomats for several minutes? Or did they, in more traditional Soviet fashion, assume that the foreigners had merely stopped off the road to relieve themselves, disguise the fact that several minutes were unaccounted for, and say nothing at all? It is impossible to know the answer to this question, but it is easy to guess it.

From the car boot, Rachel and Arthur Gee could hear muted grunts and bumps, as Gordievsky struggled to remove his clothes in the constricted space. Then a distinctive gush, as he decanted his lunchtime beers. Rachel turned up the music: Dr. Hook's *Greatest Hits*, a compilation of the American rock band's records that included 'Only Sixteen', 'When You're in Love with a Beautiful Woman' and 'Sylvia's Mother'. The style of Dr. Hook's music is often described as 'easy listening'. Gordievsky did not find it easy. Even crammed into the boiling boot of the car, fleeing for his life, he found time to be irritated by this lowbrow schmaltzy pop. 'It was horrible, horrible music. I hated it.'

But it was not the noise their secret passenger was making that most worried Rachel, it was the smell: a mixture of sweat, cheap soap, tobacco and beer, rising from the rear of the car. It wasn't unpleasant exactly, but it was most distinctive, and quite strong. 'It was the smell of Russia. It's not something you would have found in an ordinary English car.' The sniffer dogs would surely register that something in the back of the car smelled quite different to the passengers in the front.

By a process of contortion, Gordievsky managed to remove his shirt and trousers, but the exertion left him clutching for breath. The heat was already intense, and the air inside the boot seemed to thicken with each gulp. He swallowed a sedative pill. Gordievsky imagined the scene that would take place if the border guards found him. The British would feign surprise, and claim that the fugitive had been planted as a provocation. They would all be hauled off. He would be taken to the Lubyanka, forced to confess and then killed.

Back in Moscow, the KGB must have been aware that it had a problem. Yet it still did not move to close the nearest land border, or make the connection between Gordievsky's disappearance and the two British diplomats who had slipped away from an embassy function the previous evening to drive to Finland. Instead it was at first assumed that Gordievsky must have killed himself, and was probably lying at the bottom of the Moscow River, or else drunk in a bar. Weekends are lethargic times in all large bureaucracies, when the second-tier staff comes to work, and the boss relaxes. The KGB began looking for Gordievsky, but without particular urgency. After all, where could he possibly run to? And if he had committed suicide, what could be clearer evidence of guilt?

On the twelfth floor of Century House, Derek Thomas, the Deputy Under-Secretary for Intelligence from the Foreign Office, had joined the PIMLICO team in P5's office to wait for Shawford's telephone call, and learn the outcome of the 'fishing expedition' in Finland. At the Foreign Office, David Goodall, the Permanent Under-Secretary, gathered his senior advisers to await word from Thomas. At 1.30 in the afternoon, 3.30 in Russia, Goodall, a devout Roman Catholic, looked at his watch and declared: 'Ladies and gentlemen, they should be crossing the border around now. I think it would be appropriate to say a small prayer.' The half-dozen officials bowed their heads.

The traffic crawled through Vyborg. If the KGB was going to flush them out by staging a traffic accident and ramming one of the cars, then it would take place in the centre of town. The Zhiguli had vanished. Then the police cars peeled off. 'If they're going to get us, they'll get us at the border,' Gee thought.

Rachel remembered the training they had undergone, at Veronica Price's insistence, in Guildford woods, squeezed into a car boot under a space blanket, hearing the sounds of the engine, the music from the cassette deck, the unexpected jolts, halts and Russian voices. 'It had seemed crackers at the time.' Now it appeared inspired: 'We all knew what he was going through.'

Gordievsky swallowed another pill, and felt his mind and body slacken a little. He pulled the space blanket over his head. Even stripped to his underwear, the sweat was running down his back and pooling on the metal floor of the boot.

Ten miles west of Vyborg, they reached the perimeter of the militarized border area, a wall of mesh fencing, topped with barbed wire. The border zone was roughly twenty kilometres in width. Between here and Finland were five separate barriers, three Soviet and two Finnish.

At the first border check, the frontier guard gave the party 'a hard look' but then waved them through without a document check. The border authorities had clearly been told to expect the diplomatic party. At the next checkpoint Ascot scanned the faces of the guards, 'but sensed no special tension in the air directed specifically at us'.

In the other car, Arthur Gee was focused on a different anxiety. He was having what might be termed a 'Have I left the iron on?' moment. He could not remember whether, in his haste, he had locked the car boot. Indeed, he was not even sure he had closed it properly. Gee had a sudden, horrible vision of the boot lid popping open as they passed through the border area, to reveal the spy, in foetal position, curled up inside. He stopped the car, jumped out, headed to the edge of the forest and urinated in the bushes. On the way back he checked, as casually as he could, that the boot was locked — which it was, just as the iron is always off. The delay had taken less than a minute.

The next checkpoint brought them to the border itself. The men parked the cars side by side in the fenced parking lot of the immigration holding area, and then joined the queue at the customs and immigration kiosk. Filling out paperwork for leaving the Soviet Union could be a time-consuming business. Rachel and Caroline prepared for a long wait. No sound came from the boot of the car. Rachel remained in the passenger seat, trying to look bored and in pain. The baby Florence was fractious, helpfully providing distraction and covering noise with her wails. Caroline took her out of her car seat and stood talking to Rachel through the open door, gently rocking the baby. Border guards passed between the lines of cars, looking left and right. Rachel braced herself to 'throw a wobbly' if they attempted to search the car. If they insisted, Ascot would then present his copy of the letter of protest and the terms of the Vienna Convention. If they still seemed determined to open the boot, he would throw his own diplomatic wobbly, and insist they were immediately driving back to Moscow to launch a formal protest. At that point, they would probably all be arrested.

Two tourist coaches were parked nearby, the passengers asleep or staring idly out of the windows. Around the edges of the wired enclosure, wild willow herb grew in purple profusion. The smell of fresh-cut hay wafted across the car park. The woman official in the customs and immigration kiosk was grumpy and slow, complaining bitterly about the extra work created by the youth festival and the influx of drunk young foreigners. Ascot made Russian small talk, fighting the urge to hurry her. The border guards were carefully searching the other cars, mostly Moscow-based businessmen and Finnish visitors returning home.

The air was hot and still. Rachel heard a low cough from the boot, and Gordievsky shifted his weight, rocking the car very slightly. Unaware that they were already inside the border zone, he was clearing his throat, attempting to ensure there would be no involuntary spluttering. Rachel turned up the music. 'Only Sixteen' by Dr. Hook echoed incongruously around the concrete lot. A dog-handler appeared, and stood, eight yards away, looking intently at the British cars and stroking his Alsatian. A second sniffer dog was inspecting a container lorry. The first dog approached, eager and panting, straining at its chain. Rachel reached casually for a packet of crisps, opened it, offered a crisp to Caroline, and dropped a couple on the ground.

The British cheese and onion crisp has a most distinctive aroma. Invented by the Irish potato crisp magnate, Joe 'Spud' Murphy, in 1958, cheese and onion is a pungent artificial cocktail of onion powder, whey powder, cheese powder, dextrose, salt, potassium chloride, flavour enhancers, monosodium glutamate, sodium 5'ribonucleotide, yeast, citric acid and colouring. Caroline had bought her imported Golden Wonder crisps from the embassy shop, which stocked Marmite, digestive biscuits, marmalade and other British staples impossible to obtain in Russia.

The Soviet sniffer dogs had almost certainly never smelled anything like cheese and onion crisps before. She offered a crisp to one of the dogs, which wolfed it down before being yanked away by the unsmiling handler. The other dog, however, was now snuffling at the boot of the Sierra. Gordievsky could hear muffled Russian voices overhead.

As the dog circled the boot, Caroline Ascot reached for a weapon that had never been deployed before in the Cold War, or any other. She placed Florence on the car boot directly over the hidden spy, and began changing her nappy — which the baby, with immaculate timing, had just filled. She then dropped the soiled and smelly diaper next to the inquisitive Alsatian. 'The dog duly slunk off, offended.' Olfactory diversion was never part of the plan. The nappy ruse had been completely spontaneous, and highly effective.

The men returned with the completed paperwork. Fifteen minutes later a border guard appeared with their four passports, checked them against the occupants, handed them over and politely bid them goodbye.

A queue of seven cars had formed at the last barrier, a belt of barbed wire, with two elevated lookout posts, and guards armed with machine guns. For about twenty minutes they inched forward, aware that they were being closely scrutinized through binoculars from the posts. Gee was now ahead of Ascot. 'It was a nerve-racking moment.'

The final Soviet hurdle was passport control itself. The Soviet officers seemed to scrutinize the British diplomatic passports for an age, before the barrier was raised.

They were now technically in Finland, but two more hurdles remained: Finnish customs and immigration, and Finnish passport control. It would require only a single telephone call from the Soviets to turn them around. The Finnish customs officer studied Gee's documents, and then pointed out that his car insurance would be out of date in a few days. Gee remonstrated that they would be returning to the Soviet Union before that. The official shrugged and stamped the document. Gordievsky felt the driver's door close, and a jolt as the car moved off again.

The cars funnelled towards the final barrier. Beyond lay Finland. Gee posted the passports through the grille. The Finnish official examined them slowly, handed them back and came out of his kiosk to raise the barrier. Then his phone rang. He returned to the kiosk. Arthur and Rachel Gee stared ahead in silence. After what seemed like an eternity, the border guard returned, yawning, and raised the barrier. It was 4.15, Moscow time; 3.15 in Finland.

Inside the boot, Gordievsky heard the fizz of tyres on warm asphalt, and felt a judder as the Ford picked up speed.

Suddenly classical music was blasting out of the tape deck at top volume, no longer the soupy pop of Dr. Hook, but the swelling sounds of an orchestral piece he knew well. Arthur and Rachel Gee still could not tell their passenger, in words, that he was free; but they could do so in sound, with the haunting opening chords of a symphonic poem written by Finnish composer Jean Sibelius in celebration of his native land.

They were playing *Finlandia*.

Twenty minutes later, the two British cars nosed onto the forestry road, and into the woods. The area looked completely different from the photographs Ascot had studied back in London: 'Several new tracks had been made into the forest and there seemed to be too many smart new cars parked in the lay-bys around the area with stony-faced men, whom I had never seen before, staring at us.' These were the Danes, Eriksen and Larsen, 'ready to ram hostile Soviet pursuit'. Ascot was not the only person alarmed by the sudden activity in this usually secluded spot. A battered brown Mini appeared, containing an elderly Finnish woman apparently on a mushroom-collecting expedition. 'She understandably took fright and smartly drove off.' Through the trees, Ascot caught sight of Martin Shawford, 'an unmistakable blond figure'. As he drove past the beige Volvo and prepared to stop, he saw Price's face, pressed to the window. She mouthed the words: 'How many?' Ascot raised a single finger.

Gordievsky felt the car bump over the forest track.

The scene that now played out was like a slow-motion dream, in silence. Brown and Price ran forward. The Danes held back. Brown opened the boot of the car. There lay Gordievsky, soaked in sweat, conscious but dazed. 'He was semi-naked, in this pool of water: and I immediately felt it was like I was seeing a new-born child in amniotic fluid, and some extraordinary rebirth.'

Gordievsky was momentarily dazzled by the sunlight. All he could see was blue sky, clouds and trees. He staggered out and onto his feet, helped by Brown. Veronica Price did not approve of emotional displays, but she was visibly moved, 'her expression a mixture of recognition and love'. She wagged her finger, in mock admonition, as if to say: 'Gosh, You really have been up to something.'

Gordievsky seized both her hands, raised them to his lips and kissed them, an unmistakably Russian gesture of gratitude and liberation. Then he walked shakily over to where Caroline Ascot and Rachel Gee stood side by side. Bowing from the waist, he kissed their hands too, first one and then the other. 'All we had seen was this great bull coming out of the bushes, and then suddenly there was this courteous, very delicate gesture.' The space blanket was still draped over his shoulders. 'He looked like an athlete who had just run a marathon.'

Veronica Price took his arm, and gently guided him away, a dozen yards into the forest, out of range of any microphones in the British cars.

Now, at last, he spoke, addressing her by the alias she had always worn: 'Jean, I was betrayed.'

There was no time for more.

At the second rendezvous point, Gordievsky was swiftly dressed in fresh clothing. His dirty clothes, shoes, bag and Soviet papers were bundled up and placed in the boot of Shawford's car, along with the false passports for Leila and the girls, and the redundant syringes and clothes. Price took the wheel of the Finnish hire car, while Brown and Gordievsky climbed into the back seat. She turned onto the highway heading north. Gordievsky waved away the sandwiches and fruit juice Price had carefully packed. 'I wanted whisky,' he said later. 'Why didn't they give me whisky?' Brown had expected him to be hysterical with exhaustion, but instead Gordievsky seemed 'perfectly controlled'. He began to tell his story, describing the drugged interrogation, how he had evaded surveillance and the mysterious way the KGB had followed but not arrested him. 'As soon as he was able to talk – he was straight into analysis of the case, and how we'd misjudged it.' Brown gently raised the question of his family. 'It was too much of a risk to bring them,' Gordievsky said flatly, and stared out of the window at the passing Finnish countryside.

At the petrol station on the road to Helsinki, Shawford met Ascot and Gee, heard a swift account of the escape, and headed for the telephone box. The phone rang on P5's desk in Century House. The entire PIMLICO team clustered around the desk. The Sovbloc controller snatched up the receiver.

'How is the weather?' he asked.

'The weather's excellent,' said Shawford, as the Sovbloc controller repeated the words to the team clustered round the desk. 'The fishing has been very good. The sun is shining. We have one extra guest.'

The message caused momentary confusion. Did that mean another escaper, in addition to the four family members? Had Gordievsky brought along someone else? Were there five people heading for Norway, and, if so, how would the 'guest' get across the border without a passport?

Shawford repeated. 'No. We have ONE guest. In total.'

The team whooped in unison as the call ended. But the joy was uneven. Sarah Page, the MI6 secretary who had done so much to maintain the nuts and bolts of the case and was now six months pregnant, felt a lurch of empathy for Leila and the children. 'Oh the poor wife, and his daughters,' she thought. 'They have been left behind. What will happen to them?' She turned to another secretary and muttered: 'What about the human cost?'

P5 called 'C'. 'C' called Downing Street. Charles Powell told Margaret Thatcher. The Sovbloc controller drove to Chevening House, the Foreign Secretary's country residence in Kent, to inform Geoffrey Howe that Gordievsky had crossed the Russian border. At the last moment, he decided not to take champagne – a wise decision, for Geoffrey Howe, who had never been fully behind PIMLICO, was not in celebratory mood. He had a large map of Finland spread out on a table. The MI6 man pointed to the road where Gordievsky must now be travelling north. 'What are your plans in the eventuality that a KGB hit squad is on his trail?' asked the Foreign Secretary. 'What if it goes wrong? What about the Finns?'

That night, on the top floor of the Klaus Kurki, the smartest hotel in Helsinki, Shawford hosted a dinner for the MI6 exfiltration team. They dined on roasted ptarmigan and claret; for the first time, out of microphone range, the Moscow MI6 staff discovered PIMLICO's real name, and what he had done. If the KGB was still watching, they would have noticed that Rachel Gee's bad back had miraculously recovered.

The two escape cars drove on through the night, heading towards the Arctic Circle. They stopped only briefly, to fill up with petrol and, once, to allow Gordievsky to shave off three days of stubble in a mountain stream, using a wing mirror. He got halfway through shaving before the mosquitoes drove him back to the car. 'We were still in semi-hostile territory. The Russians could have mounted something if they wanted to. It was perfectly within their capabilities. But the further we got from the border, the more confident we became.' The Danish PET officers stuck close. The Arctic sun dipped briefly below the horizon and then rose again. Gordievsky dozed, half awake and semi-bearded, and barely spoke. Shortly after eight o'clock on Sunday morning, they reached the Finnish–Norwegian border at Karigasniemi, a single-pole barrier across the road. The border guard barely bothered to examine the three Danish and two British passports before waving the cars through. At Hammerfest, they spent the night in an airport hotel.

No one paid much attention to Mr Hanssen, the rather tired-looking Danish gentleman, and his British friends, who boarded the flight to Oslo the next morning, and then caught the connecting flight to London.

On Monday evening, Gordievsky found himself in South Ormsby Hall, a grand country house in the Lincolnshire Wolds, surrounded by servants, candlelight, splendid panelled rooms and admiring people, eager to congratulate him. The seat of the Massingberd-Mundy family since 1638, the Hall had 3,000 acres of surrounding parkland and a complete absence of inquisitive neighbours. Its owner, Adrian Massingberd-Mundy, was an MI5 contact and happy to host a welcoming reception for an honoured guest of the Service. He was staggered to be told who his guest really was, and sent an aged retainer on a bicycle into the nearby village, to hang around the pub and 'check for any signs of loose talk'.

Just forty-eight hours earlier, Gordievsky had been lying in a car boot, drugged, half naked, drenched in his own sweat, sick with fear. Now he was being waited on by a butler. The contrast was too much. He asked if he could telephone his wife back in Russia. MI6 told him he could not. A call would alert the KGB that he was in Britain, something the British wanted to reveal only when they were good and ready. Exhausted, anxious, wondering why he had been taken to this English palace in the middle of nowhere, Gordievsky retired to a four-poster bed.

That evening, MI6 sent a telegram to the Finnish spy chief, Seppo Tiitinen, explaining that British intelligence officers had smuggled a Soviet defector to the West via Finland. The message came back: 'Seppo is content. But he wants to know if force was used.' The exfiltration, MI6 reassured him, had been completed without recourse to violence.

The consequences, fallout and benefits from Britain's most successful Cold War spy case began to be felt long before news broke of Gordievsky's astonishing escape.

After a day in Helsinki, during which Gee's car was thoroughly cleaned to try to remove any evidence that Gordievsky had been in its boot, the exfiltration team drove swiftly back to Moscow. They knew they would be declared *persona non grata* and thrown out of the Soviet Union as soon as the KGB uncovered what had happened. But they were elated. 'I've never felt such a sense of complete exhilaration,' said Ascot. 'We were going back into the evil empire, and we'd licked them. After two and a half years of being intimidated, in a system that you knew always won, we'd miraculously dodged them.' David Ratford, the *chargé d'affaires*, performed a five-minute jog of jubilation around the embassy. The ambassador, however, did not.

A few days later, Sir Bryan Cartledge formally presented his credentials to the Kremlin: a ceremonial photograph was taken, with the staff of the embassy surrounding the new ambassador, dressed in full diplomatic uniform. Ascot and Gee were there – fully aware, as was the ambassador, that they would not be there much longer.

Mikhail Lyubimov was waiting at Zvenigorod Station to meet the 11.13 train on Monday morning. But Gordievsky was not in the last carriage. Nor was he on the next train from Moscow. Irritated but worried, Lyubimov returned to his dacha. Was Gordievsky lying blotto in his flat, or had something worse happened to his old friend, once so punctual and reliable? 'Drinking entails optionality,' he reflected sadly. A few days later, Lyubimov was summoned to KGB headquarters for questioning.

Rumours of Gordievsky's disappearance had begun to swirl around the KGB, accompanied by wild speculation, and some deliberate misinformation. For weeks, Directorate K remained convinced that he must still be in the country, drunk or dead. A search of the Moscow area was launched, including lakes and rivers. Some said he had slipped out through Iran, using false papers and in heavy disguise. Budanov claimed that Gordievsky had been spirited into a British safe house after escaping from the KGB sanatorium, knowing full well that he had returned from Semyonovskoye weeks before his disappearance. Leila was brought back from the Caspian, and taken to Lefortovo prison for questioning: the interrogation, the first of many, continued for eight hours. 'Where is your husband?' they asked, again and again. Leila replied with asperity: 'He's your officer. You tell me where he is.' When the interrogators revealed that Gordievsky was suspected of working for British intelligence, she refused to believe it. 'That seemed so crazy to me.' But as the days turned into weeks, with no word or sighting, the grim truth took root. Her husband had gone. But Leila flatly refused to accept what she was hearing about her husband's treachery. 'Until he tells me himself I will not believe it,' she told the KGB interrogators. 'I was very calm, I was strong.' Gordievsky had warned her not to believe any accusations made against him, so that is what she did.

Gordievsky was moved from South Ormsby Hall to Fort Monckton (1MTE, standing for Military Training Establishment), the MI6 training base at Gosport. Above the gatehouse of the Napoleonic fort, he was lodged in a guest suite habitually used by the chief, simple but comfortable. Gordievsky did not want to be lauded and spoiled; he wanted to get to work, and demonstrate – to himself above all – that the sacrifice had been worthwhile. Yet at first he seemed almost overwhelmed by his sense of loss. During the first, four-hour debriefing he focused almost exclusively on the circumstances of his escape, and the fate of his wife and children. He drank endless cups of strong tea, and bottles of red wine, preferably Rioja. He repeatedly asked for news of his family. There was none.

For the next four months, Fort Monckton would be his home, private, secluded and well defended. The need-to-know principle was strictly applied to the identity of the mystery occupant of the gatehouse, but soon many of the staff came to understand that this long-term visitor was someone of importance, to be treated as an honoured guest.

The case was awarded a new codename, its last, and one in keeping with the moment of jubilation. SUNBEAM, alias NOCTON, alias PIMLICO, was now, and henceforth, OVATION. As SUNBEAM, Gordievsky had supplied intelligence on the KGB's Scandinavian operations; as NOCTON, in London, he had produced information that significantly affected strategic thinking in Downing Street and the White House; but as OVATION the case would enter its most valuable phase. Much of the intelligence Gordievsky had produced over the years had been too good to be used, because it was too specific and therefore potentially too incriminating. To protect his security, it had been chopped up, repackaged, disguised and distributed, with extreme parsimony, to only the most restricted readership. During the London phase alone, the case had produced hundreds of individual reports – ranging from long documents to political reporting to detailed counter-intelligence briefs – only a few of which had ever been shared outside British intelligence, and then only in edited form. Now the French could be informed of all intelligence directly relating to France; the Germans could be told of just how close the world had come to disaster during the ABLE ARCHER scare; the full story of how Treholt, Haavik and Bergling had fallen under suspicion could be revealed to the Scandinavians. With Gordievsky now safe in Britain, and the operational case ended, the vast trove of intelligence gathered over the previous eleven years could be exploited to the full; it was finally time to cash in the winnings. Britain had secrets to trade in abundance. The Fort Monckton apartment became the setting for one of the most extensive intelligence gathering, collating and distribution exercises ever undertaken by MI6, as a succession of officers, analysts, secretaries and others harvested the fruits of Gordievsky's espionage.

With the successful exfiltration, a host of new questions arose. When should the CIA, and other Western allies, be told of MI6's coup? Whether to inform the media, and, if so, how? And, above all, how to manage relations with the Soviet Union? Would the improved understanding between Thatcher and Gorbachev, so painstakingly built up with Gordievsky's secret help, survive this dramatic turn of events in the spy war? Above all, MI6 pondered what to do about Leila and the two girls. Perhaps, with careful diplomacy, Moscow could be persuaded to release them. The sustained, intensely secret campaign to try to reunite Gordievsky with his family was code-named HETMAN (a historical term for a Cossack leader).

MI6 never doubted Gordievsky's honesty, yet some found elements of his story hard to swallow. In Whitehall, a handful of sceptics wondered whether 'Gordievsky might have been turned into a double agent during his time in Moscow, then deliberately sent back to Britain.' Why had he not been arrested and imprisoned the moment he arrived in Moscow? The analysts put that down to KGB complacency, a legalistic approach, a determination to entrap the spy and his handlers in the act, and fear. 'If you're in the KGB, and you're going to shoot somebody, you have to have absolute proof, because it may be your turn next. They tried too hard to get hard evidence: that is what saved him, and his own sheer, desperate courage.' But Gordievsky's description of being drugged and interrogated at the First Chief Directorate dacha seemed scarcely credible. 'There were doubts about the sequence of events. It just seemed so melodramatic.' Finally, hanging over the entire case, was the most unsettling question of all: who had betrayed him?

Confirmation that Gordievsky's story was true arrived, a week later, from an unexpected quarter: the KGB.

On 1 August a KGB officer named Vitaly Yurchenko walked into the US embassy in Rome, and announced that he wished to defect. The Yurchenko case is one of the strangest in intelligence history. A KGB veteran of twenty-five years' standing, General Yurchenko had risen to become head of Department Five of Directorate K of the FCD, investigating suspected espionage by KGB officers. Additionally, he was involved in 'special operations abroad' and the use of 'special drugs'. In March 1985 he had become Deputy Chief of the First Department, responsible for coordinating KGB efforts to recruit agents in the United States and Canada. He was succeeded by Sergei Golubev, one of the men who had jointly interrogated Gordievsky.

Yurchenko remained plugged into the activities of Directorate K, and had good relations with Golubev.

Yurchenko's motives remain murky, but his defection appears to have been spurred by a failed love affair with the wife of a Soviet diplomat. He would re-defect back to the Soviet Union four months later, for reasons that are still unclear. The Soviets later claimed he had been kidnapped by the Americans, but they were equally uncertain what to make of him. Yurchenko may have been unhinged. But he knew a number of very important secrets.

Yurchenko's defection was hailed as a major triumph for the CIA, the agency's biggest KGB catch to date. The officer appointed to debrief the Russian defector was the CIA's Soviet counter-intelligence expert, Aldrich Ames.

At first, Ames was worried by the news of a senior KGB defector. What if Yurchenko knew he was spying for the Soviets? But it swiftly became clear that the Russian was unaware of Ames's espionage. 'He didn't know anything about me,' Ames said later. 'If he had, I would have been one of the first persons he would have identified in Rome.'

Ames was waiting at Andrews Air force Base near Washington when Yurchenko was flown in from Italy on the afternoon of 2 August.

The first thing he asked the defector, before they had even left the airport tarmac, was the question every intelligence officer is trained to ask a walk-in spy: 'Are there any important indications that you know of that the CIA has been penetrated by a KGB mole?'

Yurchenko would identify two spies inside the American intelligence establishment (including one CIA officer), but his most important revelation, that very evening, concerned his former colleague Oleg Gordievsky, the KGB *rezident* in London who had been summoned back to Moscow as a suspected traitor, given a truth serum, and grilled by the investigators of Directorate K. Yurchenko had heard on the KGB grapevine that Gordievsky was now under house arrest, and liable to be executed. He did not know that Gordievsky had since escaped to Britain; and nor, of course, did Ames. The Russian defector also did not know who had betrayed Gordievsky to the KGB. But Ames did.

Ames's reaction to the news that Gordievsky had been arrested was indicative of a man whose parallel lives had so completely merged that he could no longer tell them apart. Ames had sold out Gordievsky to the KGB. But his first instinct, on discovering the consequences of his own action, was to warn the British that their spy was in trouble.

'My first thought was, *Jesus Christ, we've got to do something to save him! We've got to get a cable to London and tell the Brits.* I had given the KGB Gordievsky's name. I was responsible for his arrest . . . I was genuinely worried about him, yet at the same time I knew I had exposed him. I know that sounds crazy, because I was a KGB agent too.' Perhaps he was being deliberately disingenuous. Or perhaps he was still only half a traitor.

The CIA dispatched a message to MI6: a newly arrived Soviet defector was reporting that a senior KGB officer, Oleg Gordievsky, had been drugged and interrogated as a suspected British spy. Could MI6 shed any light? The CIA did not reveal that it knew perfectly well Gordievsky had been spying for the British. The cable from Langley came as a relief to the OVATION team: here was independent verification of Gordievsky's story. But it also meant that the Americans would have to be told that he had escaped.

Two MI6 officers flew to Washington that afternoon. At the airport, they were met by a driver and taken to Langley. Accompanied by Burton Gerber, the CIA's head of Soviet operations, they were then driven to the Maryland home of the CIA's Director, Bill Casey, for an early dinner cooked by Casey's wife, Sophia. The Caseys were going to the theatre later. The two British officers provided a detailed account of the Gordievsky case: from recruitment, through more than a decade of valuable service to MI6, and finally his breathtaking escape. America also owed him an enormous debt, they explained: the RYAN intelligence, accurately reflecting Kremlin paranoia at a perilous moment in East–West relations, had come from Gordievsky. Halfway through the account, Sophia interrupted to say that it was time to leave for the theatre. 'You go ahead,' said Casey. 'This is the best show in town.' For the rest of the evening, the American spy chief listened with admiration, gratitude and wonder. The appreciation was entirely genuine; the surprise was not. Bill Casey did not reveal that the CIA already had a file on Gordievsky, codenamed TICKLE.

On 16 September a military helicopter skimmed over the sea towards Fort Monckton. 'C' and a handful of his senior officers were waiting by the helipad as it touched down. Out stepped Bill Casey. The veteran CIA chief had secretly flown to Britain to pick the brains of Britain's newly exfiltrated spy. A lawyer from New York, Casey knew England well from the war, when he had served in London in the Office of Strategic Services (OSS), the CIA's wartime precursor, directing spies in Europe. After running Ronald Reagan's election campaign, he was appointed to head the CIA with responsibility, in Reagan's words, for 'rebuilding America's intelligence capability'. A stooped figure with the face of a bloodhound, Casey was about to become embroiled in the Iran–Contra affair and would die of a brain tumour within two years. But at this moment he was probably the most powerful spy in the world, with an acute appreciation of his own abilities. 'I'm on top of all facets of the job,' he declared, early in Reagan's second term. 'I have a capacity to size up a situation once I get the facts, and to make decisions.' Casey was in Fort Monckton to get some facts from Gordievsky, and make some decisions. Reagan would soon be meeting Mikhail Gorbachev for the first time, at the superpower summit in Geneva. Casey wanted an expert KGB opinion on what he should say to the Soviet leader.

Over lunch in the guest suite above the gatehouse, with only 'C' in attendance, Casey quizzed Gordievsky about Gorbachev's negotiating style, his attitude to the West and his relations with the KGB. The American scribbled notes on a large yellow pad with blue lines. Occasionally Casey's American drawl and false teeth left Gordievsky perplexed; 'C' found himself in the odd position of having to translate American-English into English-English for the Russian. Casey listened attentively, 'like a schoolboy'. Above all, the CIA's Director wanted to understand Moscow's attitude towards nuclear deterrence, and in particular the Soviet view of the Strategic Defense Initiative missile defence system. Andropov had denounced the Star Wars initiative as a deliberate attempt to destabilize the world and enable the West to attack the Soviet Union without fear of retaliation. Would Gorbachev feel the same? Casey suggested some role-playing, and an odd little Cold War drama now played out in MI6's secret training base.

'You are Gorbachev,' he said. 'And I am Reagan. We would like to get rid of nuclear weapons. To inspire confidence, we will give you access to Star Wars. What do you say?'

In place of mutually assured destruction by nuclear weapons, Casey was effectively offering mutually assured defence against them.

Gordievsky/Gorbachev pondered for a moment, and then answered emphatically, in Russian.

'*Nyet!*'

Casey/Reagan was taken aback. In his imagined exchange, the US was effectively proposing to end the threat of nuclear war by sharing the technology to render it obsolete.

'Why *nyet*? We're giving you everything.'

'I don't trust you. You'll never give us everything. You'll hold something back which will give you the advantage.'

'So what do I do?'

'If you drop SDI altogether, Moscow will believe you.'

'That's not going to happen.' Casey slipped out of character for a moment. 'It is President Reagan's pet project. So what should we do?'

'All right,' said Gordievsky. 'Then keep it up. You keep up the pressure. Gorbachev and his people know they can't outspend you. Your technology is better than theirs. Keep it up.' Moscow would beggar itself trying to match Star Wars, he added, pouring money into a technological arms race it could never win. 'In the long term SDI will ruin the Soviet leadership.'

Some historians see the meeting in Fort Monckton as another pivotal moment in the Cold War.

At the Geneva summit the following November, the American President refused to budge on the Star Wars programme, just as Gordievsky had advised, describing it as 'necessary defence'. The first test of the SDI system was announced while the summit was underway. Later described as the 'fireside summit', reflecting the warmth between the two leaders, Reagan 'stood firm' on his pet project.

Gorbachev left Geneva believing the world was a 'safer place', but also convinced that the USSR would have to reform, and quickly, to catch up with the West. Glasnost and perestroika followed, and then a wave of tumultuous change that, in the end, Gorbachev was powerless to control. Gordievsky's accurate interpretation of Kremlin psychology in 1985 did not cause the collapse of the Soviet Union; but it probably helped.

The lunch with Bill Casey was only the first of many meetings with the CIA. Just a few months later, Gordievsky flew to Washington under tight security for a secret meeting with senior officials of the State Department, the National Security Council, the Defense Department and the intelligence agencies. Gordievsky was bombarded with questions, which he answered patiently, professionally and in unprecedented detail – no mere defector but a long-term, deep-penetration agent with an encyclopaedic understanding of the KGB. The Americans were impressed and grateful. The British were proud to share the expertise of their star spy. 'The information from Gordievsky was very good,' said Caspar Weinberger, Reagan's Defense Secretary.

But there was one question he could not answer. Who had betrayed him?

At CIA headquarters in Langley, Gordievsky was wheeled out to give a series of briefings to senior officers. At one of these, he was introduced to a tall, bespectacled man with a thin moustache, who seemed particularly friendly, 'quietly and patiently listening' to his every word. Most CIA officers struck Gordievsky as rather formal, even a little suspicious, but this one 'seemed different: his face radiated gentleness and kindness. I was so impressed by him that I thought that I had encountered the embodiment of American values: here was the openness, honesty and decency of which I had heard so much.'

For a dozen years, Gordievsky had lived a double life, a dedicated professional intelligence officer who was secretly loyal to the other side, playing a part. He was very good at it. But so was Aldrich Ames.

# EPILOGUE

# 16.   Passport for PIMLICO

A month after Gordievsky's escape, the scientific counsellor at the Soviet embassy in Paris was surprised to be invited to tea at the Alliance Française by a British diplomat he only vaguely knew. He turned up, on the afternoon of 15 August, to be greeted by an Englishman he had never seen before. 'I have a very important message for you to give the head of your KGB station,' the stranger said.

The Russian turned pale. He was about to be dragged into something very murky.

The Englishman calmly informed him that a senior KGB officer, until recently the *rezident* in London, was alive and well and living in the UK under close protection. 'He is very happy, but he would like his family back.'

So began Operation HETMAN, the campaign to get Leila and the girls to the UK, and reunite the Gordievsky family.

Within MI6 there was a debate about how to play the situation. A formal letter setting out a deal with the KGB was rejected as too risky. 'Any written document might have been doctored and played back at us in some way.' It was agreed to deliver an oral message to a *bona fide* Soviet diplomat outside the UK, and the luckless counsellor had been selected as the best recipient.

'I've never seen a man look so frightened,' said the MI6 message-bearer. 'He went away trembling.'

The terms were straightforward. Thanks to Gordievsky, the British now knew the identities of every KGB and GRU officer in Britain. These would have to leave. But Moscow could 'withdraw people gradually, over a long period, provided the Gordievsky family was set free'. That way the Kremlin would save face, its spies discreetly ejected without a diplomatic fuss, and the family would be reunited. If Moscow rejected a deal, however, and refused to release

Leila and the girls, then the Soviet spies in London would be expelled *en masse*. The KGB had two weeks to respond.

Gordievsky's fears for his family grew by the day. His pride at having bested the KGB was coupled with a soul-crushing guilt. The people he loved most were now prisoners of the Soviet Union. Margaret Thatcher's offer to strike a secret deal with Moscow was highly unorthodox, as Gordievsky acknowledged in a letter sent to the Prime Minister: 'To set aside procedures and allow the unofficial approach to go forward was a unique act of great generosity and humanity.'

It did not work.

The offer of a secret arrangement was received in Moscow with disbelief, and then fury. In the month since Gordievsky's disappearance, the KGB had scoured the country, unwilling to believe he could have escaped. Leila was repeatedly interrogated about her husband's whereabouts, as were other members of his family, including his younger sister and mother. Marina was petrified. Olga Gordievsky was stunned. Every colleague and friend was grilled. Leila maintained a dignified front, insisting that her husband was the victim of some plot, or a terrible mistake. She was tailed everywhere by six KGB surveillance officers. Her daughters were even watched in the school playground. Almost every day she was hauled into Lefortovo Prison for more questions. 'How did you not know he was spying for the British?' they asked, again and again. Finally, she snapped. 'Look. Let's be clear. I was a wife. My job was to clean, cook, shop, sleep with him, have children, share the bed and be his friend. I was good at it. I'm grateful he didn't tell me anything. For six years of my life I was a perfect wife. I did everything for him. You, the KGB, you have thousands of people with salaries whose job was to check up on people; they checked him and checked him and cleared him. And you come to me and blame me? Don't you think that sounds stupid? You didn't do your job. It wasn't my job, it was yours. You ruined my life.'

Over time, she got to know her interrogators. One day, one of the more sympathetic officers asked her: 'What would you have done if you *had* known that your husband was planning to escape?' There was a long pause before Leila answered: 'I would have let him go. I would have given him three days and then, as a loyal citizen, I would have reported it. But I would have made sure he had gone for sure before I did so.' The interrogator put down his pen: 'I think we will not put that in the report.' Leila was in enough trouble already.

Mikhail Lyubimov was brought in for questioning by Directorate K. 'Where could he be?' they demanded. 'Is he with some woman? Is he holed up in a hut somewhere in the Kursk region?' Lyubimov, of course, had no idea. 'Every aspect of my relationship with Gordievsky was combed through, looking for clues to his treachery.' But Lyubimov was as mystified as everyone else. 'My theory was simple, and based on his appearance when I last saw him: I thought he must have had a nervous breakdown, and possibly committed suicide.'

Ten days after the meeting in Paris, a message came back from the Centre, conveyed by the luckless scientific counsellor, in the form of a 'long tirade of abuse'. Gordievsky was a traitor; his family would remain in Russia; there would be no deal.

Britain prepared its response, Operation EMBASE. In September the Foreign Office released the news of Gordievsky's defection (though not, yet, the sensational details of his escape). Dramatic headlines splashed across every newspaper: 'The Biggest Fish Ever Netted', 'Friend Oleg, Master Spy', 'Russia's Ace of Spies; the Super-Spy Who Went West', 'Our Man in the KGB'. On the same day, the British government expelled twenty-five KGB and GRU officers identified by Gordievsky: a wholesale purge of Soviet spies. That day, Thatcher wrote to Ronald Reagan: 'We are making it clear to the Russians, on my personal authority, that while we cannot tolerate the sort of intelligence actions which Gordievsky has revealed, we continue to desire a constructive relationship with them. In the meantime, I think it is no bad thing that he [Gorbachev] should have presented to him so starkly, early in his leadership, the price to be paid for the scale and nature of KGB activities in western countries.'

Moscow's riposte was immediate. The ambassador, Sir Bryan Cartledge, was summoned to the Foreign Ministry by Vladimir Pavlovich Suslov, head of the department responsible for dealing with foreign embassies. On the desk in front of him, Suslov had the photograph of the new ambassador surrounded by his staff: with a leaden look, he placed two fingers on the heads of Roy Ascot and Arthur Gee. 'These two men are political bandits,' he said. The KGB had begun to piece the story together. Cartledge played dumb: 'What's all this about?' Suslov condemned the 'blatant activities' of British intelligence officers in the embassy, adding that the Soviet authorities 'know of the role assigned in this to first secretaries Gee and Ascot'. Suslov was particularly enraged that Rachel Gee had 'acted the part' of a woman with a bad back. He then read out the names of twenty-five British officials, including the two MI6 officers and their secretary, Violet Chapman, and stated they should leave the Soviet Union by the third week of October, the same deadline Mrs Thatcher had given for the expulsion of KGB staff in London. Most of these people had nothing to do with intelligence, let alone the exfiltration.

Sir Bryan Cartledge met Ascot in the safe-speech room, and blew off steam at gale force 12. The ambassador knew the Prime Minister had given her personal stamp of approval to the escape operation, but the fallout was only just beginning. 'He was absolutely furious,' recalled Ascot. 'He said we had wiped out his embassy, at a time when Thatcher was getting on with Gorbachev (partly because of our friend, but I couldn't tell Bryan that). There are people who are most eloquent when most angry. He told me how my great-grandfather, the Prime Minister, would be turning in his grave.' Actually, if Ascot's famous ancestor was doing anything in his grave, he was probably hooting with pleasure and pride.

In vain, Cartledge sent a most undiplomatic telegram to London, urging an end to the tit-for-tat expulsions: 'Never engage in a pissing match with a skunk: he possesses important natural advantages,' he wrote. (His fury rose another notch when that message found its way, verbatim, to the Prime Minister's desk.) But Thatcher had not finished her pissing competition with the Soviets. Her Cabinet Secretary, Sir Robert Armstrong, proposed four more expulsions. She did not consider this 'adequate', and insisted another six Soviet officials be thrown out. Sure enough, this prompted the immediate expulsion of six more British diplomats, bringing the overall total to sixty-two evictions, or thirty-one apiece. Cartledge's fears had been fully realized: 'I lost all my Russian speakers at a stroke . . . we'd lost half our embassy.'

Gordievsky remained in hiding at the fort. Occasionally, he would leave the building and explore the surrounding area, but always under heavy protection. He took a daily jog around the fort perimeter, or through the New Forest, accompanied by the MI6 officer Martin Shawford. But he could not make any new acquaintances, or contact old friends in Britain. MI6 attempted to make this life seem almost normal, but his only social contact was with members of the intelligence community and their families. He was always busy, but deeply lonely. The separation from his own family was a perpetual torment, the complete absence of news about them a source of anguish that occasionally erupted in bitter recrimination. To overcome his misery, he threw himself into the debriefing process, insisting on working long into the night. He veered between resignation and hope, pride in what he had achieved and despair at the personal cost. He wrote to Thatcher: 'Although I had prayed for an early reunion with my wife and children, I fully accept and understand the reasons for taking decisive action . . . I must, however, go on hoping that some way can be found to secure the release of my family as, without them, my life has no meaning.'

Thatcher replied: 'Our anxiety for your family remains and we shall not forget them. Having children of my own, I know the kind of thoughts and feelings which are going through your mind each and every day. Please do not say that life has no meaning. There is always hope.' Saying that she wished to meet him one day, the Prime Minister added: 'I am very conscious of your personal courage and your stand for freedom and democracy.'

Within the KGB, the news that Gordievsky had escaped to Britain set off a firestorm of mutual recrimination and buck-passing. Chebrikov, the KGB chief, and Kryuchkov, the head of the First Chief Directorate, blamed the Second Chief Directorate, which was theoretically responsible for internal security and counter-intelligence operations. The FCD bosses blamed Directorate K. Grushko blamed Gribin. Everyone blamed the surveillance team, which, since it occupied the lowest rung of the pecking order, had no one else to blame. The Leningrad KGB, responsible for surveillance of the British diplomats, was held directly accountable, and many senior officers were either sacked or demoted. Among those affected was Vladimir Putin, a product of the Leningrad KGB who saw most of his friends, colleagues and patrons purged as a direct consequence of Gordievsky's escape.

Embarrassed and enraged, and still uncertain exactly how Gordievsky had made his getaway, the KGB responded with a campaign of disinformation, planting fake news to the effect that he had been smuggled out of the embassy during the diplomatic reception, heavily disguised, or issued with false papers. His rank and importance were downplayed. The KGB would later claim – as MI6 had once claimed of Philby – that they had suspected him of disloyalty all along. In his memoirs, the former Foreign Minister Yevgeny Primakov suggested that, under interrogation, Gordievsky had offered to switch sides yet again. 'Gordievsky was close to confessing when he began to probe the possibility of actively operating against the British, and even offered various guarantees that he could work successfully as a double agent. The KGB leadership was informed that day. Foreign-intelligence officers were confident he would admit everything the next day. But suddenly an order came from above to stop the debriefing, remove outside surveillance, and send Gordievsky to a health centre . . . from there he fled across the Finnish border.' Primakov's gloss does not make sense. If Gordievsky only came 'close' to confessing, he plainly did not actually do so; and if he did not admit to being a British agent, how could he have offered to be a double agent?

Both Primakov and Viktor Cherkashin, Ames's first KGB handler, insisted that the KGB had been alerted to Gordievsky's betrayal by an unnamed source months before his return to Moscow. But, for all the bluster and fakery, the KGB leadership knew the truth: it had held the most significant spy of the Cold War in its grasp, and then let him slip through its fingers.

Two days after the Anglo-Soviet diplomatic bloodbath, a long column of passenger cars, some twenty in all, trundled along the Leningrad to Vyborg highway. Eight were British diplomatic cars, and every other car was a KGB surveillance vehicle. The diplomats were being expelled through Finland: Ascot and Gee were retracing the escape route, only now they were escorted out of the country 'like prisoners being paraded in triumph'. In his luggage, Gee had carefully packed a Harrods bag, and a tape of Sibelius's *Finlandia*. As they reached the lay-by with its distinctive rock, the KGB cars slowed, and the Soviet officers all swivelled in their seats and stared at the spot as they drove slowly past. 'They had worked it out.'

The KGB, legalistic to the last, had not quite finished with Gordievsky. On 14 November 1985, he was tried *in absentia* by a military tribunal, convicted of treason, and sentenced to death. Seven years later, Leonid Shebarshin, who had succeeded Kryuchkov as head of the FCD, gave an interview in which he said he hoped Gordievsky would be assassinated in Britain, and issued what sounded like a public threat to do so. 'Technically,' he said, 'it's nothing very special.'

**Oleg Gordievsky** became a one-man intelligence roadshow. He travelled the world, accompanied by a series of MI6 minders, explaining the KGB and demystifying that most mysterious of organizations. Among other countries, he travelled to New Zealand, South Africa, Australia, Canada, France, West Germany, Israel, Saudi Arabia and throughout Scandinavia. Three months after his exfiltration, a gathering was held at Century House, to which representatives of all the intelligence services were invited, along with selected government officials and allies, to examine the Gordievsky haul and its implications for arms control, East–West relations and future intelligence planning. The hundreds of individual reports were piled up on a single conference table, 'like a huge buffet', over which the assembled spies and spymasters browsed and gorged for two solid days.

In Britain, MI6 bought a house for him in the London suburbs where he lived under a false name. MI6 and MI5 took the death threats seriously. He gave lectures, listened to music, and wrote books with the historian Christopher Andrew, works of detailed scholarship that still stand as the most comprehensive accounts of Soviet intelligence to date. He even gave television interviews, disguised in a faintly absurd wig and false beard. The KGB knew what he looked like, but it was not worth taking chances. As Gorbachev's reforms began to sweep the Soviet Union, and the communist empire started to totter, his expertise was ever more sought after.

In May 1986, Margaret Thatcher invited him to Chequers, her

official country residence. For nearly three hours, she interviewed the man she had known as Mr Collins: on arms control, Soviet political strategy and Gorbachev. In March 1987 he briefed her again, this time in Downing Street, before she made another successful visit to Moscow. The same year, he met Ronald Reagan in the Oval Office, where they discussed Soviet espionage networks and posed for the cameras. The meeting lasted twenty-two minutes (four minutes longer, Gordievsky gleefully noted, than the Labour leader, Neil Kinnock, had enjoyed with the leader of the free world). 'We know you,' said Reagan, putting an arm around the Russian's shoulder. 'We appreciate what you've done for the West. Thank you. We remember your family, and we'll fight for them.'

For the first years of liberty, he was exceedingly busy, but often profoundly miserable.

Gordievsky's family remained captives of a vengeful KGB. In a recurrent dream, he saw his wife and daughters returning at the arrivals hall in Heathrow to a joyful reunion, only to wake up to the knowledge that he was alone.

In Moscow, Leila lived under effective house arrest, kept under close surveillance in case she, too, somehow managed to flee. Her telephone was tapped. Her letters were intercepted. She could not find a job, and depended on her parents for support. One by one, her friends seemed to melt away. 'There was an absolute vacuum. Everyone was frightened to see me. I changed the children's names to Aliyev, because Gordievsky is such a distinctive name. My daughters would have been ostracized.' She stopped cutting her hair, and declared she would not cut it again until she was reunited with her husband. When, years later, she was asked by a journalist how she felt when she heard he had defected to Britain, she said: 'I was simply glad to know he was alive.' Under the terms of Gordievsky's conviction for treachery, their combined property was confiscated: flat, car, luggage and the video recorder brought from Denmark. 'The camp bed with the holes in the mattress, the iron. They especially liked the iron because it was an imported one, a Hoover,' Leila said.

Gordievsky tried to send her telegrams, but these never reached her. He bought presents, including expensive clothes for the girls, which he lovingly wrapped and sent to Moscow. All were seized by the KGB. When a letter finally arrived from Leila, he read the first few lines and realized it had been dictated by the KGB. 'They've forgiven you,' she wrote. 'You can easily get another job.' Was this a trap to lure him back? Was she conspiring with the KGB? He managed to smuggle a letter to her, through a Soviet official, in which he stuck to the claim that he was the victim of a KGB plot, perhaps thinking this would protect her. Leila was appalled. She knew it was not true. 'He told me: I'm not guilty of anything. I'm an honest officer, I'm a loyal citizen and so on, and I had to flee abroad. Why he lied to me again I don't know. It was surreal. I tried to understand. There were some words about the children, and he said he still loved me. But I thought: "You did what you wanted to do – I am still here with the children. You ran, but we are prisoners."' They were deceiving each other. Perhaps they were deceiving themselves. The KGB told Leila that her husband was having 'an affair with a young English secretary'.

Leila was informed by the KGB that if she formally divorced Gordievsky, her property would be returned, including the iron. 'They said I should think of the children.' She agreed. The KGB sent a taxi to take her to the divorce court, and paid the divorce tax. She reverted to her maiden name. She believed she would never see him again. 'Life went forward,' she said. 'The children went to school, they had some joy. Never did I dare to cry in front of my children or show what was in my soul. I always had a proud mind and a smile on my face.' But she told a sympathetic Western journalist who managed to secure a brief interview that she still loved her husband, and longed to be with him. 'Even if I am not his wife on paper, I am still his wife in spirit.'

The campaign to get the family out continued for six years, relentlessly and fruitlessly. 'We tried to approach them through the Finns and Norwegians, but we had no cards,' said George Walker, the MI6 officer in charge of Operation HETMAN and now one of Gordievsky's main points of contact with the Service. 'We spoke to people in neutral countries, and human rights people. We got the French, the Germans, the New Zealanders, everybody, to organize and try to build pressure for their release. The Foreign Office was constantly bringing it up through the ambassadors in Moscow.' When Margaret

Thatcher met Gorbachev in March 1987, she immediately raised the issue of Gordievsky's family. Charles Powell observed the Soviet leader's reaction. 'He went white with anger and refused to respond at all.' They would meet twice more over the coming years. On both occasions, Thatcher raised the matter again, and was rebuffed. 'But it didn't deter her, it never did deter her.'

The KGB would not relent. 'Oleg had made absolute fools of them,' said Walker. 'The only punishment they could inflict on Oleg was not to let his wife and children go.'

Two years after the escape, a letter from Leila arrived in London, brought out by a Finnish lorry driver who posted it to London from Helsinki. The letter, in Russian on three pages of foolscap, was not written under KGB direction. It was honest, and furious. Walker read it: 'It was the letter of a very strong, able, very angry woman saying: "Why didn't you tell me? How could you abandon me? What are you doing to rescue us?"' Any hope that the story might have a fairy-tale ending began to fade. Betrayal, extended separation and KGB misinformation had eroded what little marital trust remained. Occasionally they managed to make telephone contact, but the conversations were strained, as well as overheard and recorded. The girls were shy and monosyllabic. The stilted exchanges on a crackling line seemed only to magnify the distance, both physical and psychological. Walker observed: 'I knew from the start it wasn't going to be an easy reconciliation. It would have been extraordinarily difficult under any circumstances. But once I'd read the letter it was clear that it was very unlikely that there was going to be a reunion.' Operation HETMAN continued nonetheless. 'My job was to make sure that we still remembered this woman.'

The escape had stunned and deeply embarrassed the KGB, but the heads that rolled were, as always, the smaller ones. **Nikolai Gribin**, Gordievsky's immediate boss, was demoted, even though he had no responsibility for what had happened. **Vladimir Kryuchkov**, the head of the First Chief Directorate, became Chairman of the KGB in 1988. As his deputy, **Viktor Grushko** rose with him. **Viktor Budanov**, who had led the investigation, was appointed head of Directorate K and rose to the rank of general. After the collapse of communism, Budanov founded Elite Security. In 2017, it was announced that Elite had won a $2.8 million contract to guard the US embassy in Moscow, an irony that amused Mikhail Lyubimov, who pointed out that the Russian embassy in Washington would be quite unlikely to hire a company with links to the CIA.

The Berlin Wall, the barrier that had triggered the first stirrings of rebellion in Gordievsky, came down in 1989, following a wave of anti-communist revolutions in Eastern and Central Europe. With glasnost and perestroika, the KGB began to loosen its grip on the disintegrating Soviet Union. The hardliners of the Kremlin were increasingly unhappy with Gorbachev's reforms, and in August 1991 a group of plotters, led by Kryuchkov, attempted to seize power. He doubled the pay of all KGB personnel, ordered them back from holiday, and placed them on alert. The coup collapsed after three days. Kryuchkov was arrested, along with Grushko, and charged with high treason. Gorbachev moved quickly against his enemies in Soviet intelligence: the KGB's 230,000 troops were placed under Defence Ministry control, Directorate K was disbanded, and most of the top leadership was fired – with the exception of **Gennadi Titov**, now a general. 'The Crocodile' happened to be on holiday when the coup was launched, and was promoted to head of counter-intelligence. 'Spying has become much harder than it used to be,' he said wistfully, a few days after the attempted putsch.

Kryuchkov was replaced by Vadim Bakatin, a democratic reformer who set about dismantling the vast espionage and security system that had terrorized the Soviet Union for so long. 'I am presenting the President with plans for the destruction of this organization,' said Bakatin. The new head of the KGB would also be its last. One of his first acts was to announce that the Gordievsky family would be reunited. 'I felt it was an old problem, which should be resolved,' said Bakatin. 'When I asked my generals, they all categorically said "No!" but I decided to ignore them, and regard this as my first major victory in the KGB.'

**Leila Aliyeva Gordievsky** and her daughters, Maria (Masha) and Anna, landed at Heathrow on 6 September 1991, and were flown by helicopter to Fort Monckton, where Gordievsky was waiting to take them home. There were flowers, champagne and presents. He had tied yellow ribbons, the American symbols of homecoming, through-out the house, bought fresh new linen for the girls' beds, and turned on every lamp to create a 'cheerful blaze of light'.

Three months after the family was reunited, the Soviet Union was dissolved. The newspapers published posed photographs of the family, strolling happily through London, a picture of domestic harmony and the power of love at a time of tumultuous political upheaval in Russia. Here was a convenient romantic symbol for the end of communism. But after six years of enforced estrangement, there was also deep pain. Masha, now aged eleven, barely remembered her father. To his ten-year-old younger daughter, Anna, he was a stranger. Oleg expected Leila to slot back into the marriage just as before. He found her critical and hostile, 'demanding explanations'. He accused her of making the children deliberately dependent on her. For Leila, the return to Britain was just the latest chapter in a story over which she had no control. Her life had been destroyed by politics and the secret choices made by a man she had loved deeply, and trusted completely, but had never fully known. 'He did what he believed in, and I respect him for that. But he didn't ask me. He involved me without my choice. He didn't give me an opportunity to choose. From his point of view he was my saviour. But who put me in the shit-hole? He'd forgotten the first part. You can't kick someone off a cliff and then put out a hand and say: "I saved you!" He was so bloody Russian.' Leila could not forget, or get over, what had happened to her. They tried to reassemble a family life, but the marriage that existed before the escape was from another world, another time, and could not be wished back to life. In the end, she felt Gordievsky's loyalty to an idea had taken precedence over his love for her. 'The relationship between a person and the state is one thing, and the relationship of two loving people is completely different,' she said, many years later. The marriage, already over in the eyes of Soviet law, came to a swift and bitter end. 'There was nothing left,' Oleg wrote. They parted for ever in 1993, their relationship destroyed by the battle between the KGB and MI6, between communism and the West. The marriage had been conceived amid the impossible contradictions of Cold War espionage, and died just as that war was ending.

Leila divides her time between Russia and the UK. Their daughters, Maria and Anna, attended British schools and universities, and remain in Britain. They do not use the name Gordievsky. MI6 continues its duty of care to the family.

Gordievsky's friends and colleagues in the KGB could not forgive him either. **Maksim Parshikov** was brought back from London, investigated by the KGB, and then fired. He spent the rest of his life wondering why Gordievsky had taken the leap into betrayal. 'It's true that Oleg was a dissident. But who in the USSR in his sober mind wouldn't be a dissident in the 1980s, at least to a certain extent? The majority of us in the London *rezidentura* were a bunch of dissidents to different degrees, and we all liked life in the West. But it was only Oleg who turned out to be a traitor.' **Mikhail Lyubimov** took the betrayal as a personal injury: Gordievsky had been his friend, they had shared secrets, music and the works of Somerset Maugham. 'Immediately after Gordievsky's flight, I felt the fist of the KGB. Almost all former colleagues immediately broke contact with me, and shied away from meetings . . . I heard rumours that menacing KGB orders referred to me as the main culprit in Gordievsky's betrayal.' Only now did he understand the clue Gordievsky had given him on the eve of his escape by referring to 'Mr Harrington's Washing'. Though he never succeeded in becoming the Russian Somerset Maugham, Lyubimov wrote novels, plays and memoirs, and remained a most distinctive hybrid of the Cold War: Soviet in loyalty, old-school English in manner. He deeply resented that he had been used to divert the attention of the KGB at the crucial moment in the escape, and made into what he called, in English, a 'red herring'. Gordievsky had outraged his sense of British fair play. They never spoke again.

Sir **Bryan Cartledge** was surprised how quickly, after the tit-for-tat spy expulsions, relations between Britain and the Soviet Union resumed their former warmth. He completed his ambassadorship in the Soviet Union in 1988. Looking back on the case, he described the exfiltration as 'an extraordinary victory'. Gordievsky had supplied 'a compendium of knowledge of the KGB's structure and modus operandi . . . enabling us comprehensively to frustrate them, probably for years'. **Rosemary Spencer**, the researcher at Conservative Central Office, was shocked to discover that the charming Russian diplomat she had grown so close to, at the behest of MI5, was working for MI6 all along. She married a Dane, and moved to Copenhagen.

Gordievsky's MI6 case officers and handlers maintained their bond, a secret cell inside the secret world. The other officers – **Richard Bromhead, Veronica Price, James Spooner, Geoffrey Guscott, Martin Shawford, Simon Brown, Sarah Page, Arthur Gee, Violet Chapman, George Walker** – stayed in the shadows, where they remain, at their own request, because these are not their real names. At a secret audience with the Queen, **Ascot** and **Gee** were each appointed an OBE, and Chapman was appointed an MBE. **Philip Hawkins**, the Scotsman who had been Gordievsky's first case officer, gave a typically dry response when he learned of the escape: 'Oh, he was genuine after all, was he? I never believed he was.'

**John Deverell**, the head of K Section, went on to head MI5 in Northern Ireland. He was killed in 1994, along with most of Britain's other Northern Ireland intelligence experts, when their Chinook helicopter crashed on the Mull of Kintyre. In March 2015, after **Roy Ascot** had taken his seat in the House of Lords, a fellow peer, the historian Peter Hennessy, spectacularly blew his cover: 'Although I know that he is too discreet to mention it, the noble Earl possesses a special place in intelligence history as the officer who spirited that remarkable and brave man, Oleg Gordievsky, out of Russia and into Finland.' Ascot's daughter, whose dirty nappy had played such a strange role in the Cold War, became an authority on Russian art. The KGB could never quite believe that MI6 had taken along a baby as cover on an exfiltration operation.

**Michael Bettaney** was released on parole in 1998, having served fourteen years of his twenty-three-year sentence. In 1987, **Stig Bergling**, the Swedish spy, was let out of prison for a conjugal visit with his wife, and escaped to Moscow, where he lived on a handsome stipend of 500 roubles a month. He moved on to Budapest a year later, and then Lebanon, where he worked as a security consultant to Walid Jumblatt, the leader of the Druze militia. In 1994 he called the Swedish security service and announced he wanted to come home. After serving three more years, he was released on the grounds of ill-health. Bergling died of Parkinson's disease in 2015, soon after shooting and wounding a nurse in his care home with an air gun. **Arne Treholt** was released and controversially pardoned by the Norwegian government in 1992 after serving eight years in a maximum-security prison. His case remains a source of dispute in Norway. The Norwegian Criminal Cases Review Commission reopened an investigation into the conviction and concluded in 2011 that there was no basis to suggest evidence had been tampered with, as Treholt's supporters claimed. After his release, he settled in Russia and then Cyprus, where he works as a businessman and consultant. **Michael Foot** sued the *Sunday Times* in 1995 over an article, serializing Gordievsky's memoirs, with the headline: 'KGB: Foot was our agent'. Foot described the article as a 'McCarthyite smear', and was paid substantial damages, some of which were used to finance the running of *Tribune*. Foot died in 2010 at the age of ninety-six.

For Western intelligence services, the Gordievsky case became a textbook example of how to recruit and run a spy, how to use intelligence to inform and improve international relations, and how, in the most dramatic circumstances, a spy in peril could be saved. But the question of who had betrayed him still lingered. Gordievsky had his own theories: perhaps his first wife, Yelena, or Standa Kaplan, his Czech friend, had given him away; perhaps Bettaney had worked out who had exposed him as an MI5 mole; or was it the arrest and trial of Arne Treholt that had alerted the KGB? It did not occur to him, or MI6, to suspect the friendly American officer who frequently sat across the table during his marathon CIA briefings.

After a stint in Rome, **Aldrich Ames** was assigned to the CIA's Counterintelligence Center Analysis Group and given access to fresh information on the agency's Soviet agents, which he passed straight to the KGB. The death toll mounted, as did the balance of his Swiss and American bank accounts. He bought a brand new silver Jaguar, and then an Alfa Romeo. He spent half a million dollars, in cash, on a new home. He had his nicotine-stained teeth capped. Rosario's aristocratic airs provided cover, since he claimed the money came from her wealthy relatives. The KGB assured him that it could help him escape if he ever came under suspicion: 'We were prepared to do in Washington what the British had done in Moscow with Gordievsky,' said his KGB handler. Ames earned a grand total of $4.6 million from the Soviets, a figure only slightly more astonishing than the fact that his monogrammed shirts and gleaming new teeth had passed unremarked by his CIA colleagues for so long.

On the surface, Gordievsky and Ames behaved in similar ways. Both turned against their respective organizations and countries, and used their intelligence expertise to identify spies for the other side. Both betrayed the oath they had made at the start of their careers, and both appeared to live one life, while living another in secret. But there any similarity ends. Ames spied for money; Gordievsky was driven by ideological conviction. Ames's victims were rooted out by the KGB and, in most cases, killed; the people Gordievsky exposed, such as Bettaney and Treholt, were watched, intercepted, tried by due process, imprisoned and eventually released back into society. Gordievsky risked his life for a cause; Ames wanted a bigger car. Ames chose to serve a brutal totalitarian regime for which he felt no affinity, a country where he would never have considered living; Gordievsky tasted democratic freedom, made it his mission to defend and support that way of life and culture, finally settling in the West at huge personal cost. In the end, the difference between them is a matter of moral judgement: Gordievsky was on the side of the good; and Ames was on his own side.

The CIA initially put the loss of so many of its Soviet agents down to causes other than an internal spy, including a bug in CIA head-quarters, or a broken code. The lingering trauma from Angleton's mole-hunts in the 1960s and 1970s made the possibility of betrayal from within too painful to contemplate. But finally it became clear that only treachery could explain the level of attrition, and by 1993 Ames's lavish lifestyle had finally attracted attention. He was placed under surveillance, his movements tracked and his rubbish searched for clues. On 21 February 1994, Rick and Rosario Ames were arrested by the FBI. 'You're making a big mistake!' he insisted. 'You must have the wrong man!' Two months later he pleaded guilty to spying, and was sentenced to life in prison; in a plea bargain, Rosario got five years for tax evasion and conspiracy to commit espionage. In court, Ames admitted that he had compromised 'virtually all Soviet agents of the CIA and other American and foreign services known to me' and had provided the Soviet Union and Russia with a 'huge quantity of information on United States foreign, defense and security policies'. Rick Ames, Prisoner 40087-083, is currently imprisoned at the Federal Correctional Institution in Terre Haute, Indiana.

Gordievsky was staggered to discover that the man he had regarded as a model American patriot had tried to murder him. 'Ames blew my career and life into shreds,' he wrote. 'But he did not kill me.'

In 1997 the American television journalist Ted Koppel interviewed Ames in prison. Gordievsky was interviewed in England beforehand, and Koppel brought the videotape with him to show to Ames, and gauge his reaction. The betrayed man directly addressed his betrayer. 'Aldrich Ames is a traitor,' said Gordievsky, as Ames, dressed in prison garb, intensely studied the footage on a screen. 'He only worked for money. He was simply a greedy bastard. He will be punished by his own conscience until the end of his days. You can say: "Mr Gordievsky has nearly forgiven you!"'

Koppel turned to Ames as the tape ended: 'Do you believe him that he has nearly forgiven you?'

'I think so,' said Ames. 'I think everything he said there certainly strikes me very strongly. I said once that the men I betrayed had made similar choices and taken similar chances. Any reasonable person hearing me say that is going to say: "What arrogance!" But that was not an arrogant statement.' Ames's tone was self-justifying, almost smug, as he insisted on the moral equivalence between his actions and those of the other spy. But the sight of Gordievsky also prompted Ames to utter something that sounded close to regret: 'The kind of shame and the kind of remorse that I feel is something that is and always will be intensely personal.'

Oleg Gordievsky still lives, under an assumed name, in the detached house on a nondescript suburban street in England that he moved into soon after his escape from Russia. His home is almost entirely unremarkable. Only the high hedges around it, and the telltale ping of an invisible electronic tripwire as you approach the building, indicate that it might be different from the neighbouring houses. The execution order is still in force, and MI6 continues to watch over its most valued Cold War spy. The anger of the KGB lingers. In 2015, Sergei Ivanov, then Vladimir Putin's chief of staff, blamed Gordievsky for damaging his KGB career: 'Gordievsky turned me in. I cannot say that his shameful betrayal and recruitment by the British intelligence service broke my life but I got certain problems at work.' On 4 March 2018 a former GRU officer named Sergei Skripal and his daughter, Yulia, were poisoned by assassins using a Russian nerve agent. Like Gordievsky, Skripal had spied for MI6, but he had been caught in Russia, tried, imprisoned and then exchanged in a spy swap in 2010. Andrei Lugovoi, the former KGB bodyguard accused of murdering the defector Alexander Litvinenko a decade earlier, offered an intriguing response when asked whether Russia had also poisoned Skripal: 'If we had to kill anyone, Gordievsky was the one. He was smuggled out of the country and sentenced here to death *in absentia*.' Putin and his people have not forgotten. The security measures surrounding him were reinforced in the wake of the Skripal poisoning. His home is under twenty-four-hour surveillance.

Today Gordievsky seldom leaves the house, though friends and former colleagues in MI5 and MI6 frequently visit him. New recruits are occasionally brought to meet a legend of the secret services. He is still considered a potential target for retribution. He reads, writes, listens to classical music, and closely follows political developments, particularly in his native land. He has never returned to Russia since the day he crossed the Finnish border in 1985, and says he has no desire to do so: 'I am British now.' He never saw his mother again. Olga Gordievsky died in 1989, at the age of eighty-two. To the end she insisted that her son was innocent. 'He is not a double agent, but a triple agent, still working for the KGB.' Gordievsky never had the opportunity to tell her the truth. 'I would dearly have liked to let her have my version of events.'

As the afterlives of so many spies attest, espionage extracts a heavy price.

Oleg Gordievsky still lives a double life. To his suburban neighbours, the bowed, bearded old man living quietly behind the tall hedges is just another old-age pensioner, a person of little consequence. In reality he is someone else entirely, a figure of profound historical importance, and a remarkable man: proud, shrewd, irascible, his brooding manner illuminated by sudden flashes of ironic humour. He is sometimes hard to like, and impossible not to admire. He has no regrets, he says, but from time to time he will break off in mid-conversation, and stare darkly into a distance only he can see. He is one of the bravest people I have ever met, and one of the loneliest.

In the 2007 Queen's birthday honours, Gordievsky was appointed Companion of the Most Distinguished Order of St Michael and St George (CMG), for 'services to the security of the United Kingdom' – the same gong, he likes to point out, as that awarded to the fictional James Bond. The media in Moscow reported, wrongly, that former Comrade Gordievsky would henceforth be 'Sir Oleg'. Gordievsky's portrait hangs in Fort Monckton.

In July 2015, on the thirtieth anniversary of his escape, all those involved in running the case and exfiltrating him from Russia gathered to celebrate the 76-year-old Russian spy. The original cheap imitation leather holdall, with which he escaped to Finland, is now in the MI6 museum. At the anniversary celebration he was presented, as a souvenir, with a new travel bag. It contained the following: a Mars bar, a plastic Harrods bag, a map of Western Russia, pills 'for the relief of worry, irritability, insomnia and stress', mosquito repellent, two bottles of chilled beer and two cassette tapes: Dr. Hook's *Greatest Hits* and Sibelius's *Finlandia*.

The final items in the bag were a packet of cheese and onion crisps, and a baby's nappy.

# Codenames and Aliases

| | |
|---|---|
| ABLE ARCHER 83 | NATO war game |
| BOOT | Michael Foot (KGB) |
| COE | Bettaney case (MI5) |
| DANICEK | Stanislaw Kaplan (MI6) |
| DARIO | Unidentified KGB illegal (KGB) |
| DISARRANGE | Exfiltration of Czech intelligence officer (MI6) |
| DRIM | Jack Jones (KGB) |
| ELLI | Leo Long (KGB) |
| ELMEN | Joint MI5–MI6 Bettaney counter-intelligence operation (MI5/MI6) |
| EMBASE | Expulsion of KGB/GRU personnel after Gordievsky's detectim (UK) |
| FAREWELL | Vladimir Vetrov (Direction Générale de la Surveillance du Territoire) |
| FAUST | Yevgeni Ushakov (KGB) |
| FOOT | Expulsion of KGB/GRU personnel (MI5/MI6) |
| FREED | Czech intelligence officer (MI6) |
| GLYPTIC | Josef Stalin (MI5) |
| GOLDFINCH | Oleg Lyalin (MI5/MI6) |
| GOLFPLATZ | Great Britain (German) |
| GORMSSON | Oleg Gordievsky (PET) |
| GORNOV | Oleg Gordievsky (KGB) |
| GROMOV | Vasili Gordievsky (KGB) |
| GRETA | Gunvor Galtung Haavik (KGB) |
| GROUND | Cash transfer to DARIO (KGB) |
| GUARDIYETSEV | Oleg Gordievsky (KGB) |
| HETMAN | Campaign for release of Leila Gordievsky and daughters (MI6) |

| | |
|---|---|
| INVISIBLE | Exfiltration of Czech scientists (MI6) |
| KOBA | Michael Bettaney |
| KORIN | Mikhail Lyubimov (KGB) |
| KRONIN | Stanislav Androsov (KGB) |
| LAMPAD | Joint MI5-MI6 liaison (MI5/MI6) |
| NOCTON | Oleg Gordievsky (MI6) |
| OVATION | Oleg Gordievsky (MI6) |
| PIMLICO | Gordievsky exfiltration operation (MI6) |
| PUCK | Michael Bettaney (MI5) |
| RON | Richard Gott (KGB) |
| RYAN | Raketno-Yadernoye Napadeniye (Soviet Union) |
| SUNBEAM | Oleg Gordievsky (MI6) |
| TICKLE | Oleg Gordievsky (CIA) |
| UPTIGHT | MI6 (CIA) |
| ZEUS | Gert Petersen (KGB) |
| ZIGZAG | Eddie Chapman (MI5) |

# Acknowledgements

This book could not have been written without the wholehearted support and cooperation of its subject. Over the last three years, I have interviewed Oleg Gordievsky, at the safe house, on more than twenty occasions, amassing more than 100 hours of taped conversations. His hospitality has been endless, his patience boundless and his memory prodigious. His cooperation came without strings attached, or any attempt to shape the writing of this book: the interpretation of events and the mistakes it contains are entirely my own. Through Gordievsky, I was able to speak to every MI6 officer involved in the case, and I am hugely grateful to them for their help. These agreed to speak freely, on condition of anonymity. Living former MI6 officers, and some former Russian and Danish intelligence officers, appear here under pseudonyms, including several individuals who have already been publicly identified. All other names are real. I have also benefited from the generous help of many of the former KGB, MI5 and CIA officers involved in the Gordievsky case. This book was not authorized or aided by MI6, and I have had no access to the files of the Intelligence Service, which remain classified.

Two people have been particularly helpful: arranging meetings with the different participants, attending interviews with Gordievsky, checking the manuscript for factual accuracy, providing nourishment, spiritual and gastronomic, and generally ensuring that a complex and potentially fraught operation has been completed with efficiency and endless good humour. They deserve far greater credit than I can give them; but, to their credit, they do not want it.

I also wish to thank Christopher Andrew, Keith Blackmore, John Blake, Bob Bookman, Karen Brown, Venetia Butterfield, Alex Carey, Charles Cohen, Gordon Corera, David Cornwell, Luke Corrigan, Charles Cumming, Lucie Donahue, St John Donald, Kevin Doughton, Lisa Dwan, Charles Elton, Natasha Fairweather,

Emme Fane, Stephen Garrett, Tina Gaudoin, Burton Gerber, Blanche Girouard, Claire Haggard, Bill Hamilton, Robert Hands, Kate Hubbard, Lynda Jordan, Mary Jordan, Steve Kappas, Ian Katz, Daisy Lewis, Clare Longrigg, Kate Macintyre, Magnus Macintyre, Robert McCrum, Chloe McGregor, Ollie McGregor, Gill Morgan, Vikki Nelson, Rebecca Nicolson, Roland Philipps, Peter Pomerantsev, Igor Pomeranysev, Andrew Previté, Justine Roberts, Felicity Rubinstein, Melita Samoilys, Mikael Shields, Molly Stern, Angus Stewart, Jane Stewart, Kevin Sullivan, Matt Whiteman, Damian Whitworth, Caroline Wood.

My friends and colleagues at *The Times* have been an endless source of support, inspiration and deserved mockery. The late Ed Victor, my brilliant agent for twenty-five years, was there at the inception, and Jonny Geller took over the reins magnificently. The teams at Viking and Crown have been superb. Finally, my thanks and love to my children, Barney, Finn and Molly, the kindest and funniest people I know.

# Select Bibliography

Andrew, Christopher, *The Defence of the Realm: The Authorized History of MI5*, London, 2009

—, *Secret Service: The Making of the British Intelligence Community*, London, 1985

Andrew, Christopher, and Oleg Gordievsky (eds.), *Instructions from the Centre: Top Secret Files on KGB Foreign Operations 1975–1985*, London, 1991

—, *KGB: The Inside Story of Its Foreign Operations from Lenin to Gorbachev*, London, 1991

Andrew, Christopher, and Vasili Mitrokhin, *The Mitrokhin Archive: The KGB in Europe and the West*, London, 1999

—, *The World was Going Our Way: The KGB and the Battle for the Third World*, London, 2005

Barrass, Gordon S., *The Great Cold War: A Journey through the Hall of Mirrors*, Stanford, Calif., 2009

Bearden, Milton, and James Risen, *The Main Enemy: The Inside Story of the CIA's Final Showdown with the KGB*, London, 2003

Borovik, Genrikh, *The Philby Files: The Secret Life of Master Spy Kim Philby – KGB Archives Revealed*, London, 1994

Brook-Shepherd, Gordon, *The Storm Birds: Soviet Post-War Defectors*, London, 1988

Carl, Leo D., *The International Dictionary of Intelligence*, McLean, Va, 1990

Carter, Miranda, *Anthony Blunt: His Lives*, London, 2001

Cavendish, Anthony, *Inside Intelligence: The Revelations of an MI6 Officer*, London, 1990

Cherkashin, Victor, with Gregory Feifer, *Spy Handler: Memoir of a KGB Officer*, New York, 2005

Corera, Gordon, *MI6: Life and Death in the British Secret Service*, London, 2012

Earley, Pete, *Confessions of a Spy: The Real Story of Aldrich Ames*, London, 1997

Fischer, Benjamin B., 'A Cold War Conundrum: The 1983 Soviet War Scare', https://www.cia.gov/library/center-for-the-study-of-intelligence/csi-publications/books-and-monographs/a-cold-war-conundrum/source.htm

Gaddis, John Lewis, *The Cold War*, London, 2007

Gates, Robert M., *From the Shadows: The Ultimate Insider's Story of Five Presidents and How They Won the Cold War*, New York, 2006

Gordievsky, Oleg, *Next Stop Execution: The Autobiography of Oleg Gordievsky*, London, 1995

Grimes, Sandra, and Jeanne Vertefeuille, *Circle of Treason: A CIA Account of Traitor Aldrich Ames and the Men He Betrayed*, Annapolis, Md, 2012

Helms, Richard, *A Look Over My Shoulder: A Life in the Central Intelligence Agency*, New York, 2003

Hoffman, David E., *The Billion Dollar Spy: A True Story of Cold War Espionage and Betrayal*, New York, 2015

Hollander, Paul, *Political Will and Personal Belief: The Decline and Fall of Soviet Communism*, New Haven, Conn., 1999

Howe, Geoffrey, *Conflict of Loyalty*, London, 1994

Jeffery, Keith, *MI6: The History of the Secret Intelligence Service 1909–1949*, London, 2010

Jones, Nate (ed.), *Able Archer 83: The Secret History of the NATO Exercise That Almost Triggered Nuclear War*, New York, 2016

Kalugin, Oleg, *Spymaster: My Thirty-Two Years in Intelligence and Espionage against the West*, New York, 2009

Kendall, Bridget, *The Cold War: A New Oral History of Life between East and West*, London, 2018

Lyubimov, Mikhail, *Записки непутевого резидента* (*Notes of a Ne'er-Do-Well Rezident or Will-o'-the-Wisp*), Moscow, 1995

—, *Шпионы, которых я люблю и ненавижу* (*Spies I Love and Hate*), Moscow, 1997

Moore, Charles, *Margaret Thatcher: The Authorized Biography*, vol. 11: *Everything She Wants*, London, 2015

Morley, Jefferson, *The Ghost: The Secret Life of CIA Spymaster James Jesus Angleton*, London, 2017

Oberdorfer, Don, *From the Cold War to a New Era: The United States and the Soviet Union, 1983–1991*, Baltimore, 1998

Parker, Philip (ed.), *The Cold War Spy Pocket Manual*, Oxford, 2015

Philby, Kim, *My Silent War*, London, 1968

Pincher, Chapman, *Treachery: Betrayals, Blunders and Cover-Ups. Six Decades of Espionage*, Edinburgh, 2012

Primakov, Yevgeny, *Russian Crossroads: Toward the New Millennium*, New Haven, Conn., 2004

Sebag Montefiore, Simon, *Stalin: The Court of the Red Tsar*, London, 2003

Trento, Joseph J., *The Secret History of the CIA*, New York, 2001

Weiner, Tim, *Legacy of Ashes: The History of the CIA*, London, 2007

Weiner, Tim, David Johnston and Neil A. Lewis, *Betrayal: The Story of Aldrich Ames, an American Spy*, London, 1996

Westad, Odd Arne, *The Cold War: A World History*, London, 2017

West, Nigel, *At Her Majesty's Secret Service: The Chiefs of Britain's Intelligence Agency, MI6*, London, 2006

Womack, Helen (ed.), *Undercover Lives: Soviet Spies in the Cities of the World*, London, 1998

Wright, Peter, with Paul Greengrass, *Spycatcher: The Candid Autobiography of a Senior Intelligence Officer*, London, 1987

# References

The majority of source material for this book derives from interviews with the participants, officers of MI6, the KGB and the CIA, most of whom cannot be named; and interviews with Oleg Gordievsky, his family and friends, and his memoir, *Next Stop Execution*, published in 1995. Other sources and significant quotations are cited below.

## 1. *The KGB*

'**There is no such thing**': Vladimir Putin, speaking to an FSB audience, December 2005, http://www.newsweek.com/chill-moscow-air-113415.

'**Better that ten innocent people**': quoted in Sebag Montefiore, *Stalin*.

'**the Russian Harvard**': quoted in *Encyclopedia of Contemporary Russian Culture* (ed. Tatiana Smorodinskaya, Karen Evans-Romaine and Helena Goscilo), Abingdon, 2007.

'**The intelligence officer's behaviour**'; '**To make it into**': Leonid Shebarshin, 'Inside the KGB's Intelligence School', 24 March 2015, https://espionagehistoryarchive.com/2015/03/24/the-kgbs-intelligence-school/.

'**an Englishman to his fingertips**': Mikhail Lyubimov, quoted in Corera, *MI6*.

'**I did not hesitate**': Philby, *My Silent War*.

## 2. *Uncle Gormsson*

Mikhail Lyubimov's memoirs are contained in *Notes of a Ne'er-Do-Well Rezident* and *Spies I Love and Hate*; for Vasili Gordievsky's activities in Czechoslovakia, see Andrew and Mitrokhin, *Mitrokhin Archive*.

## 3. SUNBEAM

The recruitment of Gordievsky is described in an unpublished memoir by Richard Bromhead, 'Wilderness of Mirrors' ('Gerontion', T. S. Eliot).

## 4. Green Ink and Microfilm

'**Search for people who are hurt**': Pavel Sudoplatov, cited in Hollander, *Political Will and Personal Belief*.

'**Intelligence agents, in my experience**': Malcolm Muggeridge, *Chronicles of Wasted Time*, part 2: *The Infernal Grove*, London, 1973.

'**a marvellous man**': Borovik, *Philby Files*, p. 29

The Haavik and Treholt cases are described in Andrew and Mitrokhin, *Mitrokhin Archive*. For the activities of the Copenhagen *rezidentura*, see Lyubimov, *Notes of a Ne'er-Do-Well Rezident* and *Spies I Love and Hate*.

## 5. A Plastic Bag and a Mars Bar

'**There were those who were recruited**': Cavendish, *Inside Intelligence*.

'**Fear by night**': Robert Conquest, *The Great Terror: A Reassessment*, Oxford, 1990.

'**as improbable as placing**': Helms, *A Look Over My Shoulder*, quoted in Hoffman, *Billion Dollar Spy*.

'**very few Soviet agents**': Gates, *From the Shadows*, quoted in Hoffman, *Billion Dollar Spy*.

'**reliable intelligence**': CIA assessment, 1953, quoted in Hoffman, *Billion Dollar Spy*.

'**grey, black, white and dull**'; '**Money for information**': cited in AFP report, 28 June 1995.

'**Ashenden admired goodness**': W. Somerset Maugham, *Ashenden, or, The British Agent*, Leipzig, 1928.

## 6. Agent BOOT

'one of the world's greatest trade union leaders': Gordon Brown, *Guardian*, 22 April 2009.

'prepared to pass to the Party'; 'confidential Labour Party documents': cited in Andrew, *Defence of the Realm*.

'passed on all he could get': ibid.

'I rather enjoyed the cloak and dagger'; 'Like many other journalists': Richard Gott, *Guardian*, 9 December 1994.

Details of the BOOT files are contained in interviews conducted with Gordievsky, held in the *Sunday Times* legal archive.

'The Lyubimov and Boot': Mikhail Lyubimov, in Womack (ed.) *Undercover Lives*.

'I am as strong': Michael Foot, http://news.bbc.co.uk/onthisday/hi/dates/stories/november/10/newsid_4699000/4699939.stm.

'Foot freely disclosed information': Charles Moore, interview with Gordievsky, *Daily Telegraph*, 5 March 2010.

'The actions of the Russians': Michael Foot, speaking at Hyde Park rally, June 1968.


## 7. The Safe House

The principal sources on the life of Aldrich Ames are Earley, *Confessions of a Spy*; Weiner, Johnston and Lewis, *Betrayal*; and Grimes and Vertefeuille, *Circle of Treason*.

'Thanks to the excessive zeal': Gates, *From the Shadows*.

'There is no business like it': quoted in Bearden and Risen, *The Main Enemy*.


## 8. Operation RYAN

Key sources on Operation RYAN are Barrass, *Great Cold War*; Fischer, 'Cold War Conundrum'; Jones (ed.), *Able Archer 83*.

'the man who substituted': Ion Mihai Pacepa, in *National Review*, 20 September 2004.

'**No such plans existed**': Andrew, *Defence of the Realm*.
'**The Soviet leadership really did**': Howe, *Conflict of Loyalty*.
Maksim Parshikov's account is contained in an unpublished memoir.
'**I am no spy**': *The New York Times*, 2 April 1983.


# 9. Koba

For the Bettaney case, see Andrew, *Defence of the Realm*, and contemporary
    newspaper accounts.
'**He dressed like a bank manager**': *The Times*, 29 May 1998.


# 10. Mr Collins and Mrs Thatcher

For Margaret Thatcher's views on Gordievsky, see Moore, *Margaret
    Thatcher*.
'**leave Marxism–Leninism on the ash heap**': Ronald Reagan to the
    Houses of Parliament, 8 June 1982.
'**the joy of total self-righteousness**': Henry E. Catto, Jr, Assistant Secre-
    tary of Defense, quoted in the *Los Angeles Times*, 11 November 1990.
On ABLE ARCHER, see Barrass, *Great Cold War*; Fischer, 'Cold War
    Conundrum'; and Jones (ed.), *Able Archer 83*.
'**most dangerous moment**': Andrew, *Defence of the Realm*.
'**Gordievsky left us in no doubt**': Howe, *Conflict of Loyalty*.
'**I don't see how they could believe that**': cited in Oberdorfer, *From the
    Cold War to a New Era*.
'**Three years had taught me**': cited in the *Washington Post*, 24 October 2015.
'**My first reaction**': Gates, *From the Shadows*.
'**Gordievsky's information was an epiphany**': see Jones (ed.), *Able
    Archer 83*.
'**treated as the holy of holies**': Corera, *MI6*.
'**For heaven's sake**': Moore, *Margaret Thatcher*.
'**What can I say?**': AP, 26 February 1985.
'**Guk has always been**': Andrew, *Defence of the Realm*.
'**a barrel-chested bear**': Bearden and Risen, *Main Enemy*.

'The idea of leaving the country': quoted in Gareth Stedman Jones, *Karl Marx: Greatness and Illusion*, London, 2016.

'I grew up in a family of KGB officers': radio interview with Igor Pomerantsev, Radio Liberty, 7 September 2015.

'a unique opportunity': Moore, *Margaret Thatcher*.

'Is there conscience in the Kremlin?': https://www.margaretthatcher. org/document/105450.

'I certainly found him a man': Thatcher to Reagan, note released to UK National Archives, January 2014.


## 11. Russian Roulette

'The information reaching the CIA': see Jones (ed.), *Able Archer 83*.

'Burton Gerber was determined': Bearden and Risen, *Main Enemy*.

'a Danish intelligence officer': see Earley, *Confessions of a Spy*.

For KGB handling of Ames, see Cherkashin, *Spy Handler*.

'all the earmarks': Grimes and Vertefeuille, *Circle of Treason*.

Interview with Viktor Budanov, 13 September 2007, http://www.pravda report.com/history/13-09-2007/97107-intelligence-0/.

For the DARIO case, see Andrew and Gordievsky (eds.), *Instructions from the centre*.


## 12. Cat and Mouse

'Never confess': Philby, *My Silent War*.

'the rest and cure of leaders': *The New York Times*, 8 February 1993.

For OG's state of mind, see Lyubimov, *Notes of a Ne'er-Do-Well Rezident* and *Spies I Love and Hate*.


## 13. The Dry-Cleaner

'I would have let him escape': radio interview with Igor Pomerantsev, Radio Liberty, 7 September 2015.

'**When sorrows come**': *Hamlet*, Act IV, scene V.

'**The art of bowing to the East**': Kari Suomalainen, https://www.visa-vuori.com/fi/taiteilijat/kari-suomalainen.

'**man has always found it easier**': W. Somerset Maugham, 'Mr Harrington's Washing', in *Ashenden, or, The British Agent*, Leipzig, 1928.

'**tedious waste of time**': *Daily Express*, 14 June 2015.

## 14. Friday, 19 July

'**Here, in the homeland**': Gorbachev's speech at 12th World Festival of Youth, 27 July 1985: https://rus.ozodi.org/amp/24756366.html.

## 15. Finlandia

For further information on cheese and onion crisps, see Karen Hochman, 'A History of the Potato Chip', http://www.thenibble.com/reviews/main/snacks/chip-history.asp.

South Ormsby Hall is open to the public, http://southormsbyestate.co.uk.

On Yurchenko, see 'The spy who returned from the cold', *Time Magazine*, 18 April 2005.

'**I'm on top of all facets**': *The New York Times*, 7 May 1987.

'**The information from Gordievsky**': see Jones (ed.), *Able Archer 83*.

## 16. Passport for PIMLICO

For correspondence between Thatcher and Gordievsky, see National Archives, http://www.nationalarchives.gov.uk/about/news/newly-released-files-1985-1986/prime-ministers-office-files-prem-1985/.

For the diplomatic fallout, see interview with Sir Bryan Cartledge, Churchill Archive Centre, https://www.chu.cam.ac.uk/media/uploads/files/Cartledge.pdf.

'**Gordievsky was close to confessing**': Primakov, *Russian Crossroads*.

'**Technically it's nothing very special**': *The Times*, 10 March 2018.

'**Life went forward**': radio interview with Igor Pomerantsev, Radio Liberty, 7 September 2015.

'**Spying has become much harder**': *Los Angeles Times,* 30 August 1991.

On Vadim Bakatin dismantling the KGB, see J. Michael Waller, 'Russia: Death and Resurrection of the KGB', *Demokratizatsiya*, vol. 12, no. 3 (Summer 2004).

Ted Koppel interview with Ames, http://abcnews.go.com/US/video/feb-11-1997-aldrich-ames-interview-21372948.

Sergei Ivanov's exposure by Gordievsky, *The Times*, 20 October 2015.

'**If we had to kill anyone**': Andrei Lugovoi in the *Sunday Times*, 11 March 2018.

# Index